BIRDS
OF BRITAIN AND EUROPE

*A comprehensive illustrated guide to
over 360 species*

KAREL ŠŤASTNÝ
EDITED BY DAVID CHRISTIE

Picture Acknowledgements
The figures in brackets indicate the numbers of photographs.
J. Anderle (8), F. Balát (6), A. Bardi, Panda photo (3),
S. Benucci, Panda photo (4), A. Boano, Panda photo (2),
J. Bohdal (5), P. Bürger (4), G. Cagnucci, Panda photo (10),
M. Chroust (6), S. Chvapil (5), F. Cianchi, Panda photo
(1), Š. Danko (12), J. Elmelid (10), J. Formánek (50),
F. Framarin, Panda photo (1), Grupo Tichodroma (5),
J. Hanzák (5), P. Harris, Panda photo (2), S. Harvančík (11),
L. Hauser (2), J. Hlásek (59), L. Hlásek (159), T. Karlsson
(1), G. Kovácz (1), I. Lipták (1), P. Macháček (5), J. Mihók
(4), G. Molnár (1), J. Motyčka (1), P. Pavlík (55), E. Perez,
Panda photo (4), A. Petrelli, Panda photo (4), P. Podpěra
(22), V. Podpěra (4), F. Pratesi, Panda photo (1), J. Rys (5),
M. Sara, Panda photo (1), J. Scheufler (1), E. Studnička (2),
M. Šebela (1), J. Ševčík (11), Z. Veselovský (1), WWF,
Panda photo (1), J. Zumr (1).

Text by Karel Šťastný
Translation by Margot Schierlová
Illustrations by J. Čepická, Z. Hedánek, K. Hísek,
L. and J. Knotek, P. Rob, E. Smrčinová, M. Váňa
Graphic design by Michal Burda

This edition published 1995 by
Sunburst Books, Deacon House,
65, Old Church Street,
London SW3 5BS

Copyright © 1990 Aventinum, Prague

ISBN   1 85778 085 X
Printed in Slovakia

3/19/04/51-02

Contents

A short introduction to the life of birds

Typical characters of birds as a class

In all their organ systems, birds (Aves) display a mixture of characters inherited from reptile ancestors, from which they evolved over millions of years, and adaptive characters which developed later and enabled them to conquer the air.

The first feathered and winged bird-like creatures appeared on the Earth at the end of the Jurassic period in the Mesozoic Era, about 150 million years ago. They have been preserved as clearly discernible imprints in upper Jurassic slates in Bavaria and are known under the name *Archaeopteryx*. These primitive birds possess both reptilian and avian characteristics. They were the size of a pigeon, had jaws with teeth instead of a beak, and had three free toes on their fore feet; their tail, which was longer than their body, was composed of 23 vertebrae. On the other hand, they were already feathered (their tail feathers grew in two rows, one pair to each vertebra), they had wings (though they were able only to glide), and their legs were already like a bird's. Later on, during the Cretaceous period (some 60 to 125 million years ago), we come across groups of toothed birds belonging to the genera *Hesperornis* and *Ichthyornis,* whose members looked much more like recent birds than *Archaeopteryx*. They were piscivores (fish-eaters) and bore a resemblance to divers and gulls. Members of the orders we know today appeared on the Earth in the early Cenozoic Era.

The most characteristic features of birds, evident at first glance, are their plumage, completely biped locomotion, the ability to fly, conversion of the fore limbs to wings, loss of the caudal vertebrae, and the development of a beak. The accompanying illustrations, with the names of the various parts of a bird's body, will give a better idea of its structure (Figs. 1 and 2).

Birds have a completely septate heart divided into an arterial and a venous half and they have tubular lungs with a system of air sacs. Further characteristics include a very high metabolic rate, associated with a high and stable body temperature, and oviparity (reproduction through egg-laying).

Let us now take a closer look at some of these characteristics. The bird's feather is a very complex structure (Fig. 3). Its axis is a tough shaft (rachis, Fig. 3a), which at the base becomes a hollow quill (calamus) where the feather is anchored in the skin. On either side of the shaft is the vane (vexillum); in the wing (flight) feathers,

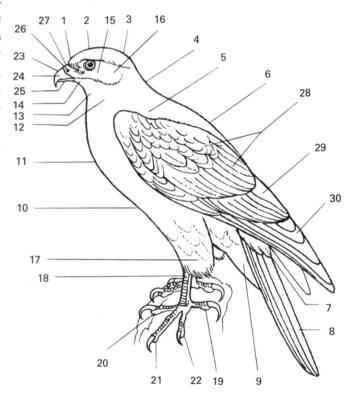

Fig. 1. *Body topography of a bird of prey:*
1 forehead, 2 crown, 3 hind neck, 4 nape, 5 shoulder, 6 back, 7 upper tail-coverts, 8 tail, 9 undertail-coverts, 10 belly, 11 breast, 12 neck, 13 throat, 14 chin, 15 ear-coverts, 16 ear region, 17 thigh, 18 tarsus, 19 hind toe, 20 inner toe, 21 middle toe, 22 outer toe, 23 bill ridge, 24 upper mandible, 25 lower mandible, 26 nostril, 27 cere, 28 wing-coverts, 29 secondaries, 30 primaries.

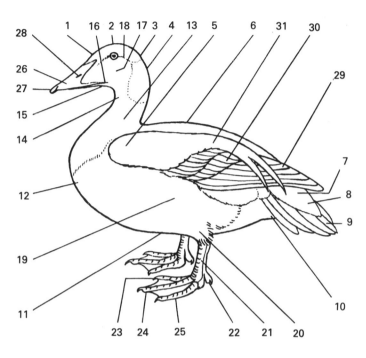

Fig. 2. *Body topography of the Eider:*
1 forehead, 2 crown, 3 hind neck, 4 nape, 5 shoulders, 6 back, 7 rump, 8 uppertail-coverts, 9 tail quills, 10 undertail-coverts, 11 belly, 12 breast, 13 neck, 14 throat, 15 chin, 16 lores, 17 ear-coverts, 18 ear region, 19 flank, 20 shank, 21 tarsus, 22 hind toe, 23 inner toe, 24 middle toe, 25 outer toe, 26 bill, 27 nail, 28 nostrils, 29 primaries, 30 secondaries, 31 scapulars.

which are the most highly developed feathers on the whole of the bird's body, it is the vane that forms the supporting surface in the air. The vane is composed of barbs (rami, Fig. 3b) joined together by interlocking barbules (radii, Fig. 3c) held together by large numbers of fine hairs and hooks (hamuli, Fig. 3d). The wing feathers, the tail feathers (used for steering and for altitude regulation) and the contour feathers (the pennae, Fig. 4, which give the bird's body its typical form) all have this structure. Down consists of feathers (plumae) with short, soft shafts whose barbs and barbules are not interconnected (Fig. 5); it is important for keeping the body warm. In adult birds down grows beneath the contour feathers, but in young birds it forms their first plumage (neoptile) and covers the whole of their body. Powder-down is a specialised type of down composed of feathers with a shaft and long side filaments whose tips release fine particles (powder) which help to keep the other feathers in good condition. Filoplumae, which may or may not have a small vane at their tip, are another

Fig. 4. *Contour feather.*

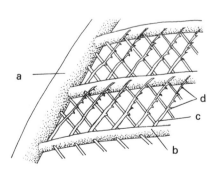

Fig. 3. *Structure of bird's feather:*
a — shaft (scapus), b — barbs (rami), c — barbules (radii), d — hooks (hamuli).

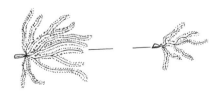

Fig. 5. *Down.*

Typical characters
of birds as a class

specialised type of feather which grow free or at the base of the contour feathers. The vibrissae, bristle-like feathers which grow mainly at the corners of the beak and around the eyes and nostrils, have a tactile function. The feathers surrounding the cloaca and the duct of the preen gland, etc, can also have special functions.

The feathers are a product of the skin, which is completely devoid of glands. There are no sweat glands, because the body is cooled by large subcutaneous air sacs. The only skin gland is the sebaceous preen gland (glans uropygialis), whose secretion is used for keeping the plumage well oiled. It is most highly developed in aquatic birds, whose feathers must be protected from becoming wet. In some groups (e.g. pigeons and parrots) it is severely reduced and in flightless running birds (ratites) it is actually absent.

Flight is closely associated with reduction of body weight. The bird's skeleton is highly pneumatic and the bones are mostly hollow and filled with air; this does not, however, detract from their strength. The body is made buoyant by air sacs which lead from the lungs and pervade the whole body; these take the place of the lungs as air reservoirs. The air sacs play an important role in respiration. When air is breathed in, it passes through the lungs into two pairs of large inspiratory air sacs situated in the abdominal cavity. From here it is driven by muscular contractions into three pairs of expiratory sacs in the anterior part of the body cavity and then back to the lungs and out again. The air sacs enlarge the body without increasing its weight; they reduce intermuscular friction (their processes stretch between the viscera, below the skin, between and into the bones and between the muscle layers), they are of great significance in thermoregulation and they act as resonators in the amplification of vocal sounds. Another factor which helps to reduce body weight is the absence of a urinary bladder; urine is released continuously into the cloaca in a crystalline (i.e. not a liquid) form and is quickly excreted without first having to collect in a bladder. The gonads are also very economically constructed. In males they are fully developed and functional only in the reproductive season; as soon as nesting time is over, they shrink to almost microscopic proportions. For instance, in December the testis of the House Sparrow *Passer domesticus* measures only 0.5 mm, but in May it measures up to 15 mm and its volume in the spring increases about 400-fold. In females, only the left ovary functions as a rule.

The fore limbs are used for flying and are consequently highly modified, especially in the region of the scapular girdle; the digits, which have become superfluous on these limbs, are also strikingly reduced. Certain modifications have likewise taken place on the hind limbs. The femur is short and is usually withdrawn into the body, while the fibula is rudimentary and is attached to the tibia. The metatarsals and the tarsus have fused to form a single bone, the tarsus. Of the toes, the fifth is always missing and the first is also sometimes missing.

In birds, the jaws are drawn out to form a beak with a horny covering. The beak plays the main role in the capturing and breaking up of food and its shape varies with the type of food.

Compared with the heart of other vertebrates, the bird's heart is extremely large. In pigeons and sparrows it accounts for 13% of body weight, in humming birds for as much as 27%, but in man for only 4% of body weight. Small birds have a relatively larger heart, in keeping with their greater activity. They also have a much faster heart rate than large birds or other vertebrates. For instance, Ostriches have a heart rate of $60-70$ beats per minute, but in small songbirds it is over 1,000 per minute. Heart size and the heart rate are associated in birds with the very high metabolic rate, which in turn is associated with high activity and a high body temperature (the latter is higher than in other warm-blooded vertebrates). The resting body temperature is about 40°C, but temperatures of about 44°C have been measured during intensive activity.

Reproduction

Birds reproduce in a different way from other vertebrates. They lay eggs as do amphibians and reptiles, but, unlike most of these, they look after the eggs and keep them warm — incubate them — with the heat of their own body until the young are hatched. The only birds which do not sit on their eggs, but bury them in warm volcanic sand or in rotting plant débris, are mound-builders, gallinaceous birds of the family Megapodiidae. The avian egg is a very complex structure. The main part is the yolk, which is actually the egg cell (incidentally, the largest one known among vertebrates), the very beginning of the future organism. It consists of formative yolk in the shape of an embryonic spot or germinal disc (blastodisc) at one pole of the yolk sphere, and of nutritive yolk, which provides the developing embryo with the necessary nutrients and comprises the rest of the yolk sphere. The nutritive yolk is not homogeneous, but is composed of alternating layers of transparent white yolk and denser yellow yolk. The yolk as a whole is wrapped in a fine cytoplasmic membrane known as the vitelline membrane. The yolk swims in a thick layer of transparent egg white, which likewise provides the embryo with nutrients and is also arranged in denser and thinner layers. The yolk, which is situated in a roughly central position, is kept in place by spiral bands (chalazae) anchored in the denser egg white. The yolk and the white are held together by a thin parchment-like membrane with two layers. The entire egg is enclosed in a shell formed of calcium carbonate, calcium phosphate, keratin and other components and is riddled with large numbers of pores through which the embryo receives air. At the blunt end of the egg, the two layers of the parchment membrane separate to form a large air chamber (Fig. 6).

By the phrase nesting time or breeding season we mean the time from the start of egg-laying to the end of the care of the young. This does not take into account certain species (e.g. geese, ducks) whose families do not break up until the autumn, nor eggs laid to replace a lost clutch, when the nesting time is likewise prolonged. It should further be borne in mind that the time when nesting begins depends on the latitude, and that in Europe it can vary by as much as six weeks. The nesting times given for the various species apply chiefly to central and west European conditions; in the north the birds nest two to three weeks later and in the south two to three weeks earlier.

The reproductive period for European birds falls in the spring and the early summer. The Crossbill *Loxia curvirostra*, which also nests in the winter, at the time of the conifer-seed harvest, is an exception, although other species are likewise known to nest occasionally in the autumn or even in the winter, if they can find sufficient food (e.g. the Barn Owl *Tyto alba* in prolific vole years). The size of the clutch is influenced by the climate and the food supply. For instance, about 30% of the House Sparrows in central Europe nest four times a year and some pairs five times, while beyond the Arctic Circle

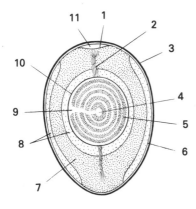

Fig. 6. *Cross section of non-incubated bird's egg: 1 egg membrane, 2 chalaza, 3 shell, 4 latebra, 5 yellow yolk layer, 6 shell membrane, 7 gelatinous semi-solid albumen, 8 viscous liquid albumen, 9 blastodisc, 10 vitelline membrane, 11 air space.*

Reproduction

they nest only once or twice, but in India seven times a year. The number of eggs in the clutch increases in a south-to-north direction, evidently as compensation for the smaller annual number of clutches. For example, in Hungary the clutch of the Collared Flycatcher *Ficedula albicollis* averages 5.5 eggs, in the Czech Republic 5.7 and in Poland 6.1 eggs.

Nesting is preceded by the formation of pairs. Some pairs remain together for only a single season, others for a lifetime; in the case of the Greylag Goose *Anser anser,* for instance, if one of the partners dies, the other may sometimes remain alone for the rest of its life. Pair formation and mating is associated, in birds, with a courtship ritual. This is the outward expression of sexual excitation of the males (and sometimes of the females), which try in this way to rouse the interest of the opposite sex. It occurs in every species; in some it is barely discernible, but in others it is very complicated and fascinating, as in different grouse genera (*Tetrao, Bonasa*). It may be performed on the ground, on water, in a tree or on the wing, and individually or collectively. If the males perform collectively, they sometimes fight real duels, when feathers fly in all directions; sometimes, however, the duels are only token battles. The courting male does its utmost to make its appearance striking and attractive to its partner. It spreads its wings and its tail, bows and hops, trails its wings on the ground, scrapes with its feet, puffs itself up and performs a range of symbolic movements. This display of movement and posturing is accompanied by vocal manifestations in the form of distinctive songs and calls. Some birds make good a lack of vocal expression by 'playing' on a 'musical instrument'; for example, woodpeckers (Picidae) 'drum' on resounding wood and snipes *Gallinago* with their own vibrating tail feathers, while storks (Ciconiidae) make clattering sounds with their beak.

Nests are built in a wide variety of situations – on the ground, on water, in a tree hole or a hole in the ground, on the branches of trees and

Fig. 7. *Example of nidicolous young.*

Fig. 8. *Example of nidifugous young.*

bushes, between stems of reeds, grasses and similar plants, and on rock faces; sometimes the eggs are laid on the bare ground or in a depression, but some birds build very intricate and elaborate nests. As a rule, the female builds the nest, while the male supplies the material. In some species the eggs are incubated solely or mostly by the female, in others the parent birds take the duty in turns; in rare cases (e.g. among phalaropes) the male hatches the eggs. In most species, the female waits until the clutch is complete before beginning to sit on the eggs, but among raptors and owls it is often usual for the bird to begin incubating the first egg and in the meantime lay others. In that case the young are hatched in succession, since the eggs all need to be incubated for the same length of time. The young hatched from the first eggs are thus well ahead of their later siblings in terms of their development.

The embryos need a temperature of about 38–39°C for their development. Incubation is aided by brood patches, bare patches on the underside of sitting birds, which are formed automatically at the beginning of the nesting season through loss of the feathers and hypervascularisation of the skin. These 'inflamed' patches heat the eggs directly. Instead of brood patches, some aquatic birds acquire particularly soft, warm down at nesting time. When the young bird is ready to leave the egg, it breaks its way out of the shell by means of its egg tooth — a hard, horny point at the tip of its upper mandible, which is shed soon after hatching. The newly hatched young of nidicolous birds are generally poorly developed, naked, blind and deaf; they are hardly capable of movement and are completely dependent on the care of their parents, which consists mainly of feeding them, keeping them warm and cleaning the nest: e.g. songbirds (Passeriformes) (Fig. 7) or birds of prey (Falconiformes). The newly hatched young of nidifugous birds are much better developed, are covered with a thick coat of down and in a few hours can leave the nest, run about or swim and gather food themselves: e.g. ducks, geese and swans (Anseriformes) and game birds (Galliformes) (Fig. 8). The mobile and independent young of semi-nidicolous birds remain in the vicinity of the nest and are fed by the parents: e.g. terns (Sternidae) and gulls (Laridae).

Fig. 9. *The powerful beak of the Parrot Crossbill, which lives on the seeds of hard pine cones.*

Fig. 10. *Beak of a Red Crossbill picking out seeds from spruce cones.*

Fig. 11. *Beak of a Two-barred Crossbill picking out seeds from soft larch cones.*

Food

The activity of birds and their high rate of metabolism (the highest known among vertebrates) necessitate a high food intake. The smaller the bird, the relatively greater are its body area and the consequent heat losses and the greater therefore is its food consumption. For example, birds of prey and owls have a daily food consumption of 25—30% of their body weight, while tits (Paridae), goldcrests *Regulus* and other insectivorous birds consume roughly the equivalent of their own weight. Big birds are able to go for fairly long periods without food. This applies especially to birds of prey, where it is a biological necessity, since they may not catch anything for several days. Conversely, in small insectivorous songbirds, only a few hours' deprivation of food during the winter, when energy output is higher, can lead to death from starvation. For instance, this may happen to tits or goldcrests on a dull, inclement winter's day if they are unable to find an adequate amount of food.

Birds live on a wide variety of diets and as a rule we distinguish omnivorous, insectivorous, carnivorous, piscivorous, herbivorous, granivorous and frugivorous species. These distinctions are not absolutely strict, however. For instance, many insectivorous birds, such as warblers (Sylviidae), also live for part of the year (chiefly in the late summer and the autumn) on berries, while most granivorous birds, such as sparrows, feed their young on insects. The adult birds' diets likewise change strikingly in the course of the year. In the spring, for example, Starlings *Sturnus vulgaris* live mainly on animal food, but in the summer they increasingly switch over to fruit and large flocks can destroy the whole of a cherry or grape harvest. Some species, however, are strictly specialised. These include crossbills, which live almost entirely on the seeds of conifers. Their adaptation to this diet is manifested in the crossed tips of their mandibles, which are a classic example of environmental adaptation. In the various species of crossbill, food specialisation and associated adaptation of the shape of the beak actually go still further. The Parrot Crossbill *Loxia pytyopsittacus,* whose diet consists chiefly of the seeds of hard pine cones, has a large, powerful beak (Fig. 9), while the Two-barred Crossbill *Loxida leucoptera,* which devours the seeds of soft larch cones, has a more slender beak (Fig. 11); intermediate between these two species is the Red Crossbill *Loxia curvirostra,* which lives mainly on the seeds of spruce or fir cones (Fig. 10).

Birds, especially those which eat easily digestible plant food such as fleshy fruit, digest their food very quickly (mistletoe berries pass through the digestive tract of Waxwings *Bombycilla garrulus* in only seven to ten minutes). The digestion of hard grain takes much longer, partly because the seeds are retained quite a long time in the crop, to allow them to swell and soften (hens need 12−14 hours to digest grain). Flesh is also digested more slowly; for example, the Great Grey Shrike *Lanius excubitor* takes about three hours to digest a mouse.

Undigested elements such as fur, feathers, bones, claws, scales or chitinous insect remains are regurgitated in the form of pellets, which, if analysed, furnish a wealth of interesting information on the composition of the bird's diet.

Communication

During countryside walks, especially in the spring, we can hear voices and sounds with every step we take. Most of them belong to birds. It is a well-known fact that birds are hardly ever silent. The sum total of their calls gives rise to a 'bird language' in which every call serves a special purpose. We may differentiate two basic groups of calls: those which are to be heard the whole year round, and the specific songs, which are heard only or at least mainly in the spring, at breeding time. These are supplemented by 'instrumental' sounds, such as rapid taps of the beak on dry branches (woodpeckers), vibrations of the tail feathers (snipes) or clattering sounds of the beak (storks).

The commonest vocal manifestation of social species, for example of most songbirds which live in flocks after the nesting season is over, is the contact call, a stereotyped and generally simple call by which birds of the same species draw attention to themselves and summon and entice one another. It is uttered as a reflex response to incite the others to fly up or descend again and to maintain contact in the air. It is very striking in flocks of Siskins *Carduelis spinus,* Redpolls *Carduelis flammea* and crossbills *Loxia;* waders (Charadriiformes), especially sandpipers *Tringa,* also call when they fly up into the air. One species may have several contact calls. There is likewise a warning or alarm call, which draws attention to danger. Like the contact call, it is species-specific and is inborn, so that the young can react to it soon after they are hatched. The best-known warning calls are those of the Blackbird *Turdus merula* and the Jay *Garrulus glandarius* and other birds and even mammals frequently react to them. Among the wide range of further calls, there are some which express anxiety or distress, the calls of the young and begging calls, etc. The number of these calls, which varies with the species, is sometimes extremely high: for in-

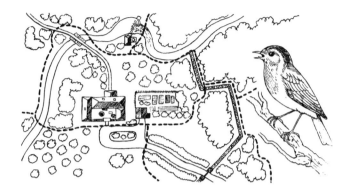

Fig. 12. *Illustration of nesting areas occupied by male robins.*

stance, the Pied Flycatcher *Ficedula hypoleuca* and the Collared Flycatcher were found to have 50 different vocal manifestations; 48 of these were common to both species and only two (song and the warning call) could be differentiated with any certainty.

Song is the most highly developed and the most striking form of vocal expression. It is generally confined to the males, and the number of species whose females also sing is very small (e.g. the Bullfinch *Pyrrhula pyrrhula*). The purpose of song is often interpreted as being solely to attract and appease the female. This is indeed its intention, but at the same time it informs other males that this particular neighbourhood has already been chosen as a nesting site and that it is being guarded (Fig. 12). If, despite the warning, an intruder comes along, a fierce battle ensues and continues until one of the males is driven away. The fight is thus not one between 'jealous' males for the female, but a fight for the nesting site. The reason for this defence of a certain area is to ensure that the two partners of a pair have an adequate supply of food and are able to rear their offspring in peace. Unlike the other calls, song is only partly inborn and the young have to complete their vocal repertoire later by ear. As a result, the song of males of the same species is not always the same: good singers can be distinguished from poor singers and various local 'dialects' can be identified. The songs of medi-

ocre singers (e.g. leaf warblers *Phylloscopus*, treecreepers *Certhia*) are largely inborn and do not develop any further. The best singers (e.g. nightingales *Luscinia*), whose song is a complex melody divided into several verses, have to learn by ear. To be able to master the song of their own species perfectly, they need to listen to the best singers, which are to be found in densely populated areas, where fierce competition between the males leads to intensive singing contests. The song of some species consists almost entirely of imitation of the voices of other species, as in the case of the Icterine Warbler *Hippolais icterina*, for example.

Distribution

The region where a given species occurs is known as its range or area of distribution. In our case this applies only to the territory where the species nests (its breeding distribution), and not where it spends the winter. Similarly, if we speak of the home or the country of a given species, or the places it inhabits, it is always the region where it nests that is meant.

Birds' ranges do not have fixed borders; on the contrary, they change fairly frequently and the only place where they are really stable is where they coincide with the coastline. Changes in the distribution of a species are usually accompanied by quantitative changes, i.e. by an increase or a decrease in its numbers over a given area. Population changes and regional changes are generally caused by environmental factors, such as climatic changes or interference by man. In recent years, the influence of man's activities on changes in nature has increased to such an extent and so fast that it has led to an increase in the rate of changes in the distribution of individual species. Obviously, pollution of the environment, manifested in the death of forests over huge stretches of central and western Europe, has, together with rapid mechanisation and urbanisation, a tremendous — and primarily a negative — effect on the distribution of birds and of other animals and plants.

Changes in the distribution of birds are usually of a dual nature. Relatively short-term changes in range size (oscillation), over the space of a few years, have lately been observed in central Europe in the case of the Nightingale *Luscinia megarhynchos,* the Bee-eater *Merops apiaster,* the Night Heron *Nycticorax nycticorax,* the Purple Heron *Ardea purpurea* and several other species. Permanent and long-term changes include expansion and decline. Among the expanding species in central and western Europe today we have the Raven *Corvus corax,* the Redpoll, the Syrian Woodpecker *Dendrocopos syriacus,* the Tufted Duck *Aythya fuligula* and the Black Stork *Ciconia nigra.* The expansion of some species, such as the Serin *Serinus serinus* (Fig. 13)

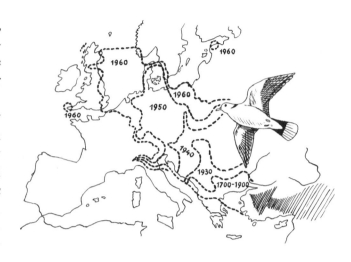

Fig. 14. *Expansion of the Collared Dove.*

crake *Crex crex,* the Quail *Coturnix coturnix,* the Grey Partridge *Perdix perdix* and forest game birds.

Although the majority of species are widely distributed, there are relatively few which inhabit almost all the continents and can be described as cosmopolitan. They are mainly species bound to an aquatic environment, such as the Great White Egret *Egretta alba,* the Glossy Ibis *Plegadis falcinellus,* the Black-winged Stilt *Himantopus himantopus,* and the Osprey *Pandion haliaetus,* together with the Barn Owl and the Peregrine. Other birds have much smaller distribution areas.

Fig. 13. *Spread of the Serin in Europe.*

and the Collared Dove *Streptopelia decaocto* (Fig. 14), has been so forceful that the size of their distribution area has increased by over a million square kilometres within just a few years. Species which are now declining, over practically the whole of Europe, include the Peregrine *Falco peregrinus,* the Roller *Coracias garrulus,* the Hoopoe *Upupa epops,* the Corn-

Migration

Birds are divided, by a standard and known criterion, into migratory, nomadic and resident birds. Migratory birds actually have two homes: in the northern hemisphere, one in the north, where they breed and rear their young, and one further south, where they spend the winter but do not nest. They often have to fly a long way to find conditions sufficiently satisfactory to tide them over the months while their nesting places are uninhabitable. Many species — and even individual birds — winter in the same place every year and return to the same nesting site (even the same nestbox). Every year they travel from their nesting place to their winter quarters and back again, sometimes covering over 10,000 km on each journey (e.g. the Swallow *Hirundo rustica* and the White Stork *Ciconia ciconia*). The full-grown young of gulls, herons and various other species undertake pre-migratory excursions before actually setting out for their winter quarters. Very often, different populations of the same species display different degrees of migration. For instance, Starling populations living in the north are migratory, whereas those in the south are resident. In the case of the Blackbird, some forest birds are migrants and others are residents (such populations are known as partial migrants), but town-dwelling birds are all resident. Resident birds remain in the same spot the whole year round and do not leave it even when the breeding season is over. Intermediate between these two groups are nomadic birds, which remain in the region of their breeding place · during the winter, but roam about over a wide radius, which may be as much as 100 km or even more. There are also birds which appear in given regions only once in several years, but then in the form of a large-scale invasion; these are known as irruptive birds. Such invasions have been recorded in the case of the Nutcracker *Nucifraga caryocatactes*, the Waxwing, the Rose-coloured Starling *Sturnus roseus* and Pallas's Sandgrouse *Syrrhaptes paradoxus*, for example, and they are generally due to a lack of food in the birds' normal nesting areas, sometimes in association with high production of young or with inclement weather, etc.

What is the real reason for this double annual migration? Most people would no doubt say that the birds would not survive the hard winter frosts and would not find enough to eat. This applies only to a few migrants, however, and it does not explain why many birds leave as early as the end of the summer, when plenty of food is still available. It likewise does not explain the migration of birds which would also find enough sustenance during the winter and, conversely, why the birds return again when they can still find sufficient to eat in their winter quarters. Several theories attempting to elucidate and explain the causes of migration have been put forward.

According to one theory, the whole of the northern hemisphere was originally inhabited by resident birds. The glacial periods in the Pleistocene led to cyclical deterioration of environmental conditions, since large parts of Europe, Asia and North America were covered with a sheet of ice. The winters became so severe that birds were obliged to fly far to the south every year and were unable to return to their original abodes until the winter was over. In time, these annual movements became genetically fixed. This theory does not, however, explain why some birds migrate far to the other side of the equator, sometimes even as far as the Antarctic, and why they sometimes migrate within the limits of the tropical belt.

Another theory claims that in ancient geological ages birds lived only in the tropical (and possibly the subtropical) belt. Here they overproliferated and were consequently obliged to spread northwards at nesting time, to regions which were not yet inhabited and where it was therefore easier to find food. Another cause of these migrations could have been the short tropical day, which, at the equator, lasts only 12 hours. In central Europe the day lasts 14−16 hours in the summer and the birds thus have far more time to look for food and rear their numerous offspring. This theory appears to be confirmed by species which come to central and northern Europe for only a short time ($3-3\frac{1}{2}$ months) during the summer to rear their young, species such as the Golden Oriole *Oriolus oriolus* and the Swift *Apus apus*.

Migration

Fig. 15. *An untidy flock of Starlings.*

According to a third theory, the factor responsible for migration is photoperiodicity, i.e. regular lengthening of the period of daylight in the spring and its diminution in the autumn. An increasing amount of light and lengthening of the day stimulate development of the gonads and maturation of the germ cells, while a decrease has the reverse effect. This theory holds the migratory instinct to be dependent on hormones secreted into the body. Not one of the existing theories has, however, resolved the question of the origin of migration satisfactorily and definitively.

Some birds, such as swallows *Hirundo* and Rooks *Corvus frugilegus,* migrate in flocks; others such as the Golden Oriole and *Phylloscopus* warblers, singly; and there are species whose males and females migrate at different times. It is often said that old, experienced birds show young birds the way and also the dangers on long journeys. Although this is often indeed the case, there are nevertheless species whose innate sense of direction is so strongly developed that the young birds can set out on their first journey to their winter quarters alone and unaided (e.g. the Cuckoo *Cuculus canorus* and the Red-backed Shrike *Lanius collurio*). Many birds migrate at night, so that their migration passes unnoticed; they are very often diurnal insectivorous birds and in this way they can still gather food by day and escape the attention of birds of prey by night.

The speed of flight has often been overestimated. First of all there is a 'cruising' speed, which does not fatigue the bird and is used for long-distance flights, especially during migration. Birds seldom develop a high to maximum speed, but if they do it is usually to escape from danger or in pursuit of prey. For instance, the cruising speed of the Sparrowhawk *Accipiter nisus* has been found to be only 41 km per hour, of the Hooded Crow *Corvus corone cornix* 50 km, of finches (Fringillidae) 52 km, of Starlings *Sturnus* 74 km and of geese about 70–90 km per hour. The bird with the fastest cruising speed was found to be the Swift, at 160 km per hour. As a rule, the daily distances covered are not particularly long; in the autumn they are usually short – in the case of the White Stork about 110–150 km – and in the spring, when the birds are hurrying to reach their nesting places, they are longer. Aquatic birds generally follow the coastline in the autumn and take a short cut across the continent in the spring.

The height at which birds fly is also often overestimated. Small songbirds fly mostly less than 100 m above the ground, but they can normally master heights of about 1,500 m. It is evidently rare for birds to fly much higher, except when crossing mountain ranges, when they may be forced up to altitudes of about 7,000 m.

Fig. 16. *A flock of Swallows.*

Fig. 17. *Typical flight formation of ducks.*

With most species (e.g. songbirds), migration takes place over an extensive stretch of territory, i.e. along a wide front, which occasionally, in mountain passes, in river valleys or on tongues of land by the sea, shrinks to narrow corridors. Many birds, such as Swallows or Starlings, migrate in seemingly unorganised flocks (Figs. 15, 16), while others fly in special formations, each characteristic of the given species. The best known of these are the regular arrow formations of wild geese or cranes; the streaming lines of gulls or wild ducks (Fig. 17) are less familiar.

The question of orientation and the ability of birds to return to exactly the same spots is naturally extremely interesting. Although it has not yet been fully resolved, we know that birds are guided partly by the position of the sun and stars, in conjunction with an internal time rhythm, which we can best describe as their biological 'clock'.

Birds and their environment

For bird-watchers it is very important to know where given species of birds are to be encountered. The gift of flight makes birds exceptionally mobile, so that they are generally not bound to a strictly defined type of environment as mammals and other animals are. Nevertheless, they have a preference for a particular type of habitat where they can find sufficient food, suitable conditions for nesting and adequate refuge from enemies. We can thus be sure that it would be useless to look for marsh birds at the top of mountains, or open country species in dense woods. As soon as a bird-watcher knows which birds occur in what type of habitat, their identification becomes much easier and allows the group to which a given bird belongs to be determined, if not the actual species itself.

The above conditions apply mainly in the nesting period, when birds have a firm relationship to their nesting sites. Outside the nesting season, and especially when the birds are migrating, i.e. in the autumn and the spring, we must expect to catch sight of many species in places where they would never be able to nest. That, of course, makes their identification much more difficult.

Another factor which must be taken into account is that many birds nest in one environment and hunt in another. The Buzzard, for instance, nests in woods, but hunts in open country (meadows, fields and pastures). The Grey Heron likewise nests on tall trees in woods, but catches its food in ponds and marshes, often many kilometres away. Many birds nest and hunt in the same type of environment, which can be very variable, however. For example, the Hedge Sparrow may nest in a continuous wood, a hedge or an overgrown garden in a town. In addition, the habitat requirements of a species may undergo long-term changes. This occurs in the case of the Blackbird, which has changed from a bird of the woods to an inhabitant of towns, and the same applies in central Europe to the Redpoll, which lived in mountainous regions and peatbogs.

The descriptions of the individual species in this book also state which habitats they prefer. Illustrations of typical examples of various habitats are given on pp. 18–24, together with the names of their most characteristic bird inhabitants.

Rock faces

Rocks falling away steeply into the sea and sheer rock faces and cliffs on islands in the north Atlantic and the North Sea furnish accomodation for huge colonies of sea birds which sometimes number tens or hundreds of thousands of individuals. The birds nest on shelves of rock, while the surrounding sea is a virtually inexhaustible source of food. The most important rocks are to be found on the British Isles and the coasts of Scandinavia and France and they provide shelter for over three quarters of all the gannets and razorbills in existence. Various kinds of guillemots and, less commonly, puffins are further characteristic species, but they require grassy slopes on islands and the seashore rather than bare rock. The colonies are usually formed of several different species. At one time they included the Great Auk or Garefowl, which was exterminated by man in the middle of the last century.

Parks and gardens

In parks and gardens we can encounter species which are at home in woods (the Great and Lesser Spotted Woodpecker, the Great Tit and the Blue Tit, the Treecreeper, the Nuthatch, the Robin and the Spotted Flycatcher) and others inhabiting open country with scattered bushes and trees (the Whitethroat, Lesser Whitethroat, Yellowhammer, Linnet and Greenfinch, etc). The highly heterogeneous environment, with both native and exotic trees and shrubs, and the large quantity of herbaceous plants and grasses, provide ample food, nesting sites and shelter and often attract quite unexpected species. In old, spreading parks and large overgrown gardens we may therefore find a greater number of different birds than in woods and if a small lake or one or two ponds are present, they may further be inhabited by a few species of aquatic birds, especially ducks.

Human settlements

The number of birds which are strongly attached to a human environment is relatively small. The best known species is the House Sparrow, which would be unable to live anywhere else and inhabits the biggest stone and concrete jungles without even a touch of green. Original mountain species, such as the Black Redstart and the House Martin, nest on buildings, whose stone walls take the place of precipitous rocks for them. The Swallow, Jackdaw and Barn Owl nest inside buildings. The Blackbird and Collared Dove appear as long as there are just a few trees available, while the Greenfinch and other species will even nest in small gardens.

The number of species which have attached themselves to man, i.e. synanthropic species, has increased in recent years. Alongside the Song Thrush, such unexpected species as the Redpoll and the Scarlet Rosefinch have penetrated further and further into central European towns and villages and the Wood Pigeon and Collared Dove are now quite common birds in the cities of western Europe. In eastern Europe, the Hooded Crow today normally inhabits towns.

Fields

A great many birds live in open country, but even there they usually need at least a solitary tree, a group of shrubs or a hedge. In central Europe, however, these once familiar features of the countryside are fast disappearing, since the farmers cut down trees, do away with small copses, drain and fill up morasses and join small fields together to make larger ones. Such huge expanses of land, which are sometimes termed 'cultivated steppe' and are used for large-scale, mechanised agriculture, provide conditions for only a few species whose habitat requirements are modest in the extreme. The Skylark, Tawny Pipit, Stone Curlew and Great Bustard are typical inhabitants of such environments. In Britain, small fields separated by hedges suit the Yellowhammer, Corn Bunting, Pheasant, Partridge and Quail. Among the birds of prey, Montagu's Harrier is known to nest in large cornfields, and kestrels fly in open country in search of food.

Flowing water

Birds living beside flowing water can be differentiated according to whether they prefer torrential mountain streams or slow-flowing water at low altitudes. Fast mountain and submontane streams and rivers can be inhabited only by certain, highly adapted species. The songbird the best adapted to a life beside — and actually in — swiftly flowing water is the Dipper, whose pairs, under optimal circumstances, usually occupy about 1 km of the stream. The nesting density of the Grey Wagtail is double this value or even more. The Common Sandpiper nests on gravelly and sandy banks overgrown with grass and shrubs, from lowlands to high up in the mountains, and the pairs often nest no more than 200–400 m apart from one another. The Little Ringed Plover and certain species of terns inhabit gravelly and sandy coastland at low altitudes. Slow-flowing lowland rivers are a very convenient environment for birds, especially if they are bordered by abundant vegetation. Here we can find various kinds of warblers, the Reed Bunting, the Sedge Warbler, the Pied and the Yellow Wagtail and, among aquatic birds, the Mallard. In addition, the Kingfisher and Sand Martin nest in steep clayey and sandy river banks.

Ponds and lakes

Stagnant water, especially if it is not too deep and if there are plenty of water and swamp plants around its edges, are very rewarding to the ornithologist the whole year round. Grebes, ducks, geese, swans, gulls, terns, Coots and other aquatic birds all nest here and their nest concentration is very high, especially on islands in the water, where tens to hundreds of duck nests and several hundred to a thousand gull or tern nests can often be found over an area of only 1 ha. Dense littoral growths of reeds, bulrushes, sedge and shrub willows are literally alive with birds. In such environments, we usually become aware of their presence through their voices, before we actually see them. Reed and other kinds of warblers, Reed Buntings, Bearded Tits, rails, Bitterns, Little Bitterns, Moorhens and several species of herons are typical inhabitants of such environments, where tens to hundreds of nests can be found over a vegetation area of 1 ha. During their autumn migration, flocks of birds from the north also settle on stagnant water, which, if it does not freeze, can provide them with enough food to see them through the winter. Deep lakes poor in food and lacking vegetation are usually inhabited only by divers and ducks.

Mountains

This section comprises environments from the upper edge of the tree-line to the snow-line. The characteristic vegetation is dwarf trees and shrubs, stunted by the harsh climate, which become shorter with increasing altitude. In the true alpine belt we encounter short grasses and creeping shrubs. Just below the snow-line we find denuded rocks and rubble, with islands of sturdy plants, and permanent snow and ice. The Ring Ouzel, Redpoll, Coal Tit, Hedge Sparrow and Crossbill are typical birds at the upper limit of the tree-line, while the Meadow Pipit and Skylark inhabit the alpine belt and the Wheatear, Golden Plover, Dotterel, Raven and Snow Bunting live among the rocks and rubble. The Golden Eagle and other birds of prey such as Peregrine and Buzzard have been displaced from lower altitudes to inaccessible rock faces. Game birds, such as the Ptarmigan, are also important mountain-dwellers. Young Choughs and Hooded Crows ascend to the limit of the permanent snow and are often observed by mountaineers in the vicinity of their highest camps.

Beechwoods

Natural mountain beechwoods are composed mainly of beech, but in mainland Europe sometimes contain silver fir and sometimes Norway spruce and not infrequently stretch to an altitude of 1,100−1,300 metres. They also occur in lowlands and at medium altitudes. Dominant beechwoods generally lack a shrub layer and often a herbaceous layer, because the crowns of the trees form a continuous, dense green vault through which very little light can penetrate to the ground. The only exception is the springtime, when the trees are bare and the woods are carpeted with spring flowers. Beechwoods provide shelter for a number of interesting birds. Perhaps their most characteristic − though a not very common − songbird is the Wood Warbler, together with a whole series of other hole-nesters, such as the Pied Flycatcher, Stock Dove, Great Spotted Woodpecker and Lesser Spotted Woodpecker. Some species of owls, in particular the Tawny Owl, nest typically in forests of a virgin character. Predators include certain birds of prey such as the Sparrowhawk, which chiefly inhabit lowland forests allowing them to make excursions into open country in search of food.

Firwoods

Natural firwoods predominate both in the boreal type of evergreen conifer forests and in the montane or submontane type of conifer forest. Although not represented in Britain, this habitat is fascinating and in Europe, fir growths generally form the upper limit of the coherent forest belt.

Rapid growth of fir seeds and the ease with which seedlings could be cultivated led, in the 18th and 19th century, to a fashion for planting out fir monocultures throughout the whole of Europe. The typical birds of firwoods are grouse (the Capercaillie and Black Grouse). The most important representatives of the songbirds in British plantations are the Crossbill, the Coal Tit and Crested Tit, the Goldcrest and Firecrest, the Siskin and the Bullfinch. In Europe, firwoods are further inhabited by the Pygmy Owl and Tengmalm's Owl, however more characteristic predators which like to nest in firwoods include the Goshawk and the Sparrowhawk. The distribution of the Nutcracker and the Three-toed Woodpecker in Europe is linked to both latitude and altitude. In the north they often occur in lowland firwoods whereas further south they only frequent forested mountains.

Pinewoods

When we speak of pinewoods, it conjures up a picture of open conifer forests. Pines are explicitly photophilic and form fairly loose growths which let in plenty of light. Pinewoods are usually poor in undergrowth, especially on dry, sandy soil. An abundance of herbaceous undergrowth is usually a sign that the pine originally grew here only as one of various kinds of trees and not in pure pine growths. Because of the hardy nature and quick growth pines, like firs, are grown on a large scale in monocultures, again at the expense of mixed and deciduous woods. This is particularly the case in several countries in central and southern Europe, where forest fires contributed to the spread of the pine-tree. It is hard to think of any birds which frequent nothing but pinewoods. Perhaps we could name the Crossbill, which lives entirely on pine cones. Further characteristic species include tits (chiefly the Coal Tit and Crested Tit), the Siskin and — in dry, sandy pinewoods — the Wood Lark. Otherwise, in pinewoods we mainly find general woodland species like the Chaffinch, Tree Pipit, Treecreeper and Great Spotted Woodpecker.

Scattered structures

When we speak of 'scattered structures', we mean any type of growth of trees or shrubs scattered about in open country. They can thus be solitary trees, groups of trees, shrubby hillsides, roadside avenues and greenery growing alongside running water. This environment or ecotone (the transition zone between two overlapping habitats) is one of the very richest, since it also contains species living only or mainly in the ecotone. The number of avian species represented here is large and the number of nesting birds per area unit is high. This tendency to greater species variety and density in the contact area of adjacent habitats is known as a marginal effect. Such predominantly ecotonal species include practically all the warblers (which require trees and bushes both for nesting and as a source of insects), together with the buntings, thrushes, linnets and greenfinches, which gather food in open spaces.

Explanatory notes to the text

The species depicted in this book are birds living in the western part of the Palaearctic region, that is to say in the whole of Europe as far as Iceland in the north, to the Ural Mountains and the Caspian Sea in the east and also south to North Africa and Asia Minor. They are all birds which nest in the given region, or appear there more or less regularly as passage migrants or vagrants.

I have tried to include as many regular nesting birds as possible, together with others which live on the outskirts of this region and are thus not familiar to ordinary amateur ornithologists, in particular species living at the eastern or south-eastern end of the western Palaearctic. I have also added species which were brought to Europe from other parts of the world and have since become so thoroughly acclimatised and adapted that in some European countries they now live and breed freely in the wild.

The photographs all show the adult birds, generally in their breeding plumage; in some cases both sexes are illustrated and occasionally the birds are depicted in their non-breeding plumage.

An adult bird is a full-grown and sexually mature bird. In their first few months of life the young still wear down and from their first autumn until they reach sexual maturity they still do not acquire their proper plumage. Gulls and birds of prey in particular have various intermediate plumage, which are known as first-winter plumages or second-summer plumage, etc, so that the birds are often quite hard to identify. Breeding (nesting or spring) plumage is the plumage worn at nesting time and it is fully developed in the spring. When the breeding season is over, most birds moult, their appearance changes and they don their plainer winter plumage, in which even the once brightly coloured males often resemble the females. Differences between the various plumages are pointed out in the text. Where no difference is emphasised, the description refers to both the male and the female. In some species (e.g. birds of prey), there are no differences between the non-breeding and the breeding plumages.

In the illustrations, males are denoted by the symbol ♂ and females by the symbol ♀.

Birds' voices are one of their most important identification marks in natural surroundings and often they are actually the only possible means of identifying the species. This applies particularly to birds which lead a secretive existence (e.g. rails), to birds which are active mainly at dusk or at night (owls, nightjars) and to species very similar in appearance to one another (*Phylloscopus* warblers, reed warblers, treecreepers). The description of most species therefore includes a description of the voice, despite the difficulties of making it comprehensible to the reader. I have tried to resolve the problem by transcription, i.e. by expressing the voice in certain syllables or sounds, or by comparison with other, familiar sounds. Transcription does not render birds' voices with absolute accuracy, but if we are at least just a little acquainted with them we find that transcription gives us a fair idea of the sounds and that it is a useful guide. The best way, of course, is to learn birds' voices in the company of an experienced ornithologist. Another way is to study them from gramophone records or tape recordings.

The area of breeding distribution in the maps is marked in black. The regular area of winter distribution is marked by a line. In some cases the wintering area is found outside the maps (mostly in the south), and sometimes the same occurs with the breeding distribution. In both cases there is an arrow marking their location.

25

Diving birds

Divers
Grebes

These two orders comprise aquatic birds which spend practically the whole of their life on or beneath the surface of water. Their shape and structure are excellently adapted for movement both in and under water. Divers have a long, cylindrical body, much of which is submerged when they are swimming (Fig. 1); grebes have more rounded contours and a longer neck (Fig. 2). The legs are situated at the very rear end of the body (Fig. 3). The tibiae are immovable and do not project from the body at all; the only free parts of the legs are the short, flat-sided tarsi and the toes. In divers, the three front toes are joined together by wide webbing; the first toe is rudimentary (Fig. 4). In grebes, each toe has a separate, continuous edging of tough skin, which is joined to the edging of the adjacent toes only at the base; the claws are flat and nail-like (Fig. 5). On land, divers and grebes are very awkward, holding themselves erect and walking with tiny steps. In the water, however, it is a pleasure to watch them. The features which are a handicap on dry land become an advantage in the water, and penguins are probably the only birds better adapted to an aquatic existence. When swimming under water they hold their wings tightly against their body, while their legs project sideways, striking out simultaneously and forcing the water behind or above the body. Diving is further made easier by the fact that their bones are not filled with air.

Another form of adaptation to an aquatic environment is their very dense plumage, which is generously oiled with the secretion of the highly developed preen gland and at the same time ensures complete thermal insulation. When the birds moult, they lose all their flight feathers at once and are thus, for some time, unable to fly. This does not appear to matter to them, however, since in any case they are not often seen in the air.

Fig. 3. *In grebes, the legs are attached at the end of the body.*

Fig. 1. *Divers (Gaviiformes).*   **Fig. 2.** *Grebes (Podicipediformes).*   **Fig. 4.** *A diver's foot, with wide webbing.*

The only time they undertake long journeys is during migration, when they fly fast, in a straight line. Their short, narrow wings, long neck and short tail are very noticeable in the air (Fig. 6). Because of the shape and size of their wings, divers in particular have difficulties with taking off and landing; they run a long way over the surface before rising, and when they alight they skim the water for several metres on their breast and belly, with their legs stretched out behind them.

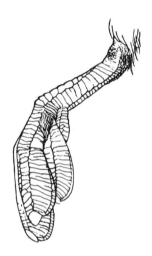

Fig. 5. *Foot of a Great Crested Grebe; the toes are bordered with leathery skin and have flat nails instead of claws.*

Fig. 7. *The floating nest of a grebe.*

Fig. 6. *The Great Crested Grebe in flight.*

Divers build their nest at the water's edge and all they have to do is slip off it. Grebes build floating nests made of rotting aquatic plants (Fig. 7). Before they leave the nest they cover it with the same material, so that to the eye of the uninitiated − and especially to potential nest-robbers, such as crows − it appears to be deserted. In addition, the heat produced by the rotting material evidently helps to keep the eggs at the right temperature when the parents are absent from the nest. The young are nidifugous, i.e. their development is well advanced at hatching and they do not remain in the nest. They are immediately able to swim and dive, but the parents catch food for them, and in fact feed them and care for them in general for a very long time. Young grebes spend much of their infancy riding on their parents' backs, since their own thermoregulation is not yet properly developed and they do not tolerate long periods swimming in cold water; the Great Northern Diver *Gavia immer* has also been seen to carry its young on its back. The members of both orders live mainly on fish, supplemented by aquatic invertebrates. Adult grebes also give their young feathers plucked from their own body or gathered from the surface of the water; their own stomach likewise always contains a good-sized ball of feathers. According to some experts, this provides internal protection against injury by fish bones, while others consider that it acts as a 'plug' and prevents partly digested food from passing too soon from the stomach to the intestine. Grebes sometimes leave their nesting area in search of food and carry the fish back to the nest in their beak.

Grebes do not lay many eggs and the result is fluctuation in the size of their populations. Divers lay even fewer eggs and many pairs fail to rear their brood at all. As a rule, the males and females are the same size and are similar in coloration.

A pair of Great Crested Grebes (Podiceps cristatus) *near their floating nest.*

Red-throated Diver, Red-throated Loon
Gavia stellata

The Red-throated Diver occurs in the tundras and in parts of the forest belt of Eurasia and North America. It inhabits stagnant inland waters, often with little vegetation, at both low and montane altitudes. The birds return to their Arctic nesting sites, already paired, in March or in April. If they find the lakes still frozen, they wait off the coast until the ice has melted. They nest singly or in small colonies. Their peculiar mating call can be heard over long distances; it begins with short cackling sounds of mounting frequency, which change into a long series of plaintive notes. Mating is accompanied by a nuptial dance on the surface of the water. The nest is merely a depression in a pile of floating aquatic plants, or lies on the shore at the water's edge. The birds nest from May to July. The parents take turns to sit on the 2 olive-green to brown eggs with blackish-brown speckles (2), which they incubate for about 25 days. The young are able to swim only 10—12 hours after they are hatched and at 40 days they already have their contour feathers, but are not yet adult size. The families stay together until the autumn and between October and December they fly southwards in search of ice-free water. Sometimes they winter on the coast, near their inland nesting sites, but sometimes they fly as far afield as the Mediterranean and the Black and Caspian Seas. They live mainly on small fish, supplemented by molluscs, crus-

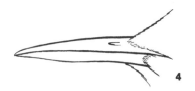

taceans and large aquatic insects. In its breeding plumage (1) the Red-throated Diver has a grey head and neck and a reddish-brown triangular patch on its throat; in its winter plumage it is greyish-brown, with a white-mottled back. It has a slightly uptilted beak (3), in contrast to the Black-throated Diver *Gavia arctica* whose beak is down-curved (4).

Little Grebe
Tachybaptus ruficollis

The Little Grebe inhabits practically the whole of Europe (except the most northerly part), southern Asia, Australia and part of northern Africa. In western and southern Europe it is a bird of passage or a resident bird; in central and eastern Europe it mostly migrates southwestwards for the winter. The pairs are evidently permanent and even in the winter they mostly remain together. They usually arrive at their nesting sites — sheets of water of every possible type and size — in March or April. Their courtship is noticeable for the prolonged trills ('bibibibee') given by both partners. The male is very aggressive and drives away from its chosen nesting site birds much larger than itself. Both sexes participate in the building of the nest, which is no more than a pile of rotting aquatic plants hidden in dense vegetation. The eggs, at first white, are stained by the nest material and gradually turn brown. Little Grebes produce two broods a year. Each clutch contains 4—6 eggs, which the parent birds incubate in turns for 20—21 days; they likewise care assiduously for the young for over two months. If danger threatens, the adult birds dive with tremendous force, sending showers of water over the enemy. The grebes generally leave their nesting sites between August and October. They catch their food — insects, molluscs, crustaceans, worms and small fish — under water. The Little Grebe is the smallest of its family; in its breeding plumage it has a chestnut-brown neck and a greenish-yellow spot around the corners of its beak (1), while in the winter it is greyish-brown with a white underside (2).

2

1

31

Great Crested Grebe
Podiceps cristatus

The Great Crested Grebe inhabits large parts of Eurasia and also occurs in Africa, Australia and New Zealand. North and east European birds are migrants; they winter in the southwest and the south, along the Atlantic and the Mediterranean coasts. They migrate by night, so that their appearance on ponds, lakes and creeks may be sudden and unexpected. Their arrival at their

adult birds' backs and, although they can already swim and dive, they let themselves be carried about for the first six weeks. The parents first of all feed them directly on insects and small invertebrates, to which they later add small fish. At 10—11 weeks the young are still completely dependent on their parents. The families do not break up until it is time for them to disperse or

nesting sites — usually in March or April — is followed by courtship, in which the birds circle each other on the water, shake their heads and ruffle their forked crests and collars; in the final phase they 'tread water', breast to breast, holding in their beaks aquatic plants brought up from the bottom (2). The nest, which is made from aquatic plants and is built between April and July, is either hidden in the littoral vegetation or floats on the open water; it is a simple structure and looks like a small or large heap

of plants. The nests usually occur singly; nesting colonies are not very common. The 3—5 eggs (3) are incubated for 25—29 days, the parents taking turns to incubate them. When their feathers have dried, the young climb on to the

3

migrate, in August or September. In their breeding plumage the birds have a gleaming white breast, two erectile 'horns' and an expansible ruff (1). In the winter their horns and ruff are barely detectable and their plumage is greyish-brown. These grebes, which are almost the size of a wild duck, are the largest members of the family. Their normal call, which can be heard over long distances the whole year round, is a barking 'gorr'; their mating call is a repeated 'kek kek kek'.

Red-necked Grebe
Podiceps grisegena

The Red-necked Grebe inhabits chiefly eastern Europe, but also occurs in parts of central and northern Europe. It also lives in eastern Asia and the north of North America. Some of its populations are migratory. For instance, north European birds winter on the shores of the Atlantic and east European birds in the Mediterranean and Black Sea region. For nesting they choose

family, i.e. they carry them on their back and place food directly in their beak. In about six weeks the young are able to gather food themselves, but the adult birds still look after them for a further four weeks. The main components of their diet are insects, insect larvae, small crustaceans, molluscs and small fish. Red-necked Grebes migrate in September and October; the adults

large sheets of water which have at least some dense vegetation. The nesting sites are occupied in March or April, sometimes later. The courting rituals are accompanied by loud 'neighing' calls ('er-er-er-er') which have been compared with the cries of a foal. The pairs always nest singly. Each pair works on the nest together, building it usually in growths of aquatic plants, but sometimes in the open. The nest

is a simple pile of decaying plant material and mud. In May or June, 3–5 eggs appear in the shallow bowl; the parents take turns to incubate them, from the very first egg, and the young are hatched asynchronously in 22–27 days. Very often the male tends the first offspring, while the female still incubates the remaining eggs. Red-necked Grebes care for their young in the same way as other members of the

generally leave sooner than the others. In its breeding plumage (1), this bird has a striking russet-coloured neck, whitish-grey cheeks and throat and a black-capped head with only vestigial 'horns'. Its winter plumage (2) is predominantly greyish-brown and there is no superciliary stripe between the black cap and the eyes. The Red-necked Grebe is only slightly smaller than the Great Crested Grebe.

Slavonian Grebe, Horned Grebe
Podiceps auritus

The Slavonian or Horned Grebe nests on stagnant inland waters, preferably with luxuriant littoral vegetation, although it will also make do with thinly overgrown reservoirs. The floating pile of decaying plant material which constitutes the nest is built by the combined efforts of both sexes. As a rule, the nests are placed singly in the waterside vegetation, but sometimes there will be they crawl into the feathers on their parents' backs, where they spend most of their early life. It is quite normal for the adult birds to dive with their offspring clinging to their back. They are very attentive parents and keep the young well supplied with the larvae of aquatic insects, crustaceans, aquatic gastropods and later small fish. The Slavonian Grebe inhabits northern Europe, Asia spring, the adult birds have a conspicuous russet neck and a black head with rusty-yellow side stripes terminating at the back of the head in erectile tufts of feathers (1). In the winter, the black cap is sharply separated from the white cheeks (2). In the nesting season their call is a trilling 'beebeebeebee'. Slavonian Grebes are roughly the same size as Black-necked Grebes.

several together, forming a small colony. Nesting time lasts from May to July. The parent birds take turns to sit on the eggs, which they incubate for 20–25 days. Like other grebes, if they both leave the nest, they cover the clutch with rotting plants so that it will not be seen by predators (particularly crows) on the look-out for eggs. As soon as the newly hatched young are dry, and North America. In most of Europe it is to be seen only on migration or during the winter (usually from October to April). North European birds generally migrate southwestwards to western Europe and on a smaller scale to the Mediterranean. In the

Black-necked Grebe, Eared Grebe

Podiceps nigricollis

The Black-necked Grebe was originally a native of southeastern Europe, but at the end of the last century it began to spread westwards and northwestwards, so that today its range stretches to France and Spain and to the south of Scandinavia. It also lives in various parts of Africa and Asia and in the west of North America. It is a very gregarious bird and usually nests in colonies which may number up to several hundred pairs. Very often it nests in gull colonies and the bond between the two species is so strong that, if the gull colony breaks up, the Black-necked Grebe colony likewise ceases to exist. The birds arrive at their nesting sites in March or April, already paired. As a rule they frequent large reservoirs with an adequately large area of open water and abundant decaying plants. In this species, the male brings the material and the female does the actual building. The 3—4 eggs are incubated for 20—21 days by both parents in turn. The young spend most of the early part of their life on their parents' backs or under their wings. Their diet is the same as that of other grebes. Black-necked Grebes are slightly smaller than Coots. In spring they have a black

littoral vegetation, where they hide their inconspicuous nest, which is built between April and June and is the usual heap of neck and fan-shaped tufts of golden-yellow feathers on the sides of their head (1); their eyes are like coral beads. In the winter they resemble Slavonian Grebes, but the dividing line between their black cap and white cheeks is not so sharp and they have a differently shaped, slightly uptilted beak (2). Their calls are a melodious 'beebeeb' and a whistling 'poo-eep'.

35

Gliding birds and Fishing birds

Tubenoses
Pelicans and Allies

Tubenoses are excellent and enduring fliers accustomed to stormy sea winds and to looking for their food on the surface of the water as they fly. All day long they roam the seas and the only time they visit the shore is in the nesting season. They glide low down, close to the surface, utilising in a masterly manner differences in the velocity and direction of the wind on the lee and windward slopes of high waves (this is known as dynamic gliding). Gliding is facilitated by the extent of their wings, whose ulnar and humeral bones (the arm) are particularly long, rather than the manus (hand), as in gulls for instance. The Wandering Albatross *Diomedea exulans,* the

largest bird capable of flight, has a wingspan of up to 3.5 m (Fig. 1) and possesses 37 arm feathers (secondaries), instead of the usual 10–12. Some petrels (the Storm Petrel is the smallest seabird frequenting European shores) check their fluttering flight on the surface by spreading their webbed feet and dipping them into the water (Fig. 2). Their easy and enduring flight is made possible by the large amount of air in their bones.

The nostrils of tubenoses are visible as tubular formations on the top of the beak, the horny covering of which is composed of small platelets (Fig. 3). The size of their nasal cavities, whose surface is covered with olfactory mucosa, is enlarged still further by the convolutions of their nasal conchae, and the exceptionally large olfactory lobes of their brain testify that these modifi-

Fig. 1. *Silhouette of a flying albatross, showing the exceptionally long ulnar part of the wing.*

Fig. 2. *Mode of flight of the Storm Petrel, almost skimming the water.*

37

cations are associated with a very fine sense of smell (rather unusual in birds). The tubular nostrils are evidently responsible for perception of wind velocity and they also contain the ducts of salt-excreting glands. In pelicans, on the other hand, the nostrils are vestigial or completely overgrown, to prevent water from entering them. There is no sexual dimorphism either in size or in coloration.

Pelicans and allies are famed for their skill at catching fish. They also swim and dive extremely well, aided by their paddle-like feet; the first toe points forwards and all the toes are joined together by webbing (Fig. 4). All the members of this order live on fish, but they catch their prey in different ways. Gannets plummet down to the surface from a height (Fig. 5); they dive to considerable depths and remain under water for a long time; there are even reports of Gannets having been caught in fishermen's nets at depths of down to 30 m. Cormorants catch their food by

Fig. 3. *The beak of a Storm Petrel is composed of platelets and has tubular nostrils (viewed from the side and from above).*

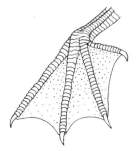

Fig. 4. *On the foot of members of the order Pelecaniformes, all four toes point forwards and are joined together by webbing.*

Fig. 5. *The Gannet catches its food by diving headlong on to the surface of the sea.*

diving from the surface to depths of about 9 m and remain under water for up to 70 seconds, swimming with simultaneous strokes of their feet and steering with their tail and wings. They can even hunt in turbid water and, since blind cormorants in good physical condition have sometimes been found, it was postulated that when catching fish they may also be guided by their sense of hearing. Pelicans are equipped with an enormous pouched bill for catching fish. All the members of this order are skilled fliers or gliders (Fig. 6). Pelicans and Gannets have a fully pneumatic and buoyant skeleton (almost all their bones are hollow). In Gannets, the air sacs under their skin evidently have the function of buffers, reducing the force of the impact of their body with the water when they dive to catch fish. In cormorants, however, these modifications would be a hindrance to diving and the pneumatisation of their body and bones is therefore very restricted.

In both the above orders an aquatic mode of life is also associated with an extremely well-developed uropygial (preen) gland, which means that the feathers are always kept properly oiled (the plumage of some species is so saturated with

A colony of White Pelicans (Pelecanus onocrotaιus).

oil that even old stuffed museum specimens and the eggs have an unpleasant smell). The only exceptions are cormorants, which dry their wet wing and tail feathers in the air when perched, occasionally flapping their half-spread wings to speed the process.

The members of both orders generally nest gregariously in colonies. The incubation of the eggs takes a very long time; for example, fulmars sit on their eggs for an average of 53 days. The nidicolous young are completely naked when hatched and their eyes are closed. The parents keep them so well supplied with food, and for so long, that for a time they may actually weigh more than the adult birds. The young of some tubenose species are left to fend for themselves before they are fully developed; they then live on their own fat reserves until they are able to fly out to sea.

Fig. 6. *Silhouette of a flying pelican, with broad wings suitable for gliding.*

39

Fulmar
Fulmarus glacialis

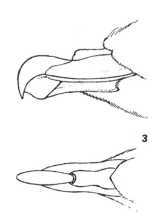

The Fulmar is at home in the northern part of the Pacific and Atlantic Oceans, and breeds in large numbers on the coasts of Britain and Ireland. In the autumn and winter, however, it appears regularly off other coasts of western Europe and very occasionally it is driven inland by gales. The whole of its life is closely associated with the sea and it visits the land only to sleep and to nest. Its large nesting colonies are usually situated high up on rocks or steep slopes overlooking the sea. The nest is in a crack in the rocks, or in a hole excavated by the parent birds in the shelter of a boulder; it is merely a shallow depression lined sometimes with grass and sometimes with small stones. The single white egg is laid in May or in the first week of June; the parents take turns to incubate it (the incubation time, 48—57 days, is exceptionally long) and they care for the young bird for roughly the same length of time. For the first 14 days, one of the parents always remains with the offspring, while the other flies far out to sea in search of food; this consists chiefly of dead creatures floating on the surface, cephalopods, crustaceans, jellyfish and fish. The young bird is fed only once a day, on a partly digested, oily liquid which makes it enormously fat. In the last phase of the yong Fulmar's growth the parent birds stop feeding it, and until it is fully fledged it lives on its accumulated fat reserves. It is not capable of breeding until it is seven years old. Fulmars are larger than the Black-headed Gull; they are white, with silvery-grey wings, back and tail (1), but there is also a dark, grey-coloured phase (2). They have a characteristically shaped beak (3). In the breeding season they utter grunting sounds.

Cory's Shearwater
Calonectris diomedea

Cory's Shearwater inhabits the shores and islands of the Mediterranean, the northern part of the Atlantic and evidently the Indian Ocean also. It spends almost the whole of its life over the waves and the only exception is the breeding season, when it seeks out deserted coasts and islands to nest. The birds nest in colonies in holes and fissures in the rocks, or in burrows up to 50 cm deep which they excavate themselves. The nest is sometimes almost bare of any lining, but sometimes the partners bring twigs, grass, small stones and shells found in the neighbourhood. At the end of May or the beginning of June the female lays a single white egg, which is incubated by both the parents in turn; they also both take care of the young, which remains in the nest until it is fully fledged. The young are usually hatched between the middle of July and the beginning of August and leave the nest between the middle of October and the beginning of November, so that the total period for the incubation of the eggs

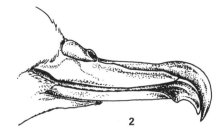

2

and the care of the young amounts to a full five months. The birds live mainly on cephalopods, but also on other molluscs, crustaceans and animal remains floating on the water. Some Cory's Shearwaters winter in the Mediterranean region, but the majority migrate to the coasts of southern Africa. They set out between October and December and return to their nesting sites in March. Cory's Shearwater (1) is a little larger than a Common Gull. It has a greyish-black back, a light brown crown and a whitish underside; its beak (2) is yellow. When nesting, it utters a long-drawn-out, gull-like 'yeh-gow, yeh-gow'.

Storm Petrel
Hydrobates pelagicus

The Storm Petrel (1), the smallest seabird on European coasts, is about the same size as a swift. It is completely greyish-black, with a white rump, a whitish band across its wings and a straight-ended tail (2). It utters calls only while nesting, when it makes squeaking and growling sounds terminating in a characteristic 'hiccup'. It is strictly a seabird and the only time it is to be found on land is in the breeding season. It nests in colonies, generally on islands and less often on the coast. The nest is in a crack in a rock, in a hole in the ground, in a rabbit burrow or under a stone; sometimes the birds dig a hole themselves. They usually arrive at their nesting sites at the end of April and generally nest from the end of May to July. The single white egg, marked with dark brown speckles at its blunt end, is incubated for 38–41 days by both the adult birds in turns; sometimes, however, they take a break for one or two days, during which time the egg does not come to any harm. The parents tend their offspring for 54–68 days. For the first week or so, one of them always stands guard, but from about the sixteenth day onwards the young bird is left in the nest on its own, while the parents scour the sea for food — small coelenterates, molluscs, crustaceans and the floating fatty remains of marine animals. They do not return to the nest until nightfall (usually one hour or more after sunset) and return to the open sea again about one hour before sunrise. The Storm Petrel's home is the eastern part of the north Atlantic and the Mediterranean Sea. In the winter it migrates to the west and south coast of Africa, although many birds remain in the vicinity of their nesting areas the whole year round.

2

Leach's Petrel
Oceanodroma leucorhoa

Leach's Petrel (1) is a small sea-bird about the size of a swallow. It has a blackish-brown body, a white, grey-centred rump and a slightly forked tail (2). It 'hops' over the surface of the water, looking for oily remains of marine animals and refuse from ships, but it also catches crustaceans, molluscs and small fish. It is almost voiceless, except in the

2

June or up to the middle of July, but sometimes as late as the first half of August. Its incubation takes 42 days and the parents sit in turns, at intervals of four to six days. The young bird is 63—70 days old before it is fully fledged. These petrels usually leave their Atlantic nesting sites in October; most of them spend the winter between the tropic of Cancer and

breeding season, when its chirping 'pure wheat, pure wheat' can be heard from its nesting sites. Leach's Petrel inhabits the north Atlantic and the north Pacific and is seen on land, on rocky shores and on islands, only in the breeding season. It is very gregarious and some of its colonies number thousands and even tens of thousands of nests. It nests in rock crevices or holes in the ground, which the male excavates itself. The birds almost always return to the same hole each year. The burrows are usually over 30 cm, and sometimes as much as 120 cm, deep and the nest chamber is lined with plant débris. The single white egg, whose blunt end is marked with a few red spots, is usually laid in the equator, but many cross the equator and some actually find their way to Antarctic waters. On the other hand, many winter near their nesting areas, to which they all return in March or April.

43

Gannet
Sula bassana

The Gannet inhabits coasts and islands in the northern part of the Atlantic. In Europe it nests in Iceland, the Faroe Islands, Norway, Britain and Ireland (British and Irish birds form over 70% of the total world Gannet population), the Channel Islands and northwest France. It is a gregarious bird and nests in huge colonies, the largest of which, on St Kilda, in the Outer Hebrides, numbered 59,000 pairs in 1974. The colonies are situated on small islands or on precipitous rocks descending straight into the sea. The nest is made of seaweed, grass and fragments of wood. The single bluish egg is laid between March and May and is incubated by the male as well as the female, for a period of 43—45 days. The adult birds both feed the young on fish, which they push into its beak with their own. They feed their offspring so assiduously, and even at night, that in ten weeks or so it is exceptionally plump and weighs about 4,500 g — that is to say, about 1 kg more than its parents. The excess fat comes in very useful, however, since the parents abandon the young bird and leave it to provide for itself. While still unable to fly, it launches itself from the cliff into the water and very often it swims tens of kilometres before rising for the first time, on its own wings, into the air. This usually takes place when it is about 15 weeks old. After that it learns to catch fish in the typical gannet manner, by dropping, head first, on to the surface of the sea. Gannets are partial migrants. Birds from northern and western Europe migrate in September or October, as a rule to waters off west Africa

and to the Mediterranean, and return to their nesting sites between February and April. The adult birds, which are about the same size as geese, are white, with a yellowish head, a bluish beak and black-tipped wings (1). The young are dark brown, speckled with white; later, according to their age, they are variably mottled with brown and white spots (2).

Cormorant, Great Cormorant

Phalacrocorax carbo

The area inhabited by the Cormorant is exceptionally extensive. It comprises all the continents except South America and stretches both south of the equator and far to the north. Birds from southern and western Europe are nomadic and resident; the remaining European birds are migrants. Cormorants frequent both fresh water and the sea. They consume large quantities of fish and settle on well-stocked rivers, fishponds, lakes and coastal waters. Their colonies, which are sited on rock or cliff ledges or on tall trees, can number several thousand birds. In time, the trees generally dry up, probably because they are plastered with the birds' droppings. The nest, which is made of sticks and twigs and is lined with grass, reeds and stalks, is built by both the partners together. In mixed colonies, Cormorants often take over the nests of various kinds of herons. The 3—4 light blue eggs, which are laid between March and May, are covered with a thick layer of chalky substance. The parents take turns to sit and the incubation period is 23—29 days. The young are hatched asynchronously; they are naked and they do not open their eyes for three days. The parents first of all feed them on partly digested food, but later bring them fresh fish and water, which they carry in a pouch in their throat. The young are fledged at two months. They begin to leave the colony in August and the older birds follow in September; the non-resident populations migrate mainly to the Mediterranean region. The way in which Cormorants catch fish is particularly interesting. Very often several birds hunt together in a row, driving the fish into shallow water, where they are easier to catch. Adult Cormorants are black, with a white throat and (in the breeding season) a white thigh patch; they are about the same size as a goose. The young are blackish-brown with a whitish belly (1).

45

Shag
Phalacrocorax aristotelis

The Shag (1) resembles the Cormorant, but is completely black, with a green lustre; the young are brown and generally lack the whitish belly. Part of the breeding plumage is a short crest, pointing forwards, on the head. As in other cormorants, the short legs are situated far back on the body and the feet are wholly webbed, showing that their owner may be clumsy on land but is an excellent swimmer and diver. The Shag lives almost entirely on fish, which it catches by diving from the surface; sometimes it remains under water for almost three minutes. As a rule, it hunts in the open sea, within sight of land, and comes into the mouths of rivers and to quiet lagoons only in stormy weather; it is thus a typical seabird. It nests on the coasts of northern, western and southern Europe and of North Africa. Approximately from Britain southwards it is a resident bird; birds which nest further north sometimes spend the winter along the European shores of the Atlantic. The Shag's nesting colonies are to be found on rock faces and on cliffs, often in more or less inaccessible holes and hollows. The site is chosen by the male and old males usually return each year to the same site. New nests are generally built only by young males, which fetch the material (mainly rotting seaweed, twigs, leaves − often green − and heather), while the females make the actual nest. Between March and May the female usually lays 3 light blue eggs (2), which the adult birds both incubate in turn for 30−33 days. The young remain about 50 days in the nest, but are dependent on the parents for a further two to four weeks. The young generally do not start to breed until they are three to four years old.

2

Pygmy Cormorant
Phalacrocorax pygmeus

The Pygmy Cormorant is only about half the size of the Cormorant and is thus no larger than a large pigeon. In its breeding plumage (1) it has a dark russet head and neck, while the rest of its body is black, with a green lustre, and with white feathers scattered among the black. When the breeding season is over, the white spots disappear. This species has a shorter beak and a longer tail than the Cormorant, which it otherwise resembles as regards its habits, although it does not form such large colonies and is not so timid. It often perches on shrubs and hanging branches. It occurs in southeastern Europe (former Yugoslavia, Romania and Bulgaria) and in southwestern and central Asia. It is nomadic and a migrant; birds from southeastern Europe spend the winter on the shores of the Aegean Sea and the Adriatic. It nests beside lakes and the arms of large rivers and in swamps extensively overgrown with rushes and willows. It likes company and therefore nests in colonies, often together with other birds such as various species of herons and cormorants. The deep nest is made of dry twigs and reeds and is built on a tree, in a bush or on flattened rushes, and the 3—5 bluish eggs are laid between the end of April and the middle of July. The male helps the female to incubate the eggs and the young are hatched in 27—30 days. Both the parent birds participate in the feeding and rearing of the young, but it is not yet known just how long this takes. The Pygmy Cormorant lives predominantly on fish measuring 10—15 cm, which it catches very skilfully under water. Unlike other cormorants, it also catches its food in narrow channels and small stretches of water.

47

White Pelican
Pelecanus onocrotalus

In Europe, the White Pelican now nests regularly only in the Danube delta, on the shores of the Black Sea. From here its range extends to Asia Minor and central Asia and to northeastern, tropical and southern Africa. It is a nomadic and a migratory bird, which leaves in September or October to fly southeast to Asia Minor, Egypt or further still, to southwestern Asia and India. Very rarely – generally between July and September, when the breeding season is over – it appears far to the west (as far as Spain) and to the north (as far as Finland). For nesting it prefers large lagoons, river deltas and large inland lakes with dense and extensive growths of reeds and rushes. It usually returns to its nesting sites between the end of March and May and settles there in colonies varying in size from a few to several hundred birds. The nest is no more than a large pile of reeds and grass blades. The eggs, of which there are almost always 2 and which are laid in April, May or June, have a thick, yellowish chalky covering. They are incubated by both the parents in turn for about 33 days. The adult birds likewise both feed the young, on half-digested fish, which the chicks obtain by pushing the whole of their head down into the older bird's gullet. Small pelicans venture out on to the water while still in their downy plumage and at ten weeks they make their first attempts to fly. Pelicans often hunt in flocks; the birds swim in a row, beating the water with their wings and driving the fish into shallow water, where the

pelicans have no difficulty in catching them in their enormous pouched beaks, which function like dip-nets. The White Pelican (1), which is larger than a swan, has white (sometimes pink-tinted) plumage except for the primaries and their coverts, which are blackish-brown. It has only a narrow pointed strip of feathers on its forehead (2), but its most striking feature is its

huge beak with the bright yellow-red pouch; its feet are flesh-pink and it has red irises. White Pelicans fly in regular lines, and on such occasions the black-bordered hind edge of their wings can be seen from below (3).

Dalmatian Pelican
Pelecanus crispus

Today, the Dalmatian Pelican is to be found in southeastern Europe only in the Srebrno reserve in the north of Bulgaria and in mixed pelican colonies in the Danube delta in Romania. Further east it nests on the shores of the Sea of Azov and the Caspian Sea and in scattered colonies as far as the Aral Sea and Mongolia and in Asia Minor. European birds are migrants; they leave

their nesting sites as early as August and migrate mainly to North Africa, to the Nile. The first birds return in March and the last in May. They nest in similar habitats to the preceding species, but also ascend to lakes high up in the mountains. After arriving at their nesting sites, they at first associate in small flocks, but gradually pair off and begin to build their nests. The male uses its beak to tear away reed blades or whole clumps of grass from the previous year, swims back to the nest with them and presents them to the female, which almost always uses an old nest as the foundation of the new one. At the same time as the White Pelican, it usually lays 2 white eggs which vary greatly in shape: one of the eggs may be long and narrow and the other one short and round. Both the parents incubate the eggs and the young are hatched in 30–32 days. At about $2\frac{1}{2}$ weeks they leave the nest and all collect in the centre of the colony; at four to five weeks they are able to swim in the vicinity of the nest and at 14–15 weeks they are completely independent. These pelicans live on fish weighing up to 1.5 kg and their daily consumption amounts to about 3 kg. The Dalmatian Pelican (1) is silvery-grey; it has yellow irises, grey feet and curled feathers on its head and neck. When flying, it shows the white underside of its wings (2). Its forehead is completely covered with feathers (3).

Long-legged beauties

Herons and Allies
Flamingos

CICONIIFORMES

PHOENICOPTERIFORMES

These two orders comprise slender-bodied, long-legged and long-winged birds of a wide range of sizes. Two of the largest are the White Stork, which weighs about 3 kg and has a wingspan of 1.65 m, and the Greater Flamingo, which is about the same weight and from head to toe measures over 170 cm; the Little Bittern, which weighs 0.14 kg and has a wingspan of 0.5 m, is one of the smallest. Their legs, especially the tarsus and the tibia, are very long and their toes are very flexible. They are adapted for wading in shallow water (although sometimes the birds wade in water up to their belly), for striding over marshy ground and for walking on clumps of reeds. In addition, flamingos are good swimmers,

stretched out behind them and their equally long neck either stretched forwards (storks, Fig. 1; flamingos, etc, Fig. 2), or curved like a letter S (herons, Fig. 3). Flamingos, which have short wings, are unable to glide and merely flap their wings.

These birds have a well-developed preen gland, and in herons large patches of powder-down play an important role in the care of the plumage. These produce large quantities of a fine powder, which is dusted over the contour feathers and keeps the plumage in good condition. Large species have stiff, close-fitting contour feathers, but small species and flamingos have soft plumage. In the courtship period, many

Fig. 1. *Flight silhouette of a White Stork, with its neck stretched straight out in front.*

Fig. 2. *Flight silhouette of a flamingo, with the long neck extended in front and the long legs stretched out behind.*

with incomplete webbing on their front toes. Although the members of both orders have long legs, they do not use them for running; on the contrary, they have a slow, deliberate gait. In the presence of danger they do not run away, but instead take to the air. The majority of these birds fly extremely well and many of them glide very skilfully. When flying, they hold their long legs

Fig. 3. *Flight silhouette of a heron, with the neck held curved like a letter S.*

herons acquire decorative feathers on various parts of their body as part of their display plumage. There is no obvious sexual dimorphism, but the males are usually a little larger than the females.

The skeleton is light and highly pneumatic. The long and very flexible neck is composed of 16–20 vertebrae. In many herons, special modification of the sixth vertebra allows the birds to fold their neck in an S-shaped curve and this, together with their strong cervical muscles, explains their ability to 'harpoon' their prey (Fig. 4). Species which catch fish have a thick, straight and pointed beak with sharp edges (herons, Fig. 5; storks, Fig. 6); those which catch crustaceans and worms have a long, thin and downcurved beak (ibises, Fig. 7) and the beak of spoonbills (Fig. 8) and flamingos (Fig. 9) is adapted for sloshing about in mud to catch food. No other bird has a beak anything like the flamingo's. As distinct from the beak of other birds, the upper mandible is smaller and looser than the lower mandible and is bent at an angle of 60 degrees. This enables the flamingo to walk with its upper mandible skimming over the bottom sediments, to stir up the mud and, by means of the dense horny platelets along the edge of its beak and with the aid of its fleshy, sensitive tongue, to catch small aquatic animals living in the mud.

Fig. 5. *The sharp, pointed beak of the Grey Heron.*

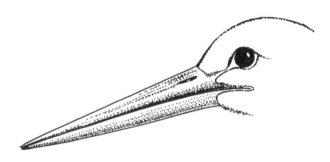

Fig. 6. *The thick, straight beak of the White Stork.*

Fig. 7. *The thin, arching beak of the Glossy Ibis.*

Fig. 8. *The flat, spatulate beak of the Spoonbill.*

Fig. 4. *Sigmoidal flexion of a heron's neck – functional adaptation for harpooning prey.*

The members of both the above orders are monogamous and the pair-bonds are often permanent. They are all very sociable and therefore nest gregariously in colonies, which are sometimes composed of several hundred – and in the case of flamingos several thousand – pairs. The nests are built in trees or in reeds. The flamingo's nest, however, is completely atypical, since it is

The Black Stork (Ciconia nigra) *is a typical forest species whose boundary is spreading steadily further westwards.*

Fig. 9. *The hooked beak of a flamingo, with a smaller upper mandible and a built-in filter apparatus.*

only a pile of mud, mixed with feathers and vegetation, standing in shallow water or on mud by the waterside and left to harden. Herons' and flamingos' eggs are not spotted. The young hatch with their eyes open, but are otherwise completely helpless. The parents feed their offspring by regurgitating food directly into their beaks or into the nest; many of them fly tens of kilometres in search of food.

The vocal organ (syrinx) of these birds is generally reduced to varying degrees, except in herons, which have the most pronounced vocal manifestations and whose syrinx is equipped with 'song' muscles. Many storks, however, are voiceless, but make good their vocal deficiency by mechanical means, i.e. by rattling their beak.

53

Bittern

Botaurus stellaris

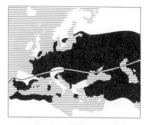

The Bittern, which inhabits extensive reedbeds and marshes, is heard more often than seen. It has a most unbird-like deep, booming, far-carrying call, which it usually repeats three to six times. The way in which it utters these sounds was long a subject of controversy. At first it was thought that the bird thrust its beak into water when calling, but much later it was found that it stretched and lowered its neck and inflated its gullet, which thus acted as a soundbox. In the courtship period (April to June), the male calls mainly at night (less often in the daytime), to mark out its nesting area. The nest is an untidy heap of reeds, rushes and other aquatic plants, with a shallow basin in which the female lays 4—6 brownish eggs (2). The female alone incubates the eggs; the male apparently shows no interest in the nest and, on the contrary, it seems to turn its attention to other females. At only about 14 days, the young leave the nest if disturbed; they are fully fledged at about two months. Bitterns live mainly on insects and insect larvae, supplemented by frogs, newts, fish and small mammals. They inhabit most of Europe (in the north as far as southern Scandinavia), a large part of Asia and northern and southern Africa. In western and southern Europe they are resident birds. Bitterns from other parts of Europe winter in southwestern Europe and northern Africa; in the spring they migrate from February to April, in the autumn from August to October. Both the males and the females are marked with lon-

gitudinal rows of blackish-brown spots (1). If they stand among the previous year's reeds in their rigid defensive 'pole' position, with their body erect and their beak pointing skywards (3), they are virtually invisible. They are slightly larger than a pheasant.

3

2

54

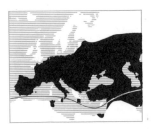

Little Bittern
Ixobrychus minutus

up to 5 cm. The Little Bittern is distributed over most of Europe except Scandinavia and the British Isles; it also occurs in the western part of Asia and in northern and southern Africa, southern Australia and possibly New Zealand. It is a migratory bird; between August and October it migrates to equatorial Africa and returns between the end of March and the beginning of May. Among herons and their allies, sexual differences in coloration are not usual, but here the male is black and very pale ochre (1), while the ochre-coloured female is marked with dark brown spots (2). The Little Bittern, which is about the same size as a Jay, is the smallest European heron.

2♀

The Little Bittern frequents growths of reeds and rushes in ponds, swamps and river creeks and clumps of short willows and alders. It prefers extensive reed-beds, but will also nest on small ponds. It is a retiring, secretive bird, except in the spring, when the male betrays the position of its nesting site by its incessantly repeated call ('hogh-hogh'), which can be heard for hours, especially after dusk and at night and less often in the daytime (when it is usually heard before rain). The male begins to build the nest and the female, with the male's assistance, completes it. The nest is an untidy structure made of dry reed blades or twigs, lined with softer material. The 5—6 eggs are laid between May and July and the parents take turns to sit on them, at irregular intervals; the incubation period is 16—19 days. At only one week, the young, still in their ochre-yellow downy plumage, are able to climb the reeds in the vicinity of the nest; they are fledged at about three weeks. At first, the parents regurgitate the food for the young birds into the nest, but in a few days the young can take it straight from their beaks. The food consists mainly of aquatic and terrestrial insects, molluscs, small fish and frogs measuring

Night Heron, Black-crowned Night Heron

Nycticorax nycticorax

The Night Heron is distributed over the whole of the globe, with the exception of Australasia. Birds which nest in Europe are all migratory and winter in equatorial Africa. They nest in regions with fishponds, marshes and

When a pair has been formed, the female completes the building of the nest, aided by the male. The 3—4 bluish-green eggs (3) are incubated for 20—23 days by both the adult birds, which also brood the newly hatched young

over a radius of many kilometres. The adult birds are about the size of a crow. In their breeding plumage (1) they have a black crown and back, a white underside and ash-grey wings and tail. At the back of their head they have two

slow-flowing rivers and with extensive growths of shrubs and trees, since they are typical shrub- and tree-nesters and are seldom to be found among reeds. They nest in colonies, often together with other herons and even with Ravens. They return at the end of March and during April, in several waves, so that their nesting season lasts from April to July. The males build the foundations of the nest and then, using special displays and calls, attract the females.

for several days. For the first few days they feed them on largely digested pulpy food, and later regurgitate fish, amphibians and various insects for them; the young are independent in about 50 days. Night Herons set out for their winter quarters during August and September. Their vernacular name ('Night' Heron) is not very apt, however, since they are active mostly after dusk and early in the morning, when they fly off to their hunting grounds on rivers, streams and fishponds,

to four erectile plumes, which are shorter on birds in winter plumage. The juveniles are dark brown, with yellow drop-shaped spots (2).

Squacco Heron
Ardeola ralloides

The Squacco Heron inhabits southern Europe and the south-western part of Asia; it nests in northern Africa and in various parts of the rest of that continent south of the Sahara. European birds are migrants and spend the among reeds on a bush standing in water or high up in a tree. The male fetches the material (reed blades and stems) from nearby and presents it to the female, which puts it in place. The nest is lined with fine plant fibres. The early evening, beside the water and in shallows. In August and September the herons leave for the winter. The Squacco Heron grows to roughly the same size as a crow. In its breeding plumage (1, 2) it is ochre-yellow, with

2

winter in Africa. Outside its nesting areas the Squacco Heron is generally a rare accidental visitor seen only during the period before the birds leave for the winter. It nests in swamps, in reedbeds beside ponds and lakes and in flood-prone regions alongside large rivers, where it gathers in colonies, often together with other herons, ibises or spoonbills. It returns from its winter quarters in April or May and the eggs are laid between April and July. The nest is usually built clutch usually consists of 4—5 bluish-green eggs, which are incubated for 21—24 days, mostly by the female and only occasionally by the male. The young remain in the nest for at least one month. They can leave the nest before they are fully fledged, but always return to it to be fed. The parents both participate in the care of the young, for which they catch mainly terrestrial and aquatic insects and their larvae, small fish and frogs; they hunt their prey during the daytime and white wings; its crown and its long-plumed crest are streaked with brownish-black. When it moults, the ornamental plumes are shed and longitudinal stripes can be seen on its head and neck.

57

Great White Egret, Common Egret

Egretta alba

2♂

The Great White Egret is a great traveller. In Europe it inhabits only the southeastern part and in other regions it is, as a rule, only an accidental visitor during its pre-migratory wanderings; it also occurs on all the other continents. Its migration from southeastern Europe takes it to the coast of southern Europe, northwestern Africa and southern Asia. It is less sociable than other herons, although it nests together with them quite regularly. Its colonies generally comprise only three to eight nests and quite frequently the birds nest singly. The Great White Egret has a preference for marshy regions and swamps, fishponds with dense reedbeds and rushes and river deltas. It generally arrives at its nesting sites in March; the nest is built by both the partners between April und June, generally on broken reeds or rushes and less often on a shrub or a tree. The building material — reed and rush stems or dry sticks — depends on where the nest is situated. The eggs are a lighter blue than those of other herons and both the sexes incubate them in turn for 25—26 days; they likewise both feed the young for about six weeks, until they are fledged. Migration to winter quarters takes place from September to November. Great White Egrets live largely on fish and amphibians, which they can catch 40 cm below the surface — a depth that no other heron is able to reach. This egret is the same size as the Grey Heron, but is snow-white and has no long plumes on its head. In its breeding plumage, the ornamental plumes on the male's back are up to 50 cm long (the female's are far shorter) and form a kind of mantle (2); they are soon shed, however (1). At one time, these plumes, like those of the Little Egret, were a fashionable accessory to women's fashions and in the 19th century the demand for them brought these birds to the verge of extinction.

1

Little Egret
Egretta garzetta

2

aquatic arthropods and less frequently small mammals, nestling birds, molluscs and worms. They gather food during the daytime in or beside shallow stagnant water and, like other herons, will fly as much as 10—12 km in search of it. Their departure for their winter quarters is spread over the period from September to November. The Little Egret is about the size of a Night Heron; it is pure white, with a black beak and black, yellow-toed legs. In its courtship plumage (1) it has two

or three long, ribbon-like feathers on its head and on its back there are 18—21 long, curling ornamental plumes whose discontinuous vanes are formed of loose, filamentous barbs (2).

3

The Little Egret is a bird of warm climates, inhabiting southern Europe and southern Asia, Indonesia, New Guinea, northern and eastern Australia and a large part of Africa; it is not often seen in central and northern Europe. It arrives at its nesting sites in marshy and fishpond regions, or in flooded riparian woods, between March and May. Being gregarious, it nests almost entirely in colonies, often together with other herons. The nest is generally built on a tree or a shrub and less often among reeds. The male brings the nest material (long sticks or dry reed blades), while the female does the actual building and defends the nest against neighbours who might consider that the twigs would come in useful for their own nest. The nesting season is very long and lasts from April or May to July or August. The parents take turns, for 21—25 days, to incubate the 3—5 light blue eggs (3), and they also share the rearing of the offspring, to which they chiefly bring fish, amphibians and

1

Grey Heron
Ardea cinerea

The Grey Heron inhabits a large part of Europe, the temperate and subtropical part of Asia and northern, southern and eastern Africa. West European birds are residents; those which nest in the north and east migrate in September or October to the Mediterranean and sometimes as far as South Africa. They usually return in May to their nesting sites beside lakes, fishponds and large lowland rivers, in river valleys and streams and even high up in the mountains. The nesting colonies, which are sometimes several hundred pairs strong, are usually situated on tall trees, but sometimes in reedbeds; isolated single nesting pairs can likewise often be found. The male displays to the female by holding itself erect in a special posture, by ruffling its feathers, by uttering harsh croaks and (later) by symbolic modifications of the nest. The nest, which is built by both the birds together, is made of twigs, but is lined with finer material. Some nests are used for several years, in which case material is added every year, so that the difference between old and new nests is very pronounced. The 4—5 bluish-green eggs (2) are laid between March and May and are incubated for 25—28 days by both the parents in turn. Since they begin incubating with the first or the second egg, the young are hatched asynchronously, and since the youngest is also the weakest it seldom survives. Its siblings push it away from food, so that it does not grow, and finally it is pecked to death or thrown out of the nest. The herons live entirely

on animal food — mainly fish and, to a lesser extent, amphi-

2

bians, small mammals, reptiles, molluscs and insects. The Grey Heron is somewhat smaller than a stork. When adult (1), it has a grey back and a whitish underside. Its black eye-stripe terminates in long ornamental feathers, which are often missing from its winter plumage. Its harsh, croaking 'kray-eek' can be heard mainly from birds in flight and also from the nesting site.

Purple Heron
Ardea purpurea

The distribution of the Purple Heron coincides largely with that of the Grey Heron, but its range does not extend so far to the north. European birds are migrants, young birds leaving in August and the older ones in September. Sometimes they spend the winter in southern Europe, but generally they go on to western and eastern Africa. They return during April, already

paired, and settle in lowland regions with swamps and fishponds. They nest from April to June in small colonies in dense growths of reeds or rushes and less often in waterside bushes or on trees. Accordingly, the nest is either an untidy platform of reed or rush blades, or is made of twigs. It is built by both the partners, which also both incubate the 3—4 bluish-green eggs (2) and care for the offspring, which are hatched in 24—28 days. From the age of three weeks the young herons undertake reconnaissance expeditions in the surrounding reedbeds, which become interwoven by a dense network of paths, bridges and resting places. Their progress over the broken stems is facilitated by their strikingly long toes. The parents bring them food in their throat sac and either let the young 'help themselves' or disgorge the food into the nest; their diet is the same as that of other herons. The young are independent at about two months. The Purple Heron is about the size of a stork. It is mainly rusty-brown and black, with long ornamental feathers on its head and shoulders; its winter and breeding plumages are basically the same (1). In the air, all herons can be identified by their retracted, S-shaped neck and their legs, which protrude far beyond the end of their tail (see the silhouette). Seen from in front, their wings are strikingly arched (3).

Black Stork
Ciconia nigra

The distribution of the Black Stork forms a wide band stretching from central Europe to the Pacific coast of Asia, with an outpost in Spain. During the past few decades it has spread distinctly westwards, so that today the Black Stork nests in the middle of France. Unlike the White Stork, it is a typical forest bird and shuns the neighbourhood of human habitations. It inhabits extensive deciduous and conifer woods with rivers, streams or

stretches of water in the vicinity, at both low and high altitudes. Black Storks arrive at their nesting sites in March or April, usually already in pairs. During the nuptial rituals they often circle above the nesting site and continue the ceremony on the nest by revolving around each other, with the white undertail-coverts spread. The nest is generally situated on an old tree and less often on a ledge of rock. It is built by both the partners in April or in May, first of thick and then of thin twigs, and is lined with turf with grass, moss and lichen growing on it. The 3—5 white, green-tinged eggs are incubated in turn by both the parent birds for 30—34 days; they also both share the task of tending the young, which do not leave the nest for 60—70 days. The young are fed mainly on fish (less on frogs, reptiles and small mammals); the adult birds carry the food in their throat sac and regurgitate it into the nest, where the nestlings pick it up themselves. Prey is caught in shallow water and in streams, sometimes as far as 20 km away from the nest. In August and September, Black Storks migrate to southern and eastern Africa. The young do not reach maturity until their third year. The adult birds (1) are completely black, except for their white underside and their red beak and legs. The juveniles have a greyish-green beak and legs and brownish-black plumage (2). Unlike herons, storks fly with their neck stretched straight out in front of them.

White Stork
Ciconia ciconia

The White Stork's distribution is confined to central and southern Europe, a small area of Asia and North Africa. In Europe it is a very popular bird; people protect it in every way possible and encourage it to nest by providing it with solid foundations on roofs, chimneys and trees. Today, the number of storks nesting in their original environment in forests and on rocks is much smaller than those living together with man. Storks use the same nests for many years, so that sometimes they grow to huge proportions. The largest nest on record was 225 cm across and 280 cm high and weighed 990 kg; a case of a nest used for over 400 years is also known. Stork 'marriages' are usually permanent, the reason, of course, being fidelity to the nest, not to the partner. The male is generally the first on the scene and it will calmly accept another female, should one be willing, before its original mate arrives. Sometimes there are fierce battles between females over the occupation of the nest. The 3—5 eggs, which are laid in April or May, are incubated by both the parent birds in turn; they also both care for the young, which hatch after 30-34 days. Their care is so thorough that, on hot summer days, they give the nestlings shower-baths with water brought in their beak. In August or September, White Storks gather together and migrate, like Black Storks, to eastern and southern Africa, some by a southwestern and others by a southeastern route (2); they return in March or April. The White Stork lives mainly on

2

frogs, small mammals and insects and less on other vertebrates and invertebrates. The adult birds (1) are white, with black wing feathers, red legs and a red beak. The juveniles have brownish to greyish-black legs and their beak is at first blackish and later light red. The best-known sound made by White Storks is the loud clattering of their beak.

Glossy Ibis
Plegadis falcinellus

The Glossy Ibis is a rare bird in Europe. It nests only in the southeast and, sporadically, in Spain, Italy, Hungary and former Yugoslavia, and breeds in scattered areas of Asia, Australia, America and Africa. In Europe it is strictly a migrant, and between August and October it moves to tropical and southern Africa. In April, when it returns, it settles in swamps, beside lakes or slow-flowing rivers or in river deltas with dense reedbeds or bushes. It nests in May, usually in colonies sometimes numbering up to 1,000 pairs and often together with herons, spoonbills, cormorants and even Ravens. The nest, which is built by both sexes, is usually situated in a reedbed and less often on bush; depending on where it is placed, it is made of reeds or of twigs. The sexes also share the 15—18 days' incubation of the 3—5 dark bluish-green eggs. When the young are hatched, the male is kept very busy catching crustaceans, molluscs, worms and insects in shallow water; it brings the food to the nest and presents it to the female, which then divides it among the nestlings. After the young leave the nest, the adult birds still look after them until they are about 30 days old. The Glossy Ibis is about the size of a crow, but has long legs and a thin, curved beak. It is entirely reddish-brown, adult birds (1) having a pronounced greenish to purple lustre. In flight it holds its neck and its legs extended and intersperses the flapping movements of its wide, round-tipped wings with stages of gliding. When ibises move in flocks, they often fly side by side. The Glossy Ibis is a silent bird, except for the grunting sounds which it usually makes only at the nesting site.

The Bald Ibis (1) has a somewhat curious appearance. It is the same size as the preceding species, is black, with a blue, green and purple lustre, and around its neck it sports a ruff formed of long, narrow feathers. The skin on its head and part of its neck is bare and red in colour (brick-red on the crown). Its long, downcurved beak is bright red. Today there are evidently only two places where the Bald Ibis still survives. In Asia Minor, on the upper Euphrates, about 1,300 birds were found in 1953, but in 1976 there were only 39; while in Morocco, in 1940, there were still at least 1,500 birds at 38 nesting colonies, but in 1975 these numbers were only 600—650 and 18 respectively. At one time this bird also nested in southern Europe, and its most northerly limits stretched to southern Germany, Switzerland, Austria and Hungary. Its disappearance from Europe was probably due to climatic changes and to the many-sided negative effects of human activities. In its present areas, the Bald Ibis is a resident, nomadic and migratory bird. It arrives at its nesting sites in February or March, and as early as the end of June migrates southwestwards again. It inhabits more or less bare rock faces and precipitous cliffs and used to nest in ruined castles and human habitations. Its food — insects, worms, amphibians, reptiles and small mammals — is caught in the surrounding steppes, meadows and marshes, on river banks and on the seashore. The nest, which is placed in a hole or a recess in a rock, is built by both sexes and is made of grass and straw. The 2—4 bluish, brown-speckled eggs are laid in March or in April and are incubated for 27—28 days by both the parents in turn. The adult birds also share in the rearing of the young, which remain in the nest for 46—51 days and do not breed themselves until they are five or six years old. There have recently been proposals to re-introduce the Bald Ibis in Europe, in the Alpine countries to which it historically belongs.

Spoonbill
Platalea leucorodia

In Europe, the Spoonbill nests only in the southeast, with isolated nesting areas also in Hungary, Holland and Spain. Its breeding range continues into southern and central Asia and to eastern Africa. The Spoonbill nests beside lowland lakes and fishponds and in swampy regions and river deltas with abundant vegetation in the form of reeds and shrubs. It arrives in April or in May and, being a so-

2

ciable bird, it settles in colonies, which may consist entirely of Spoonbills, but may be mixed and include herons, ibises and cormorants. The nest is built by both sexes together; if it is on a tree or a bush it is made of sticks and twigs, while on the ground it is made of reed and rush blades. Since the nest is used several years in succession, it grows to quite considerable proportions. In large colonies several nests may be joined together, so that two or three pairs nest on the same heap. In April, May or June the female lays 3—5 white eggs with rusty-brown spots (2) and, together with the male, incubates them for 21—25 days. When feeding, the young thrust their beak deep into the parent bird's gullet; their diet consists chiefly of aquatic insects, crustaceans, molluscs, worms and (less often) small frogs and fish. Prey is caught in a rather unusual manner; as the adult birds wade through shallow water, churning up the mud, they describe quarter circles with their wide-tipped bill a little way below the surface and literally 'spoon' it up. In August or September, Spoonbills migrate to tropical Africa. The adult birds are about the same size as a stork. In their breeding plumage (1), they are pure white, with a yellow patch on the breast, and their head is adorned with a long-plumed crest; their non-breeding plumage lacks the crest and the patch of colour. Their legs and beak are black, but the beak has a yellow tip. The juveniles have black-tipped wings, and their legs and beak are pale yellow to grey.

Greater Flamingo
Phoenicopterus ruber

Few birds are as attractive as flamingos. The adults, which are about the size of a Grey Heron, have mainly white, pink-tinted plumage, with bright red wings and black flight feathers; the juveniles are dingy white, with brown wings. Apart from their very long neck and legs, their most striking feature is their thick beak, bent at an obtuse angle in the middle. The beak is edged with tightly packed lamellae; as the flamingo catches small aquatic animals living in shallow water and mud, these lamellae, with the aid of the fleshy tongue, filter out the water and mud, leaving the food behind. When gathering food (2), the flamingo holds its beak upside down, rakes its upper mandible over the bottom and churns up the mud with rapid movements, often stamping its feet to stir up food. Flamingos' nests are also out of the ordinary. They are conical piles of mud, reinforced with feathers and fragments of plants, and the cup is a shallow depression at the top. They are usually 15—50 cm high and 50 cm across and, since flamingos are very sociable birds, there may be up to three nests to one square metre. The 1—2 yellowish-green eggs are thickly coated with a chalky substance; they are laid between the second half of April and the beginning of June and the female incubates them for 30—32 days. About four days after they are hatched, the young climb down from the nest and soon after gather in a crèche, where they are all reared together. They are fed on a red-coloured substance containing carotenoids and blood

cells, which is secreted by the first part of the adult birds' alimentary tube. At two weeks, their beak begins to acquire a hooked shape and they learn to gather food themselves. They are

not fledged for several months, however, and do not attain maturity until their third year. The Greater Flamingo occurs in three subspecies scattered over regions with extensive shallow brackish and salt water in Eurasia and North and South America. In Europe, the subspecies *P.r. roseus* (1) lives only in the Camargue in the south of France and, less regularly, in the south of Spain.

Unrivalled swimmers

Ducks, Geese and Swans

ANSERIFORMES

The members of this order are moderately large to large birds. Their largest representative is the Mute Swan, whose males weigh up to 16 kg, have a wingspan of 2.4 m and measure up to 160 cm in length; one of the smallest, the Garganey, weighs only 0.4 kg. Their short, but strong legs are adapted for swimming. The three front toes are joined together by wide webbing; the hind toe is situated somewhat higher than the others (Figs. 1, 2). A particular beak structure is common to all species. The beak is covered with soft skin and terminates in a wide, horny plate, known from its shape as a 'nail' The sides of the beak are equipped with horny outgrowths, whose structure is adapted to the way in which the bird obtains its food (Fig. 3). Species which filter their food from mud have dense lamellae along the sides of their mandibles; in fish-eating species the lamellae have been converted to sharp-edged processes for gripping fish; while in herbivorous species the lamellae are tooth-like structures, making it easier to tear plants. The length of the neck also has something to do with the way food is obtained. Swans, which reach the greatest depths, when dabbling for food, have 25 cervical vertebrae, while geese have 18 and mergansers, which chase fish below the surface, only 16.

Ducks, geese and swans have dense plumage and the whole of their body is covered with a thick layer of down, their main insulation against the cold water. They keep it well oiled with the oily secretions of their preen gland, so that not a drop of water reaches their skin. We need only to watch them and see how much time they spend in preening. They fly extremely well, and some of them very fast; for instance, Eiders have been reliably recorded to fly as fast as 76 km per hour. This allows them to fly many kilometres every day in search of food and also to migrate

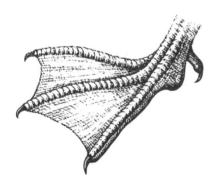

Fig. 1. *Foot of a dabbling duck; the middle toe is the longest and the hind toe is not bordered by webbing.*

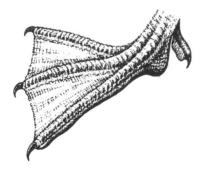

Fig. 2. *Foot of a diving duck; the outer toe is the longest and the first (hind) toe is bordered by webbing.*

Fig. 3. *Duck's or goose's beak, with horny lamellae along the sides and a nail at the end.*

69

long distances. One of the characteristics of this order is the sudden temporary loss of all the flight feathers during the complete summer moult, as a result of which they are unable to fly for about three weeks. They spend this vulnerable period hidden away in the safe shelter of reeds and rushes.

Most ducks are characterised by pronounced sexual dimorphism, the male being much more gaudily coloured than the inconspicuous female. The reason is evidently that the female sits on the eggs and that its plainer colouring offers better protection. Ornithologists divide ducks into dabbling and diving species. Dabbling ducks have an elongate body and a relatively small 'draught', so that their rear end is always left sticking up out of the water (Fig. 4). They have no webbing on their hind toe and their middle toe is longer than

Fig. 4. *Silhouettes of dabbling duck on water and on land.*

Fig. 5. *Silhouettes of diving duck on water and on land.*

Fig. 6. *Dabbling ducks take off directly from the surface of the water.*

the others (Fig. 1). They obtain food by dabbling just below the surface and filter out water and mud particles by means of dense lamellae along the sides of their beak and the ragged edges of their fleshy tongue. They fly straight up from the water (Fig. 6), and in flight a brightly coloured patch (speculum), usually with a metallic gloss, can be seen on the secondaries of each wing. Diving ducks are plumper and shorter; they have a greater 'draught' and on the water their tail is roughly level with the surface. Their legs are situated well back on their body, which makes walking difficult and obliges them to hold the front of their body upright (Fig. 5). Their hind toe is distinctly lobed and their outer toe is the longest (Fig. 2). They dive and catch their food well beneath the surface, often on the bottom. They are also good underwater swimmers, striking off with both their feet at once (and in some species with their wings). Some are perfect divers, capable of remaining under water for up to three minutes and reaching a depth of 60 m. Diving ducks have greater difficulty in rising from the surface and need to take a running start over the water (Fig. 7). They have no speculum on their wings.

Ducks, geese and swans usually lay a large number of eggs, which are incubated entirely by

Fig. 7. *Diving ducks need a running start before taking off from water.*

A flock of geese and ducks above their assembly ground.

the female, but male geese and male swans help to tend and teach their offspring. The chicks of all three groups are among the most highly developed of nidifugous young. At hatching they are already thickly covered with down, and almost as soon as they are dry they leave the nest, are active on land and in the water and are able to look for food themselves.

Mute Swan
Cygnus olor

The Mute Swan inhabits a continuous area stretching from Ireland, Britain and the south of Sweden to central Europe; further east, in the rest of Europe and in Asia, it is found mostly in scattered localities. During the past few decades its numbers in most of Europe have shown a marked increase. It is a partial migrant and spends the winter on ice-free water and seashores in western, central and south-eastern Europe. Because of its majestic appearance, it has been kept since time immemorial in a tame or semi-tame state on ponds in the grounds of mansions and in parks. In the wild state it inhabits stagnant or slow-flowing waters. The pair-bond, which is formed in the autumn, is permanent. Both sexes build the nest, which is situated near the surface of the water in a reedbed or in rushes, or in the open on an island or by the waterside. The male tears up plants growing in the vicinity and places them within reach of the female, which arranges them around itself. This gives rise to a large heap of plant material with a shallow depression in the centre. Here, in April or May, 4—7 grey-green or greyish-white eggs are laid (in the case of domesticated or semi-domesticated swans there may be as many as 9—12). The female, largely unaided, incubates them for about 35 days. The young are not fledged until four or five months old; at two or three years they make attempts at nest-building, but they are not fully adult until their fourth year. Adult birds (1) have pure white plumage, an orange-red beak with a black pro-tuberance at its base and black legs. On water they characteristically hold their beak pointing obliquely downwards, their neck curved in an S shape and their wings slightly raised (see the silhouette). The juveniles are greyish-brown (later with white patches) and have greyish legs. The downy plumage is grey, but among semi-wild swans we occasionally come across young in completely white down (the mutant *'immutabilis'*, known as the Polish Swan), which have pale pinkish-grey legs when adult. In flight, the slow, powerful strokes of their wings produce a clear whistling sound. Otherwise, as its name implies, the Mute Swan is not very vocal, except for the infrequent occasions when it emits high-pitched whimpering, snorting and hissing sounds.

Bewick's Swan
Cygnus columbianus

Bewick's Swan is an Arctic species inhabiting the far north of Europe and Asia, from the Kola Peninsula in the west to the Chukchi Sea in the east. It nests in swampy tundra country with lakes and rivers. The nest, which is built on an elevation near water, is a pile of moss, lichen and grass with a shallow cup lined with down; it is built entirely by the female. The 2—4 yellowish eggs, which are incubated for 29—30 days, again entirely by the female, grow steadily darker. The young develop considerably faster than young Mute Swans. They generally hatch in June or July and often leave the nest area as early as September, when the water starts to freeze. Their regular winter quarters in Europe are the coastal regions of the North Sea and in Britain and Ireland, where in places their flocks number thousands of birds; elsewhere they appear only rarely and in small numbers, although they have been known to winter as far afield as the

Mediterranean. As a rule, they arrive back on their nesting sites in May or June, depending on the advent of spring. Bewick's Swan is an almost complete vegetarian and small fish or aquatic insects only occasionally find their way into its food. It is the smallest of the swans. Its general appearance and behaviour are similar to those of the Whooper Swan, but it is only three-quarters its size. The adult birds (1) are snow-white; the front half of their beak is black and separated from the yellow posterior half by a curved, jagged or square edge (3); in the Whooper Swan, the yellow forms a tapering wedge of colour (2). The juvenile birds are greyish-brown. The swan's call — a resonant 'lyook' and 'howk' — is heard both on the water and in flight.

Whooper Swan
Cygnus cygnus

The Whooper Swan likewise lives in the north. Its breeding range stretches from Iceland across Scandinavia to the Far East; it also nests patchily far to the south, near the Caspian Sea and in central Asia. Birds from the northwest of the breeding range spend the winter on the shores of the North Sea and the Baltic and are seen only locally inland. Pairs are formed in the birds' winter quarters, the bond lasts a lifetime and family life is exemplary. In the spring the pairs return to their swamps and lakes in the tundras or to bays with abundant vegetation, and on the shore, on an island or in a reedbed they begin to build the nest. This is merely a heap of plant material, with a shallow cup thinly lined with down. The 4–6 yellowish-white eggs (2), which are usually laid in May, are incu-

bated entirely by the female for 35–42 days. The male remains in the vicinity, keeping watch, and later participates very actively in the rearing of the young. When swimming, the family always remains together; the mother leads the young ones (sometimes she carries them on her back) and the father brings up the rear, to make sure that the others are safe. The parents defend their offspring with great courage and are capable of administering vicious blows with their wings (this ap-

plies to other swans as well). The adult birds live mainly on grass and aquatic plants, but the young

also eat worms, molluscs and insects. The young birds are a dingy grey (3), while the adult birds (1) are white; on the water they can be recognised by their straight neck and folded wings. They have a yellow, black-tipped beak, in which the yellow area tapers off in a wedge into the black part. In size they resemble the Mute Swan, but their wings do not produce a noise in flight. Their trumpet-like call, 'whōōp, whōōkoock', is loud and resonant.

Bean Goose
Anser fabalis

The Bean Goose inhabits the north of Europe and Asia, from northern Scandinavia to the Bering Sea; here and there, however, it breeds near mountain lakes in central Asia. It nests beside rivers and lakes or in swamps, often in forests. The nest is a simple depression in the ground, close to water, and is lined with grass, lichen and down. Only the female incubates the 4–6 dingy white eggs (2), which are laid between May and June, the incubation period being 27–29 days. The whole of the time the male stands guard and when the young are hatched he helps to rear them. In about two months the young are able to fly and at the end of August or the beginning of September they migrate southwards with their parents, as members of a flock. Bean Geese's wintering grounds in Europe start in the south of Scandinavia and the North Sea region and extend patchily to the Mediterranean and the Black Sea. The chief areas are from Denmark to Belgium and the middle of the Danube basin, where up to several tens of thousands of birds winter together, and Hartobágy Puszta in Hungary, where their flocks comprise several hundred thousand individuals. Recently, however, there has been a distinct drop in the numbers of these geese in their winter quarters. Bean Geese return to their nesting sites in February or March. They live mainly on grass and aquatic plants, but in the winter their flocks can be very damaging to autumn-sown cereal crops. The Bean Goose is about the same size as the Greylag Goose. It is predominantly greyish-brown (1) with a strikingly dark brown head and neck; its legs are orange-yellow, while its beak is yellow with a black base and with a black nail at the tip. In flight, the almost uniform colour of its wings is a useful distinction from the Greylag Goose. Its call, a ringing 'ang-owk-kayak' or 'kayayak', is different from that of the Greylag.

2

White-fronted Goose
Anser albifrons

2

The White-fronted Goose nests in the most northerly parts of Europe, Asia and North America, but spends the winter far to the south: in Europe from the south of Scandinavia to the west coast of Ireland, but also deep in central Europe and even further south, on the Mediterranean. It is one of the commoner wild geese and its winter flocks often consist of several thousand birds. For its winter quarters it chooses large areas with fields, meadows and pastures in the vicinity of large ponds and rivers, where it can rest at night and graze early in the morning. It lives mainly on grass and autumn-sown cereals. The birds nest from May to June in damp, swampy tundra country and wooded tundra, generally close to water; where conditions are favourable, they display a tendency to nest in loose colonies. The simple nest of grass, lichen and down is built on an elevation, almost entirely by the female. The 4—6 dingy white eggs (2) acquire yellowish-brown spots during incubation, which is performed wholly by the female for 27—28 days while the male keeps watch nearby; both parents take part in the rearing of the young. Immature and unpaired geese remain together the whole summer in flocks, roaming the tundra. When the nesting season is over, they are joined by families with newly fledged young, and at the end of September and (mainly) in October the geese set out on the long journey to their winter quarters. The White-fronted Goose is smaller and darker than the Greylag Goose. Adult White-fronted Geese (1) can be identified by the black barring on the underside of their body and also by the white 'blaze' on their forehead, which extends to the sides of their beak. The juveniles lack the white forehead patch and the black abdominal bars. There is no black in the pink or orange colour of the beak. The call of this goose is a high 'kow-lyoo' or 'lyo-lyok'.

ANSERIFORMES
ANATIDAE

Lesser White-fronted Goose
Anser erythropus

beginning of June. The female seeks a depression in the soil, sometimes on an elevation in marshy terrain, lines it with twigs, grass, leaves and down and then lays the yellowish-white eggs, of which there are usually 4−5. The female incubates the eggs for 25−28 days, but when the young are hatched the male also joins the family and both sexes rear their offspring together until they are fledged (in about two months). This goose feeds mainly on the soft, green parts of plants, but in the winter it also eats seeds, including grain. It has black abdominal bars and a white frontal patch, like the White-fronted Goose (2), but the white patch extends on the crown to a point level with the rear edge of its eyes (3). It has a yellow eye-ring, which is also present in the juveniles, although the white patch on the forehead is not. When on the ground, the tips of its wings extend beyond the end of its tail. The adult bird (1) is about one third smaller than the Greylag Goose. Its high, whistling call sounds like 'kyu-yut' or 'kluyu-yu-yu'.

The Lesser White-fronted Goose inhabits tundras and wooded tundras in Europe and Asia. It prefers to breed near rivers and lakes, but also lives at high altitudes and in rocky places. At the end of August or the beginning of September it migrates to winter quarters far south in southeastern Europe, in the Black Sea region and in southern Asia, although a few birds may remain on the shores of the Baltic and the North Sea. Inland, in central and western Europe, the Lesser White-fronted Goose is a rare and irregular visitor, most often encountered during its autumn migration, between September and November, or during the return journey in the spring, from March to April. The birds arrive at their breeding grounds in flocks and do not pair off and look for a place to nest until the last snow has disappeared. In north Europe the eggs are generally to be found from the end of May to the

Greylag Goose
Anser anser

The family life of the Greylag Goose is often cited as a good example for human beings. The pairs remain in a lifelong union, which is sometimes so strong that if one partner dies the other never 'remarries'. The birds return from their winter quarters in February or March and soon afterwards the female starts to build the nest, which is made of aquatic plants, twigs, grass and leaves and is situated in the vegetation beside ponds and lakes, on the bank or on an island. Nesting is accompanied by an increase in the amount of down, with which the goose covers the eggs when it leaves the nest. The 4—8 dingy white eggs (2) are incubated entirely by the female, but the male is never very far away. The goslings hatch in 27—29 days. When they enter the water, the female always leads, while the male brings up the rear and, if need be, defends his family with fierce tenacity. In about two months the young geese learn to fly, but the families still remain together and are evidently also sometimes joined by the young of the previous year. The geese from whole regions then assemble in large flocks on suitable ponds and make ready for their departure in September or October. The Greylag Goose inhabits Iceland, the British Isles, the coast of Scandinavia and parts of central and southeastern Europe and central Asia. With the exception of the British population it is a migrant, and in Europe winters largely in the northwest and in the Mediterranean region. It lives on the same type of food as other geese. The Greylag Goose grows to the same size as a domestic goose, i.e. to a length of about 76—89 cm. It is greyish-brown and, in flight, large silvery-grey areas can be seen on the upper fore wings. West European birds (*A.a. anser*) (1) have an orange-yellow beak, east European and Asian birds (*A.a. rubrirostris*) a pink beak. Greylag Geese fly in echelon formation or in single file and their honking 'gahgagag' closely resembles the call of the domestic goose.

2

Snow Goose

Anser caerulescens

The Snow Goose is an Arctic species which nests on Wrangel Island and in the region of the Chukchi Sea, in the north of North America and in Greenland; it winters on the coasts of eastern Asia as far as Japan, and in North America as far south as Mexico. A rare visitor to Europe, it is seen most often in the western parts. In the tundra belt the Snow Goose lives near lakes and rivers, but nests in drier places, in colonies usually comprising several dozen pairs, but often several hundred. The nest is a depression in the ground lined with blades of grass and lichen from the immediate vicinity and with down. The 4–5 white eggs, which are incubated solely by the female, are usually laid at the beginning of June, when snow showers still fall and the offshore water is still frozen over. The male remains close to the nest, ready to defend it against enemies. The goslings are hatched in 23–25 days, and soon after they are dry the parents lead them to the waterside marshes;

in about six weeks they make their first fluttering attempts to fly. In July, the adult geese all moult, when they stay on the water, but as early as August they begin their migration. The Snow Goose lives chiefly on various kinds of grasses and leaves and on the seeds of tundra plants, but will occasionally also eat small aquatic animals. The adult birds (1) grow to the same size as a Greylag Goose and are completely white, except for the black tips of their wings; young birds have a brownish back. In addition to this white phase there is also a 'blue' phase (2), in which the ground colour is bluish-grey and only the head, neck, vent and undertail-coverts are white. The beak and legs are always red. The call is a raucous 'kay-ayk' or a deep 'ung-ung-ung'.

79

Canada Goose
Branta canadensis

Originally a native of North America, where it nests from the Arctic tundra to the north of Colorado and California, the Canada Goose has bred in Britain for about 300 years. It was first kept in England in the 17th century, as an ornamental bird, but since the end of the 18th century it has nested in the wild. Its populations in the British Isles are growing

ish populations are resident, but Scandinavian birds regularly migrate southwestwards to Holland and to Germany. The nesting habitats of the Canada Goose are very diverse and range from grasslands and open moorlands to forests, coastal marshes and tundra. The nest is generally just a depression in the ground, lined with twigs and

tation or by shrubs. Only the female sits on the 4−6 dingy white eggs, which are incubated for 25−30 days; the male stands guard nearby and when the young are hatched it plays a very active part in their education. For the first two days the young remain in the nest, but then follow the parent birds to the water. Canada Geese live on green food,

rapidly and by 1967−69 some 10,000 birds were recorded there. In 1929 it was introduced into Sweden (by 1965 there were about 1,500 birds) and in 1936 into Norway; it has nested in Finland since 1966, in Denmark since 1971 and in Holland since 1974. It has also nested in Germany, but the birds in question were evidently escapes. Brit-

blades of grass from the neighbourhood and with down. As a rule it is close to water (most often on an island) and is usually concealed by the waterside vege-

which they graze mostly on dry ground, chiefly in the morning and the evening. The Canada Goose (1) is the largest member of its genus and is noticeably larger than the Greylag Goose. It is predominantly greyish-brown, but its head and long neck are coal-black and its throat, cheeks, lower belly and tail-coverts are gleaming white.

Barnacle Goose
Branta leucopsis

The Barnacle Goose is an Arctic species inhabiting only the east coast of Greenland, Spitsbergen (Svalbard), the southern island of Novaya Zemlya and Vaygach Island. It spends the winter in western Europe, in exceptional cases as far south as the Iberian Peninsula; elsewhere and inland it is a very rare casual visitor. This is altogether a rare bird and in 1963

lined with down. It can be distinguished from the nests of other geese by the coherent ring of droppings around it; this is because the sitting female is unable to leave the nest, as otherwise the eggs would immediately be destroyed by gulls or skuas. Since the male also remains constantly on guard, the parent birds eat very little and lose a lot of

above the surface of the sea; when the newly hatched young are dry, some of them jump down from the cliffs straight into the water, but some are evidently carried down by the parent birds in their beak or on their back. At the end of August or in September, the geese gather together in small flocks and set out for their winter quarters, return-

its total population was estimated to be only 35,000. Being very gregarious, it nests in large or small colonies, on rocky coasts, on sloping ground beside lakes and rivers and quite often together with other seabirds on 'bird cliffs'. The nest, which is on the ground among stones or in a depression, is faced with moss, lichen and grass and is richly

weight during the incubation period. The 4—6 whitish or yellowish eggs are laid between April and June and the female incubates them for 24—26 days. The nest is sometimes quite high

ing again in May. Barnacle Geese feed on grass, twigs, buds and seeds, occasionally supplemented by crustaceans and molluscs. The Barnacle Goose (1) has grey, black and white barring on its back, a white underside, a black breast and neck, a white face and a black crown. It is a little larger than a wild duck. Its call is a barking 'gwack gwack'.

Brent Goose, Brant
Branta bernicla

The Brent Goose nests further north than any other goose, on the most northerly coasts of Europe (Svalbard, Spitsbergen and Franz Josef Land), Asia and North America. European and west Asian birds winter on the shores of the North Sea and (less

2

rearing of the young, but soon deserts the family and moults, in the company of other males. The females also moult and by the time they have finished, about half-way through August, the young are already able to fly and they all migrate southwestwards.

often) of the Baltic, and also the European Atlantic coast, very occasionally as far as the Iberian Peninsula, and a few individuals or small flocks may find their way inland. Since the beginning of the present century, an alarming decrease in the number of these birds has been observed in their known European winter quarters, and according to some authors it fell to only 10% of what it was a hundred years ago; a marked recovery has, however, been recorded over the last 25

years. The Brent Goose nests almost entirely along the coast, chiefly near the mouths of rivers, and otherwise only in the tundra, beside lakes and rivers. It arrives on its breeding grounds at the end of May and nests and eggs can be found only ten days later. The nests, which are made chiefly of lichen and are padded with down, are usually tucked away under boulders. The female incubates the 3–5 greyish eggs (2) unaided for 24–26 days. The male at first participates in the

Brent Geese live on moss, lichen, grass and, in winter, mostly algae and marine plants (occasionally molluscs and crustaceans). They are not much bigger than Mallards. The Brent Goose is darker than any other goose and is the only one with a completely black head; it also has a black neck and breast, but the narrow white mark on either side of its neck is not present in the juveniles. Its belly is either greyish-white or slate grey (1). Its call is a loud 'rrouk rrouk'.

Red-breasted Goose
Branta ruficollis

The Red-breasted Goose also inhabits a very limited area and the only place where it nests is the northern part of the West Siberian Plain from the east coast of the Yamal Peninsula to the mouth of the River Khatanga. It spends the winter in the region of the Caspian and Aral Seas, in Transcaucasia, Iran and Mesopotamia, and has lately been found with increasing frequency — and in large numbers — in Romania and Bulgaria. Very occasionally, individual birds and small flocks stray into central and western Europe, usually between October and April. In its breeding area the Red-breasted Goose inhabits dry, rocky country in tundra and wooded tundra, mainly on the banks of rivers. It generally forms small nesting colonies comprising four or five pairs. The nest, which is usually on the ground, among stones, is made of dry blades of grass and is lined with a large amount of down, with which the female covers the eggs when it leaves the nest. The 4—6 whitish, green-tinted eggs are laid about half-way through June and are incubated by the female, which sits on them unaided for about 25 days. As soon as the newly hatched young are dry, the parents lead them to the water and care for them in a generally 'exemplary' manner. During September the geese leave for the south, so thus they do not spend more than three to four months in their nesting area. Here the adult birds and the young both live almost entirely on grass, but in their winter quarters they also eat other plants, such as autumn-sown cereal crops. The Red-breasted Goose (1) has strikingly coloured plumage: its fore neck, breast and a large patch on its cheek are rusty-brown; its back, hind neck, crown and a vertical stripe through the eye are black; its belly is white and it has narrow white bands on its sides and neck, a narrow white collar and a white patch at the base of its beak. It is the same size as the preceding species. Its call is a high, sharp, rapidly repeated 'keek-ooeek'.

Egyptian Goose
Alopochen aegyptiacus

The Egyptian Goose nests over practically the whole of Africa, except the deserts and tropical forests, and also possibly in part of Asia Minor; it is most abundant in southern and eastern Africa. The ancient Egyptians worshipped it as a sacred bird, but the Greeks and Romans kept it as poultry. Feral Egyptian Goose populations also exist in several European countries, where the number of individuals is estimated at 300—400. In Holland, where they have lived in the wild since the end of the 1960s, the number of nesting pairs ranges

natural site for the nest is on a tree, to which the birds often retire to rest. The female incubates the 8—10 creamy white eggs for 28—30 days. The male keeps the female company and defends her, and also helps to rear the young; he is very intolerant of intruders and defends his territory most emphatically. By the time they are ten weeks old, the young are able to fly; they collect in flocks, which assemble on sandbars in the rivers and then, after dusk, fly out to graze in the neighbouring swamps, meadows and fields. The most

from 30 to 50. In their country of origin they occupy various habitats and nest in the most diverse sites. The nest, built from July onwards, may be on the ground in waterside vegetation, on an island, in a mammal burrow or among stones, in a hollow rock, in old ruins, in a hole in a tree or in another bird's nest up to a height of 25 m. The most striking feature of the Egyptian Goose is its long legs (2). Both sexes have yellowish-brown plumage with indistinct fine black vermiculations and with green, brown, black and white in their wings (1). They are about the size of the Greylag Goose.

Ruddy Shelduck
Tadorna ferruginea

The only parts of Europe where the Ruddy Shelduck nests are the south of the Iberian Peninsula and the east of the Balkan Peninsula; it also nests in the Atlas region of Africa and across central Asia as far as the River Amur, where the centre of its distribution is the steppes of Kazakhstan and Iran. In the Mediterranean countries it is generally resident; elsewhere it is a nomadic and migratory bird. On migration it is to be found over the whole of northern Africa and southern Asia and it has been known to stray, on rare occasions, to prac-

2♂

females (as in other species of the genus *Tadorna*) are more active than the males, which they provoke into attacks on their rivals. The nest is built in various kinds of holes and hollows — in

creamy yellow eggs are usually laid at the end of May and are incubated for 27—29 days by the female, although the male is never very far away. The rearing of the young is a joint undertaking, which continues until the young are able to fly. The Ruddy Shelduck gathers its food on dry land more often than in shallow water. It lives mainly on greenery, but also eats small crustaceans and molluscs, worms, small fish and frogs and even carrion. Both sexes are mostly rusty-brown, but the wing-coverts are white and the tips of

tically every country in Europe. It likes open country, where it frequents mainly steppes with unvegetated lakes and sometimes large rivers, but in central Asia it also settles beside mountain lakes at altitudes of over 3,000 m. In the breeding season the

a burrow, under a stone, in ruins and in trees, in exceptional cases in the abandoned nest of a bird of prey and sometimes in a nestbox. It is generally made entirely of down, reinforced with a few blades of grass and leaves, and is built by the female. The 8—12

the wings and the tail are black. The male (2) can be distinguished from the female (1) by its narrow black collar and its darker head. The Ruddy Shelduck is slightly larger than a Mallard. Its call, 'uhung', can be heard over long distances.

Shelduck, Burrow-duck, Bergander
Tadorna tadorna

The Shelduck nests almost exclusively in burrows 1–2 m long; sometimes it excavates these itself, but at other times it takes over abandoned rabbit burrows or the dens of foxes and other mammals. Occasionally it will nest in a crack in a rock, among stones, in a hole in a tree or in the shelter of dense shrubs. It inhabits the seashore and salt and brackish inland lakes. The pairs sometimes arrive at their nesting sites in February, but usually in March. The nest is lined with down and the 7–12 creamy white eggs are laid between April and June. They are incubated for 27–29 days by the female, while the male stands guard near the nest and sometimes right in the entrance. As soon as the newly hatched young are dry, the parents take them to the water. Shelducks live almost entirely on small molluscs and crustaceans, worms, insects and small fish and only rarely on plant material. This duck breeds on the coasts of the whole of northern and western Europe and here and there on the shores of the Mediterranean and the Black Seas, east of which its range extends, unbroken, from the Caspian Sea to the steppes of inner Asia. In the south it is a resident bird, but in the north and west and in most of Asia it is a nomad and a migrant. In August and September European migrants move to the Atlantic coast of western Europe and to the Mediterranean, returning to their breeding areas in March or April. On migration this duck occasionally appears inland in Europe, on lakes or large rivers. The Shelduck (1), which is the same size as the Mallard, has contrastingly coloured white, black and chestnut plumage; its beak is bright red, with a prominent knob at the base in the male. The young (2) have a dark grey back and a whitish underside. The call is a rapid 'ak-ak-ak' and in the breeding season the male utters a high-pitched whistle, 'khee-oh'.

2

Wood Duck
Aix sponsa

1

The Wood Duck originates from the eastern half of North America, where it was almost exterminated by the beginning of the present century; it was not until after 1918, when its shooting was prohibited and a number of other measures (artificial breeding, the provision of nestboxes) were introduced, that its numbers rose again. In Europe it has been kept as an ornamental bird since the 18th century. Today it lives freely in various parts of Britain and the first wild-breeding experiments were carried out there in about 1870; it has also been introduced into many other countries. It generally lives beside inland lakes, fishponds and running water surrounded by deciduous woods. From March onwards, individual pairs explore the woods, looking

3

for a suitable nest site. Very often they use nestboxes, but are sometimes content with a crack in a rock. The nest is lined with down and the 10–14 cream-coloured eggs (3) are incubated for 28–32 days by the female. In response to the female's calls,

2♀

the newly hatched young jump from the nest and are led to the water; they are seldom joined by the drake, who generally does not help in the care of the offspring. The families remain together until the autumn. In the autumn Wood Ducks feed mainly on acorns, beechnuts and other seeds, while in the spring and summer they live chiefly on the green parts of plants, supplemented by small aquatic animals. The drake (1) has a flattened crest; its upperparts are predominantly green, blue and black, with white markings, and its underparts are white and yellow. The female (2) lacks the crest and its plumage is mainly brownish to greyish-green. The adult birds are slightly smaller than the Teal.

Mandarin Duck
Aix galericulata

The Mandarin Duck lives in southeast Asia, from the lower reaches of the Amur to northeastern China, and in Japan. It was brought to Europe in the first half of the 18th century and has been kept there as an ornamental bird ever since. It has been successfully released in Britain, where some 300–400 or more (perhaps as many as 1,000) pairs now live in the wild; it also nests in the

2♀

wild in Holland (three to eight pairs), Denmark (two or three) and the northern part of Germany, and is found fairly regularly in other European countries. The Mandarin Duck is a true forest duck. It darts among the crowns of the trees, lands safely on a branch and then runs nimbly along it. It nests chiefly in tree holes (and also occupies nestboxes), less often in rock fissures or on forked branches, and occasionally on the ground in the shelter of shrubs. The 7–12 creamy brown eggs are incubated for about 30 days by the female. Their thick down and small weight allow the ducklings to drop to the ground from heights of over 10 m without coming to harm; it has been demonstrated experimentally that *Aix* ducklings – as distinct from ducks which nest on the ground – do not fear heights. The female alone is responsible for the care of the young, which are able to fly at about six weeks. This species lives on various aquatic plants, molluscs, insects and worms; in the autumn it also eats large quantities of acorns, beechnuts and rice. The drake (1) is conspicuous for its orange-chestnut 'sails' (the extremely wide inner vanes of the tertials curve sharply upwards), for its cinnamon 'side-whiskers', its helmet-like crest and the marked contrast between its dark violet breast and its yellow flanks. The duck (2) is mainly a plain greyish-brown colour. Both sexes are the same size as the Wood Duck.

1

Wigeon, European Wigeon

Anas penelope

The Wigeon inhabits the north of Europe and Asia from Iceland and Britain to the Pacific coast. It is strictly a migrant and winters throughout western Europe, around the Mediterranean, in parts of northern Africa and in the whole of southern Asia. Its spring migration takes place in March and April, its autumn migration between September and November. In their northern breeding areas, Wigeons frequent large rivers and lakes with luxuriant waterside vegetation,

3♂

2♀

marshy country and swamps. They arrive already paired. In the courtship ceremony the drake swims around the duck with ruffled head feathers and raised flight feathers; from time to time its head jerks up and it emits a loud whistle. The female conceals the nest in the waterside vegetation and under shrubs close to the water; it is made of dry plants and is later lined with ash-grey down. From the second half of May (in Britain from the end of April) to July, the female lays 7–10 yellow or brownish eggs (4) and incubates them for 22–24 days. Soon after they are dry, the young are taken to the water, but although they are joined there by the male most of the work of rearing them falls on the female. Wigeons live mainly on plant food supplemented only occasionally with molluscs and insects. The Wigeon can be identified, even at a distance, by its rounded head (with bulging forehead) and its short, bluish-grey beak. In its breeding plumage the drake (1) has a reddish-brown head, with a creamy yellow patch on the forehead and crown, and a pinkish breast. In flight (3), a large white area can be seen on the fore part of its wings and a gleaming green speculum on the secondaries. The duck (2) is brown and speckled, with a whitish belly. Both sexes are smaller than the Mallard.

1

4

89

Gadwall
Anas strepera

built more painstakingly than the nests of other ducks. During incubation of the eggs, the amount of dark grey, white-tipped down, from which the nest can be identified, increases. The 7–12 eggs (2), which are distinctly smaller than those of the Mallard, are tinged yellow or pink. The female sits for 26–28 days unaided, and also cares for the young until they are fledged, at the age of seven to eight weeks. Gadwalls feed largely on the green parts of plants and in the winter chiefly on seeds; the amount of animal food is very small and is important only in the summer. The Gadwall lives primarily in central and eastern Europe and nests only patchily or sporadically in northwestern Europe; it also breeds across central Asia and North America. West European birds are partly resident and partly nomadic; the rest are migratory. The winter quarters of European Gadwalls lie mainly in the Mediterranean region and particularly in northern Africa, although some birds winter in western and southeastern Europe. They leave the breeding areas between September and November and return in March or April. In the spring, the male (1, in foreground) is grey to greyish-brown, with fine black vermiculations, a bluish-grey beak and a black 'stern'. The female (1, behind) is inconspicuously marked with brown spotting and speckles. In both sexes, the white specula on the wings are clearly visible in flight. This species is smaller than the Mallard.

The Gadwall prefers to nest beside large ponds and lakes with abundant waterside vegetation, but will make do with any large patch of open water. The birds return to their nesting sites already paired and the eggs are laid between April and June. The nest is generally near water, well concealed in nettles, grass or sedge stands or under the branches of shrubs. After excavating a hollow in the ground,

the female makes a nest of dry plants, grass and leaves, which is

2

Teal,
Green-winged Teal
Anas crecca

The Teal nests over the whole of Europe except the southeast, in the cold and temperate parts of Asia and across northern North America. It frequents ponds, swamps and the banks of slow-flowing rivers bordered by dense vegetation. The birds appear on the breeding grounds in the spring, as soon as the snow has melted; they return in pairs formed from about February onwards among the winter flocks, which during courtship are made obvious by the bell-like voices of the males. The female conceals the nest in thick grass, sometimes below a bush and even quite a long way from water. The nest is a shallow depression faced with dry grass or the stems of plants gathered from the immediate vicinity and during nesting lined with down; the down is dark grey, but that in the sides of the nest is whitish and indistinctly spotted. The 6—12 eggs (2), which are creamy-yellow or grey, with a greenish tinge, are laid mainly at the end of April and in May. The female incubates them for 22—25 days, sitting very determinedly and if disturbed not flying away until the very last instant. The male takes no part in caring for the family. The young birds begin to fly at the age of about one month. At the end of the summer and in the autumn, Teals assemble in large flocks, sometimes numbering several thousand birds, and in September and October they set out for their winter quarters in southern and western Europe. In the spring and summer Teals live mainly on aquatic animals and in the autumn and winter on seeds.

1

2

With a length of only 35 cm, the Teal is the smallest European duck. In its breeding plumage, the drake (1) has a chestnut and green head, a narrow white horizontal stripe above the wings and a yellow patch on the underside of its tail. The duck is brown and finely speckled. Both sexes have bright green specula on their wings. The male's call is a ringing 'krit', the female's a rapid 'quack-quack-quack'.

91

Mallard
Anas platyrhynchos

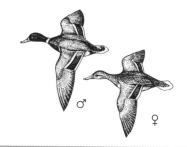

The Mallard inhabits the whole of the northern hemisphere, where, despite its enormous range, it forms only a few subspecies. The chief reason is that Mallards, unlike the majority of other birds, choose their mates in the winter quarters and the drakes then follow the ducks to their nesting sites, so that the populations are constantly being mixed. The Mallard prefers stagnant water with abundant vegetation, but will also nest beside rivers and streams and even frequents water flowing through large towns. Very often the nest is built quite a long way from water and sometimes in a very unlikely spot, such as the abandoned nest of a bird of prey, a hole in a tree or the roof of a house; however, it is much more likely to be found close to water, in the marginal vegetation or hidden by shrubs. The nest is a small depression hollowed out by the female's breast; it is lined with dry plants and later with a quantity of the female's own down. The 7—11 greenish or yellowish eggs (2) are generally laid in April or May and the ducklings are hatched in 22—28 days. In the autumn, Mallards assemble on large sheets of water in flocks that number up to several thousand birds, and at night spread out over the countryside in search of food, in which the plant component preponderates. They spend the winter on ice-free water and on the coast; some populations are migrants, others are resident birds. In the spring, the drake (1, in front) has a green head separated from its reddish-brown breast by a white collar; the female (1, behind) is brown and speckled. Both sexes have characteristic violet-blue specula. The adult birds measure 58 cm. The duck utters a loud 'quarkquark quack', the drake a wheezy 'quek ek'.

2

1

The Pintail inhabits northwestern Europe, northern Asia and North America, but occasionally nests much further south. In Europe it is partly (and elsewhere wholly) a migrant. In the winter, some birds migrate to quiet bays along the Atlantic coast and others to the Mediterranean and northern Africa, where they are one of commonest ducks in the Nile basin. In the breeding season Pintails undertake characteristic nuptial flights, in which they almost skim the surface of the water, holding their necks curved like a letter S. In March and April they settle in swamps and on

the nest. The care of the young, which lasts about six weeks, is entirely the province of the female. Between September and November the birds leave for their winter quarters. Pintails feed on seeds and the green parts of plants and on insects, worms, tadpoles and small fish. They have a long, thin neck and long, tapering tail feathers, which are particularly noticeable on the male in flight (4). In its breeding plumage, the drake (1) has a brown head with a white neck stripe and white underparts, while the female (3) is inconspicuously speckled. They are slightly smaller than the Mallard. The courting male utters muted whistles.

lakes and fishponds with luxuriant aquatic vegetation. The nesting site is chosen by both sexes, but the duck builds the actual nest, which is always on the ground, hidden in grass or sedge or standing almost exposed in a field; it is made of a small amount of dry grass or leaves and is lined with smoky-brown down, the feathers of which have a light-coloured tip and base. The 6—12 yellowish or greenish eggs (2), which are generally laid in April or May, are incubated for 22—23 days by the female, while the male keeps watch in the vicinity. In the event of danger, the drake flies around in circles until the duck has left

Garganey,
Summer Teal
Anas querquedula

♂ ♀

1

The Garganey inhabits Europe and Asia, but not so far to the north as the Teal — in Europe only to the southern half of Britain and Scandinavia. Over the whole of its range it is strictly a migrant, some birds spending the winter in the Mediterranean region but the majority in tropical Africa. They migrate early — at the end of July or in August — and return, already in pairs, to their breeding areas in March or April. The courting drake swims behind his mate, his head level with her tail, his beak in the water and his head feathers and long scapulars ruffled, rhythmically nodding his head. From time to time he throws his head right back and utters vibrant sounds like the noise made by a child's rattle. The males also undertake characteristic flights close to the water, rapidly flourishing their wings after they land on the surface. The Garganey frequents

3

reservoirs and gently-flowing water richly overgrown with vegatation, swamps, meadows around ponds and drainage channels. The female builds the nest in tall grass, sedge or reeds beside water or in a meadow. It

2

closely resembles the Teal's nest, but the down feathers have a single, compact dark spot in the middle. The female sits very determinedly on the 8—11 yellowish or brownish eggs (3), which are not green-tinged; these are generally laid between April and June and are incubated for about 23 days. The ducklings are taken to the water within one day after they hatch. In July the families gather together in small groups; they never form such large flocks as the Teal. The Garganey drake is the only drake with a white superciliary stripe; in its breeding plumage (1) it has a brown head and breast and trailing ornamental scapular plumes on its back. The female (2) resembles the female Teal, but has more pronounced stripes above, below and through its eyes and less distinct specula on its wings. The adult birds are both a little larger than the Teal.

Shoveler
Anas clypeata

The Shoveler prefers to nest beside stagnant or slow-flowing water with shallows and with standing vegetation, in swamps and in flooded meadows. Its choice of habitat is closely related to its feeding habits, since it lives largely on small planktonic organisms strained out of water and mud from the shallows. For this it has a perfect filter apparatus, composed of long, dense lamellae, along the sides of its beak. The birds arrive at their breeding sites in March or April, already paired. The drake courts the duck by swimming around her in circles, turning the back of his neck towards her. The nest, which is no more than a hollow in the ground, is generally in grass or sedge, often some distance from the water. After the eggs have been laid it is lined mainly with ash-grey, pale-spotted down. The 7–12 greenish-grey or cream-coloured eggs (3), laid between April and June, are incubated entirely by the female. The young hatch after 23–25 days and are able to fly about six weeks later. The Shoveler nests in lowland areas in Iceland, Ireland, Britain and France, and from there across much of Europe with the exception of the southern peninsulas and the north of Scandinavia, in the greater part of Asia and in the west of North America. Over most of its range it is a migratory bird; European populations migrate between September and November to the Mediterranean region, northern Africa and the Atlantic region. West European Shovelers are partly migratory and partly resident. In its breeding plum-

age the drake (1) is very brightly coloured, with a green head, a white breast, reddish-brown belly and flanks and pale blue fore wings. The brown-speckled female (2) has blue fore wings and green specula. The adult birds are about the same size as the Mallard.

Marbled Duck, Marbled Teal

Marmaronetta angustirostris

The Marbled Duck occupies a very restricted area. In Europe it nests regularly only in the south of Spain, and occasionally on some of the Mediterranean islands and in southern France; otherwise it lives in a small strip of northern Africa and in the Middle East and southwest Asia. It is an irregular short-distance migrant and often does not leave its breeding area even in the winter, when it generally frequents the seashore and the shallows of lakes. The pairs are formed during the winter; in the breeding season they frequent small, shallow lakes richly overgrown with vegetation, quiet river arms and salt water with tamarisks and other shrubs growing beside it. The nest is generally situated in dry, hard grass or under a low shrub beside a lake or reservoir, or in a damp meadow; in the Volga delta the Marbled Duck also nests in old nests of crows. Egg-laying generally starts at the beginning of June and continues into July. The nest usually contains 7—12 yellow or brownish eggs, which are incubated by the female for 25—27 days. Meanwhile, the drakes collect in small flocks to moult, and display no interest at all in their families. The females lead the newly hatched young to the water and care for them until they are able to fly. Knowledge of this duck's diet is still incomplete, but it lives partly on the green parts of plants and on seeds, together with aquatic insects and their larvae and molluscs. The Marbled Duck is somewhat larger than the Teal. It is light brown in colour, with whitish spots, and has a dark patch on either side of its head; there are no specula on its wings. In the male (1, 2), the plumes at the back of the head are elongated, forming a short crest.

2♂

1

Red-crested Pochard
Netta rufina

The Red-crested Pochard is intermediate between a diving duck and a dabbling duck. It remains almost the whole time on the surface of the water, but from time to time it dives. It lives mainly on aquatic plants, about 30% of which it gathers by diving, about 40% by dabbling and the remaining 30% while swimming; it never seeks food on dry land. It nests chiefly beside freshwater lakes and ponds with dense marginal vegetation and an adequately large free surface; it also inhabits ponds which are almost devoid of vegetation but have plenty of small islands, and it even nests beside shallow brackish and salt water with practically no vegetation. The ducks return from their winter quarters in March or April, already in pairs. The male sometimes courts the female by offering her green plants. The nest is built close to the water; it usually has strong sides made of dry plant material from the immediate vicinity, and its height is increased during nesting by the addition of a quantity of grey and brown down. The 6—12 greyish-yellow eggs (2), which are laid in April, May or June, are incubated for 26—28 days entirely by the female, which also cares for the young for about eight weeks. The only continuous areas inhabited by the Red-crested Pochard are the steppes to the north of the Caucasus and the steppes of western and central Asia. In southern and central Europe it nests only in isolated areas, although in some countries of central Europe its numbers have increased considerably in recent years. In the Mediterranean region it is a resident or nomadic bird; elsewhere it is a migrant or a partial migrant. It migrates to the Mediterranean from September to November. In the spring, the drake (1, on left) has a crimson beak, a rusty-golden head with a strikingly high forehead and a black breast. The duck (1, on right) is greyish-brown, with whitish cheeks and a brown-capped head. In flight (3), both sexes have a conspicuous broad white bar running the whole length of the rear part of their wings. They are about the same size as Mallards.

♂

♀

3

2

1

Pochard
Aythya ferina

2♀

The Pochard has a preference for large sheets of deep stagnant water and, although it sometimes nests on small ponds and in swamps, it usually takes the newly hatched young to the nearest large stretch of open water. For nesting it requires the presence of marginal vegetation and

1

also of aquatic plants, which provide it with food; in addition, it eats, in smaller amounts, molluscs, crustaceans and aquatic insects. Flocks of Pochards arrive at their nesting sites in March or April. The courtship ceremony is less striking than that of dabbling ducks. One or several males swim around the female, throwing their head back until it touches their back and inflating their neck and stretching it flat on the water. The duck builds the nest in the shelter of plants growing close to the water and often on an island. Sometimes a large number of nests are built in the same place and, as in the case of the Tufted Duck, the eggs may be laid in another bird's nest or on the ground outside. The normal clutch consists of 5–12 large greyish or greenish eggs (3) with a very thin shell which feels greasy. They are generally laid in May and are incubated for 24–26 days by the female, which also rears the young. The Pochard's range extends from the British Isles to central Europe and from there to central Asia; in recent years a marked extension of range has been noted in central and western Europe. Birds from the Atlantic and the southern parts of the range are resident or nomadic; the rest are migratory. Between September and November the latter birds migrate to the Atlantic coast and (on a smaller scale) to the Mediterranean region. In its breeding plumage, the drake (1) has a chestnut head and neck, a black breast and a silvery-grey back; the female (2) is mainly greyish-brown. Both are slightly smaller than the Mallard. The male calls to the female with a soft 'wibwibwib' and the female answers with a guttural 'kur-r-r'.

3

Ferruginous Duck
Aythya nyroca

The Ferruginous Duck is a warm-climate species nesting from south and southeastern Europe to central Asia and northern Africa. In central and western Europe it is a sporadic and irregular nester. South European populations are partly nomadic and partly resident, while birds from further north are migrants, which winter mainly in the Mediterranean region, returning to their breeding areas at the end of March or in April, already paired. The courtship is similar to that of the Pochard. The birds nest beside still water (lakes, reservoirs, ponds, dead arms of large rivers) with abundant marginal vegetation. The nest, which is usually close to the water, is built by the female. Like the nest of other pochards, it is made both of dry plants and of fresh green plants which dry up after it has been built. In time, the amount of greyish-brown down in the nest also increases. The yellow or brownish yellow-green eggs, of which there are generally 6—12, appear in the nest in May or June. They are incubated by the female, the male remaining near the nest only for the first few days. The ducklings hatch in 25—28 days and one day later they are already active swimmers and skilled divers. By the time they are two months old they are able to fly. Autumn migration sometimes begins in August and continues up to the end of October or the beginning of November. The Ferruginous Duck is predominantly a vegetarian, living on the green parts and seeds of aquatic plants; it dives in search of its food. In the spring, the drake (1) is chestnut-brown, with a white belly and white undertail-coverts, and in flight shows a striking white wingbar. The female's coloration (in flight) is duller, but otherwise the same; both are the same size as the Tufted Duck. The drake has white irises, the duck brown.

1

99

Tufted Duck
Aythya fuligula

The Tufted Duck originally inhabited northern and northeastern Europe and northern Asia; it appeared in central Europe at the beginning of the present century and in many places is now one of the commonest ducks there. Its southward spread is continuing, so that it already breeds in Austria and former Yugoslavia. Birds from northwestern Europe are mostly nomadic or resident;

usually contains a quantity of dark brown down. The 5–12 greenish-grey or yellowish-grey eggs (3) are laid in May or June and the female incubates them for 23–25 days; at the age of about seven weeks the young are already able to fly. Autumn movements begin in September and normally reach a peak in October. Tufted Ducks feed mainly on snails and molluscs, often

other populations are migratory. The winter quarters of this species extend from the shores of the Atlantic to the Mediterranean. The birds arrive at their nesting sites in March or April, usually already in pairs. They prefer stagnant water with rich marginal vegetation, but will also nest in peat-bogs and beside water with practically no vegetation at all (e.g. gravel-pits); in some large European cities, such as London and Hamburg, they live on ponds in public parks. The

nest is generally right next to the water, often on an island or among plants actually standing in water. It is a simple hollow lined with plant material from the immediate vicinity and towards the end of the incubation period it

3

diving to depths of 2–3 m in search of them. They are roughly three quarters the size of a Mallard. In its breeding plumage, the male (1) is deep black, with gleaming white flanks and belly; on the top of its head it has a thin, drooping crest. The female (2) is dark brown, with paler flanks and belly and often with a narrow white area at the base of its beak, and has a rudimentary crest. When viewed at close quarters, both can be seen to have bright yellow irises.

Scaup, Greater Scaup
Aythya marila

The Scaup inhabits cold coastal and tundra regions in the far north of Europe, Asia and North America; in Europe its southerly limits are north Scotland and the north of Poland, where it nests only sporadically. It is a migrant and its main wintering areas lie in the North Sea and the Baltic, where it sometimes forms flocks numbering upwards of a thousand birds. A smaller pro-

The nest is situated close to water, in grass, in sedge or under a bush. On dry ground it is a simple depression lined with dry grass, but on wet ground it is a huge structure measuring about 25 cm across and up to 15 cm in height. It is always lined with, and surrounded by, a thick layer

of dark brown down. On some islands Scaups nest in colonies. The 6—9 brown or greenish eggs (2) are laid in May or June and are incubated for 24—28 days, entirely by the female. Autumn migration usually starts at the beginning of September and attains its peak in October. Scaups gather their food mainly by diving; they live chiefly on molluscs, small crustaceans, worms and insects,

portion of the population moves to the Mediterranean and the Black Sea. In some years, usually when the winter is particularly severe, it also appears on large inland lakes and rivers. It nests beside stagnant water in tundra, in wooded tundra and on the northern edge of the taiga, often preferring large lakes with abundant vegetation; further south it also nests in bogs. As a rule, the birds return to their breeding areas in April, already in pairs.

supplemented by the green parts of aquatic plants and by seeds. In its breeding plumage the male (1) has a deep black, green-glossed head, a black neck and breast, white flanks and belly, and a light grey back with dark grey vermiculations. The female closely resembles the female Tufted Duck, but the white patch around its beak is larger and it also has a white spot on the rear ear-coverts. The adult birds are roughly the same size as the Mallard.

Eider,
Common Eider
Somateria mollissima

The young, together with the females, form large flocks sometimes numbering over a hundred birds; if attacked by gulls or skuas, they defend themselves by splashing water over their attackers and by synchronised diving. Eiders live on a specialised diet of molluscs, mainly edible mussels of the genus *Mytilus,* which they swallow whole and then crush in their muscular gizzard; the daily consumption of these robust ducks, which weigh some 2.5 kg, is about 150—250 mussels. Eiders nest on the northern coasts of Europe, Asia and North America. In the far north they are migrants, but populations further south are resident or nomodic. In the winter they assemble in large flocks on the coasts of northern and northwestern Europe, but a few venture inland (e. g. Austria, Switzerland) and occasionally they stray to the Mediterranean region. Their autumn migration takes place in October or November and their spring migration in April. The Eider is the largest European diving duck and is the same size as a Mallard. It has a very characteristic profile and a substantially longer beak (4) than the King Eider *Somateria spectabilis* (3). In its breeding plumage the male (1) has a white back, a black belly, a pink-tinged breast and a green patch on the nape; the female (2) is brown, with dark brown barring.

For its warmth and lightness, eider down has for years been the most sought-after — and the most expensive — filling of quilts ('eiderdowns') and sleeping-bags. A single quilt, however, requires the down from dozens of nests, since one duck does not produce more than 28—35 g. Eiders nest in colonies, which sometimes comprise hundreds and even thousands of pairs. The nests are situated on stony or sandy coasts with little vegetation, often in colonies of terns and small gulls, and occasionally beside inland lakes. In the second half of May or in June, the female lays 4—6 greyish-green or greyish-yellow eggs (5), which it incubates, unaided, for 27—28 days. It sits very resolutely, and if a human being approaches it moves only a little way off or even allows itself to be stroked.

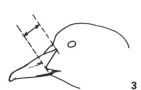

Long-tailed Duck, Hareld, Oldsquaw
Clangula hyemalis

The Arctic Long-tailed Duck nests in the most northerly parts of Europe, Asia and North America. It is a migratory bird and many spend the winter on the Atlantic coast of northern Europe, the North Sea coast and around the Baltic, where it is perhaps the commonest winter bird; small numbers also appear inland. It leaves for its winter quarters between September and November and returns to its nesting sites in tundra and wooded tundra in April or May. The birds migrate chiefly at night. In their breeding areas they frequent mainly freshwater lakes and sluggish rivers, but also nest in sheltered bays. The nest, close to the water or on an island, is carefully hidden in swamp vegetation or tall grass, under a shrub or among stones. It usually has a fairly deep cup thinly lined with grass, twigs or leaves and with a quantity of dark down. The brownish-yellow to greyish-green eggs, of which there are generally 5—9, are laid between the end of May and July; the female incubates them for 23—24 days, unaided and very tenaciously. Long-tailed Ducks feed mainly on molluscs, crustaceans and aquatic insects and occasionally on small fish. They are excellent divers and reach depths of as much as 60 m in search of food; they supplement their main diet with green shoots, moss and algae. The Long-tailed Duck is characterised by a rounded head and a short beak, and the male also by very long feathers in its tail. In its breeding plumage, the male is predominantly blackish-brown, with a smaller amount of white; in the winter,

the reverse is the case (1 and 2). The female is at all times brown and white. Both sexes are noticeably smaller than a Mallard. The drake courts the duck with a loud 'ow-ow-owdlow' call, while the female answers with guttural sounds.

2♂

Velvet Scoter,
White-winged Scoter
Melanitta fusca

1

The Velvet Scoter's distribution in Europe is confined to the north and west of Scandinavia and the northern part of the former USSR. It is a migrant, leaving in October and November for its winter quarters in the coastal regions of the western Baltic and the North Sea and on west European coasts as far south as the Bay of Biscay; single birds or small groups (generally females or young birds) sometimes winter further inland. Velvet Scoters return to their breeding sites in the taiga and tundra in April or May, already paired. They frequent lakes and sluggish rivers and streams, but also nest on small islands and on the seashore. Their display is characterised by circling flights. The female builds the nest, which is made of plant material and down and is placed on the ground, in grass or moss, under a bush or between stones. The 6–10 brownish-yellow, pink-tinted eggs are laid in May or June. The female incubates them unaided for 26–29 days and also looks after the young, which are not fledged until September. The Velvet Scoter feeds mainly on molluscs, together with aquatic insects, worms, crustaceans and the buds and roots of aquatic plants, and can dive to considerable depths in search of food. In its breeding plumage, the male is black, with white secondaries and a white mark beneath each eye; its irises are greyish-white, and its legs are red with black webbing. Its mainly orange beak has a black protuberance at the base of the upper mandible. The female (1) is blackish-brown, with white secondaries and two white spots on the side of its head. Although not a very vocal species, the drake utters whistling 'whoo-or, or' calls and the duck makes growling sounds.

Common Scoter
Melanitta nigra

The Common Scoter lives in the north of Europe and Asia, and in a few isolated pockets in North America. It is a migratory bird and winters in the coastal regions of the whole of northern and western Europe, but particularly in the North Sea and the Baltic; some birds reach the coast of northwest Africa. In coastal regions the Common Scoter can be seen migrating, in the evening and at night, as early as July, when males preponderate; from about September onwards the ratio changes, and by December females and young birds clearly predominate. In Europe, Common Scoters are seen inland only exceptionally and in very small numbers, usually between September and April. The birds generally return northwards to their nesting sites in May (in Britain in March or April), already in pairs.

They settle on lakes or slow-flowing water in the tundra (sometimes in the taiga) and also nest in peat-bogs. Common Scoters are skilled swimmers and divers, but on land they are very awkward and walk with a stiff upright gait. That is presumably why they nest close to water, usually in the waterside vegetation or under a bush. The nest is a simple depression in the ground, thinly lined with dry stalks, moss and lichen, to which down is added later. The 6−10 yellowish or brownish eggs are laid in May or June and the female incubates

2♀

them for 28−30 days. As soon as the young are hatched, the mother takes them to the water and looks after them for six to seven weeks. Common Scoters live mainly on molluscs, crustaceans and aquatic insects, supplemented by aquatic plants (chiefly the roots and buds). The male Common Scoter (1) is the only duck with completely black plumage (the Velvet Scoter has white on each wing and below each eye). It has a protuberance at the base of its beak and a large orange spot on its upper mandible; its legs are brownish-black and its irises brown. The female (2) is dark brown, with a paler underside and a whitish throat and cheeks. Both sexes are about one fifth smaller than a Mallard. The courting male utters a fluty 'coorlee', and the female a raucous 'kr-r-r'.

105

Barrow's Goldeneye
Bucephala islandica

Barrow's Goldeneye closely resembles the Goldeneye. The male's breeding plumage (1, in front) is strikingly black and white, but its white facial spot is crescent-shaped and its back is completely black except for some white spots. Since the female (1, behind) is almost indistinguishable from the female Goldeneye, it is best, in the field, to go by the accompanying drake. This is very much a northern duck: in Europe it nests only in Iceland; it probably breeds in southwest Greenland, but in North America it is more widely distributed. In western Europe it is an accidental visitor. Barrow's Goldeneye nests beside mountain lakes surrounded by conifer forests, or on rocky coasts with large numbers of small, wooded islands. In mountains with conifer forests in the subalpine zone it ascends to altitudes of 1,800 m. Its courting displays are similar to those of the Goldeneye and it likewise usually nests in a hole in a tree, although sometimes the nest is in a rock fissure, in a hole in the ground or in a wall, or even in a deserted house. The female always lines the nest with soft white down and the 10—14 bluish-green eggs are laid at the end of May or in June. The young, which hatch after about 30 days, are very active and soon jump down from the nest, without coming to any harm. The female cares for them for about two months, with no assistance from the male. These diving ducks live almost entirely on aquatic insects, molluscs and crustaceans. With the advent of winter, only some of the birds leave for the coast. The greater part of the population is resident, but in the depth of winter may retreat to the nearest ice-free river or sea.

Goldeneye, Common Goldeneye
Bucephala clangula

The remarkable courtship of the Goldeneye begins with the first sunny days in the spring. The male swims around the female, with its head and neck just above the surface, and then throws its head right back (1), uttering wheezy sounds. It jerks its ruffled head forwards and backwards, at the same time flailing its feet, so that with every nod of its head it sends jets of water flying backwards. The nest is usually built in a hole in a tree or in a nestbox, sometimes as high as 20 m above the ground and up to 2 km away from water. The hole, which may be over 2 m deep, is lined only with wood débris, but in time an increasing amount of white down is added. The 4-14 bluish-green eggs (3) are laid between the end of April and the beginning of June and are incubated for 30 days by the female. The newly hatched young, hardly dry, are incredibly agile; they can jump to a height of up to half a metre and, with their sharp

claws, are expert climbers. When called by the mother, they scramble up into the opening of the nest and then jump down. The female accompanies them on the water until they are able to fly, i.e. for about two months. Goldeneyes live almost entirely on animal food, in which molluscs

3

and aquatic insects predominate. They breed in the north of Europe, Asia and North America, but they also nest occasionally in central Europe. Everywhere they are migrants, some birds wintering in the North Sea and Baltic region, some in central Europe and others in the area of the Mediterranean and the Black Sea. Their spring migration takes place from February to April, their autumn migration from September to November. The Goldeneye is a little larger than a Tufted Duck. In its breeding plumage, the male is strikingly black and white, with a large, white oval spot on its green-glossed black head. The female (2) has a chocolate-brown head, which is separated from its brown-tinted, whitish-grey body by a broad white collar. In flight, the Goldeneye is characterised by the loud whistling sound made by its wings, which is audible over a considerable distance.

Smew
Mergus albellus

The Smew nests from the northern part of Scandinavia, across the whole of Siberia, as far as Kamchatka; western populations spend the winter in western Europe, including England, on the northern shores of the Mediterranean and around the Black and Caspian Seas. In Europe, it also winters quite often on ice-free inland rivers and ponds, where it is usually to be found from October to April. Courtship generally begins during spring migration, in February and March. In the breeding season, the Smew frequents inland lakes and rivers in wooded regions, where it normally nests in old, hollow trees. Sometimes, however, the nest is built among stones or between the roots of trees; nestboxes are also accepted. The nest is lined only with feathers and a quantity of greyish-white down. The creamy yellow eggs, of which there are usually 6—9, are laid in the second half of May or in June. Smew eggs and Goldeneye eggs are sometimes found in the same nest. The female sits on the eggs for about 30 days and also cares, unaided, for the young, which leave the nest within one day after hatching. By the time they are about ten weeks, old, the young are able to fly and to look after themselves. The Smew, which is the same size as a Tufted Duck, is the smallest member of the genus *Mergus;* it has a shorter and thicker beak than other species, but this has a hooked tip and sharp, serrated edges and is thus excellently adapted for catching live prey, such as aquatic insects and small fish, under water. In its breeding plumage, the male (1) is lighter in colour than any other duck. It is pure white, the only contrast being the eye-masks, the markings on the back of its head, the thin stripes on the side of its breast, and its back and primaries, all of which are black. The female (2) is grey, with a white throat and face and a brown-capped head. The courting male utters a growling 'krr-ek' and the female a monosyllabic 'regg'.

2♀

Red-breasted Merganser
Mergus serrator

The Red-breasted Merganser nests in northern Europe, throughout the whole of northern Asia and in a large part of North America. Some birds are resident and spend even severe winters on fast-flowing ice-free rivers or on the sea, from Iceland to the shores of the North Sea and the Baltic. Other Red-breasted Mergansers migrate much more regularly, and in larger numbers, than the Smew or the Goosander, and move to the North Sea or to the Mediterranean and Black Sea regions. Autumn migration takes place in September and October; spring migration occurs primarily in April and continues into May. The first signs of courtship can be seen at the end of the winter and pairs are formed mostly in the birds' winter quarters, but partly in their breeding areas. The nest is usually on the ground, hidden in dense waterside vegetation or very often under a bush; it may be a long way from water. The female lines the shallow cup with dry and green parts of plants from the immediate neighbourhood. While the female looks for a nesting site, and also while it is building the nest, the male remains close at hand on the water. The 5–12 yellowish or olive-brown eggs (2) are incubated for about 32 days by the female. One or two days after they hatch, the female leads the young to the water and looks after them for a further eight to nine weeks. Fish, both freshwater and sea, form the chief component of the Red-breasted Merganser's diet. The most striking feature of the male's breeding plumage (1, in foreground) is its green-glossed black head, which has a double

2

occipital crest and is separated from the rust-brown breast by a white 'clerical' collar; in flight, two black bands can be seen across the white inner part of the wing. The female (1, in background) has a greyish-brown back, a whitish underside and a brownish head, likewise with a double crest.

109

Goosander, Common Merganser

Mergus merganser

The Goosander has a similar distribution to the Red-breasted Merganser, but isolated breeding areas also exist in Mecklenburg (Germany) and in the French, Swiss and Austrian Alps. For nesting, it seeks out large, clear inland lakes and rivers with from water; in Switzerland it has actually been known to nest in large towns. The birds use the same nest for many years — sometimes for over 40. The 7–12 yellowish or brownish eggs are laid from April to the beginning of July; the young hatch in appears on the water, which is usually in October or November. It winters throughout most of northwest Europe and inland in western and central Europe. Its diet consists almost entirely of fish. In its breeding plumage, the male (1, in front) has a white,

an abundant supply of fish, bordered by trees with suitable holes and hollows. It prefers deciduous and mixed woods and will even make do with groups of trees or old single trees. If there are not sufficient holes in the trees, it nests in holes and crevices in rocks, in the ground or in the walls of deserted buildings, and sometimes even in empty nests of birds of prey up to 1 km away 32–35 days and the mother remains in the nest with them for a further two days or so. The young then jump down to the ground and the female leads them to the water. They are able immediately to swim and dive, but if they are tired they climb on to the mother's back and allow her to carry them. The Goosander is a partial migrant and a migrant and leaves as soon as ice pink-tinted breast and flanks; its back and its outer wings are black, and on the back of its greenish-black head it has a short, rounded crest. The female (1, behind) closely resembles the female of the preceding species, but its occipital crest points downwards and it has a sharply demarcated white area on its chin. Goosanders are slightly larger than a Mallard.

White-headed Duck
Oxyura leucocephala

The White-headed Duck inhabits a fragmented area from south Europe to central Asia, but its incidence is sporadic. It is a rare nester in Spain, North Africa, the Balkan Peninsula, part of the former USSR and Italy and some of the Mediterranean is-

tation. The nest, which is usually close to the water, is made of reed stalks and rotting plant material. The old nests of Coots and grebes are often used, but material is always added to them. The nest of the White-headed Duck has a characteristic, very

responsible for the care of the young. White-headed Ducks feed mainly on the young shoots and seeds of aquatic plants, plus a small proportion of aquatic insects, molluscs and crustaceans. This species' most typical features are its strikingly long

lands. European birds are evidently resident, but in some regions they move further south for the winter, chiefly to the shores of the Mediterranean. In central and western Europe the White-headed Duck is an accidental visitor, usually seen between October and March. In the nesting season it frequents shallow freshwater and mildly saline lakes with dense marginal vege-

deep cup, in which the eggs often lie on top of one another. The 5-10 large greyish-white or slightly greenish eggs are laid at the end of May. They are incubated for 25−27 days by the female, which is able to leave them for relatively long intervals, because the embryos have some capacity for thermoregulation and continue to develop in the heat generated by the rotting nest material, without the added warmth of the female's body. The female is probably also entirely

tail, which is held erect over the back if the bird is excited, and its large beak with its 'swollen' base. In its breeding plumage, the male (1) is russet-coloured, with a blackish-brown neck and crown; the rest of its head is white. The female is dark brown, with a white throat and a dark horizontal band across the cheeks. The adult birds are somewhat smaller than a Mallard.

Masters of the sharp beak and talons

Birds of prey

Birds of prey form a group characterised by the shape of their beak and the structure of their feet. The upper mandible is hooked and terminates in a sharp point; it overhangs the lower mandible and has sharp edges, enabling the bird to cut and tear away the flesh from the body of its prey. In some species there is a sharp 'tooth' on the upper mandible (Fig. 1). The base of the beak and the

Fig. 1. *Head of falconine bird of prey with a characteristically hooked beak with a tooth at the tip and cere at the base.*

area around the nostrils are covered with a tough membrane (the cere). The prehensile feet have long, flexible toes with long, curved, sharp claws (Fig. 2a, eagle; 2b, hawk). Sexual dimorphism is generally expressed in size rather than in coloration, the females sometimes being a third or more larger than the males; for instance, the male Peregrine weighs about 600 g, but the female over 900 g.

All European birds of prey are carnivorous and live mainly on warm-blooded vertebrates, which they generally catch alive. Some take fish (the Osprey, Fig. 3), others chiefly snakes (the Short-toed Eagle) or insects (the Honey Buzzard). There is also a large group of birds − the vultures − which do not catch their prey alive, but feed on carrion; they have a longer neck, with 17 vertebrae (instead of the usual 14), making it easier for them to extract the entrails from the carcases of large mammals. In keeping with their feeding habits, birds of prey have a voluminous, thin-walled stomach capable of accepting a large amount of food at once; when it is full, the birds can still take in extra reserves, which they store in their crop. They can even digest bones, and so the only indigestible parts of their food, regurgitated from their stomach in pellet form, are fur and feathers.

Most birds of prey are fast and skilful fliers, owing largely to the amount of air in their bones. The shape of their wings and the way they fly tell us a great deal about how they catch their prey. Very fast fliers, such as falcons (Fig. 4), which mainly catch birds on the wing, have long, narrow wings for speed and agility. An attacking falcon may develop a speed of over 180 km per hour, more than any other bird. Hawks (Fig. 5) have short and rounded wings, enabling them, with the aid of their long tail, to make fast turns in the air; this they need to do since they often hunt in woods, among trees and bushes, and usually catch their prey by sudden attack, not by pursuing

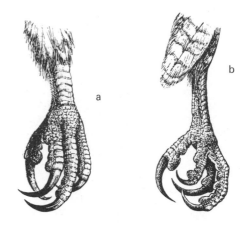

Fig. 2. *Foot of a bird of prey, with sharp, curving talons (a − eagle, b − Goshawk).*

it. Large birds of prey (buzzards, eagles, vultures) have long, broad wings (Fig. 6) and are masters in the art of soaring and gliding (they make use of the air currents formed by an increase in the temperature of the air over the land). They catch only slow prey, usually on the ground, or scan the countryside from a height, on the look-out for carrion.

The majority of birds of prey have strongly developed supraorbital ridges, which give their face its characteristic expression and whose purpose is probably to protect their eyes from dazzle. This is very necessary, since vision is their keenest sense and they are very dependent on it when hunting. As a rule, the big eyes are directed largely forwards and they can see exceptionally

Fig. 3. *Osprey making an attack on a fish.*

Male Kestrel (Falco tinnunculus) *with prey.*

Fig. 4. Characteristic silhouette of a falcon, with long, narrow wings and a narrow tail allowing exceptionally fast flight.

Fig. 5. Characteristic silhouette of a Sparrowhawk, with short, rounded wings and a long tail, allowing the bird to change direction abruptly.

Fig. 6. Flight silhouette of eagle (vulture), with long, broad wings suitable for gliding.

well. For instance, a falcon can see a flying pigeon 1.5 km away and a sitting pigeon 1 km away, while a kestrel can sight a sitting mouse from a height of 50 m.

Large birds of prey lay only one or two eggs, small species up to six. The incubation period is relatively long and in large species can amount to 50–60 days. Incubation usually begins with the first egg, so that the young are hatched asynchronously. The young are nidicolous, but lack some of the typical characteristics of such chicks since their vision and hearing are good right from the outset. They are at first completely white and look like little balls of down. The parents feed them by tearing the food into small fragments and putting it directly into their beak; only vultures feed their offspring with partly digested food regurgitated from their crop. The young grow slowly, so that rearing them takes the parents a long time. Fig. 7 shows the development of the young Peregrine; the numbers represent the age in days.

Fig. 7. The development of the nidicolous young of birds of prey takes a very long time. The drawings illustrate the young of a Peregrine at the ages of 1, 10, 20, 25 and 30 days.

115

Honey Buzzard
Pernis apivorus

The Honey Buzzard (1) lives mainly on the larvae and pupae of wasps and bumble-bees, whose nests it rakes open with its short, flat claws, but it also catches adult wasps, bumble-bees and other insects and even small vertebrates. It inhabits wooded country, interspersed with fields and meadows, in lowlands and uplands in practically the whole of Europe except the far north and west and the extreme south; in the east it extends to western Siberia. It is strictly a migrant and between August and October it migrates to tropical Africa; it does not return to its breeding areas until April or May, usually already in pairs. The first two or three weeks are devoted to the courtship displays; flying in wide circles, without flapping their wings, the

birds rise higher and higher, drop obliquely downwards and then rise again, carried by the impetus, and rapidly raise their wings several times high above their body so that they almost touch. The nest, which is generally situated high up on a tree, is sometimes a new one built by both sexes together; sometimes, however, they use the abandoned nest of another bird of prey or a crow as the foundation. The edge of the nest is always faced with green twigs from deciduous trees and/or conifers. The nesting period lasts from

2

May to July, the parents taking turns to sit on the 2 reddish-brown eggs (2), which are incubated for 30-35 days. After the young are hatched, the mother remains with them, sitting on the edge of the nest for two to three weeks, while the father brings honeycombs containing larvae, or other prey, which the mother first examines before giving to the young. After about 40 days the young leave the nest and disperse locally. Adult Honey Buzzards are the same size as Buzzards. Their upperparts are usually grey-brown, but their underparts are very variably coloured. In flight they can be distinguished from Buzzards by their smaller, more protruding head and longer tail with two narrow bands at the base and a single, broader terminal band.

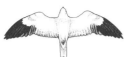

Black-winged Kite,
Black-shouldered Kite

Elanus caeruleus

In Europe, the Black-winged Kite lives only in the south of Portugal, with a few pairs also in Spain; otherwise, it inhabits most of Africa and much of southern Asia, from Arabia across India, Indo-China and southern China to the Philippines and New Guinea. It is a resident bird and its excursions into western and central Europe are exceedingly infrequent. In its home area it frequents flat, open country with open woods, groups of trees and gardens near human settlements. It builds a fairly large, flat nest on a tree, at various heights, but in some places it also nests on cliffs. The nest is made of dry branches, stalks, turf and palm fibres and is lined with moss, feathers and fur. The eggs are laid in the spring, but in India the birds nest at any time of year. The usually 3–5 (in Arabia only 1–2) dingy white eggs are marked with indistinct reddish-brown spots. They are incubated for 25–28 days, as a rule entirely by the female, and the young remain 30–40 days in the nest. Black-winged Kites live mainly on small mammals and birds, large insects (especially locusts, whose swarms they often follow) and beetles; they also take dead fish. The Black-winged Kite is a little larger than a Kestrel. In flight, its long wings are held bent at an angle and can be seen to be black-tipped below; the tail is relatively short and often slightly forked. This kite frequently hovers in the same manner as a Kestrel. Its call is a soft, whistling 'kree-ay'. The adult birds (1) have a greyish-blue back and a white underside and tail; their upperwing-coverts are contrastingly black. The young have a grey-brown back and a brownish underside marked with faint longitudinal streaking.

Black Kite
Milvus migrans

2

The Black Kite breeds in Europe (except Britain and most of Scandinavia), the whole of the southern and temperate part of Asia, Africa (except the Sahara) and Australia. Wooded regions with fields and meadows are its favourite environment and it shows a distinct preference for rivers or large ponds and other wetland areas. It is a migrant in the north; the birds leave for their winter quarters in tropical and southern Africa and Asia in August or September, and return in pairs in March or April. In their courtship flights, they circle high above their nesting site, make mock attacks on each other and sometimes actually lock talons together. Quite often they settle in the nesting colonies of herons or other colonial birds, and sometimes several pairs of kites nest together. The nest, which is built by both the partners, may be completely new, or it may be the adapted nest of some other bird. It is made of branches, grasses, moss and twigs, but the strangest materials, such as paper, rags, string and strips of plastic, can be found in its lining. The 2—3 whitish eggs, which are marked with sharply defined brown spots (2), are laid in April or May. They are incubated largely by the female, which the male keeps supplied with food. The young are hatched in 30—32 days, but the smallest one is generally pushed aside by its stronger siblings and dies. If the parents are disturbed while on the nest, they may drop food to the young from the air. The young leave the nest after 42—46 days. Black Kites live largely on carrion (often dead fish) and refuse; they obtain much of their food by molesting other birds of prey, or even herons, but they also catch small vertebrates themselves. The adult birds (1) have a dark brown back, a grey head and a rusty-brown underside. Their tail is only slightly forked, so that when it is fully spread the fork disappears. The call is a melodious series of trills: 'queeū-kiki-kiki-kik,' Both this and the next species are the same size as a buzzard.

Red Kite

Milvus milvus

The Red Kite inhabits western, southern and central Europe and the north of Africa. It lives in both flat and hilly wooded country interspersed with open areas and is less dependent on the presence of water than the Black Kite. In Europe, it also used to nest in towns. In southern Europe and in Wales Red Kites are largely resident birds; elsewhere they migrate southwards to the Mediterranean in the winter, although in recent years more and more of them have tended to remain behind. Migrants return to their breeding sites in March or April, when their courtship flights — prolonged circling at great heights — immediately draw attention to them. In most places they nest singly, but in Spain they

2

may still form small colonies together with the Black Kite. Sometimes they take over and adapt the nests of other birds of prey or of crows, while at other times they build a new nest, which likewise incorporates an assortment of turf, moss, rags, paper, bones, pieces of leather and finally sheep's wool. In April or May the female usually lays 3 whitish eggs with indistinct grey or

brown spots (2), which it incubates, almost unaided, for 28—30 days, while the male fetches food. After the young are hatched, the male keeps the family supplied for the first two weeks with food, which the female tears and divides out. The young are able to leave the nest in about 40—50 days. The Red Kite catches small invertebrates and also eats carrion and refuse. It employs its flying skill to attack other birds of prey, which it compels to relinquish their prey. The adult birds (1) are rusty-red, with a greyish-white head. When gliding, they can be identified by the white patch on either wing and by their deeply forked tail. Their call is a sharp 'heea' and a trilling 'heea-hi-hi-hi-hi-heea' at nesting time.

119

White-tailed Eagle

Haliaeetus albicilla

With a wingspan of about 2.5 m, the White-tailed Eagle is the largest eagle in Europe. The adult birds are greyish-brown, with a white tail and a yellow beak; the juveniles (1) are blackish-brown, with a dark beak and tail, on which white spots appear as the bird grows older. The White-tailed Eagle circles persistently on its wide, board-like wings, the primaries spread out like fingers; in flight, it also shows the wedge-shaped appearance of its tail. As it circles around its nesting site, it repeatedly calls 'kyee-kyee-kyee'. The White-tailed Eagle always settles near water — a large river, a pond, a lake or the seashore — from Greenland, Iceland and Scandinavia to central and south-east Europe (where it occurs only sporadically) and across practically the whole of northern Asia to North America. It has been re-introduced to Scotland. It is a partial migrant, and some birds from the most northerly parts of its range sometimes spend the winter in central and southern Europe. The courtship flights may begin in December, but usually at the end of January. The screeching birds fly up in circles, high into the air, where the male makes a headlong drop on to the female, which turns over on to its back to greet it with outstretched talons. The nest, which is built by both sexes, is placed on a tree, on the seashore, on a cliff or, in the tundra, on the ground. It is used and added to year after year, until it sometimes acquires huge proportions (it has been known to be 3 m high and to weigh almost half a ton). The 1—2 eggs appear in the nest in February or in March; they are incubated mainly by the female, helped by the male. The young are hatched in 35—40 days; at first they are fed only by the mother, on food brought by the father, but from the fourth or fifth week they are also fed by the father. The young eagles remain in the nest for 80—90 days, but even after they leave it they still beg food from the parents for a further four to five weeks. It is five or six years before they are able to breed themselves. The White-tailed Eagle lives on fish, mammals and birds and it also scavenges carrion.

Bearded Vulture, Lammergeier
Gypaetus barbatus

Today the Bearded Vulture lives only at one or two sites in the Iberian Peninsula, in the Pyrenees, in the south of the Balkan Peninsula, on one or two large islands in the Mediterranean, in North Africa, the Middle East and in southern-central Asia. In the last century it still nested in the Alps and the Carpathians and during the past few decades it has again begun, fairly regularly, to frequent the Salzburg Alps. It is a resident bird nesting in the rocky parts of mountains. The pair-bonds are permanent and the same nest is used for years. It is built on a cliff ledge or in a small cave, is made of branches and is lined with grass, moss and animal hairs. The rusty-brown, thickly russet-speckled eggs, of which there are usually 2, are laid as early as the end of December or during January and are incubated for 55–60 days by both the parents in turn. Since the second egg is laid four or five days after the first, the younger bird, being much smaller, is generally crushed to death. The young do not attain adulthood until their fifth or sixth year. A great deal has been written about the feeding habits of the Bearded Vulture, including the statement that it attacks human beings and carries off large mammals. In actual fact, it lives mainly on carrion, although it can also catch young chamois, lambs and goats. Its great strength and the large supporting surface of its wings enable it, as distinct from other vultures, to carry large food items to the nest in its feet. It also eats large, thick bones, which it either breaks into pieces on stones, or drops from a considerable height on to the rocks; tortoises are cracked open in the same manner. The adult Bearded Vulture (1), which is larger than the White-tailed Eagle, is blackish-brown, with a rusty-yellow to whitish underside, a whitish head and a striking long, black 'beard'; the young birds are dark brown, with a black head. Prominent during flight is the long, wedge-shaped tail; the wings are relatively narrow, pointed, and bent at an angle.

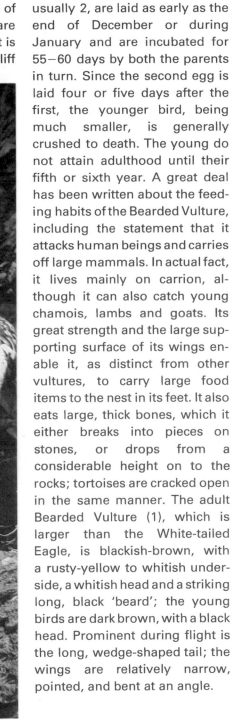

Egyptian Vulture
Neophron percnopterus

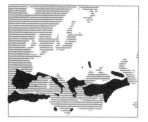

where young birds evidently remain until they are adult. In Africa, this species is regarded as one adapted to life in the desert, but in Europe it also lives in damp environments at quite high altitudes. It returns to its European nesting sites in March or April. It nests singly or in small colonies, generally on cliffs or crags and even on buildings, but seldom on trees. The nest is a large structure made of dry branches and lined with malodorous material of animal origin and with refuse. Nesting begins from February (in Africa) to April (in Europe). The 1−2 yellowish-white eggs, thickly marked with rusty-brown speckles, are incubated for about 42 days, both parents taking turns to sit. The young leave the nest in 10−12 weeks and in September or October they depart for their winter quarters, together with the adult birds. The Egyptian Vulture lives chiefly on organic rubbish, carcases and even excrement and is consequently often to be found near or in human settlements. It also uses implements, since it is able to crack large eggs with a stone. The adult birds (1) are a little larger than a buzzard. Their plumage is dingy white, with black and white wings. They have a bald yellow head and an elongated, only slightly hooked beak. Their white, wedge-shaped tail is very noticeable in flight. The young are completely brown and black; they turn white gradually and at the same time the bald patch on their head grows larger, but they do not attain maturity, complete with adult plumage, until their fifth year.

The Egyptian Vulture inhabits southern Europe, northern and tropical Africa, Asia Minor and the Middle East to India. At the end of the last century it still nested as far north as Switzerland. European birds migrate across the straits at the eastern and western end of the Mediterranean and across the Sahara, following the routes of the caravans, to northern tropical Africa,

Griffon Vulture
Gyps fulvus

The Griffon Vulture inhabits the regions of southern Europe around the Mediterranean, Asia as far as India and parts of northern Africa. It prefers dry, mountainous country, but extends into the lowlands. It is a resident and gregarious bird, which nests in colonies sometimes numbering up to 100 pairs. The nest is usually built on an inaccessible rock face, but sometimes on the ground. It is made of dry branches and is lined with thin twigs and dry grass. The single white egg, marked with cloudy dingy yellow or brownish spots, is laid between January and March; it is incubated by both the parents equally and they relieve each other every one or two days. The young bird is hatched in 50–52 days and the adult birds feed it with partly digested, regurgitated food. It grows very slowly and does not leave the nest for over three months; even then, the parents still look after it for several weeks more. It evidently does not reach maturity until it is four or five years old. Griffon Vultures live mainly on the carcases of large mammals; they rip open the abdomen with their beak and devour first of all the entrails and then the flesh from inside, until only the bones and skin are left. They collect around the carcase in dozens, circling down quickly and not, like some other vultures, dropping straight down like a stone. With a wingspan of about 2.5 m and a weight of up to 11 kg, the Griffon Vulture (1) is one of the

largest European birds. It has a long, white neck covered with down and surrounded at the base by a collar of white feathers. In flight, its long, broad black wings and black tail (which is rounded at the end) contrast with the yellowish-brown of its body and wing-coverts. The juveniles have a light brown collar.

123

Black Vulture
Aegypius monachus

The Black Vulture (1) weighs up to 12 kg and has a wingspan of 2.75 m. Its plumage is blackish-brown, except for the feathers on its head and in its ruff-like collar, which are light brown; the naked part of its head and neck is bluish. In flight, it can be distinguished by its huge size, its dark plumage and, in warm regions, in grass-lands. It nests singly and in colonies, which are not, however, so large as those of the preceding species. The pairs remain together the whole of their lives. The nesting season is in February and March and the nest, which is made of dry branches, is built on both the parents in turn. The young bird is fed beak-to-beak on partly digested food; it remains for $3\frac{1}{2}$ months in the nest and two more months near the nest, still cared for by the parents. It is capable of breeding itself at the age of five or six years. The Black Vulture also lives mainly on car-

and its long, slightly wedge-shaped tail. It is a resident bird; it lives in Europe only in a few countries around the Mediter-ranean (Spain, Greece, Turkey, the former USSR and Yugoslavia) and over an unbroken area in south-central Asia as far as China; at one time it nested in the Alps and the Carpathians. It is found in mountains and foothills, a tree, sometimes in bushes and very occasionally on a cliff. The single brown-spotted egg (2) is incubated for 51—53 days by

2

rion, which it finds by scanning the countryside from a consider-able height. It opens up carcases, however, at the highest point, and eats chiefly the flesh, to-gether with the bones, skin and hairs; the indigestible parts are disgorged later. If insufficient carrion is available, the vulture will attack lambs; it also catches ground squirrels and reptiles.

Short-toed Eagle
Circaetus gallicus

The Short-toed Eagle lives mainly on snakes, both venomous and non-venomous, which, once it has killed them, it swallows head first; when it carries one to its nest, the tail can often be seen dangling from its beak. It inhabits the warmer parts of eastern, southern and western Europe, southwestern Asia and northern Africa, where it frequents woods broken by glades, clearings and meadows. It winters in Africa in the regions just south of the Sahara, for which it sets out in September or October. It does not return until April or May and soon afterwards begins building the nest, which is a joint undertaking by both sexes; sometimes the old nest of another bird is used as the foundation. The nest is always lined with green branches from deciduous trees and conifers. The single white egg is laid at the end of April or in May; the reason why there is only one egg is that, if there were more young, it would be impossible to keep them all supplied with snakes. (Birds of prey of this size — it is distinctly larger than a buzzard — generally lay more eggs.) The eggs are incubated mainly by the female, helped, however, by the male. The young bird hatches after about 35 days. The male at first fetches food for mother and offspring; for about the first three weeks the female tears the snakes into small pieces, but later both parents catch food and feed it whole to the young. The young eagle leaves the nest in 9—11 weeks. Towards the end of the nesting period, the father's interest in his offspring seems to wane. The Short-toed Eagle (1) has a strikingly large head with a greyish-brown back and black flight feathers. In flight, its dark brown breast and throat contrast with the often almost white underside of its body and wings, which are marked only with a few large spots; the dark coloration and spots are sometimes missing, however. On the tail there are three or four indistinct, blackish-brown bars, of which the terminal one is the widest. The male's call is a loud 'yeeoo-ok', the female's a mewing 'kewiiay-yoh'.

125

Marsh Harrier
Circus aeruginosus

The Marsh Harrier nests in reed-beds beside ponds and lakes and in marshes and occasionally in meadows and fields. The pair generally draws attention to the position of the nest by its spring courtship displays, which are accompanied by loud calling, headlong dives and neck-breaking somersaults. The nest is usually in flattened or broken reeds from the previous year, in sedge or in an osier bed. It is made of reed or sedge stems, twigs and grass and is built sometimes by both sexes, sometimes by the female. The 4—5 dingy white eggs (3), which are laid between April and June, are incubated for 31—34 days by the female, which is often fed while sitting by the male. After the young have hatched, the male is responsible for procuring food, which it passes to the female in the air or near the nest. The young are fed only by the mother, and if she dies they also perish. The father continues to bring prey — small birds and mammals — but does not divide it up and share it out between the young, which eventually die of starvation. When only 26 days old the young harriers wander about in the reeds and at 40 days they are able to fly, but the mother still looks after them for several weeks. In August or September Marsh Harriers migrate to the Mediterranean region or to equatorial Africa, they return in March or April. They inhabit almost the whole of Europe (except Iceland, Ireland and the greater part of Britain and Scandinavia), a large portion of Asia, northern Africa and even the Australasian region and Madagascar. The male (1) is brown, with a lighter head and a brown-streaked breast, a grey tail and large grey areas on its wings. The female (2) is chocolate-brown, with a yellow head and shoulders. Both sexes are a little smaller and slimmer than a buzzard.. Their flight is slow and wavering, and when gliding they hold their wings above their body in a shallow V. Their call is a high 'kwee-ay'.

Hen Harrier, Marsh Hawk

Circus cyaneus

The Hen Harrier inhabits much of Europe, the northern half of Asia and North and South America. It is mainly a migrant; in Europe it winters regularly in western and central areas and its most distant winter quarters lie in the Mediterranean region and northern Africa. In the winter it is a common visitor to farmland, heathland, marshes and meadows, but it nests on wet ground, in peatbogs and on moors, in glades and clearings in the depths of young coniferous woods, and in the north in the tundra. It arrives on its breeding grounds in April, when the pairs are formed to the accompaniment of interesting courtship flights, in which the male circles upwards and then drops, turning somersaults as it falls. The relatively small nest, which is made of twigs, dry grass and the stems of herbaceous plants, is built on the ground by the combined efforts of both sexes. The 4−5 round white eggs are laid between April and June and are incubated for 29−30 days by the female, while the male keeps watch and fetches food; the male later brings food for the young, but they are fed only by the female, which also generally cares for them unaided when they are older. The young remain five to six weeks in the nest and are fed outside it for a further two to three weeks. The adult birds catch mostly small mammals and, on a smaller scale, small birds on the ground, lizards, amphibians and insects. When looking for prey, they flutter close to the ground and frequently settle on it. In August the nests are already deserted, but migration takes place mainly in September or October. The male is light grey, with black-tipped wings; the female (1) has a dark brownish-grey back, and a whitish or rusty-brown underside evenly streaked with dark brown. From above, both birds have a white rump. They are both a little smaller than the Marsh Harrier. The courting male utters a rapid 'ke-ke-ke'; another call is a sharp 'pee-eh'.

Montagu's Harrier

Circus pygargus

Montagu's Harrier has a very slim body and long, narrow, pointed wings; it is smaller than a buzzard. The male (1) is ash-grey, with black-tipped wings of sticks and stems, is built by both birds together on the ground. The 4—6 round, white eggs are laid in May or June and are incubated for 27—30 days entirely by the female. The male brings food, which the female receives in the air or on the ground. When the young birds have hatched, the female hardly

with a narrow black wingbar. The female (2) is very hard to distinguish from the female Hen Harrier, since both have the same coloration. Montagu's Harrier inhabits Europe north to the south of Scandinavia, Asia as far as central Siberia, and North Africa. It nests in damp meadows, swamps, heaths, cornfields, young conifer plantations and large clearings in riparian woods. In its courtship flights, the male swoops headlong on to the female, which turns over on to its back and greets it with spread talons. The nest, which is made

leaves them and the family is supplied with food by the male; the female hunts later in the season. Because of their slender talons, harriers are unable to cope with large prey and therefore catch only small mammals and birds, frogs and lizards. The young are able to fly by the time they are about four weeks old, but leave the nest before that. Montagu's Harrier is a migrant. It leaves for its winter quarters, mainly in tropical and southern Africa, in August or September and returns to its nesting sites in April or May.

Goshawk
Accipiter gentilis

The Goshawk inhabits almost the whole of Europe, northern and central Asia and North America. It is a resident species and in Europe only birds from the far

made of broken branches from the surrounding trees and are lined with dry grass and stalks; during nesting, the edges of the nest are raised by adding green

to death. From about the fortieth day onwards, the young leave the nest, but the parents still look after them until they are about 70 days old. Goshawks live mainly

north migrate further southwards for the winter. It nests in every type of wood and the pairs generally always nest in the same place. The male begins its courtship flights at the end of the winter; it soars up with powerful wingbeats and then drops like a stone. The nest is always built high up in a tree; the male evidently lays the foundations and the work is completed by the female. One pair usually builds several nests in its own particular territory, which it uses and re-adapts as required. They are

twigs. The 3—4 light green or grey-tinged eggs, which are laid in April or May, are incubated for 35—40 days by the female, relieved from time to time when the male brings food. For the first ten days or so after the young have hatched, the female hardly leaves them; she keeps them warm and feeds them on morsels of prey brought by the male. Since the male has no experience in feeding them, the death of the female during this time means that the young also are doomed

on birds and less on mammals. The adults (1) have greyish-brown upperparts and heavily barred, greyish-white underparts; they have orange-coloured irises. The juveniles have a light ochre underside, heavily streaked, and light yellow irises. The male is often one third smaller than the female, which is the same size as a buzzard. Their call in the nesting season is a loud 'giggiggiggik-geeah-geeah'. In flight, the Goshawk can be identified by its relatively short, rounded wings and its long tail.

Sparrowhawk
Accipiter nisus

The Sparrowhawk is a smaller version of the Goshawk, with a similar greyish-brown back and barred underside. The male, which is not much bigger than a Collared Dove, is one quarter smaller than the female, but its barring is rusty-brown and its cheeks have a russet tinge; the female (1) usually lacks the russet shade. The Sparrowhawk has short, broad wings and a long, straight-ended tail. Like the Goshawk, it flies by alternating a few strokes of its wings with brief stages of gliding. It also

times nests in deciduous woods. The nest is most often found among conifers, close to the trunk of the tree. It is built mostly by the female, but the male brings material — dry and sometimes green twigs — from the neighbourhood. The 4—5 thickly brown-speckled eggs (2) are laid in May or June and are incubated

for 31—35 days by the female. At first, the female remains the whole time in the nest with the young, warming and feeding them, while the male keeps the family supplied with food. Later on the female also hunts, but continues to feed the offspring herself, since the male is unable to; all the male can do is to hand the prey over, usually on the spot, where the female always plucks it. The young fly in about five weeks. The Sparrowhawk inhabits the whole of Europe, the forest belt of Asia and northern

weaves its way skilfully between trees and bushes. It pounces suddenly on its prey and no small bird in its area is safe from attack. The Sparrowhawk has a distinct preference for the edges of conifer or mixed forests, but some-

Africa. Over most of its range it is a nomadic and migratory bird, but in Britain and Ireland it is almost entirely a resident. Autumn migration takes place in September and October, spring migration in March and April.

Buzzard
Buteo buteo

The Buzzard inhabits Europe and a large part of Asia. It nests in any type of forest, especially with clearings and adjoining meadows and fields. The courtship flights take place early in the spring, with prolonged circling and sudden dives accompanied by a frequent mewing 'peeiōō'. The nest is usually built in the forest, and rarely on an isolated tree or on the ground; in Britain the birds nest fairly regularly on cliffs or rock crags. The nest is made of branches and is lined with small twigs, moss or a little

the young are hatched, the female hardly leaves them, while the male hunts and brings them food. The young leave the nest in six or seven weeks, but are still fed by the parents long afterwards. The greater part (about 70%) of the Buzzard's prey consists of voles; small mammals, birds, frogs and insects form the rest. In Europe, the Buzzard is

variably resident, nomadic and migratory; in the latter case it leaves in September or October and returns in March or April. Marked shifts in search of food are also known in the middle of the winter. The Buzzard's coloration (1), particularly below, varies widely, from almost white to brown-and-white-spotted and completely dark brown; the adult bird measures 51—56 cm. In flight it can be recognised by its broad wings (the dark spot at the bend of the wings is often hardly noticeable) and its relatively

grass; during nesting, the birds raise its edges by adding dry and green twigs. The 3—4 grey-and-brown-spotted eggs (2) are laid between March and May. They are incubated for 33—35 days, the parents taking turns to sit. When

2

short, broad, inconspicuously rounded tail with indistinct barring and a dark band at the end. Its flight is slow and rather cumbersome and is frequently interrupted by gliding and circling.

Rough-legged Buzzard, Rough-legged Hawk

Buteo lagopus

The Rough-legged Buzzard (1) closely resembles the Buzzard. It is likewise very variably coloured, but the commonest form is white below, with dark areas on the belly, the bend and the tips of the wings and the end of the tail. The head is usually also white, with dark brown streaks. The legs are feathered right to the toes. In flight, the striking dark round spot at the bend of the wings, a brown band across the breast and the dark terminal band on the tail are obvious, and when the bird turns the white base of the tail can be seen. The Rough-legged Buzzard is an Arctic species nesting in wooded tundra and tundra in Europe, Asia and North America. Since it would starve there in the winter, in October and November it regularly migrates, European birds moving to central Europe, sometimes in the form of a mass invasion, returning north again in February and March. It nests on the ground, on rock ledges and in some areas on trees. The nest is made of both thick and thin sticks and is lined with bilberry leaves, grass and lichen. The eggs, of which there are generally 3—4 and which resemble those of the Buzzard, are laid in May or June; they are incubated for 31 days by the female. The nestlings are fed by the female, while the male keeps them supplied with food. In six to seven weeks the young are able to fly and leave the nest. In their northern breeding areas Rough-legged Buzzards live mainly on voles and lemmings, which play an important role in their reproduction. In prolific lemming years the buzzards may lay up to 7 eggs, are able to rear the young without losses, and the result is an invasion of central Europe by Rough-legged Buzzards in the winter.

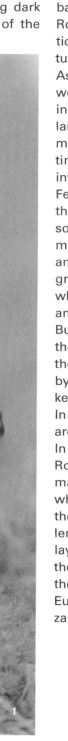

Lesser Spotted Eagle
Aquila pomarina

The Lesser Spotted Eagle occupies two very small areas, one in eastern and southeastern Europe and the other in India and Burma. European birds are migrants and in November they fly southeastwards to equatorial and southern Africa. They return in March or in April, already in pairs, and settle in forested regions broken by meadows and pastures. In their courtship flights, both birds circle high up in the air in wide spirals, without moving their wings; occasionally the male folds its wings and falls headlong, but then suddenly spreads them and rises again in a steep curve. The courting displays are accompanied by yapping 'kyee-kyee-kyee' calls. The eyrie is always situated in the crown of a tall tree; it is made of branches and the cup is lined with grass and green twigs. The nesting season is in April and May, when the female almost always lays 2 brown-speckled white eggs, which it incubates for 38—40 days with practically no help from the male. The first — and larger — nestling, which is about three days older than the second, is initially very aggressive and in four or five days pecks the younger one to death or pushes it out of the nest. If the weaker chick is reared artificially for a time and is then put back into the nest, the parents can rear both their offspring successfully, since the older one has meanwhile lost its aggressiveness. The female always feeds the young and the male is responsible for supplying them with food, which consists mainly of small mammals, reptiles and insects. The young leave the nest at the age of about eight weeks, but they do not attain maturity until their third or fourth year. The adult birds (1) are brown, with paler wing-coverts and whitish areas at the base of the primaries and on the uppertail-coverts. Juveniles have whitish spots, usually arranged in rows, on their wings. This eagle is slightly larger than a buzzard.

Steppe Eagle
Aquila rapax

The adult Steppe Eagle (1) is entirely brown, with a fairly long rounded tail marked with indistinct grey bars and markedly barred flight feathers. It often has a rusty-yellow spot at the back of its head and never has white upperwing-coverts. Immatures have obvious pale wingbars and white uppertail-coverts. This eagle is almost the same size as a Golden Eagle. It frequently settles for long periods on the ground, but seldom on trees. It rarely glides, but flies close to the ground. At all ages, its beak always has bright yellow corners which stretch much further back (past the eyes) than in other eagles. Unlike the Spotted Eagle (2), it has elliptical nostrils. Its call, a high-pitched 'kow-kow-kow', is not often heard. In Europe it nests sporadically in Romania and in the steppes of the Ukraine, and otherwise in central Asia, India and China (other races occur in Africa). When not nesting it is migratory and nomadic, its wanderings taking it chiefly southwards, so that it is hardly ever seen in central and western Europe. It prefers large stretches of flat, open country with no more than a few shrubs, such as steppes and semi-desert regions. The large nest, measuring up to 1 m across, is usually built on the ground, but occasionally on a tree or a bush, not very high up, and even on a haystack. It is made of branches and twigs and is often lined with such odd materials as horse or camel dung and pieces of leather or paper. The eggs, usually 2, are laid between April and June. They are small and dingy white, thickly spotted and speckled, and are incubated for 40–45 days by the female, which is kept supplied with food by the male. The young are fed by both the parents and are nest-bound for about 60 days. Steppe Eagles live chiefly on ground squirrels and other rodents. The eagle hunts by waiting in front of its victims' burrows, or walking along looking for them; it is not averse to eating carrion.

2

1

Imperial Eagle
Aquila heliaca

The Imperial Eagle prefers open flat and hilly country, where deciduous woods alternate with spreading plains and wide valleys; it is not found in high mountains. It inhabits the Iberian peninsula, southeastern Europe and parts of Asia as far as Lake Baikal. In the most northerly parts of its area it is a partial migrant, in the south it is resident. The spring courtship flights of this eagle are accompanied by loud, barking calls ('krok-krok-krok'). The pairs usually employ the same eyrie for several years. The nest, built by both sexes, is made of thick branches and is lined with dry grass, to which green twigs are often added. The 2—3 greyish-white eggs, faintly marked with grey and brown spots, are generally laid in April and are incubated for 42—45 days by both the parents in turn. The adult birds also both look after the young and catch food for them. At first they give them partly digested food from their own crop, and later feed them on small pieces of flesh. The young remain 65—77 days in the nest, but the parents continue to feed them for some time afterwards outside it. The young evidently stay with their parents for practically a whole year and do not leave them until the next breeding season comes around. Imperial Eagles fly in search of food over a radius of 10 km. They feed chiefly on medium-sized mammals and birds and occasionally on carrion. The Imperial Eagle (1), which is somewhat smaller than a Golden Eagle, is almost completely blackish-brown, with a pale yellow or white crown and nape and white shoulder patches; the Spanish subspecies *A. h. adalberti* also has a white leading edge to the wing. The juveniles are light yellowish-brown, with dark brown arrow-shaped spots, and have almost black flight feathers and tail.

Golden Eagle

Aquila chrysaetos

When people refer to the eagle as the king of the birds, they usually have in mind the Golden Eagle, a powerfully built, majestic bird which is able like no other to make use of air currents and to glide effortlessly for miles on its outspread wings. When it catches sight of prey, however, it folds its wings and swoops like lightning. It can catch a lamb or a small chamois without breaking its flight, sometimes hurling it down from the rocks in a sudden attack, and even a fox is not strong enough to defend itself against it. The Golden Eagle inhabits rocky country and mountain ranges in much of Europe, Asia, North America and northern Africa. The pairs remain together permanently and in the courtship period they chase each other in the air, circle, dive and swoop and roll in flight. The eyrie is generally on an inaccessible ledge of rock or on a tall tree; the nest is basically of thick branches, which the eagles break off trees in the vicinity and 'cut to size' with their beak or by dropping them from a height, and is lined with grass, heather, ferns and green twigs. After years of use, repair and addition, the nest may be over 2 m high and 2−3 m across. It is built by both sexes together and they both (but usually mostly the female) incubate the 2 eggs, which are dingy white with grey-brown spots and are laid in March or April. The young hatch after 40−45 days, but only one is generally reared successfully. At first they are fed only by the female, but later by the male

also. The adult Golden Eagle (1) is dark brown, with golden-yellow feathers on the top and back of its head. It measures 75−88 cm and is thus about one third larger than a buzzard. The juveniles have a white tail with a black terminal band, and large white patches on the wings, especially on the underside. The eagle's calls are a hoarse 'twee-oh' and a barking 'kyä'. The Golden Eagle is mainly a resident, but partly a nomadic bird.

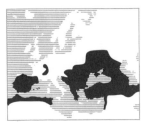

Booted Eagle
Hieraaetus pennatus

The Booted Eagle nests in south-west and southeast Europe, the Middle East, central Asia and North Africa. It is a migrant and in September or October it migrates to Africa south of the Sahara and to southern Asia, returning again in March and April. It generally occupies deciduous and mixed woods in both plains and mountains, especially where they alternate with open country. Courtship is characterised by acrobatic displays. The Booted Eagle sometimes uses other birds' nests and sometimes builds its own. The nest is generally sited at the top of a tall tree (but sometimes on a cliff) and is made of branches and thin twigs; green twigs are added to the edges during nesting, which takes place from April to May. The 2 whitish or green-tinged eggs are incubated for 35–38 days, mainly by the female; the male brings food both before and after the young are hatched; when the young have grown a little, the female also hunts. The young are fledged at two months. The Booted Eagle flies fast and skilfully, catching its prey like a hawk. It lives mainly on birds, together with small mammals, lizards and insects. The Booted Eagle, which grows to the same size as a buzzard, occurs in two colour variants. Both have dark greyish-brown upperparts, with paler wing-coverts and uppertail-coverts and a white spot near the body on the front edge of the wings, but one has a rusty-brown (1) and the other a whitish underside. In the pale form, the almost white undertail-coverts are particularly striking during flight; in the dark form, the underside of the wings is dark brown and the tail is light brown. The call is a series of clear 'kee, kee-keekeek' notes.

137

Osprey
Pandion haliaetus

The Osprey nests on every continent except South America and the Antarctic. Birds from northern and eastern Europe are migrants; those from the Mediterranean region are nomadic and resident. A few north European

or October, when they all migrate. The Osprey lives on a specialised diet of fish, which it catches by diving headlong, feet first, into the water, where it disappears for several seconds; it is able to catch fish weighing up

Ospreys winter in the Mediterranean region, but the majority migrate to Africa south of the Sahara, or to southern Asia. In March or April they return to their nesting sites, often using the same place and the same nest for many years. In its courtship, the male soars up with powerful strokes of its wings, hovers briefly and then dives. The nest is built on a large tree standing alone or at the edge of a wood, or, in unwooded country, on a cliff, on the ground or even on a power-cable pylon, and normally near a large river, pond or lake, or on the seashore. The nesting season lasts from April to June. The large nest, which is made of branches, generally contains 3 dingy white to bluish eggs marked with dark brown spots (2); they are incubated for 34–37 days by both the parents in turn. The young leave the nest at eight to ten weeks, but the adult birds continue to feed them for a whole month afterwards. The family remains together until September to 2–3 kg. The Osprey (1) is larger than a buzzard. Except for its light buff crop, it has a pure white underside, a dark brown to black back and a white head with a broad black-brown eye-stripe. In flight it is characterised by its long, strikingly angular wings, which, on the underside, have a black bar, a black patch at the bend and black tips; like the tail, the flight feathers are narrowly barred. The Osprey's breeding call is a piercing 'tchip-tchip-tchip-cheek'.

Kestrel
Falco tinnunculus

The Kestrel is the commonest member of the falcon family, inhabiting the greater part of Europe and Asia and North Africa; further races occur in central and southern Africa. It is often seen over fields and meadows or

2

the female, which is fed the whole time by the male. The female does not hunt again until the young birds have grown a little. The young leave the nest in 27—30 days, but still return to it for a few days afterwards. The

alongside motorways, floating to and fro at comparatively low heights and frequently hovering with outspread tail, looking for voles, its most frequent prey, which form 80—90% of its diet; in addition, it catches other small mammals, small birds and insects. In Europe, it is a resident, nomadic and migratory bird, in varying proportions. Birds from northern and eastern Europe migrate regularly in September or October to the Mediterranean region or to western Africa; they usually return in March or April. They generally nest in trees, either in nests built by other birds or in tree holes, in holes or crevices in rock or clay walls, or even in nestboxes; in human settlements they nest on church towers or in recesses on high buildings. The nest is unlined and the 4—6 brownish-red, mottled eggs (2) are laid in May or June; they are incubated for 28—30 days by adult birds, which measure 34 cm, are slightly larger than a Turtle Dove. The male has a light grey head and tail (with a black terminal band) and a red-brown back marked with small black spots. The female (1) has a rust-brown back, with heavy blackish-brown spotting. In flight, the birds can be identified by their pointed, slightly angular wings and their long tail. Their call is a clear 'kli-kli-kli-kli'.

Red-footed Falcon

Falco vespertinus

The Red-footed Falcon is characterised by marked sexual dimorphism. The male (1) is slate-grey to bluish-black, with chestnut-brown thighs and undertail-coverts; its legs, cere and orbital ring are crimson. The female (2) has a bluish-grey, black-barred back, a rusty-yellow underside, crown and nape and a black-brown moustachial stripe. In size and in shape this

(3) are incubated for 22—23 days by both the parents in turn. For the first ten days or so after they have hatched, the female remains with the young, while the male keeps the whole family supplied with food; later on the female also hunts again. The young leave the nest after 26—28 days. The Red-footed Falcon feeds mainly on large insects (grasshoppers, dragonflies and

bird resembles the Hobby, but it has a longer tail and frequently hovers. In the breeding season it utters a repetitive 'ki-ki-ki-ki' similar to the call of the Lesser Spotted Woodpecker. The Red-footed Falcon is a very sociable bird and very often up to 100 pairs may nest together, sometimes in colonies of other birds such as Rooks. They usually employ the nests of corvids, but have also

been known to nest in a hollow tree and on the ground. The nesting season does not begin until May or June. The 3—4 rust-coloured, brown-speckled eggs

beetles), which it seizes on the ground or in the air and devours as it flies. It inhabits steppes, wooded steppes and open country with groups or rows of trees, in eastern Europe and the temperate part of Asia. Everywhere it is a migrant; it leaves for its winter quarters in southwestern Africa in August or September and returns to its nesting sites in April or May.

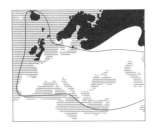

Merlin,
Pigeon Hawk
Falco columbarius

The Merlin inhabits northern Europe, northern and central Asia and North America. In Europe its range extends from Britain (whose southwestern part is its most southerly European breeding area), across Scandinavia, to the north European part of the former USSR. In Britain it is a nomadic and a resident bird, but other populations winter in western, central and southern pes. The pairs probably remain together for the whole of their lives. The nest is generally situated on a boulder, on the ground, in scrub and occasionally on a tree. The 4–5 eggs, speckled with dark brown (2), are laid in May or June and both the parents take turns to sit; the incubation period is 26–30 days. At feeding time, the male passes the food to the female, which feeds the young in the nest for 25–27 days; although not yet able to fly, the young then leave the nest. The Merlin catches its prey – mainly small birds, insects and very occasionally small mammals – in open country and on the wing. Between August and November the migrant populations move southwards. The Merlin is smaller than a Kestrel and it does not hover. Its underparts are always

Europe and in northern Africa. In March or April it returns and settles in uplands, in tundra and wooded tundra and in more open parts of the taiga; it also inhabits parts of the forest and alpine mountain belt and lives in grasslands and wooded step-

2

heavily barred. The male has a slate-grey back and a black band at the end of its tail; the female and the juveniles are dark brown above (1). The Merlin's call is a fast, high-pitched 'kik-kik-kik', rather like the call of the Kestrel.

141

Hobby
Falco subbuteo

The Hobby is perfectly constructed for flying; with its long, narrow, pointed wings and its short
tail, it looks rather like another
skilled flier – the Swift – in
outline. Its prey includes birds
and large insects, which it always
catches on the wing in open
country. In the late summer it
always takes toll of Starlings and
Swallows at their roosts beside
ponds and it often raids villages,
where it strikes terror into the
heart of even such good fliers as
Swallows and martins. The Hobby inhabits most of Europe, the
temperate parts of Asia and
North Africa. It is mostly to be
found in lowlands and hills,
where it frequents open country,
small copses and the edges of
open woods. During courtship,
the birds circle high up in the air,
suddenly dive and then soar up
again. Hobbies do not build
a nest of their own, but generally
use old nests of crows, Magpies
and Buzzards. The 2–4 yellowish-brown, thickly russet-speckled eggs (2) are laid in May or
June. They are incubated mainly
by the female, helped by the
male; the young hatch after 28
days. If they are fed on insects,
both the parents feed them; in
the case of larger prey, only the
female is responsible for feeding.
The young leave the nest in about
four weeks, but the parents continue to feed them for some time
afterwards. Hobbies migrate in
August or September, most trav-
elling as far as southern Africa.
They usually return in May. The
Hobby (1), which is the same size
as a Kestrel, has slate-black up-

2

perparts, densely streaked buff
underparts, and rufous thighs
and undertail-coverts. Its black
crown and moustachial stripe
contrast sharply with its white
throat and the sides of its neck.
Its call is a rapidly repeated
'kikikikik'.

Lanner
Falco biarmicus

whole year, and when perched on rocks they often nestle so close together that from a distance they look like one bird. The nest, which is generally in a hollow in an inaccessible rock face, is only thinly lined with the stems of plants. In southern Europe the russet-speckled eggs are laid between the middle of February and the middle of March; there are usually 3–4 and they are incubated for 32–35 days, the male apparently playing an appreciable part. Both parents care for the nestlings until they fledge after about 45 days, and also for the young some time after they have left the nest. Lanners live chiefly on birds up to the size of a duck and to a lesser extent on small mammals, reptiles, amphibians and insects. They catch their prey mainly on the wing and try to take it by surprise by flying low close to steep rock faces. The sexes very often take turns to hunt, over a radius of not more than 4 km from the nest. The adult birds (1) have a grey-brown back with large transverse spots and a pale, spotted underside. They are characterised by a rusty-brown crown and nape (in the Saker these areas are whitish), a white throat and cheeks and a narrow, dark brown moustachial stripe. The Lanner seldom perches on trees, but rather on elevations on the ground. In flight, it has a longer tail and more rounded wings than the Peregrine, but is otherwise much the same size.

The Lanner is a southern bird living mainly in Africa and Arabia (in Europe only in the eastern part of the Mediterranean region). It is evidently a resident bird and in the winter simply moves to lower altitudes. It prefers rocky country bordering on undulating fields and pastures. The pairs remain together the

143

Saker

Falco cherrug

The Saker breeds from the eastern part of Austria and Slovakia across southeastern Europe to central Asia. It inhabits deciduous and mixed woods in lowlands and mountains, with fields, meadows and pastures in the vicinity, and in Asia it also occurs on grassy plateaux at high altitudes. For nesting it requires old trees or rocks, since it takes over the nests of other birds or nests in holes and recesses in rocks. The pairs either remain near their nest the whole year round, or return to it in March. In the breeding season they draw attention to themselves by their loud 'kyack-kyack' or 'kikiki' calls. The 3—5 eggs, heavily spotted with rusty, brown or dark brown, are laid in April or May. They are incubated mainly by the female, but the male brings food and relieves the female for a short time at midday and in the evening; the incubation period is 28—30 days. At first the male procures food for the young, which the female divides into portions and shares out between them, but later both parents hunt. The young leave the nest at 40—50 days, but remain near it, under the watchful eyes of their parents, for a long time afterwards. The Saker is a very skilled hunter and is more than a match for any bird up to the size of a duck. Unlike the Peregrine, it also attacks animals on the ground, so that its prey includes small mammals such as ground squirrels and voles. It is a partial migrant, birds from northern regions wintering in southeastern Europe, to which they migrate in October or November. The Saker (1) has a reddish-brown back, and a whitish underside spotted or streaked with vivid brown. It has a yellowish or light brown head, with a narrow, inconspicuous, dark brown moustachial stripe. In flight it resembles the Peregrine in general appearance, but is larger and heavier. The Saker's outer and inner toes are the same length, while the outer toe of the Peregrine is longer.

Peregrine
Falco peregrinus

prey or of crows and herons; in the tundra they also nest on the ground. The 2–4 russet to rusty-brown, mottled eggs (2) are laid in March or April and are incubated by the female, aided by the male. The young are at first fed only by the female, but after about ten days the male also helps. Feeding time is exceedingly noisy, so that the nest is always easy to find. The young leave the nest after 35–40 days, but are still fed by the parents for a long time afterwards. At the end of July the whole family leaves the area, but during the autumn the adult birds return to the nest from time to time to re-assert their claim to it. Between October and December the birds fly west or southwest to their winter quarters. With few exceptions, the Peregrine lives mainly on birds from finch to duck size, which it almost always catches in flight, but owing to its swiftness, strength and skill it is also more than a match for geese, herons, cranes and bustards. It flies faster than any other bird and when diving after prey ('stooping') it develops a speed of 180 km per hour (perhaps more). The adult birds (1) have a dark grey back, a whitish, barred underside, a wide black moustachial stripe and a black crown and nape. The juveniles have a light yellow-brown underside heavily streaked with brown. In flight, the Peregrine can be identified by its long, pointed wings and relatively short, tapering tail. The adult female is almost the size of a buzzard; the male is roughly one third smaller.

The Peregrine is distributed over all continents of the world. Its northern populations are largely migratory, its southern populations nomadic and resident. The pairs arrive at their breeding sites in February or March, when courtship is accompanied by a constant screeching 'kek-kek-kek' as the birds chase each other high up in the air. The pairs are evidently permanent and usually always nest in the same place. They nest in holes and niches in steep cliffs, and less often in trees – in old nests of other birds of

2

145

With both feet firmly on the ground

Game birds

GALLIFORMES

Game birds or fowls are robust birds of varying sizes with a relatively small head and a strong beak whose curved upper mandible overlaps the lower mandible (Fig. 1). They have powerful, thick-toed feet with flat, blunt claws, used for raking the ground for food (Fig. 2). Their tarsi have two rows of wide plates down the front and smaller plates down the back, and in the grouse the whole leg and foot is feathered. In their feeding, nesting and other habits, game birds are essentially ground birds and can run both nimbly and fast. Nevertheless, most of them — at least occasionally — fly up into the trees to spend the night. Their wings are relatively short and rounded, which accounts for their awkward, clumsy flight; game birds generally fly only when they really have to.

On the whole, game birds have dense plumage and, evidently to compensate for the lack of down, the feathers have well-developed aftershafts (hyporhachides) (Fig. 3). Powder-down is completely absent and this is perhaps the reason why game birds are so fond of dust-baths. Conversely, they do not like water and most

never bathe in it. One characteristic feature of game birds is that the first two primaries, at the tip of the wing, are not changed at the first moult; they are not shed for a whole year and young birds can thus be told from their worn appearance. Fig. 4 shows the primaries of the Partridge at 15 months; fig. 5 represents the Partridge at over 27 months. Most game birds are characterised by pronounced sexual dimorphism. The males are often brightly coloured and have various ornamental feathers which come into play during courtship. In addition, they have brightly coloured crests, wattles and other appendages on their head and sharp spurs on their legs. Males are also usually larger than the females; for instance, the cock Capercaillie weighs up to 6 kg, the hen not more than 3 kg. Together with the Turkey, the Capercaillie is the largest European game bird; the Quail, with an average weight of 90 g, is one of the smallest. Game birds are not very intelligent and the structure of their brain ranks them among the most primitive birds.

In keeping with their diet (mainly seeds), game birds have a large, muscular stomach with a thick,

Fig. 1. *Head of a grouse, with hooked beak.*

Fig. 2. *Foot adapted for scratching.*

Fig. 3. *Feather with a hyporhachis.*

cornified lining (and usually containing a quantity of sand and grit for crushing and grinding the food), and a long blind gut in which tough plant food (buds, leaves and needles, etc, as well as seeds) can be digested. The droppings from the blind gut are excreted separately and differ from the other droppings in their homogeneous appearance and much darker colour.

Game birds are often polygamous, and the cock surrounds itself by a large number of hens. At mating time the cocks display typical courting habits characterised by specific calls and postures. As a rule, game birds nest on the ground in a simple nest; they always have a large number of eggs, which are incubated entirely by the female. The young are a typical example of nidifugous birds. When hatched, they are thickly covered with down and are immediately able to see, hear, run about and fend for themselves. All the mother has to do is to lead them to food and be responsible for their safety. The male parent seldom participates in their upbringing. The young are generally soon able to fly and their flight feathers usually grow during the first week.

Mound-builders − gallinaceous birds inhabiting Australasia and the islands of the Pacific − have a unique way of hatching their eggs: they build artificial incubators. Some species form large piles of leaves and soil and bury their eggs in the top of these 'compost heaps'. The rotting leaves produce sufficient heat for the incubation of the eggs (Fig. 6) and the birds regulate the temperature by scratching 'compost' away and then piling it up again. The young birds are not

Fig. 4. *Wing of young fowl; the first two primaries are sharp-tipped.*

Fig. 5. *Wing of old fowl; the flight feathers all have rounded tips.*

Fig. 6. *'Incubator' of mound-builders, in which the young are hatched without being brooded by the parents.*

hatched for 30−40 days, but when they do emerge they are immediately able to fly.

Game birds have provided man with the largest number of popular domesticated birds. The commonest of these are the domestic fowl, bred from species inhabiting India and the Indo-Malaysian islands, the Turkey, bred from the wild turkey of the forests of North America, and the Guinea-fowl, which originally came from Africa. The Peacock, which still lives wild in the Indian region, is sometimes kept as an ornamental bird in European parks.

Display of the male Black Grouse (Tetrao tetrix).

Hazel Hen, Hazel Grouse

Bonasa bonasia

The Hazel Hen is a typical grouse of isolated woods, where it spends most of its time in the undergrowth. It is the only monogamous European forest fowl, that is to say, the only one that lives in pairs and defends its nesting area. Its thin, high, whistling courtship call ('tsee-tsi-tseri-tsi tsi-tsui') can be heard in March and April, when it sits on the ground, on a stump or on a low branch, trailing its wings and jerking its outspread tail up and down. The hen looks after the family unaided. In April or May, it lines a shallow depression (usually at the foot of a tree, beside a boulder or under a bush) with leaves or grass and lays 8—12 reddish-yellow, brown-spotted eggs (2). The chicks hatch after 22—25 days. They develop very quickly and make their first attempts to fly at only four days. At 14 days they are able to fly properly and spend the night with their mother on a thin branch, not too high up in the tree. They may later be rejoined by the male and the parents then both rear the young until they are about three months old, when the family harmony begins to deteriorate. The young birds quarrel more and more with one another and with their parents, until finally the family breaks up. The young males look for a territory and mate of their own (their efforts are strongest at the end of September and the beginning of October), and when they have found a mate the two remain together until the courtship ceremony in the spring. Hazel Hens feed chiefly on tree buds and shoots, catkins and berries, supplemented in the summer by insects, spiders and snails. The Hazel Hen is a resident bird inhabiting the taiga of Europe and Asia and deciduous and mixed woods in central and

2

eastern Europe and the Far East. The male (1) is rusty-brown and greyish-brown, with black and white spotting, and has a white-bordered black patch on its throat. In the female, the patch is pale ochre or whitish and the plumage is predominantly brownish-ochre. Both sexes are the same size as a Partridge. The chicks are clad in yellowish-brown down and have a black eye-stripe.

Willow Grouse, Red Grouse, Willow Ptarmigan

Lagopus lagopus

The Willow Grouse is a northern bird whose southern limits in Europe are in the Baltic countries and the south of Scandinavia; it is found in similar latitudes all around the globe. A subspecies, *L.l. scoticus,* occurs in Britain and Ireland. In the ice ages the Willow Grouse extended far into central Europe, but vanished with the receding ice sheet. It is a typical resident of bogs and moors, often with scattered willows and birches growing on them. The nest, built on the ground, is usually hidden by rushes or heather. Because of the harsh climatic conditions, the birds do not nest until May or June. The 8—12 pale yellow eggs, marked with black and dark brown speckles, are incubated for 21—24 days, entirely by the female. As soon as they are dry, the chicks are led out of the nest and form large flocks, together with the adult birds. The Willow Grouse lives mainly on willow and birch buds, heather and various types of berries. The adult birds are about one fifth larger than a Partridge. Their legs are feathered to the tips of their toes. In the summer they are dark reddish-brown, with white wings (2); in the winter they are pure white, with black feathers in their tail. Characteristic of this species is that the general colouring of the plumage never changes completely (1), except in the winter, and that one moult is succeeded by the next without a break (the male moults four times a year, the female three times). Winter plumage is worn from November to March, spring plumage from March to May, summer plumage from May to August and autumn plumage from August to November. The all-brown subspecies inhabiting the British Isles remains brown during the winter, and not even its wings are white (3). For distinguishing this species from the Ptarmigan, especially in its transitional plumages, its voice — a loud, rapid, croaking 'err-rek, ok-ok-ok' — is often a help.

2

3

Ptarmigan, Rock Ptarmigan

Lagopus mutus

1

The Ptarmigan is also characterised by its adaptation to a life in polar regions, as seen from its change from brown plumage in the summer to white in the winter. In its summer plumage, the male (1) has a grey or greyish-brown, black-spotted breast and back, while the female is more yellowish-brown. Both sexes have a white belly and wings and white legs and feet, which are feathered right to the claws. Their winter plumage is white, with a black tail. The male in winter has a black eye-stripe extending to its beak (3) and distinguishing it reliably from the Willow Grouse (2); at close quarters it can also be seen to have a distinctly thinner beak. In size, the two species are practically the same. The Ptarmigan has a harsh croaking and squawking call ('ārrr', etc). It inhabits the tundra belt all around the world, but the most remarkable thing is that it also occurs in Scotland, the

Alps and the Pyrenees, where it frequents rocky slopes above the tree-line. The explanation for this broken distribution is that the birds in the mountains are relict

2

3♂

populations left there after the last ice age. The Ptarmigan is a resident bird and in the winter it descends only from inhospitable mountain crests to the shelter of the valleys. Its nesting season is May to July. The nest, which is on the ground by a bush, in heather or in rubble, is sparingly lined with blades of grass or leaves. The female sits on the 6–10 lightly brown-speckled eggs for 22–26 days, while the male stands guard nearby and tries to attract the attention of any enemies to itself. The male usually leaves the family when the young are a few days old, but sometimes returns again before they are fledged. In August the families unite in small flocks of 15–20 birds; at night they look for shelter under rocks, or make holes for themselves in the snow. Ptarmigans feed on buds, berries and the green parts of plants and in the summer they also eat insects.

♂ ♀

Black Grouse
Tetrao tetrix

The Black Grouse occurs mainly in the open taiga of northern Europe and Asia; in the west it extends to Britain and in the south to the north of the Balkan Peninsula. It frequents any kind of forest broken by clearings, growths of young trees and swamps, pastures, meadows and moors; in mountains it ascends right to the upper limit of the timber belt. In the spring, it needs the open spaces for its courtship ceremonies, for which dozens of males sometimes assemble before dawn. Courtship begins with a hissing 'whushee' call and continues with an insistent, bubbling 'ruturroo-rutoo-ur-rr-urrr-ruturroo...' The males (1) droop their wings, spread their tail, which they hold erect, run to and fro, fluttering their wings, leap up and down and sometimes engage in fierce fights, just like domestic cocks. The 'best' males naturally win the most females. The female is respon-

sible for the care of the brood. The nest is well hidden in a clump of herbaceous plants or shrubs and the 6—10 brown-speckled ochre or buff eggs (3), which are

laid in May or June, are incubated for 24—27 days. At one week the young make their first fluttering attempts at flight, but they still sleep on the ground, with the mother, up to the age of four to six weeks. In August or September the families break up and the young males embark on their own incipient courtship. The young birds live on small insects, but later, buds, catkins, shoots, berries and fruit form the bulk of their diet. Black Grouse are roughly the same size as domestic fowls. In its nuptial plumage, the male is blackish-blue, with a lyre-shaped tail, white undertail-coverts, a white wingbar and red combs above its eyes. The female (2) is rusty-brown with dark brown barring, and has a slightly forked tail. The chicks are clad in light brown down with dark brown markings, and on the top of their head there is a rusty-brown patch outlined with blackish-brown.

153

Capercaillie
Tetrao urogallus

The display of the courting Capercaillie is a sight to warm the birdwatcher's or bird-photographer's heart. The males generally perform on a horizontal branch of a spruce or a silver fir. Their song begins at dawn with a tentative tapping sound, rather like two pieces of wood being knocked together. The tapping grows faster, until it becomes a 'trill' ending in a loud 'pop', like the sound of a cork being suddenly pulled out of a bottle. Then come three to five seconds of 'grinding', like a scythe being sharpened with a whetstone,

2♀

food (ants, insects at various stages of development, spiders), which it scratches out of the ground. The young remain with the female until September and then break up into small flocks of

males and females. The adult birds live on conifer needles, shoots, buds and berries (bilberries, etc). The Capercaillie inhabits conifer forests from western Europe to Siberia. It is the largest forest gallinaceous bird. The male is the size of a turkey (up to 86 cm) and is blackish-brown, with a white spot on each shoulder and red combs above the eyes. The female (2) is smaller (up to 62 cm), rusty-brown, with a bright chestnut patch on its breast. The chicks are brownish-yellow; the top of their head is slightly spotted.

3

during which the grouse is completely deaf and the observer can quickly come a few steps closer to his target. While courting, the male grouse runs up and down along the branch, spreading its tail and drooping its wings (1). When the sun sets, it flies down to the ground to mate with the waiting females. Like the Black Grouse, the male is polygamous and therefore does not look after its family. Between April and June the female lays 6−10 ochre-coloured, brown-spotted eggs (3) in a depression in grass beside a tree or under a bush, and incubates them for 26−28 days. For the first few days after hatching the chicks are very sensitive to cold and damp, so that the female has to keep them warm, as well as taking them to look for

Rock Partridge
Alectoris graeca

The Rock Partridge is distributed from the Alps, in the southeast corner of France, across Italy to the Balkans; from there to the Middle East and central Asia it is replaced by the Chukar *A. chukar*. It likes warm, rocky localities and lives on mountainsides with rocks and groups of boulders, generally above the treeline at altitudes of 1,500−2,700 m. In the Swiss Alps, however, chicks, together with the hen bird, have been found as high as 2,860 m, while in Yugoslavia they have been found on the seashore. Outside the breeding season, the birds consort in small family flocks (coveys), which sometimes join other such flocks in the autumn to form larger groups; when nesting time comes around again, these split up into pairs. The male's courtship call is a loud 'kakabitz, kakelik' and similar sounds. The female builds the nest on the ground, among stones, or under a clump of grass or a shrub, and lines it with parts of plants or with leaves. The 8−15 yellowish-buff, brown-speckled eggs are laid between May and July and are incubated for 25−26 days by the female. The parents both care for the young, which leave the nest as soon as they are dry; the parents guard them, keep them warm and lead them to find food. The young at first live on insects, insect larvae and other small invertebrates, to which they later add seeds, buds and the green parts of plants. The Rock Partridge is a resident bird, but in the winter it descends to lower altitudes. The adults (1) have a white throat and 'bib' framed in black, a grey neck and breast, greyish-brown upperparts (with rufous tail), a light-coloured belly and black and chestnut stripes on their sides. When danger threatens, the Rock Partridge runs swiftly and nimbly uphill and then glides down into the valley, uttering shrill 'rttchi rttchi' calls to warn other members of the flock in the vicinity. Rock Partridges are a little larger than a Partridge.

Red-legged Partridge, French Partridge

Alectoris rufa

The male and female of this species (1) are the same size as a Partridge. Unlike in the Rock Partridge (3), the black band framing their white 'bib' spreads

only half the number of eggs and the female leaves the task of incubating them to the male; further eggs are laid in another nest, which the female looks after

a shallow dip in the ground, lined with a few grass blades or leaves, and incubates them for 23—24 days. The male meanwhile roams about the neighbourhood, but when the chicks are hatched it rejoins the family. The young already begin to fly at the age of one week, but even after they are independent they still remain

out in short black stripes (4). On their head, a white supercilium leads from the beak, above the eye, to the back of the neck. This partridge inhabits the southwestern part of Europe, most of southern Britain and even parts of Scotland. It was not originally a native of the British Isles. The first attempts to introduce it there were made in 1673, but the first success did not come until 1790, when the birds settled in Suffolk, after several thousand eggs had been imported from France. Although this laid the foundations for free breeding of this species in the wild, 60 further introductions were recorded between 1830 and 1958. The Red-legged Partridge prefers stony localities with plenty of shrubs, and pastures, heaths, sand dunes, vineyards and farmland. In the spring, the call of the males, a loud 'tschreck, chukor', can be heard in the distance, long before sunrise. The female usually lays the 8—16 yellowish-red, brown-speckled eggs (2) in May, in

with the parents and in the autumn the families join together in small flocks comprising about 20 individuals. Sometimes the birds nest twice in a season. In such cases the second clutch contains

herself. Over 90% of the diet of the adult birds consists of plant food (seeds, berries, the green parts of plants); the chicks live mainly on insects.

Barbary Partridge
Alectoris barbara

At a distance, the Barbary Partridge (1) is almost indistinguishable from the Red-legged Partridge. At close quarters, however, it can be recognised by its blue-grey face and 'bib' and chestnut crown, the rusty-brown spot behind its eyes and the blue, rufous-edged feathers on its shoulders; unlike other members of the genus, the 'bib' is framed not in black, but in chestnut, and is decorated with white, bead-like spots. As in related species, its legs and feet are red. Its call, a rapid 'kekkelik' and a slower 'chuk, chuk, chuk, chukar', can be heard mainly first thing in the morning and after dusk. The only places where the Barbary Partridge is found are Sardinia, Gibraltar, the Canary Islands and northern Africa, where it is the most abundant and is popular as game. It is a resident bird frequenting stony slopes thinly overgrown with shrubs, or semi-desert regions providing at least a little water and shelter in the scanty vegetation. The nest, which is built among the vegetation, is a small depression in the ground, lined with the remains of plants. The 8—15 eggs, which resemble those of related species, are incubated for about 25 days by the female. The male, however, helps with the rearing of the young, which usually leave the nest the day after they have hatched. The parents lead their offspring to their food; at first this consists mainly of insects and other small invertebrates, but later seeds, berries and the green parts of plants are added to the diet. When the breeding season is over, the birds remain together in coveys.

Partridge, Grey Partridge

Perdix perdix

female. If the female dies, the male rears the young himself until they are adult. The 10–20 greyish-green eggs (4) are laid between April and June in a small depression at the edge of a field, in clover, in corn, or on the outskirts of a wood. They are incubated for 23–25 days by the female, while the male keeps watch nearby. The chicks are at first very frail, and if the weather is cold and wet many of them die. At 16 days they are able to fly, but remain with the parents, as a small covey, until the following spring, when they occupy areas near their parents. Partridges live mainly on seeds and the green parts of plants: they devour quantities of weeds and, in the summer, insect pests. Partridges (1) are an inconspicuous greyish-brown colour, with an orange head and a rusty tail. The

Originally a steppe bird, the Partridge now inhabits almost the whole of Europe and central Asia and has become particularly well adapted to life in agricultural coutry (i.e. fields and meadows). It has also been successfully introduced into North America. During the summer and winter, Partridges live in coveys, from which pairs begin to break away in February and March, when the voice of the males ('kirr-ic') can be heard morning and evening with increasing frequency as they fight for nesting sites. The pairs are permanent and the male looks after the family just as conscientiously as the

male has a deep brown horseshoe mark on its breast; in the female the mark is very indistinct. The lesser and median coverts are a reliable distinguishing character; in the male they have one white stripe running down the shaft (2), whereas in the female they also have white cross-stripes (3). The adult birds measure 30 cm. The chicks have yellowish-brown down with dark brown markings, which are especially pronounced on the sides of the head.

Quail
Coturnix coturnix

The Quail inhabits fields and steppes throughout most of Europe (except Scandinavia), western and central Asia and a large part of Africa. It is the only migratory game bird in Europe and it spends the winter in the countries around the Mediterranean or in inland Africa. It sets out on its southward journey in September or October and returns to its nesting sites in March or April. Quails may demonstrate polygamy (one male with several females), polyandry (one female with several males) or monogamy (in pairs), according to circumstances. The male occupies its nesting site as soon as it arrives. It is very quarrelsome, pursues other birds as well as other male Quails, and sometimes even attacks its own mate. The nesting season lasts from May to July and the male's call, a trisyllabic 'quic-quic-ic', can be heard the whole of the time, often at night as well as by day. The female is responsible for the incubation of the eggs and the care of the young. The nest is a thinly lined, shallow depression made by the female in a meadow, in an empty field, in clover or in corn

and contains 10—14 brownish-yellow eggs thickly marked with blackish-brown speckles (2). The young birds, which hatch after 17—20 days, are fully fledged at 19 days. They then either leave their mother, or fly southwards with her. Quails feed predominantly on weed and grass seeds and the green parts of plants; In the summer they also catch insects. The Quail is about half the size of a Partridge. It has brown upperparts barred blackish and with buff streaks. On its throat, the male has a dark spot and dark collar marks, of which only a trace is present in the female (1). In their downy coat, the chicks have two longitudinal brownish-black bands on the top of their head. Even at this age, the male can already be told by the absence of the dark spots in the chest region and the larger size of the bald patch around its eyes.

Reeves's Pheasant

Syrmaticus reevesii

Reeves's Pheasant comes from the mountains of central and northern China. It is a forest bird and in its natural surroundings is relatively abundant at altitudes of up to 2,000 m. It lives in small family groups, from which, in the breeding season, each cock breaks away, together with one to three hens, and occupies its own territory. The hen lays 7–15 olive-brown eggs, which it incubates for 24–25 days; the young are reared and fed in the same way as those of the Pheasant. Since the 19th century, attempts have been made to introduce Reeves's Pheasant in several European countries, including Britain, France, Germany and former Czechoslovakia, with varying success. Its acclimatisation was the most successful in France, where about 1,000 lived between 1970 and 1975. In Britain, the first birds were set down between 1870 and 1890, in at least 12 counties. When in 1882, in Inverness-shire, over 100 birds were shot in the course of a single season, it was assumed that the introduction of this species would be simple and easy. The assumption proved to be wrong, however, since free-living populations were formed only temporarily (for instance, in Dorset and in Ross-shire in the 1950s and in Inverness-shire in 1973–74). The cock (1) has a somewhat larger body than a Pheasant, but has extremely long tail feathers measuring up to 180 cm in length. Its feathers are mostly golden-yellow or whitish, with black tips; its head is black, with a white crown and neck and a white spot below each eye. The hen (2) has a dark greyish-brown back with black-tipped feathers and an ochre, russet-spotted underside.

2♀

Pheasant,
Ring-necked Pheasant
Phasianus colchicus

1

2

The Pheasant is not a European bird by origin. It actually comes from central and eastern Asia, but was introduced into the Mediterranean region by the ancient Romans. A further spread, both spontaneous and artificial, occurred in Europe in the Middle Ages, so that today the Pheasant is distributed over the whole of Europe as far as the southern part of Scandinavia. Later, it was also introduced into North America, Hawaii, Japan and New Zealand. It prefers country where copses and thickets alternate with fields and meadows. In the breeding season, the cock takes possession of a nesting area and collects five to ten hens. Its crowing mating call, 'korrk-kok', forms an accompaniment to its courtship displays, during which it jumps up and down, loudly flapping its wings. The female cares for the offspring unaided. The 8—16 greyish-green eggs (2) are laid between April and June in a small hollow in a dense clump of herbaceous plants or under a bush. The young hatch after 24—25 days and as soon as they are dry they accompany their mother in search of food. At 14 days they are already able to fly up into a tree and roost there for the night, and at 45 days they are fully capable of flight. At first, the chicks live mainly on insects, but in time the proportion of seeds and the green parts of plants increases, until, for the adult birds, they form the bulk of their food. Pheasants destroy large quantities of insect pests and are even able to catch voles. The adult cock Pheasant (1) has a deep brownish-chestnut body with a purple lustre, a long, tapering tail, a gleaming greenish-blue head with long feathers resembling ears, a bare red area around its eyes and, as a rule, a white collar. In all, i.e. including the tail, it measures 66—89 cm. The hen is greyish-brown and speckled and measures 53—63 cm. The young chick, in its downy coat, has a dark brown band on its head and black stripes meeting on its forehead.

161

Golden Pheasant

Chrysolophus pictus

The Golden Pheasant comes from the mountains of inner China, where it lives in scrub, bamboo thickets and similar low, but dense vegetation on rocky slopes and in valleys. In the breeding season, the cock assembles up to eight hens around itself. When courting, it parades around the hen, making hissing sounds like a scythe being ground, and spreads its handsome 'neck cape' in her direction. The nest, under a dense bush, is sparingly lined with grass blades or leaves and contains 5–12 cream-coloured eggs, which are incubated by the hen for 22–23 days. In the autumn the birds form small flocks. The Golden Pheasant lives on berries, buds, bamboo shoots and a quantity of insects, worms and snails. Attempts have been made in some European countries to introduce it into the wild. They have been the most successful in Britain, where this species was imported as long ago as the 19th century. The first positive results were obtained in the 1890s, first of all with Golden Pheasant x Lady Amherst's Pheasant hybrids, which formed the basis of a population now living in Kirkcudbrightshire in Scotland and of a pure Golden Pheasant population in Norfolk and Suffolk. From 1968 to 1972, the total wild Golden Pheasant population of Britain numbered somewhere between 500 and 1,000 pairs; they live chiefly in conifer woods (mainly among young trees) and on a significantly smaller scale in mixed woods. The cock (1) has a golden-yellow crest, a bright orange, long-feathered collar, a red underside, a black-green and yellow back and blue-black wings; including its tail it measures about 100 cm. The hen is brown, with dark barring, and is over one third smaller than the cock.

Lady Amherst's Pheasant

Chrysolophus amherstiae

Lady Amherst's Pheasant comes from southwest China and the adjoining parts of Tibet and Burma. The cock (1) has a dark green crown terminating in a narrow red crest, and a collar formed of long, white, black-tipped feathers. Its back and breast are green, its rump is yellowish-red and it has a white belly. Its tail feathers, which are over 1 m long, are silvery grey with bluish-black bands. The plumage of the hen is greyish-brown with black vermiculations. In its original home, Lady Amherst's Pheasant lives on rocky slopes at altitudes of 2,000–4,000 m. The cock has a harem of three or four hens, and when courting he hops to and fro in front of the hen and woos her first from one side and then from the other. The 6–12 eggs are incubated for 23–24 days by the hen. The first two males of this species were brought to Europe in 1828 by Lady Amherst, the wife of the then Governor of India; everybody went into raptures over the beautiful birds, which were named after the Lady. The first time this species was bred in captivity was in 1871, but, owing to a lack of hens, Golden Pheasant hens were used and purebred Lady Amherst's Pheasants became rare. The first attempts to breed them in the open in Britain were made at the turn of the present century in Mount Stuart and Woburn, and later, in the 1930s, in Whipsnade Zoo. The Woburn and Whipsnade birds formed the basis for a population living wild in Bedfordshire, but there are also others nesting in the open elsewhere in Britain and in 1968–74 the total number of such pairs was 100–200. In some places they live together with Golden Pheasants, but, because of the danger of interbreeding, it would be better to keep the two species separate, even in the open.

A miscellaneous family

Rails and Allies

GRUIFORMES

This order comprises a varied collection of birds so different in appearance that their kinship is not evident at first glance. Some of them look like game birds (some rails) or waders (other rails) and some like ducks (coots) or storks and herons (cranes). They also differ tremendously in size. For instance, among European species the Crane weighs up to 6 kg and is up to 1.15 m tall and some male Great Bustards actually weigh about 20 kg, while, at the other end of the scale, Baillon's Crake weighs only 45 g. Because of this heterogeneity, ornithologists divide this order into several families whose members are very different from one another. The one more or less common feature of the order is the relatively short, rounded wings (Fig. 1), although of course this does not apply to cranes, which are outstanding fliers and therefore have long wings. Many of the members of this order fly seldom and unwillingly, but, despite this, the majority are migrants. They almost always have four toes and their feet (Fig. 2) are adapted for running; that is to say, the first toe is level with the other toes or is slightly higher, or else it has been severely reduced, in keeping with the principle that birds with a vestigial hind toe are generally good runners. In species adapted for swimming, the toes are edged with lobed webbing (e.g. the Coot, Fig. 3).

These birds usually have rather drab plumage. Species which are highly aquatic have particularly thick, tight-fitting plumage whose coverts generally have a varyingly developed aftershaft; they also have a well-developed preen gland. The flight feathers are moulted in succession; only rails and cranes shed them all at once (in the case of cranes every two years) and are then unable to fly for about 14 days. The Demoiselle Crane, which lives in open country, is an exception among the cranes, since its flight feathers are moulted successively, as in most other birds in general; in the open steppes, without any shelter, it would be lost if it were unable to fly. Sexual differences in colour are not pronounced among most species.

Most rails and their allies have resonant voices and often very diverse calls, and some of them have specific equipment to help them. Many males of the bustard family have 'resonance boxes' (special inflatable pouches in their neck), while cranes have an exceptionally long trachea which is twisted into a loop in the hollow ridge of their sternum and amplifies their voice so that it can be heard miles away.

Fig. 1. *Flight silhouette of bustard, with relatively short wings.*

Fig. 2. *Foot of Moorhen, with long toes and no webbing.*

165

Members of this order generally live on the ground near water or actually in water, and in dense grassland or swamps, but some live in open steppe country; none of them is a tree-dweller. They almost always nest on the ground, or possibly in shallow water. Large species lay few eggs (cranes and bustards only two), but small species about ten. The incubation period is fairly long − about three weeks in the case of small species and about one month for large birds. The young are nidifugous; many of them are clad in deep black down, with which the colour of their beak and of the feathers or skin on their head forms a sharp contrast. These features are of orientative value to the adult birds at feeding time. Rails and their allies live on various types of food, but food of animal origin always forms an important part of their diet; none shows signs of distinct food specialisation. They do not possess a crop, but have a strongly developed, muscular stomach.

During the last two centuries, several species of this order (especially among the Rallidae) have died out, owing largely to the endemic character of their distribution (on small local islands) and to interference with the biological balance of nature in their small range.

Fig. 4. *The Coot* (Fulica atra) *takes off from a running start over the surface of the water. As it flies, its long legs trail behind it.*

Fig. 5: *The courting rites of the Crane* (Grus grus) *have a dance-like character.*

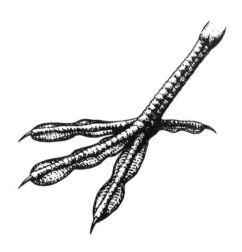

Fig. 3. *Foot of Coot; the toes are bordered by lobed webbing.*

The Water Rail (Rallus aquaticus), *an inhabitant of reed-beds.*

166

Water Rail
Rallus aquaticus

The Water Rail lives at the edge of thickly overgrown ponds and swamps. It is a very secretive bird and, since it is active mainly in the evening, we are more likely to hear it than see it. It usually betrays its presence by its repeated 'kik-kik' contact call and in the spring and summer by a high-pitched 'krooihf', reminiscent of the squealing of a piglet, which terminates in a deep growl. Nobody would believe that such a pretty little bird (it is about the size of a Partridge) could have such a loud voice. Similarly, few people know that it is a good swimmer and that it can dive if in danger. In March to May, the pairs occupy their nesting territory and defend it vigorously. The nest is woven from dry and green leaves of aquatic plants; it is carefully hidden in a clump of reeds, sedge or rushes and is generally covered with a loose conical roof made from the surrounding plants. The nesting period lasts from the beginning of April to the middle of July. The 6—12 creamy yellow, thinly brown-speckled eggs (2) are incubated by both the parent birds and the young hatch after 19—21 days. For the first few days the parents offer them food with their beak, but from the fifth to the eighth day onwards the young birds fend for themselves. The young from the first clutch accompany the parents when these attend to the brood from the second clutch, which are in another nest. Water Rails live mainly on animal food, supplemented in the autumn by small seeds and the green parts of plants. The Water Rail inhabits almost the whole of Europe, except the most northerly parts, and the greater part of Asia. In southern and western Europe it is a resident bird and in central Europe it also sometimes winters beside ice-free rivers; generally, however, central and eastern European birds migrate in September or October to the regions along the shores of the Atlantic and the Mediterranean. The adult birds of both sexes are almost identical in plumage. The salient features of this species are a long, red beak, a bluish-grey neck and breast and black and white stripes on the flanks and belly (1).

2

Spotted Crake

Porzana porzana

The Spotted Crake also lives a secretive life hidden away in luxuriant vegetation beside ponds and sluggish rivers and in marshes, swamps and wet meadows. It is less dependent on the presence of water among the plants than other *Porzana* species and is therefore also found in parts of swamps which are drying out. It is also heard rather than seen and in the

to the middle of July. The nest is carefully hidden away in the thickest clumps of sedge or reeds and is made of dry grass blades and leaves from the vicinity. The parents take turns to sit on the 7—13 yellowish or brownish, dark-brown-speckled eggs (2), which are incubated for 18—21

days; they both care for the young birds until they are fully fledged (at five or six weeks) and bring them small molluscs, crustaceans, worms and insects in their beak. The adult birds usually nest a second time before the end of August, into October. The Spotted Crake is thinly scattered over practically the whole of Europe except Ireland and the north of Scandinavia, and ex-

spring, in the evening and at night, its persistent 'whitt whitt whitt', like the swish of a cane, can be heard for hours. It is a migrant; occasionally it winters in western Europe, more often in southern Europe, but usually in tropical eastern and western Africa. It migrates at night. Between the end of March and the beginning of May it returns to its breeding areas. The breeding season lasts from the end of April

tends eastwards into inner Asia. It is the size of a thrush and its short beak is yellow or orange at the base (1). Most of its body is covered with round white spots on a brown or grey ground and it has striking brown and white striping on its flanks. The female resembles the male, but its throat is a duller grey. Like other members of the family, the Spotted Crake flies only when it is obliged to do so.

Little Crake
Porzana parva

The Little Crake inhabits the temperate parts of Europe and Asia from Spain, France, Germany and the Baltic as far as western Siberia. It is a migratory bird; sometimes it remains in the Mediterranean region during the winter, but generally it flies on to northeastern Africa. The males and females usually arrive in April at the same time and occupy nesting sites at the edge of shallow, stagnant water overgrown with reeds, rushes, sedge and other swamp plants. The nest is always well hidden in a thick tangle of waterside vegetation, right beside the water, and few people can boast of ever having found it. It is made of the dry leaves of plants from the immediate vicinity. When the family nest is finished, the male builds another one nearby for its own use, and is frequently to be found there. The eggs are yellowish or greyish and are marked with russet or brownish-grey spots; they are laid during May and June and are incubated for 17—21 days by both the parent birds, which relieve each other at short intervals. Up to the age of ten days the young are fed by the parents on insects, spiders, small molluscs and worms, which they find in old vegetation from the previous year or floating on the water, or for which they occasionally dive. By the time they are six or seven weeks old the young are able to fly and the parents can nest a second time. At the end of August or in September they all set out on the journey southwards. The Little Crake is the same size as a Starling; it has a short beak, red at the base, and green legs. The male has a brown back and a blue-grey underside, except for the undertail, which is barred with white. The female (1) has brownish-yellow underparts and a white throat. The male's display call is a descending series of 'quek-quek-quek' notes.

Moorhen, Common Gallinule
Gallinula chloropus

The Moorhen inhabits every continent except Australasia. In western and southern Europe it is resident, or at most nomadic, but elsewhere it migrates southwards or westwards in the winter. In the middle of March, Moorhens begin to return to their nesting sites in the vegetation beside ponds and sluggish rivers, in swamps and even beside artificial lakes in town parks. As soon as they have established a site, the pairs set about building the nest, which is made of dry reeds, reedmace, sedge or twigs. It is usually cleverly concealed in the marginal vegetation, but may be built in a bush or tree, sometimes fairly high above the water. The birds nest first in April or May, when the 6—10 yellow to greyish, russet-speckled eggs (2) are incubated for 19—22 days by both the sexes in turn. While the female is sitting, the male builds further nests, which the young later use to rest in. In June or July the adults nest a second time, and when the young of the second brood hatch their older siblings help the parents to look after them. Moorhens begin to leave their nesting area early in September. They live on various aquatic invertebrates and the seeds and green parts of aquatic and swamp plants. The adult birds (1) are about the size of a Partridge; they are greyish-black to blackish-brown; a white stripe runs along their flanks and their undertail-coverts are also white. Their beak has a yellow tip, but the rest of it, together with the frontal shield, is bright red. Their longish legs and very long toes are green, with a red spot above the 'knee' (the intertarsal joint). When swimming, the Moorhen has very little 'draught' and holds its tail erect. The young wear completely black down and have a red beak. The call of the adult birds is a penetrating 'kirk' or 'kirruk'.

2

1

Purple Gallinule
Porphyrio porphyrio

The Purple Gallinule (1) is about half as large again as the Moorhen. It has glossy blue plumage with white undertail-coverts, which it shows chiefly when it is alarmed and jerks its tail up and down. Its long legs, its massive beak and its frontal shield are bright red. It often climbs the reeds and rushes and runs very quickly on the ground, but it is not a very keen swimmer. In flight, it can be identified by its red, dangling legs. Its call is a screeching 'krroorr'. In Europe, the Purple Gallinule lives only in the south of Portugal and Spain and in Sardinia; otherwise it inhabits northern and southern Africa, southern Asia, Australia and New Zealand and the nearby islands. Most populations are resident, but this sometimes costs them dear. For instance, in the harsh winter of 1963—64, 90% of local birds wintering around the southern part of the Caspian Sea died. In the nesting season, the Purple Gallinule frequents the vegetation beside still inland water and bays. The nest is built in a thick clump of reeds or other aquatic plants and is generally on the water or up to 0.5 m above it. It is usually made of reed leaves and has a deep cup. The 5—7 eggs are laid between April and June; they are yellow or pinkish, with dark brown or black spots, although the pointed end is sometimes plainly coloured. The parents take turns to incubate the eggs, which hatch after 22—25 days. The chicks remain about four days in the nest and later return to it to roost. The parents both lead the young and care for them until they are able to fly. Purple Gallinules live mainly on the young shoots, seeds and flowering parts of reeds and other swamp plants, and to a smaller extent on aquatic insects, molluscs and small amphibians.

Coot
Fulica atra

1

2

The Coot is not very exacting in its choice of a nesting site. All it needs is a thinly overgrown pond, pool or swamp, or even an artificial lake in a town park. It inhabits the whole of Europe except the most northerly regions, and also a large part of Asia, northern Africa and Australasia. In eastern and northern Europe it is a migrant; in the other parts of the continent it is a resident and nomadic bird. Its most important winter quarters are in western Europe and in the Mediterranean region. In the winter, the surfaces of ice-free lakes and rivers and estuaries are sometimes black with Coots. In March, when the birds return to their breeding areas, however, the flocks immediately break up into pairs which wage fierce battles with one another for the best nesting sites. The nest, constructed by both partners, is built right on the water, at the edge of growths of aquatic plants; it is generally made of reeds or reedmace, but may be of twigs and grass. A ramp usually leads from the water to the nest. The male also builds further nests for roosting in. The parents take turns to sit on the 5—9 yellowish-grey, black-spotted eggs (2), which are incubated for 21—24 days. The male cares for the first young, while the female still sits on the remaining eggs or is busy with the second clutch. The young from the first clutch frequently help their parents to rear and feed their younger siblings. Migratory Coots move south or southwestwards in October or November. Their diet consists mainly of the green parts and seeds of aquatic plants. The adult birds (1) are almost as large as a Tufted Duck and measure about 38 cm. They are completely black, with a white beak and frontal shield, and have lobed leathery webbing on their long toes. They swim high in the water and fly somewhat laboriously, running over the surface of the water before taking off. Their call is a clear 'keff' or a piercing 'pix'. The young have an orange-red head and neck, but are otherwise completely black. The juveniles lack the bald white patch above the beak and their plumage is predominantly grey.

173

Crane
Grus grus

Not so long ago, the Crane occurred over practically the whole of Europe, but the cultivation of once extensive swampy forests and marshes has robbed it of most of its breeding sites. The only places where it is still at all numerous are the Scandinavian countries and the north of the former USSR, across to eastern Siberia. In September or October, Cranes from the western part of the range migrate to their winter quarters, which are partly in the Mediterranean region, but mostly in Africa as far as the Sudan. They return in March or April, to nest in swampy country in the middle of forests and near water. For a time they remain in flocks and perform communal courtship displays, hopping, spreading their wings and bowing ceremoniously. The pairs remain together for the whole of their lives. The nest, which is built in the middle of a swamp, is a large or smallish pile of reeds, rushes, grasses or other plants from the vicinity. In April or May, the female lays 2 brownish or grey-green eggs with a sprinkling of black speckles, which both the partners incubate in turn for 28—31 days. They likewise both look after the young for about ten weeks. While rearing the young, the adult birds lose almost all their flight feathers and are 'grounded' for about a month. Young Cranes mature very slowly and are not capable of breeding until they are five or six years old. Cranes live mainly on the green parts of plants, seeds, berries and other plant fruits, supplemented by insects, worms, molluscs and small vertebrates. The adult birds (1) are larger than storks; they are ash-grey, with a black head and neck, a long white stripe runs from the eye down the side of the neck and the long black and grey tertial feathers of the wing droop over the tail. The crown of their head is almost bald and is red. Migrating Cranes fly in echelon formation or in oblique lines. Their melodious 'kroo kroo' can be heard far and wide.

Demoiselle Crane
Anthropoides virgo

Today, the Demoiselle Crane occurs over a continuous area only in the former USSR, Mongolia and China. A small population was discovered quite recently in Turkey, at the foot of Mount Ararat, and a residual population lives in the Atlas Mountains in Morocco in northern Africa. In Europe, the largest numbers (6.000–8.000 pairs) are to be found in the Kalmyk Steppes (lowlands near the Caspian Sea). The winter quarters of this species are in northeastern Africa and southern Asia; in Europe it has been known to stray northwards to Norway, Sweden, Denmark and Germany. Lately it has begun to show signs of partial synanthropy, since it nests in pastures in the vicinity of herds of domestic animals — and in the Lower Volga region in fields. Demoiselle Cranes spend most of the year together in flocks and they also perform their celebrated courtship dances collectively. They form lifelong pair-bonds and the pair nests in the same place for many years. In April or May, the female lays 2 grey-green, grey-and-brown-spotted eggs in a shallow depression in the ground and incubates them for 27–28 days, with only occasional brief help from the male, whose real duty is to guard the nest. The Demoiselle Crane lives on the green parts of plants, seeds, insects and other invertebrates. It is the smallest member of the crane family and is the same size as a stork. The adult birds (1) are bluish-grey, the black colour of their neck extends to the elongated feathers of the breast, and the long tertials hang down over their tail. Their most distinctive feature, however, is the tuft of long white feathers on each side of their head. They have a louder and harsher trumpeting call than the preceding species.

Little Bustard
Tetrax tetrax

shuns cultivated country and frequents extensive grasslands or land which has lain fallow for a very long time. Southern and southwestern European birds are resident and nomadic; those from western and eastern Europe are mostly migrants. The Little Bustard nests in May or June. The courting male spreads its tail, droops its wings, ruffles its neck feathers and hops up and down on the spot, simultaneously flapping its wings. The nest is a poorly lined hollow in the ground and the 2—4 brownish-green eggs, sparsely marked with brown spots, are incubated for 20—21 days by the female, while the male stands guard near the nest. For about five weeks after the young are hatched, the male helps the female to rear them. Little Bustards feed on leaves, buds, seeds, insects and other invertebrates. In the autumn they form flocks. They are about the same size as a Black Grouse. In its breeding plumage, the male (1) has a grey head, a black and white neck and collar and a white underside; the rest of its body is yellowish-brown, with fine black spots. The female and juvenile lack the black and white markings on the neck. The birds fly fast, their wings producing whistling sounds, and in flight the large white areas on their black-tipped wings are conspicuous. The courting male's display call is a long-drawn-out, throbbing 'ptrrr'.

The Little Bustard has a similar distribution to that of the Great Bustard. In Europe it inhabits the Iberian Peninsula, parts of France, southern Italy and the Balkan Peninsula; it also occurs in northern Africa and across a narrow strip of central Asia to the Altai Mountains in the east. In the last century it disappeared from many of its haunts, since it

Great Bustard
Otis tarda

For most of the year, Great Bustards live in separate flocks of males and females, but in March the flocks break up and the birds' remarkable courting rituals begin. The males raise their tail and pull their neck backwards, inflate a special air sac in their neck, point their 'whiskers' straight upwards, droop their wings and literally turn them inside out, and spread their undertail-coverts and fold them over on to their back, turning themselves into a great, gleaming white ball, They stamp, 'marking time', shake themselves and occasionally utter 'ubb' sounds — all to win the favour of a female. The cock does not, however, help to look after the nest or the brood. Between April and July the female lays 2 brownish-green eggs, thinly marked with brown speckles (2), in a shallow, scarcely lined hollow in the ground and incubates them for 23—24 days. At first the young are frail and helpless; initially they are evidently fed by the female and are only later taken by her in search of food. They grow slowly and are not able to fly until they are two months old. They also take a long time to reach maturity (in the case of the males five years). The bustard's diet consists chiefly of the leaves, buds, flowers and whole plants of field crops and weeds, supplemented in the spring and summer by insects and other invertebrates; occasionally the birds also catch small vertebrates. Great Bustards are found in the Iberian Peninsula and central and southern Europe and their range then extends patchily across central Asia. To-

day the Great Bustard is almost everywhere a fast disappearing species. Over most of its range it is a resident bird, or at most

2

a partial migrant. It inhabits extensive treeless steppes and fields. Its back is brown, finely barred black, its underside is white and its neck is grey. In its breeding plumage the male (1) has 'whiskers' (which are actually long feathers) at the base of its beak. It can weigh up to 20 kg, but the much smaller female only 8 kg.

177

Denizens of swamps and marshes

Waders

CHARADRIIFORMES: CHARADRII

Members of this sub-order are mostly small to moderately large birds with a long, slender beak and long, thin legs with the tibia bare of feathers; at all events, they include some of the most 'leggy' birds of all. Their legs are adapted for wading and the hind toe, if present, is short and situated higher up than the long front toes (Fig. 1). The toes are sometimes joined together at the base by short webbing and in swimming species, such as phalaropes, they are bordered by lobed webbing (Fig. 2). In keeping with their thin legs, waders also have a slim, lightly built body. The smallest species, the tiny Arctic stints of the genus *Calidris,* weigh only 20–30 g and have a wingspan of around 30 cm, while the Curlew weighs over 800 g and has a wingspan of about 1 m.

Waders have slim, pointed, angular wings (Fig. 3) and are all fast and enduring fliers. Most of them are strictly migrants, whose winter quarters are generally a long distance from their breeding sites. Their dense, tight-fitting feathers have an aftershaft and they also have a well-developed preen gland. Sexual colour dimorphism is generally not very pronounced except in the case of the Ruff, the male of which has breeding plumage characterised by an expansible collar of long, brightly coloured neck feathers. Another interesting feature is that, in many wader species in which the male cares for the offspring, the females are more brightly coloured than the males. Many species change their breeding plumage for more plainly coloured winter plumage during a complete moult as soon as nesting is over and a subsequent partial moult. The breeding plumage is usually also quite plain, however, so that even experienced ornithologists have difficulty in identifying some waders from their appearance. Their voice is often a much better guide, since waders usually have very distinctive and clearly audible calls.

Most waders live beside water and many species inhabiting wet meadows and woods move to flooded muddy or sandy localities or tidal shores when they have finished nesting. Some species, however, live in dry regions far from any water. Courtship is generally accompanied by loud vocal manifestations and striking nuptial flights. The nest is usually on the ground, sometimes unconcealed in the open, but generally hidden by grass, and is only very exceptionally built in a tree. There are in most cases usually four relatively large, speckled eggs, tapering markedly at one end and arranged in the nest with the pointed ends in the centre. The nidifugous young leave the nest soon after they hatch and are almost immediately able to fend for themselves. They are covered with thick down with camouflage markings. When danger threatens they lie flat on the ground, while the parents attack the intruder to the accompaniment of loud cries, or try to lure it away by pretending

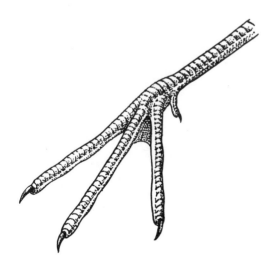

Fig. 1. *Foot of wader, with long toes joined together by short webbing and with a short hind toe situated higher up.*

The Stone-curlew (Burhinus oedicnemus) *in its typical nesting environment.*

to be lame. One curious feature of the family life of waders is that the females often abandon their family at a very early stage (in the case of phalaropes as soon as the eggs have been laid) and leave the care of the offspring entirely to the male.

Waders live on animal food, which they look for in or on water or pick out of even deep mud with their long, thin beak. They have a special mechanism which allows them to open the tip of their beak a little way when they come across prey in soft soil, since the resistance of the soil would prevent them from opening the whole of their beak. When the bird makes contact with prey, the protractor muscles on its rotating quadrate (Fig. 4a) contract and the bone moves, exerting pressure on the zygomatic arch from behind, so that the thin, flexible bones of the upper mandible are forced upwards and the beak opens at the tip (Fig. 4b). The bird is then able to seize its prey (which it feels by means of sensory cells at the tip of its beak) with these natural forceps.

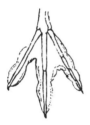

Fig. 2. *Foot of a phalarope, with lobed webbing on the toes.*

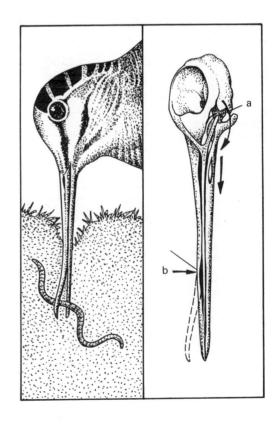

Fig. 4. *How a Woodcock extracts worms from the ground. After thrusting its beak deep into the soil, it can still open it at the tip as follows: the rotating quadrate bone (a) presses from behind on the zygomatic arch, with the result that the thin bones of the upper mandible are forced upwards at the tip (b).*

Fig. 3. *Silhouette of a flying wader, showing the slender, angular wings.*

Oystercatcher, Eurasian Oystercatcher

Haematopus ostralegus

The Oystercatcher inhabits the coasts and some inland areas of Europe and eastern Asia and shallow water in central Asia as far as the Ukraine in the west. Some British breeders are resident, but other European populations migrate regularly to western Europe and the Mediterranean region. When migrating, they almost always follow the

coastline and are therefore seen inland for the most part only as accidental visitors. Spring migration takes place from March to April, autumn migration during August and September. At the

2

beginning of the nesting period the birds perform their courting rites in groups; they hold their body in a characteristically rigid position, with their neck extended, run one behind the other or side by side and chase each other on the ground and in the air, all to the constant accompaniment of piping and trilling calls. The pairs remain together for a long time and have been known to keep the same partner and the same nesting site for as long as six years. They nest together in loose colonies on sandy, stony and muddy ground on the coast or (less often) beside lakes. The nest is a mere depression lined with pebbles or shells. The eggs, which are laid in May or June, are sandy-yellow and are marked with irregular black-brown spots (2); there are generally 3, but occasionally 2 or 4. They are incubated for 26—28 days by both the parents. At first the parents bring food to the young in their beak, but later lead them to it. They feed mainly on bivalve molluscs, whose shells they prise open (3) with their laterally flattened beak, but they also eat crustaceans, worms, echinoderms and insects. Oystercatchers (1) are adult at three years, and it has been proved by ringing them that they can live to as much as 36 years. They are about the same size as a Lapwing and have very distinctive black and white colouring, with red legs and a red beak. Their normal call is a loud 'klee-eep, klee-eep', their alarm call a vociferous, repetitive 'kip-kip-kip'.

Black-winged Stilt, Black-necked Stilt
Himantopus himantopus

Few birds are distributed over such a huge area as the Black-winged Stilt, which in Europe inhabits mainly the southern and the southeastern parts and seldom nests in the central and western parts. From there, however, its range stretches to southern Asia and across Indonesia and Australia to New Zealand, to Africa and to both the Americas.

Southern birds are resident or nomadic; those from more northerly areas, including most European breeders, migrate to the Mediterranean region or to tropical Africa as far as the equator. Everywhere they frequent fresh, brackish and salt water, generally with low marginal vegetation. The nesting sites are occupied in April or in May

4 light brown eggs, marked with dark brown spots (3), are incubated for 22–24 days by both the parent birds, which relieve each other at short intervals. The young remain only a very brief time in the nest and soon go wading or swimming in shallow water. In some years, nesting losses are enormous, largely owing to flooding. Migrant birds set out on their journey southwards between July and September. Black-winged Stilts live mainly on aquatic insects, together with small molluscs, crustaceans, worms, spiders and land insects. Their most striking feature is their exceedingly long red legs, which stretch almost 20 cm beyond the end of their tail when they fly, although their body is only a little larger than a Lapwing's; their long, slender, straight beak is black. In their breeding plumage the adult birds are distinctively black and white; the male usually has a black crown and nape (2), while in the female the crown and the neck are normally whitish (1). Their call is a clear, repeated 'kyip kyip'.

and the birds very often nest in colonies. The eggs are laid in May or June. On damp ground the nest is a fairly tall structure made of aquatic plants; on dry ground it is a shallow depression lined with only a little straw. The

2♂

Avocet
Recurvirostra avosetta

The Avocet, which is about the size of a Wood Pigeon, has an unmistakable appearance. It is black and white, with long, blue-grey legs, but its salient feature is its long, tapering, upcurved black beak, the shape of which is related to the way in which it obtains its food; it wades slowly, bill immersed, through shallow water, in which it catches insects and their larvae, crustaceans, molluscs, worms and fish fry by

scattered parts of Africa. In the southern parts of its range it is a resident or nomadic bird; in the north it migrates either to the Atlantic coast of western Europe

2

stand in a circle, bow, and run their beaks over the ground, stamping and screeching excitedly. The nest is generally a shallow depression lined with straw, shells or stones. The 4 yellowish-brown to olive-brown eggs with blackish-brown spots (2) are incubated for 24—25 days by both the parent birds in turn. When one comes to relieve the other, it observes a characteristic ceremony: it runs around the

sweeping its head abruptly from side to side. The Avocet frequents seashores and lagoons, ponds with muddy and sandy banks, salt lakes with shallow margins and river deltas. It nests patchily in western, central and southern Europe, but more continuously from the shores of the Black Sea eastwards and also in

or, more generally, to the Mediterranean region or to equatorial Africa. The birds arrive at their breeding sites between the end of March and May and the eggs are laid between the end of April and June. Avocets nest mostly in colonies and their courtship ceremonies are also performed collectively: they

nest several times, throwing small objects collected near the nest at the sitting bird, and when the latter has left it turns all the eggs over (1) before sitting on them. Autumn migration takes place between July and October. The Avocet's call is a fluty 'kloo-it'; its alarm call is a 'kit-kit-kit'.

Stone-curlew
Burhinus oedicnemus

The Stone-curlew is a nocturnal bird inhabiting open country such as steppes and wasteland, sandy and gravelly areas, pastures and large fields. It occurs in western and central Europe, in the southern half of Asia and in northern Africa. In southern Europe it is a resident bird, in the rest of Europe a migrant. Some birds winter in western and southern Europe, but the majority in tropical Africa. The pairs are lations are as a rule double-brooded. The nest is a shallow hollow lined occasionally with a little material from the vicinity, such as dry plant fragments,

2

small stones and even rabbit droppings. The 2 sandy eggs, marked with dark brown or russet spots (2), are incubated for 25—27 days by both the parent birds in turn. Soon after they are dry, the young leave the nest, but during the first week the adults still frequently warm them. At about six weeks they are already fledged and able to fly and only the male looks after them. Between July and October the birds leave their nesting sites. Stone-curlews live mainly on land molluscs, insects and worms and also, though rarely, on small vertebrates. The Stone-curlew (1) is about the size of a Wood Pigeon; it has a short, thick beak, strong yellow legs, a large head with a high forehead and striking, sul-

formed in the winter quarters and return at the end of March or in April, when they can be heard chiefly in the evening, at night and early in the morning, as they fly to and fro, or bow to each other, raising their wings. The breeding season lasts from April to July and west European popu-

phur-yellow eyes. Its sandy-brown plumage is streaked with dark brown and, in flight, two white bars can be seen on the upper surface of its wings. Its call is a plaintive 'coo-ree' or a high-pitched, penetrating 'kee-rrr-eeh'.

185

Pratincole, Collared Pratincole

Glareola pratincola

The Pratincole inhabits open country of the character of steppes or semi-deserts with sparse vegetation, such as fallow fields, pastures, dried-up mud by lakesides, drying swamps, seasonal flood regions and river deltas. It occurs in southern Europe (in central Europe as far as Hungary), southwest Asia and much of Africa. It is a partial migrant, birds from the northern parts of the range migrating to Africa. Occasionally it also appears in the countries of central and northwest Europe. A sociable bird, the Pratincole usually nests in small colonies, sometimes together with other waders. The nest is an almost unlined depression in the ground and the 3 greyish-yellow eggs thickly speckled with dark brown spots, which are laid in May or June, are incubated for 17—18 days by both the parents. The young remain only a very short time in the nest, but wander about in its vicinity under the watchful eyes of their parents; they are able to fly at about four weeks. Pratincoles live entirely on animal food, in particular insects, which they catch on the ground but mostly on the wing, in the same way as nightjars. The Pratincole (1) has an olive-brown back, an olive-buff breast, a white belly and a creamy-yellow, black-framed throat. It is about the same size as a Blackbird, but in appearance, with its forked tail and long, pointed wings, it resembles a Swallow. In flight, it can be recognised by its white rump and (in favourable lighting) the reddish brown axillaries and underwing-coverts. Its call is a loud 'kee-ik' like a tern's; its contact call in the flock is a chattering 'kitti-kirrik-kitik-tik'.

Little Ringed Plover
Charadrius dubius

The Little Ringed Plover inhabits sandy and gravelly ground beside rivers, ponds and lakes, but is also found on the beds of dried-out fishponds, and in sand-pits, gravel-pits and sludge-pits with puddles of water. It is distributed over the whole of Europe except the most northerly parts and occurs in northern Africa and most of Asia. The birds' arrival at their nesting sites in April or May is followed immediately by the male's display flights, in which it slowly flaps its wings and turns one way and then the other, to the accompaniment of rhythmic calls; it also courts the female on the ground. The male makes several nest depressions, but leaves the actual choice to the female. The scrape is lined with small stones, fragments of shells or pieces of straw. The 4 sandy-yellow eggs, which are thickly marked with blackish-brown spots (2), are incubated for 22—26 days by both the parent birds, which relieve each other at intervals lasting anything from a few minutes to several hours; when the young are hatched they care for them for a further three weeks. Little Ringed Plovers live on various insects, spiders, small crustaceans and worms; they often paddle with one foot on the sand or mud to drive them out.

2

Some birds, living mainly in the southern parts of the species' range, manage to rear two broods. In August the families leave for their winter quarters; some migrate to the Mediterranean region, but the majority move to tropical Africa. The most characteristic features of the Little Ringed Plover (1), which is about the size of a sparrow, are its short black beak and the narrow white bar above the black band on its forehead. In flight, its wings are unbarred. It runs so amazingly fast that the movements of its short legs are hardly visible and it looks for all the world like a mechanical toy. Its normal call is a frequently uttered melodious 'teeoo-teeoo'; in display flight it gives a hoarse 'chreea chreea chreeaa'.

187

Ringed Plover
Charadrius hiaticula

The Ringed Plover lives on coasts (and locally inland) in western and northern Europe, northern Asia, Greenland and northeast Canada, although in the tundra it frequents sandy ground beside rivers and lakes. Most British birds are resident; those from other regions are migrants and winter in Britain, in France or on the shores of the Mediterranean, or fly all the way to Africa. During their spring and autumn migrations they are sometimes seen much further inland, in the heart try to occupy the same site as the year before. The nest is a simple depression hollowed out by the bird's body in the sand, or a natural hole between stones, and is lined with a few broken shells or small pebbles. The 4 eggs, which are laid in April or May, are brown, with blackish-brown spots (2). They are incubated for 22−27 days by both the parents in turn, and the parents both likewise care for the young. As in the case of the Little Ringed Plover, losses during nesting are very high. In June or July the pairs nest a second or a third time, and migration takes place in August or September. Ringed Plovers live on the same diet as their smaller namesake, and often catch it by running, stopping, pecking and so on, as well as by 'foot-paddling'. The Ringed Plover (1) does not have a white border behind the black band on its forehead, but only a white line behind its eyes; the black band across its breast is wider. Its beak is yellow, with only the tip black,

of Europe. The Ringed Plover arrives at its nesting sites in April or May. Its courting habits are similar to those of the Little Ringed Plover. The birds always nest in the same area and always

and in flight a white stripe is conspicuous on the upper surface of its wings. Its call is a fluty 'tooi'; in display flight it utters a soft 'too-widdy too-widdy'.

Kentish Plover, Snowy Plover
Charadrius alexandrinus

The Kentish Plover lives beside the sea and salty inland lakes. Its distribution is very patchy, but it occurs in Europe, Asia, northern Africa and North and South America. It is mostly a migrant and in August or September European birds leave for the coast of southwestern Europe or northern or western Africa; they return again in March or April. The courting behaviour is the same as that of the two preceding plovers. In southern Europe the eggs are laid from April onwards,

parents take turns to sit on the eggs, which are incubated for 24—26 days; they also both care conscientiously for the newly hatched young and in the event of danger they try to lure the enemy away by pretending to have an injured wing. They look after the young until they are fledged, i.e. for about four weeks. The Kentish Plover feeds mainly

on insects, worms, molluscs and small crabs. It is the size of a sparrow and it always has a black beak and dark grey to greyish-black legs. The black breast band is broken in the middle, so that the centre of its breast, like the rest of its underside, is white. The black markings on its head are indistinct and are confined to a band on the fore crown, the lores and a stripe behind the eyes. The male has a reddish-brown crown; the female's crown and breast

in northern Europe in May or June. The nest is a hollow in the ground, sparsely lined with small stones, the remains of shells and broken dry stems; it usually contains 3 sandy-yellow eggs thickly speckled with black spots (2). The

patches are greyish-brown (1). Differences between the head markings of the Little Ringed Plover (3), the Ringed Plover (4) and the Kentish Plover (5) are emphasised best by a direct comparison.

189

Dotterel
Charadrius morinellus

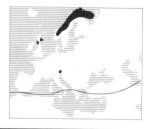

The distribution of the Dotterel is very interesting. It nests in stony tundras and northern alpine zones in Europe and Asia, but also occurs in scattered areas in dry, stony meadows on high Eurasian inland mountains. Since 1961 it has even nested on semi-dry polders (land reclaimed from shallow sea) in Holland. It is the excavation of nest hollows in the ground. The nest is usually lined with a little moss or lichen and the 3 olive-brown eggs, thickly speckled and blotched with blackish-brown, are laid in May, June or July. Here the female's duties end, and from then on the care of the brood is taken over by the male. He is Autumn migration begins in August, culminates in September and continues into November. Dotterels live mainly on insects, supplemented by spiders, worms and snails and less by seeds, berries and flowers and the green parts of plants. The adult birds are the same size as a Blackbird. In its breeding plum-

a wholly migratory bird and in the west has been known to winter beside the Atlantic and in the region from the Adriatic to northern Africa. The birds usually return to their nesting sites in April or May, before the snow has disappeared. Courtship is accompanied by much chasing, ruffling of feathers, loud calls and a very conscientious and fearless father and will allow himself to be stroked rather than leave the eggs, and will even sit on the eggs if they are held in the palm of one's hand. The eggs are incubated for 24—28 days. After the young have hatched, he protects them from enemies by feigning injury and luring the intruder away. Young Dotterels are able to fly in about four weeks. age, the male (1) has a rusty-brown breast and a black belly; its brownish-black crown is bordered by white superciliary stripes and it has a white throat and a narrow white band across its breast. The female is similar and generally brighter in colour. The call of both is a repeated, trilling 'titi-teerr'.

Golden Plover
Pluvialis apricaria

The Golden Plover has a small breeding range, which is restricted to northeast Greenland, Iceland and the northern part of Europe, from the British Isles, Germany and Scandinavia east to northwestern Siberia. It prefers large peat-bogs, high moors and swampy tundra. Some British birds are residents; the rest are migrants. North European and Siberian populations leave in August or September to winter in the region between the British Isles and Holland and the Iberian Peninsula, but many birds fly still further to the Mediterranean region and north-ern Africa. When they return, in March or April, their flocks break up into pairs and occupy nesting sites, to the accompaniment of striking nuptial flights and melodious calls. The nest is a shallow depression in heather or moss, thinly lined with leaves or grass. The 4 light brown eggs, marked with blackish-brown spots, are laid in April or May and are incubated for about 27 days by the female, with occasional help from the male. Both parents guard the eggs and the newly hatched young with a watchful eye; the young leave the nest only a few hours after they hatch and the parents lead them for four weeks. The Golden Plover lives mainly on food of animal origin — insects, molluscs, spiders and worms — supplemented by seeds and the fruits and green parts of plants. It is slightly smaller than the Lapwing; it has a relatively large, high-browed head and short legs and at all times of the year it has a blackish, gold-speckled back. In its breeding plumage (1) its underside is black from its chin to its legs; in winter and juvenile plumages its underside is buffish and white. Its call is a fluty 'tlūi'.

Grey Plover, Black-bellied Plover

Pluvialis squatarola

In size and appearance the Grey Plover somewhat resembles the Golden Plover. In its breeding plumage, the male (1) has a completely black (the female a brownish-black) underside, bordered along the sides of the neck and the breast by a wide band of white; its back is blackish-brown with silver grey barring. In its winter plumage (2) it has a grey-brown back, marked with fine greyish-white speckles, and an almost white underside. It is most easily recognised in flight, however, when it can be identified by the white bar on the upper surface of its wings, the white rump and uppertail, and its black axillaries — a feature distinguishing it from all other waders. Its call is a fluty trisyllabic 'tlee-oo-ee'. The Grey Plover is a typical bird of the Arctic tundra; it inhabits a narrow coastal strip of Europe and Asia from the

2♂

1

Kanin Peninsula eastwards, and also lives in the most northerly parts of North America. Birds which nest in northwest Eurasia migrate between September and November to the shores of the northern Atlantic and the North Sea, or continue further south as far as western Africa. They return in April or May, when they prefer to occupy the higher, less swampy parts of the tundra. The female makes a shallow scrape and lines it with pebbles, dry grass and lichen. It lays the 4 light brown eggs, marked with dark brown or black spots, in June or July and incubates them for about 27 days, with generous help from the male. Both the adult birds look after the lively chicks, which leave the nest soon after they are dry and are fledged in 30–33 days. Grey Plovers live on crustaceans, molluscs, worms and insects.

Spur-winged Plover
Hoplopterus spinosus

black and white; the top of its head, its small occipital crest and its chin, throat, breast, flanks and part of its belly are black, and the rest is white. It has a small, horny spur in the angle of its wings. It resembles the Lapwing in behaviour and habits, but its call — a disyllabic 'sick-sack, sick-seeh' — is very different. It is a very wary bird, and in danger its call acts as a warning to all the other birds in the neighbourhood. It does not hesitate to attack birds of prey and crows flying over its nest and even four-legged enemies. In Europe it inhabits only the most southerly part of the Balkan Peninsula; otherwise it lives in Asia Minor, the Middle East and northeastern and tropical Africa, and is commonest in the African part of its range. It nests in open country, such as swamps, on islands in rivers and lakes and by the waterside. The nest, a small hollow in the ground, is sometimes unlined and is sometimes lined with dry plant débris. The 2—4 yellowish brown, grey- or green-tinged eggs, which are marked with brown or blackish-brown spots, are laid in April or May. This plover lives almost entirely on insects, with a small proportion of other arthropods. The Spur-winged Plover is a predominantly resident bird, but those living in the south of the Balkans migrate still further south between the end of August and October and do not return to their nesting sites until April.

The Spur-winged Plover (1) is a little smaller than the Lapwing, but has proportionately longer legs. Its back and upperwing-coverts are greyish-buff, but otherwise it is conspicuously

193

Lapwing, Peewit, Green Plover

Vanellus vanellus

The male makes several nest hollows in the ground and leaves the choice to the female, which lines the most suitable one with straw and leaves. The 4 olive-brown eggs, which are marked with a quantity of blackish-brown spots (2), are incubated for 24—28 days by both the parent birds; they also both look after the young with scrupulous care. During the nesting time they make headlong attacks on intruders, uttering loud cries, fearlessly pursue birds of prey and draw attention away from the nest by pretending to be injured, etc. In five to six weeks the young Lapwings are able to fly; they collect in small flocks and roam the surrounding country. They live mainly on insects, spiders, worms and molluscs. The Lapwing (1) is characterised by the crest on the top of its head, which is 8—10 cm long in the male.

The Lapwing breeds in Europe, but is absent from most of the Iberian Peninsula, Italy, Greece and most regions beyond the Arctic Circle; in Asia it extends to the Sea of Japan. In western and southern Europe it is a resident bird; elsewhere it migrates between August and October to the Atlantic and Mediterranean regions. It returns very early, in February or in March, and, like the Skylark, is one of the first heralds of spring. Lapwings begin to nest as soon as they arrive. They frequent wet meadows and pastures, marshes, the beds of empty fishponds and fields with water in the vicinity. Their ac-robatic nuptial display flights (3) are characterised by curious jerking movements of their wings; they rise and fall abruptly and perform the most daring turns and somersaults, accompanied by 'swishing' or 'creaking' sounds made by their wings and by loud 'pewee-pewee, perweet-perweet' calls. Their alarm call is a resonant 'pee-wit' (hence their other vernacular name, Peewit).

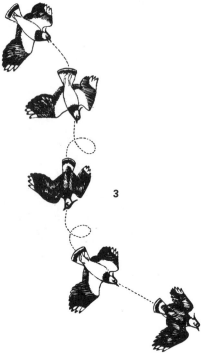

Knot, Red Knot
Calidris canutus

The Knot nests in the far north, beyond the Arctic Circle, in Greenland, on the Arctic islands of Canada, and at a few sites in east Siberia; it has bred in Spitsbergen (Svalbard). Between August and October it leaves these deserted, freezing regions and migrates mainly along the coastline, and seldom by an inland route, to the shores of the North Sea, the western part of the Mediterranean or the west coast of Africa. Some even wander as far afield as South America, the islands of tropical Asia and Australia. It nests in swampy tundra country with a little vegetation, where it arrives in May, usually already with its mate. In its display flights, the male flies straight up into the air and then, to the accompaniment of a fluting call, glides down again, with spread wings. The birds can also be heard at night. The nest, a small depression in the ground, is usually richly lined with grass and lichen. The 4 greyish-green, finely brown-speckled eggs are usually laid in June or July and are probably incubated mostly by the male; the length of the incubation period is 21—22 days.

When the nesting season is over, the birds assemble in flocks and soon afterwards they leave (the adults generally only two months after their arrival). Knots live mainly on insects, worms, molluscs and crustaceans and quite often they eat buds, seeds and fragments of seaweed and tundra plants. The Knot is a fairly robust bird the size of a large thrush. In its breeding plumage (2) it has a rufous head and underparts and a brown, black-speckled back. In its winter plumage (1) it has a brownish-grey back with white-fringed feathers, and a whitish-grey underside. Its call is a fluty 'twit-twit' or a low 'knut'.

2

Sanderling
Calidris alba

The Sanderling nests in the tundra north of the Arctic Circle, in the region from the northeastern coast of Greenland and Spitsbergen to the Arctic islands of northern Canada. When not nesting, it is to be found on the coasts of every continent and large island as far as Australia, New Zealand and South America. In Europe, on migration, it is common on sandy shores, but is rare inland. Between March and May the birds return to their inhospitable nesting areas in the tundra, where they frequent places with sparse vegetation or only with coarse-grained sand. The courting male flies from one thawed-out spot to another, flutters above each at a height of 2—3 m and utters distinctive calls. The nest is a hollow in the ground, thinly lined with grass, lichen or leaves and with catkins. The usually 4 olive-green eggs, marked with a few brown spots, are laid in June or July and are incubated for 24—27 days, whether by one or both of the parents is open to argument. Both the parent birds rear the young, however. From August onwards, Sanderlings from several breeding areas migrate for the winter to the coasts of western Europe and sometimes to western Africa. They live on small molluscs, crustaceans and insects, supplemented by buds and fragments of algae and mosses. The Sanderling is about the size of a large Skylark; its legs and its beak are short and black. In its breeding plumage (2) it has a rust-brown, black-spotted back and breast and a white belly. In its

1

2

winter plumage (1), its very pale coloration clearly distinguishes it from other waders, since it has a light grey back, with a black shoulder spot, and a white underside. In flight, a very obvious white bar can be seen on its wings. If disturbed, it utters a sharp 'twick'.

Little Stint
Calidris minuta

The Little Stint (1), which is no larger than a sparrow, is one of the smallest members of the genus *Calidris*. Its legs and its beak are short and black. In its breeding plumage it has a rusty-brown back, marked with black and white, and a mostly white underside; it also has white superciliary stripes. Juveniles have a prominent white V-shaped mark on the back. In flight, a thin white bar can be seen on its wings, together with the light border to the dark rump. Its winter plumage is largely grey-brown and white. Its normal call in flight is a short 'pit'. It is an Arctic species which nests in the tundra belt of Europe and Asia, but no further west than the north of Norway and Finland. It is a migrant, and from July until October it crosses the whole of Europe, singly or in small flocks, on its way to its winter quarters in Africa south of the Sahara; a few birds winter in the Mediterranean region. It returns north between April and June, but does not nest until June or July. It frequents swampy parts of the tundra near the coast or beside lakes and rivers and begins its courtship as soon as it arrives. The male flies over the nesting site with occasional wavering movements, like a butterfly, uttering weak whistling and chattering sounds. The nest — a depression in the ground — is sparsely lined with grass, moss and willow leaves and contains 4 yellowish-brown to olive-brown, thickly brown-speckled eggs. It is not known exactly how long the eggs are incubated or how long the parents care for the young. Sometimes both parents sit on the eggs, but sometimes the males form small parties and pay no attention to their family. Little Stints feed on small molluscs, crustaceans and insects, supplemented by the seeds of waterside plants.

197

Temminck's Stint
Calidris temminckii

Temminck's Stint has a somewhat wider breeding distribution than the Little Stint. In Europe it inhabits northern and western Scandinavia and the north of the former USSR; occasionally it also nests in the north of Britain.

fluttering its wings and uttering frequent trilling 'tirrr' calls. It is a solitary breeder and the nest is a simple shallow depression in the ground vegetation. The 4 brownish-yellow, brown-spotted eggs are laid in May or June,

reared either by one of the parent birds or by both; in 15—18 days they are already able to fly. Migration to the birds' winter quarters takes place between July and September. Temminck's Stint feeds on small molluscs, crusta-

It frequents marshy parts of the tundra with grass, shrubs and woods, and is frequently to be found beside rivers and streams. It is a migrant and its winter quarters lie between the Mediterranean and equatorial Africa. Courting begins in April or May, as soon as it returns; it flies up,

two clutches often being laid in two nests at intervals of only two to four days. In such cases the male sits on the first clutch and the female on the second, although in some instances the female takes another mate for the second clutch. The young, which hatch after 21—22 days, are

ceans, worms and insects. Compared with the similarly sized Little Stint, it has a more uniformly coloured grey-brown back and the sides of its head and neck are also greyer (1). In flight, it lacks the white V mark, but the sides of its tail, as well as of its rump, are white.

Curlew Sandpiper
Calidris ferruginea

The Curlew Sandpiper inhabits the central tundra belt of Asia beyond the Arctic Circle, westwards almost to the Gulf of Ob. It migrates to its African winter quarters via inland and coastal Europe and Asia. Older birds leave at the end of July and often travel enormous distances without stopping; young birds follow about a month later and are in less of a hurry. Relatively large numbers gather in autumn on the shores of the Mediterranean in the south of France and Spain, but the majority winter in Africa as far as its southernmost tip. In Europe, this species is to be seen regularly, though very uncommonly, during its spring migration in April or May, and in larger numbers during its autumn migration from July to September, as a rule on flat coasts or at shallow, marshy inland lakes or other wetlands. The Curlew Sandpiper nests in the Arctic tundra, usually near marshy ground and lakes with growths of grass, moss and stunted shrubs. The male's display flight involves slow wingbeats, gliding and trilling calls. The nest is a depression in the ground, lined with blades of grass, lichen and willow leaves. The 4 olive-green eggs, marked with brown spots bunched together mainly at the blunt end, are laid in June or July and are incubated by the female, helped to varying degrees by the male. The actual incubation time is unknown and the parents abandon their offspring before they are properly able to fly. The Curlew Sandpiper lives on littoral

and mud-dwelling invertebrates. It is about the size of a Starling and is recognisable by its long, downcurved beak and its white rump and, in its breeding plumage (2), by its rusty-red head and underside. In winter plumage (1), it has a brown-grey back, with darker markings, and white underparts. Its call is a clear 'chirrrip'.

199

Dunlin
Calidris alpina

The Dunlin inhabits a broad strip of coast in northern Europe, Asia and North America. It nests chiefly in the tundra, on the seashore and further inland. In the British Isles and the more southerly parts of its European range it frequents moorland and wet meadows, and in Scandinavia it lives in the alpine zone of mountains. Soon after its arrival at its nesting site, between the end of March and May, the male flutters above its chosen nest site with peculiar abrupt movements, or perches on an elevation and gives chirping calls or trills; from time to time it soars steeply upwards and then drops again. It presents the female with a few hollows and the female lines one of them with grass, moss or leaves. The nesting period lasts from the end of April until June. The clutch comprises 4 yellowish, brownish or greenish, brown-spotted eggs (2), which are incubated for 20—23 days by both the parent birds; they also both participate in the rearing of the young. The Dunlin has several times been observed to adopt other young; this applies both to birds with their own families and to birds with no offspring. The female often leaves its brood prematurely and sets off southwards, so that migration is prolonged from the end of July until October. Some birds from the

2

British Isles are residents, but most populations migrate to western Europe, the Mediterranean region and to Africa as far as the equator. On migration and in winter they form huge flocks, sometimes numbering tens of thousands of birds. Dunlins live mainly on insects, worms, small molluscs and crustaceans and occasionally on the seeds and other parts of plants. The Dunlin is the size of a Starling and has a gently downcurved beak which is distinctly longer than its head. In its breeding plumage (1) it has a rusty-brown, black-spotted back and a conspicuous large black patch on its underside; its winter plumage is greyish-brown. In the winter its call is a soft 'tree-ee'; its display call is a purring 'twirr-wirr-wirr' series.

200

Ruff, Reeve (female)
Philomachus pugnax

1

In the spring, Ruffs assemble in the middle of meadows and swamps for their collective courtship ceremonies, during which they engage in distinctive mock battles. The birds each have their own particular piece of ground, recognisable from the trampled vegetation; here they show off to the females, expanding their ruffs and their crests, spreading their wings and their tail, fluttering into the air, performing short circular flights, and lunging at each other with beak and legs. The females (the Reeves), which are usually very much in the minority, pace about among them and mate with one or more males, some of the latter being much more 'preferred' than others. Such courtship is not conducive to the formation of permanent pairs and so one male may be lucky enough to 'win' several females, while another may not win any. At the end of May or the beginning of June, in a suitable damp spot hidden by grass, the

3

female hollows out a depression for the nest with its own body, lines it with grass blades and leaves and then lays 4 yellowish, brownish or greenish, brown-spotted eggs (2), which it incu-

2

bates unaided for 21—23 days; it also cares for the brood entirely by itself. The Ruff inhabits mainly the tundra belt of Europe and Asia, but in Europe its range extends southwards to England, France, Holland, Belgium, Germany and southern Poland. The birds' autumn migration, which takes place from August to October, takes them mostly to the Mediterranean region and Africa, although some birds winter in the British Isles and on the North Sea coast. In its display plumage the male wears an expansible ruff and two prominent ear tufts. The colour of these ornaments is so variable (3) that no two males are alike, and the colour of their beak and legs also varies. The Reeve (1) and both sexes in their winter plumage have a grey-brown, pale-marked (scaly-looking) back and a whitish underside. The males are slightly larger than a Mistle Thrush, the females a little bigger than a Starling.

Jack Snipe
Lymnocryptes minimus

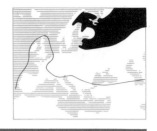

The Jack Snipe inhabits wooded tundra and taiga in Europe and Asia; in the west its range stretches to the north of Scandinavia and the Baltic region, with a small isolated population in southern Sweden. It is a migratory bird and in September or October it leaves for its winter quarters, which extend from the British Isles, across western Europe and the Mediterranean, to northern and tropical Africa; it has also been known to winter in central Europe. In its breeding area it frequents swamps and peat-bogs, to which it returns in March or April. It nests in June or July, in very damp spots — often on a slight elevation surrounded by water, or in stunted willows and birches. The nest is a shallow depression scantily lined with grass and leaves. The 4 olive-green, brown-spotted eggs are incubated for 24 days entirely by the female; apparently, no further details of the family life of this species are known. The birds live largely on worms, small terrestrial and aquatic molluscs and insects, together with small seeds and some algae. The Jack Snipe (1) resembles a small Snipe and is about the size of a Skylark. It has a brown stripe in the centre of its crown (in other snipes the stripe is buff) and a brown back with two longitudinal pale buff stripes. It is not easily flushed and prefers to lie flat on the ground; if compelled to rise, it flies slowly and usually silently in a straight line and soon drops down again. Its pointed tail, which lacks white edges, can be seen when it flies. Its display call, a rhythmic 'lok-toggi, lok-toggi', sounds like the distant clip-clop of a trotting horse.

Snipe, Common Snipe
Gallinago gallinago

The display of the Snipe (3), as it flies in wide circles and spirals above the nest, dives steeply and then rises again in a curve, is accompanied by a curious bleating sound made by the vibrating outermost feathers of the spread tail as the bird plummets down. In the spring it can be heard over wet meadows, swamps and bogs, particularly at sunset, when the females remain on the ground and watch the acrobatic display of the males. The nest is a depression in grass or a clump of sedge and is lined with dry material from the vicinity. The 4 greyish-green to yellowish-brown eggs, with dark brown spots (2), are laid between the end of March and the end of July and are incubated for 19—21 days by the female. As soon as they are dry, the newly hatched young disperse into the surrounding vegetation, where some of them are cared for by the male and the others by the female. At three weeks they are already able to fly, and at five weeks they resemble the adult. Snipe live mainly on worms and on insects, small molluscs and crustaceans. They occur in Europe and Asia (except the most southerly parts) and the north of North America. European populations winter over an area stretching from western Europe and across the Mediterranean to northern Africa. Their autumn migration takes place between August and October and they return to their nesting areas in March or April. The Snipe, which is the same size as a Blackbird, has a very long beak, but relatively short neck and legs. The members of both sexes (1) have a dark brown back with four buff stripes running down it. If suddenly flushed, the Snipe rises abruptly into the air and zigzags away, calling 'catch catch'. In the spring, its song is a repeated 'chic-ka-chic-ka', uttered mainly on the ground.

3

Woodcock
Scolopax rusticola

In the spring, shortly after sunset, male Woodcocks fly for about 20 minutes over their nesting area, following the margin of woods, clearings, paths and the courses of streams, skimming the tops of the trees and uttering a high-pitched 'tsiwick' and deep, throbbing 'orrrt-orrrt' calls ('roding' display). The females generally brown or russet spots (2), are laid at the end of April or in May. They are incubated by the female, which sits on them very assiduously for 20—24 days and also cares for the chicks for five to six weeks. If danger threatens, it flies with them to safety, endeavouring to press them to its body with its feet and beak. Some of the of Japan. It is the only true forest-dwelling European wader and it inhabits mainly deciduous and mixed woods. It is a resident in Britain and Ireland; elsewhere it is mainly a migrant, with winter quarters in western Europe and in the countries surrounding the Mediterranean. Spring migration takes place in March or April,

remain on the ground and may call softly to the males. This is followed by the less well-known phase of the courtship ceremony, in which the male performs a kind of dance around the female. One female may be courted by several males. Once they have mated, the male shows no further interest in the female. The nest is a shallow depression in grass, leaves or moss and the 4 brown eggs, marked with olive-females evidently nest a second time in June or July. The Woodcock inhabits most of Europe except the southern peninsulas, and a wide strip extending across the middle of Asia to the islands autumn migration in September or October. The Woodcock (1) has rusty-brown plumage marked with black bars and spots. It is the size of a Lapwing and has short legs and a long beak. In keeping with its nocturnal mode of life it has large eyes, which are situated high up on its head and allow it to see clearly even when its beak is plunged up to its base in soft soil as it probes for food.

2

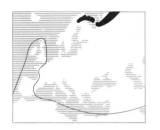

Bar-tailed Godwit
Limosa lapponica

The Bar-tailed Godwit (1) closely resembles the Black-tailed Godwit, but is smaller and has a shorter, distinctly upcurved beak. In its breeding plumage it is predominantly russet-coloured, but its back and wings are greyish-brown; in its winter plumage it is greyish-brown above, with darker markings, and has whitish underparts. In flight, it lacks the white bars on the wings, but has a white rump and dark brown barring on its tail. Its call, a raucous 'geck, eggeggeck' or 'heeheck', is heard at the nest site. The Bar-tailed Godwit in-habits the far north of Europe, Asia and Alaska; in Europe it breeds in the most northerly parts of Scandinavia and the former USSR. It nests in swampy tundra and in swamps in wooded tundra. The nest, a small depression in a clump of grass, is thinly lined with birch leaves and lichen. The olive-brown eggs, marked with dark brown spots, are laid at the end of May or in June; there are usually 4 and they are incubated for about 21 days by the male and female. The young leave the nest soon after they have hatched and are led by both the parents for about five weeks. Bar-tailed Godwits live mainly on aquatic insects and their larvae and on worms and crustaceans. At the end of July they begin to leave their nesting areas and make for their winter quarters, which include the coasts of western Europe and northwestern Africa, usually following the coastline. They take their time, however, and will remain at suitable stopover sites on the way for as long as a month. In April and May, on the return to their breeding areas in the north, they are in much more of a hurry.

Black-tailed Godwit
Limosa limosa

 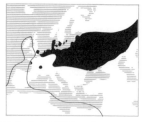

The Black-tailed Godwit breeds in scattered areas across the middle of Europe and Asia from Iceland, England and France to the southern part of western Siberia; a different subspecies breeds in eastern Asia. It is a migrant and winters in the Atlantic region of western Europe and in the Mediterranean region, but it also strays much further south, into tropical Africa. It nests mainly in wet meadows and pastures, sometimes in fields near ponds and even on dry moors. The birds arrive in March or April, often already in pairs, and their display begins soon afterwards. The male flies up steeply to a height of about 50 m and with spread tail and slow beats of its wings it circles around its nesting area, loudly calling 'greet you, greet you' in time with its wingbeats. When it lands, it holds its wings raised to show the white bars on them. Several pairs usually nest together. The nest is a small hollow lined with dry grass blades and leaves. The olive-brown eggs, which are marked with blurred dark spots, are laid between the beginning of April and the beginning of June; there are 4 to a clutch and they are incubated for 23—24 days by both the adult birds in turn. The parents also both look after the young and react very aggressively and noisily to any intruder. As soon as the young are fledged, like their parents they lose interest in their breeding meadow and all assemble on the mud of half-drained pools and ponds, where they probe for worms, molluscs and other invertebrates with their long beaks. They wander from pool to pool until, by September, the majority have migrated. The Black-tailed Godwit is about the same size as a pigeon, but it has long legs and a long, very slightly upcurved beak. In its breeding plumage (1), its neck and breast are rusty-red; in flight it shows a white bar running along its wings and a black band at the end of its white tail.

Whimbrel
Numenius phaeopus

The Whimbrel (1) breeds in the northern part of Europe, in Iceland, Scotland, Scandinavia and the Baltic republics of the former USSR, and in parts of northern Asia and North America. In the north it inhabits the tundra, further south peat-bogs and moors. The nest is a depression in dry grass or heather lined with a few grass blades and moss. The 4 olive-green to olive-brown eggs, marked with dark brown spots, are laid in the last half of May or in June and are incubated for about 24 days by both the parent birds in turn. As soon as the newly hatched young are dry, the parents lead them out of the nest and look after them very conscientiously for a further four weeks. The Whimbrel feeds mainly on insects, spiders, worms and molluscs, supplemented by berries. From the end of July until September, Whimbrels migrate southwards in small flocks; some birds winter in the southern part of the Iberian Peninsula, but the majority of west Eurasian birds fly to tropical Africa. Spring migration takes place in April or May. The Whimbrel is a smaller version of the Curlew and has the same downcurved beak, although its beak is shorter and more kinked at the tip. It has a more conspicuous superciliary stripe and dark brown and buffish-white stripes on its crown. In flight, it resembles the Curlew, but has darker wings; its call, 'titti-titti-titti-tit', uttered as it flies, is altogether different from the Curlew's.

207

Curlew
Numenius arquata

1

glide lower and lower, with their wings spread, and then rise again (3). As they rise, they utter deep, fluty tones, which grow faster as they descend and change into a bubbling trill. The nest is a straw-lined hollow in thick grass. The 4 brownish to greyish-green eggs, with dark brown spots (2), are laid at the end of March or in April or May and are incubated for 26—30 days, both the parents taking turns to sit on them. While the adult birds are sitting, they are very quiet, but after the young have hatched they are noisy and aggressive. At the end of July the families begin to leave their nesting sites. In the north, the females actually abandon their young at the age of ten days, migrate and leave the care of the young to the male. Curlews feed mainly on insects, plus spi-

The Curlew lives in the temperate belt of Europe and Asia, from Ireland, Britain and France in the west to Mongolia and China in the east. It is a migrant; some European birds spend the winter in western or southern Europe and some migrate to the heart of Africa. This species has a preference for large wet meadows and pastureland; it also occurs quite high up on peat-bogs and moors and in the east it inhabits dry steppes with water in the vicinity. Its flocks arrive in the breeding areas in March or April, the birds soon pair off and the striking courting displays begin. The males ascend to a height of 20—40 m, fluttering their wings,

2

ders, worms, crustaceans and molluscs and occasionally bilberries, cranberries and small seeds. The Curlew (1), which is the largest European wader, is the size of a slim Mallard. It has a strikingly long, downcurved beak and grey-brown, finely mottled plumage. The young at first have a straight beak, but at about three weeks it begins to curve downwards.

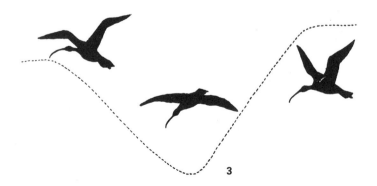

3

Spotted Redshank, Dusky Redshank

Tringa erythropus

3

The Spotted Redshank is an Arctic species nesting in swamps in tundra and wooded tundra in the most northerly parts of Europe and Asia, from the north of Scandinavia and the Kola Peninsula, across the north of the former USSR to Kamchatka. The nest, which is situated in wet, open spots, is a depression in grass, moss or lichen, thinly lined with grass, leaves or conifer needles. In northern Europe, the 4 olive-green eggs, marked with dark brown spots (3), are laid in May or June. They are incubated by both the partners, but for longer periods by the male; the exact incubation period is not recorded. Both the parents probably care for the newly hatched young, but the female soon leaves them. Spotted Redshanks feed mainly on insects, worms, crustaceans and molluscs. When the nesting season is over, the birds form flocks and between August and October they leave for their winter quarters. Some western breeders go no further than the coast of western Europe, but many fly to the Mediterranean region and probably the majority to equatorial Africa. During their migration, small flocks of Spotted Redshanks can also be encountered in various

marshy habitats, such as flood-lands, sewage-farms and lake-sides, in central Europe. They return to their nesting areas in April or May, but non-breeding birds can sometimes be seen in central Europe in June and July. The Spotted Redshank is about the size of a Turtle Dove; it has deep red legs and its thin, straight beak is red at the base. Its breeding plumage (1) is completely black, with fine white spots on the upperparts. Its winter plumage (2) is slate-grey with paler feather edges on the back; the breast and belly are white. In flight, it can be seen to have a white rump, but no white wing-bar; its legs extend noticeably beyond the end of its tail. Its call is a penetrating 'tchuitt'.

Redshank
Tringa totanus

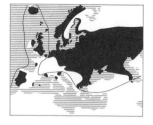

The Redshank nests in most of Europe and across the entire temperate belt in Asia. Only some British populations migrate in the autumn, but all other

2

lakes. Redshanks begin to migrate in July, and by August and September they have almost all disappeared. They feed mainly on insects, molluscs, crustaceans

1

European birds are strictly migrants. Many of them winter in western Europe, but the majority fly to the Mediterranean region or to the equatorial part of Africa. In March or April, as soon as they return, the males' melodious, yodelling 'tewlew-tewlew-tewlew' can be heard as they circle over their nesting sites in wet meadows or on marshy ground beside ponds, now gliding, now fluttering with their wings curved downwards. On the ground, the male dances around the female, trailing its wings or holding them half-raised. The nest, a small depression in grass or a sedge bed, is sparsely lined with dry blades and leaves from the vicinity. The 4 brownish eggs, strewn with blackish-brown spots (2), are incubated by the female during the daytime and by the male at night. The young hatch after 22–25 days; at five to six weeks they are independent and begin to roam the muddy banks of ponds and and spiders and occasionally peck at the green parts of plants. The Redshank (1) is about the size of a Turtle Dove; it has ashy-brown, dark-spotted plumage, orange-red legs and a straight beak with a red base. It is the only wader with a strikingly wide white margin on the rear edge of its wings (which can be seen most clearly when it flies). Its normal call is a fluty trisyllabic 'tlu-hu-hu'; its warning call is a repeated 'tewk-tewk-tewk'.

Marsh Sandpiper
Tringa stagnatilis

The Marsh Sandpiper (1) looks rather like the Greenshank, but is smaller (about the size of a thrush) and has long, dingy yellowish-grey legs, which ex- — 'tew-tew' or 'tee-eh tee-eh' — is less fluty than that of the Greenshank. In Europe, the Marsh Sandpiper inhabits the steppes between the Black Sea and the straw. The 4 pear-shaped eggs, marked with irregular dark brown to blackish-brown spots on a yellow or red-tinged ground, are laid in May or June. The

tend a long way beyond its tail in flight. Its upperparts are grey-brown, with blackish-brown speckles, its forehead is white and so is the greater part of its back, rump and tail. Its underside is likewise white, with brownish-black spots on its breast and neck (in breeding plumage). Its straight, very thin, blackish beak is longer than its head. Its call Aral Sea and it used also to nest in Hungary and former Yugoslavia. It is strictly a migrant, European birds migrating between July and September to the southern half of Africa; they return to their east European steppes, with lakes and areas of sunken, marshy ground, in April or May. The nest is in grass not far from water; it is only a small hollow lined with a little parents take turns to sit and they also both look after the young; the length of the incubation period and of the care of the young are not known. The Marsh Sandpiper feeds mainly on aquatic insects and their larvae and on molluscs; it gathers its food in the upper layer of shallow water and from aquatic plants, and seldom in the mud.

211

Greenshank
Tringa nebularia

The Greenshank (1) is one of the larger members of this genus and is about the same size as a Lapwing. In its breeding plumage, it has a blackish-brown crown, the sides of its head and its neck are light grey and finely speckled, its wings are dark greyish-brown, with black and white spots, and its underside is white; in flight, its back, rump and the base of its tail can be seen to be white. In its winter plumage, its head and its breast are whiter, the top of its head is streaked with dark brown and its wings are greyish-brown. When excited, it utters a piercing 'kyick-yick'. The Greenshank's breeding range stretches from Scotland, across Scandinavia and the rest of northern Europe and Asia, to Kamchatka. It is a migratory bird.

From August to October western populations migrate to winter quarters in Europe and the Mediterranean region, but more often to tropical and southern Africa; birds from eastern Asia migrate as far as New Guinea and Australia. The return journey

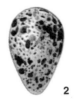

2

northwards takes place in April or May. During its migration, the Greenshank regularly appears near inland water in Europe. It nests in swampy and drier parts of the tundra and in wooded tundra. The nest is a hollow in the ground, hidden by grass and lined with a little plant material from the vicinity. The 4 yellowish-brown, brown-speckled eggs (2) are laid in May or June and are incubated for 24—25 days by both the adult birds. Within 24 hours after hatching the parents lead them out of the nest and look after them for about four weeks. The birds' diet consists mostly of insects, crustaceans, worms and molluscs; the Greenshank is also one of the few sandpipers which regularly catch small fish.

Green Sandpiper
Tringa ochropus

The Green Sandpiper has quite different nesting habits from the other members of the genus. It seldom nests on the ground and usually takes over old thrush, pigeon, jay, crow and even squirrel nests, often as much as 10 m above the ground. The nest is almost always in a wood, near marshy ground or a swamp, beside a stream or a ditch or on a bog. Nesting is preceded by a courtship display in which the male circles around the nesting site, rising obliquely above the tops of the trees with fluttering wings and then dropping with its wings held stiffly curved, constantly uttering whistled fluty notes. The birds generally return to their nesting areas between the end of March and May and the 4 brownish to greenish, finely speckled eggs (2) are laid between April and June; they are incubated for 20—22 days, both the parents taking turns to sit. A few hours after they have hatched, the young jump from the nest to the ground, where at first both the parents look after them; quite soon, however, the female leaves the care of the young entirely to the male. When the young are able to fly, they leave the forest and appear in open country on muddy ground beside ponds, where they hunt chiefly for insects, molluscs, crustaceans and spiders. Autumn migration begins as early as mid June and continues until October. The birds spend the winter in the Mediterranean region and in tropical Africa; small numbers also winter in the British Isles and in central Europe. The breeding range stretches from north-central and north-eastern Europe across the whole of Siberia to as far as the Sea of Okhotsk. This sandpiper is the size of a thrush. In its breeding plumage (1) it has a blackish-brown, white-spotted back, which contrasts strongly with its white, brown-spotted breast and belly, its white rump and the white base of its tail. In flight, its wings appear to be almost black, both above and below. Its legs and the base of its beak are green. Its winter plumage is duller and the markings are less vivid. If flushed, it gives a fluty, ringing 'tlōōi-weet-weet' while in flight.

2

Wood Sandpiper
Tringa glareola

The Wood Sandpiper occurs over a wide strip of territory in northern Europe and Asia, from Scotland, Germany, Denmark and Poland in the west, across Scandinavia and the former USSR to the Sea of Okhotsk. When nesting, it frequents swamps, bogs and wet meadows. It arrives in pairs in April or May and courtship begins immediately. The male circles around the chosen site, now fluttering up again, to the accompaniment of a loud 'tleea-tleea-tleea' display call. The nest, a sparsely lined hollow in the ground, is well hidden by grass. The 4 olive-green eggs, marked with violet-grey and blackish-brown spots (2), are usually laid in May and are incubated for 21—24 days by both the parent birds in turn. As soon as the newly hatched young are dry, the parents lead them from the nest and care for them very conscientiously; they behave very aggressively and attack any intruder who ventures into their area. After about ten days, however, the young are accompanied by only one bird — evidently the male. From the end of July the birds gradually disappear from their nesting sites and by September they

2

have all left for their distant winter quarters in Africa south of the Sahara; eastern Asian birds migrate to southern Asia and Australia. Their diet consists mainly of insects, together with spiders and small molluscs. The Wood Sandpiper (1) is a slim bird the size of a thrush. It has a brown, white-spotted back, its belly and rump are white and it has yellowish-grey legs, while above its eyes runs a pronounced white superciliary stripe. In flight, the underside of its wings is pale, with darker spots, and the whole upper surface of its tail is barred. Its winter plumage is less vividly marked. Its call in flight is a repeated clear 'chiff-iff-iff'.

Common Sandpiper

Actitis hypoleucos

The Common Sandpiper inhabits the whole of Europe and the temperate belt of Asia. It prefers gravelly and sandy stream and river banks with alluvial deposits and islands overgrown with grass, shrubs and trees. Following the water, it ascends to very high altitudes – in the mountains of central Asia to almost 4,000 m. It breeds less often beside still water and it usually avoids swampy and muddy ground. The birds arrive in April or May, already in pairs, occupy a strip of stream and defend it tenaciously against other members of the species. The male courts the female in bat-like flight, generally close to the water or level with the top of the trees, continuously uttering typical clear trills, sometimes for as long as a quarter of an hour. It makes several hollows in sand or gravel hidden by grass, under overhanging riparian plants or under a bush. The female chooses one of them, lines it with a few blades of grass and leaves and lays 4 yellowish-brown eggs marked with dark brown spots (2). The parents take turns to sit on the eggs, which are incubated for 21–22 days. While the young are being reared, the male noisily attacks every intruder, while the female leads the young away to the densest tangle of plants in the vicinity. After about 30 days the birds begin to wander about and from July to October they set out for the Mediterranean region or, in larger numbers, for equatorial and southern Africa; a few winter in western Europe. Common Sandpipers live chiefly on insects, small molluscs and crustaceans, worms and spiders. The male and female (1) are both the size of a Starling; they have dark olive-brown upperparts, with a white wingbar, white underparts, and dark patches at the sides of the breast. The Common Sandpiper flies very low over the water, alternating shallow strokes of its wings (made only from the horizontal plane downwards) with short intervals of gliding, when its wings are held curved downwards; at the same time it utters high-pitched 'twee di-dee' calls.

2

Turnstone, Ruddy Turnstone
Arenaria interpres

distances to spend the winter in northwest Europe, Africa, south Asia, Australasia and South America. On migration it makes rare appearances inland in Europe. The birds return to their nesting sites — which are always the same ones each year — between April and June. The nest, which is a small depression between or under stones and is only thinly lined with dry grass, is usually not made until after the first egg has been laid. The 4 greyish-green to brownish eggs, marked with blurred brown spots (3), are generally laid in the middle of June and are incubated for 22—24 days by both the sexes. In time, however, the female may forget its family duties and often leaves the care of the brood entirely to the male. Turnstones sometimes set out on their journey southwards at the end of July, but usually not until August or September. In their spring plumage they have rusty-brown, black and white upperparts and a white underside, with striking black markings on their mainly white head and a broad black breast band (1). In the autumn the birds lose their handsome rusty coloration and their upperparts, including the head, turn a grey-brown and black colour. Their call is a sharp 'tick-a-tick' or 'kik-kikkikkikkik'.

If we come across a bird about the size of a thrush on the seashore, engaged in the curious activity of turning over small pebbles, it can only be a Turnstone (2). It turns over one stone after another, scooping each one up with its beak and rolling it to one side or turning it right over. The stones are often much heavier than the bird itself. In the same way it overturns shells and rakes its way through layers of sea-weed, looking for small molluscs, crustaceans, worms, spiders and insects. In some places it is a common inhabitant of sandy and pebbly shores and rocky islands, and it also breeds in stony tundra country, where only moss and lichen grow. It nests from the coasts of Denmark and southern Scandinavia to the coastal tundra of Europe, Asia and North America; from there it migrates long

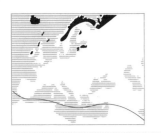

Red-necked Phalarope, Northern Phalarope

Phalaropus lobatus

In the family life of phalaropes, the normal roles of the sexes are reversed. The female is larger and more handsomely coloured than the male and it has a better-developed voice; it also plays the decisive role in mating and in the defence of the nest. It begins its display by raising its body erect, out of the water, to the accompaniment of quick, whirring strokes of its wings; it then rises for its display flight just above the surface of the water, comes down again after a few seconds and utters soft 'veddi veddi' calls. The female also chooses the place for the nest, which is a depression in a clump of grass or other plants not too far away from water and is lined by both the partners with grass, fragments of leaves or lichen. The 4 yellowish-brown or olive-brown eggs with blackish-brown spots (4) are laid at the end of May or in June. Here the female's duties end, and from now on the male takes over the whole care of the brood. It incubates the eggs for 17—21 days and then looks after and rears the young. The Red-necked Phalarope lives chiefly in the Arctic belt of Europe, Asia and North America, where it is a typical inhabitant of tundra with lakes and swamps. It is entirely a migrant and spends the winter on the coasts of Arabia, southern Asia and west-

ern South America. Autumn migration takes place from July until November and the birds return to their nesting sites in April or May. The Red-necked Phalarope lives mainly on insects and their larvae, which it catches on the surface of the water. It has a slender black beak (6), whereas the very similar Grey Phalarope *P. fulicarius* has a much thicker, broader beak (5). Both species are smaller than a thrush. In the spring, the female Red-necked Phalarope (3) has a white belly and throat, the latter bordered by

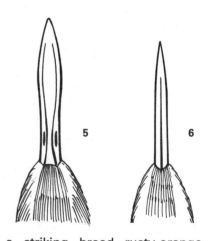

a striking broad rusty-orange band. The male (2) has much duller colouring and its neck band is more greyish-brown. In the winter, both sexes have a grey, dark-spotted back, a white underside and a black stripe behind the eye (1). Their call is a penetrating 'pit pit'.

217

Long-winged acrobats

Skuas, Gulls and Terns

CHARADRIIFORMES: LARI

Skuas, gulls and terns are a homogeneous group of moderately large birds, all very similar in appearance, with long, tapering wings whose length is determined chiefly by the long 'hand'. The primaries are so long that they alone form about half the length of the whole wing. These birds are outstanding fliers, can ride out storms without any visible effort and are masters in the art of soaring and gliding. They are also very nimble on the ground, however, and actually spend more time there than on the water, where they are less adroit and sure of themselves than ducks, for instance; they swim with their tail held erect and only a little of their body submerged (Fig. 1). Being aquatic birds, their feet are adapted for swimming; the second, third and fourth toes are joined together by webbing and the first toe is rudimentary or absent (Fig. 2). They have a moderately long beak whose upper mandible, in gulls and skuas, has a hook-like tip overlapping the lower mandible (Fig. 3); terns generally have a straight, pointed beak (Fig. 4). The smallest species are the size of a Swift (the Little Tern weighs about 50 g and has a wingspan of 48 cm), the largest the size of a goose (the Great Black-backed Gull weighs about 1.8 kg and has a wingspan of nearly 170 cm).

Since their life is associated with water, members of this sub-order have dense, close-fitting

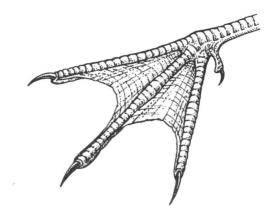

Fig. 2. *Foot of a Black Tern, with webbing and a puny hind toe.*

plumage and a well-developed preen gland. With the exception of skuas, they have mostly light-coloured plumage and there are no colour differences between the male and the female. The upper surface of the wings and the back are the same colour. The birds moult twice a year; after a complete moult in the autumn they appear in their plainer winter plumage and after a partial moult in winter they don their breeding plumage, in which in many species the whole or the top of their head is dark.

Gulls and terns frequent various types of water — fresh and salt, still and flowing. They are gregarious birds and nest together in large, bustling, noisy colonies, which are sometimes

Fig. 1. *Silhouette of a gull on the water; the small draught, with the tail held high above the surface, is characteristic.*

Fig. 3. *Powerful beak of a skua, with a hook-tipped upper mandible.*

Fig. 4. *The pointed beak of a tern.*

composed of birds of one species and sometimes of several species. The nests, which are generally on the ground, are often bare, unlined hollows; they are usually placed close together, side by side, but every pair nevertheless has its own tiny territory, which frequently stretches no further

A Great Black-backed Gull (Larus marinus) *skimming the billowing waves with masterly skill.*

than the sitting bird can peck. Nesting is mostly preceded by a lively display (Fig. 5) accompanied by striking postures and vocal manifestations and sometimes by aerial acrobatics. The clutch usually consists of two or three spotted eggs. The young are nidifugous, are covered with dense, mottled down and are able to run about soon after they hatch, but the parents generally feed them, beak to beak, for a long time. They often give them fish, but many species are omnivorous.

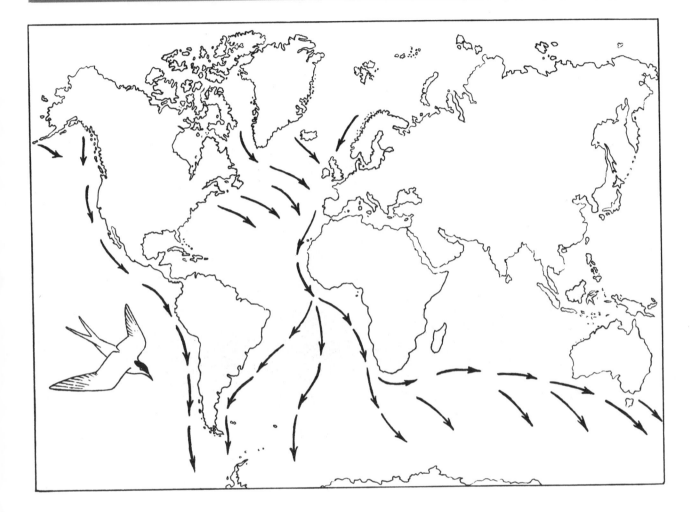

Skuas have evolved piratical habits; they violently attack other birds, forcing them to regurgitate or relinquish their prey, and then skilfully catch and swallow it in the air. After the breeding period, the birds all leave their nests and generally roam the seashore or visit inland waters. Many of them migrate extremely long distances; the best-known species in this respect is the Arctic Tern, which migrates from its nesting areas in the Arctic to the Antarctic − a distance of about 20,000 km − and actually lives almost constantly, the whole year round, in daylight (Fig. 6). Young skuas, gulls and terns generally take quite a long time to reach sexual maturity − small species two and larger species four or five years; consequently, their adult plumage also develops slowly and changes colour gradually.

Fig. 6. *The Arctic Tern covers longer distances than any other bird during its migration.*

Fig. 5. *Presentation of a nuptial gift (a fish) between terns.*

Arctic Skua, Parasitic Jaeger

Stercorarius parasiticus

The Arctic Skua nests in Iceland, in the north of Britain, on the Atlantic and Baltic coasts of Scandinavia, on the northern coast of the former USSR, and in northern Asia and North America.

Arctic Terns. During its characteristic display, it uses its flying skills to good effect, rising and falling abruptly and performing somersaults in the air. The nest is a depression in moss or grass

about 32 days. After nesting, the skuas collect in flocks and in August and September they fly southwards. The Arctic Skua seizes prey from gulls, terns, auks, petrels and shearwaters,

It is a migrant and winters on the shores or the open water of the Atlantic and the Pacific, sometimes as far afield as the southernmost points of South Africa and South America. In Europe it is the commonest skua and is seen fairly regularly inland while migrating. It nests by swamps and near overgrown freshwater lakes in the tundra, or on coastal moorland. It arrives at its breeding sites in April or May and settles in loose colonies in places with plenty of dense grass; sometimes it lives in colonies of

and the 2 greenish to olive-brown eggs, marked with dark brown spots (2), are laid at the end of May or the beginning of June. They are incubated for 24–28 days by both the parent birds, which likewise both look after the young until they are fledged, at

steals eggs and young from colonies of seabirds and catches small rodents. It occurs in two colour phases. The light phase has white underparts, often with a dark breast band, and yellowish-buff cheeks and collar; a blackish-brown cap can be seen on the dark phase (1). The central tail feathers, which are narrow and pointed, do not project more than 6.5–10.5 cm beyond the end of the tail. The bird itself is a little larger than a Black-headed Gull; its calls are a clear 'ya-wow' and a deeper 'gack-gack'.

2

Long-tailed Skua, Long-tailed Jaeger
Stercorarius longicaudus

The Long-tailed Skua is easy to tell from all other skuas because of its strikingly long, narrow central tail feathers, which project a full 20 cm beyond the end of its tail. About the size of a Black-headed Gull, it is the smallest European skua. It has a black cap, a broad white collar and a white underside, yellow cheeks and brownish-grey upperparts (1). The dark phase of this skua is very rare. Whatever plumage it is wearing, usually little or no white can be seen on its wings in flight. Its call, a sharp 'kri-kri-kri', is heard comparatively rarely. The Long-tailed Skua is an Arctic bird

inhabiting, in Europe, Scandinavia and the northern part of the former USSR; it also lives in the tundra belt in Asia and North America. North European populations winter mostly on the open sea in the southern Atlantic, but are seen on migration in the Baltic and the North Sea. The birds generally arrive at their nesting sites high up in the tundra, on rocky plateaux and on coasts in May, and in June and July they breed and rear the young. They nest singly. The nest is a mere depression in moss or

lichen or among stones and the 2 olive-brown eggs, marked with dark brown spots, are incubated for about 23 days by both the parent birds in turn. While sitting, and later, while rearing the young, the parents can be very aggressive. The young leave the nest a day or two after they hatch and in three weeks they are fully fledged, although the parents bring them food for about 30 days. They live mainly on rodents, the young and eggs of other birds, fish, insects, molluscs and worms. This species is less of a parasite than other skuas.

223

Great Skua, Skua
Stercorarius skua

able to drive falcons away from the colony and make violent attacks on human beings. When the young are full-grown, they venture out over the open sea, where they roam about with the adult birds from August to April. This skua also pirates food from Gannets, gulls, terns and auks and it terrorises bird colonies, where it robs the nests of eggs and young. It eats anything else it is able to catch and will also take carrion. The Great Skua (1) is the size of a Raven. It has a dark brown back and lighter, slightly russet-tinted underparts. At the base of its primaries it has white patches, which form a striking white flash in flight; its central tail feathers are barely longer than the others (3). When attacking, it utters a throaty 'kack kack'; other calls include a raucous 'skerrr' and a barking 'ock-ock-ock'.

The Great Skua has a most remarkable distribution. It lives on the shores of the northern Atlantic and the adjoining Arctic seas and then, on the opposite side of the globe, from the Antarctic to the southern shores of South America and New Zealand. When not breeding, it roams the greater part of the Atlantic Ocean. European populations winter mainly in the eastern part of the Atlantic, in the south as far as Nigeria.

Very occasionally the birds are driven inland by gales. The Great Skua lives singly or in small colonies, as a rule right beside the sea, preferably on a coastal upland plateau or on a rocky island covered with low vegetation. The nest is on the ground, between clumps of grass or in moss. The 2 yellowish-brown to greenish-brown, brown-speckled eggs (2) are laid in May or June and are incubated for 28—30 days by both the parents, which also both care for the young, bring them food for six to seven weeks and defend them against virtually every danger. Being skilled and powerful fliers, they are even

2

3

Great Black-headed Gull
Larus ichthyaetus

1

The Great Black-headed Gull, which grows to the same size as the Great Black-backed Gull, is one of the largest members of the gull family. It has a characteristically shaped head with a very long forehead. Its breeding plumage (1) is white, with a grey mantle, and it has a black head with two white crescents around each eye and black-tipped wings. Its most typical feature is its yellow, black-ringed beak with a reddish or orange-red tip; its legs are greenish-yellow. When it moults and dons its winter plumage (2), white patches appear among the feathers on its head. Its call is a rough, croaking 'kyow-kyow'. Its breeding range is mainly in the southeast corner of Europe, in the Black Sea region, but extends to central Asia. It is a migrant and winters in southwest Asia and the eastern Mediterranean. Its autumn migration takes place in October and November and it returns to its nesting sites in February and March. It frequents salt water and is therefore to be found on the seashore and on islands, but it also nests beside large lakes in steppe and semi-desert country and it even occurs on plateaux in the mountains of central Asia at altitudes of over 4,000 m. It generally forms nesting colonies, sometimes comprising several thousand birds, but sometimes it nests singly. The eggs are laid in April or May; there are usually 2–3 and they are greenish-grey with grey and brown spots. The nest hollow, which is in the ground, is sometimes unlined, but as a rule it is lined with a layer of stems of halophilous plants or with reed blades. The partners take turns to sit on the eggs, which are incubated for 23–29 days; the young are able to fly at 45 days. The young are fed chiefly on fish, but also on the eggs and young of other birds, small mammals, lizards and insects.

2

Mediterranean Gull
Larus melanocephalus

The breeding range of the Mediterranean Gull is very small. It lies mainly in the region of the Black Sea and the Aegean, but a few birds nest in inland Europe and on the shores of the Mediterranean and the Baltic. This gull is a partial migrant; it winters mainly in the Mediterranean region, but commonly strays to the coasts of western Europe. It nests on the coast and beside ponds and lakes. In its main nesting areas it forms large colonies; elsewhere isolated pairs nest in the colonies of other gulls or terns. The nest is made of aquatic plants from the vicinity and the 2−3 yellowish-brown eggs with dark brown spots are laid in May or June. They are incubated for about 24 days, both the parent birds taking turns to sit. The young remain in the nest or its immediate vicinity for at least a week, and the parents look after them until they are about 25 days old and able to fly. Some birds may nest at the age of one year, but the majority not until they are two or three. They live entirely on animal food − small fish, molluscs and insects.

In its breeding plumage, the Mediterranean Gull (1) resembles the Black-headed Gull and is often found in its company. It is slightly larger, however, has no black on its wings, its black cap reaches half-way down its neck and it has a white crescent above and below each eye; its beak and legs are dark red. In the winter its head and neck are white, with a blackish-brown area behind the eyes and at the back of the head. The juveniles are whitish-brown, with dark-tipped wings, but traces of black still remain in their first-year plumage, on the first to the fifth primaries. The call of this species is a 'kow' or 'keeow'.

Little Gull
Larus minutus

The Little Gull (1) nests over a broken area stretching from the shores of the Baltic to eastern Siberia and is a casual visitor in large; they are formed of not more than 50—80 pairs and sometimes occur together with Black-headed Gull and Common Tern colonies. Both sexes build the nest, which is made of swamp plants collected in the vicinity. The usually 3 brownish

to olive-green, dark-spotted eggs (3), which are laid as a rule at the beginning of June, are incubated for 20—23 days by the female, aided by the male. The young begin to fly at the age of 21—24 days and are sexually mature at three years. The Little Gull lives chiefly on insects, which it catches adroitly in the manner of terns of the genus *Chlidonias* above the water (i. e. not in meadows or fields), or collects from the surface. It also eats worms, small molluscs and crustaceans and occasionally small fish caught in shallows along the shore. The Little Gull, which is the smallest gull, is the size of a Turtle Dove. In its breeding plumage (2) it wears a black hood extending well down the back of its head. The rear edge of its wings has a white border, which is particularly conspicuous on the grey-black under-surface. In its winter plumage (1) it has a largely white head, with a blackish-grey nape and a black spot behind each eye. Its call is a loud 'kek-kek kek'.

North America. It is a partial migrant; some north European birds winter beside the Baltic and the North Sea and others on the coast of western Europe, but the majority fly to the Mediterranean region. During their spring migration in April and their autumn migration in August and September, they are commonly to be seen on inland waters. Little Gulls nest beside ponds and lakes with plenty of vegetation and in swamps, river mouths and bays. The colonies are not very

Black-headed Gull
Larus ridibundus

Hardly has the ice melted on the breeding ponds, when the first Black-headed Gulls make their appearance, often as early as March. In addition to ponds and lakes, they settle in marshes, backwaters and river deltas throughout practically the whole temperate belt of Europe and Asia. In April they are already present in noisy colonies sometimes numbering thousands of pairs. Their intricate courtship is

green with dark brown spots (6, 7). They are incubated for 22—24 days by both the parent birds, which also both care for the young (8, 9) until they are fledged at 26—28 days. Black-headed

wintering on ice-free rivers in central European cities. Birds nesting in southern and western Europe are resident and nomadic. The breeding plumage (1, 2) is characterised by a light grey mantle and a chocolate-brown head; in the winter plumage, the head is white, with only a black spot in the region of the ear (3). The wings are black-tipped, but a white border can always be seen on the front edge of the outer wing. Juvenile birds are white and brown (4, 5). Adults measure 35—38 cm. Their penetrating voice includes 'kwarr', 'krree-ah' or 'kek-kek' calls.

accompanied by characteristic ritual postures and sham attacks. The nest, which is either a shallow, lined scrape or, in wet sites, is made of reeds, bulrushes, sedge and other swamp plants, is built by the combined efforts of both partners. Older birds build inside the colony; younger latecomers are left on the fringe. Nesting starts from early April. In most cases the female lays 3 eggs, which are usually olive-

Gulls live on various invertebrates, together with fish and small mammals, and supplement this diet with fruit and grain.

The colonies begin to break up in July. This applies mainly to northern and eastern populations, which winter in the Atlantic zone of western Europe and the Mediterranean region, but in recent years there has been an increase in the number of birds

228

Slender-billed Gull
Larus genei

In Europe, the Slender-billed Gull inhabits the shores of the Mediterranean and the Black and Caspian Seas; otherwise it lives in the Middle East and Asia Minor and in other, scattered parts of southwest Asia. It is partly a resident bird and partly migratory and nomadic; sometimes it winters in the southern part of its breeding area, but it also migrates to the Mediterranean and to northwestern Africa. Migra-

inland lakes, where they form colonies, often together with terns. Their breeding season, which is quite late, usually falls in June and July. The nest is a small depression in the ground, roughly lined with the remains of halophilous plants, reed blades and rootlets. The 2–3 eggs are yellowish-white or bluish and are marked with black and grey spots; they are incubated for 22–28 days. The young are able

August or September. The Slender-billed Gull lives on small fish and various invertebrates, quite often insects. In flight, it has the same dorsal markings as the Black-headed Gull, i. e. a grey mantle and white-tipped wings with a black outer rear border. In its breeding plumage (1), however, it has a completely white head and it also has a distinctly longer and stronger dark red beak. Its underside has a pinkish

tory and nomadic birds arrive at their nesting sites in March or April. They settle on the coast, in river deltas, on islands in lagoons, in swamps and beside

to fly at the age of 30–35 days, but are fed for a further two weeks afterwards. Migrants and nomadic birds leave the colony in

tinge. Young birds have a white and brown back and a black band at the end of their tail. The adult birds are larger than Black-headed Gulls.

Audouin's Gull

Larus audouinii

Audouin's Gull is the rarest gull in the western Palaearctic. It is found only on certain Mediterranean islands and along the Mediterranean coast of southern Europe and northern Africa. It nests on sunny slopes on sandy or rocky islands not too thickly overgrown with vegetation. The nest is generally built in low vegetation or in a depression between stones; it is a relatively seek shade or shelter in the vicinity; they are fledged at five to six weeks. Audouin's Gull is a specialist at catching fish, but it also eats other marine and land animals. The adult bird (1) is the

There are only some 3,000–3,500 pairs, two thirds of which live on the northeast Moroccan Khafarinas Islands, where in 1981 the local colony numbered 2,200 pairs. It is a resident, nomadic and migratory bird, which spends the winter mainly in the north African part of the Mediterranean and on the Atlantic coast of Africa as far as Senegal. It stout structure made of grass blades and dry seaweed and it usually also contains feathers. The pairs begin to nest in April or May. The clutch generally consists of 3 olive-tinged, light brown eggs densely speckled with brown or blackish-brown spots; they are incubated for 26–33 days. The young leave the nest the day after they hatch and size of a Herring Gull; it is white, with a pearly-grey mantle and black-tipped wings, the wingtips having only a very small amount of white. It has a strong, bright red beak with a black ring and a yellow tip, but from a distance the beak appears dark. The orbital ring is red and the legs are dark olive-green. The call is a loud 'ge-ähk'.

Common Gull, Mew Gull

Larus canus

The Common Gull nests in the northern part of Europe and Asia and North America. In Europe, its numbers are increasing; first of all it spread westwards, and it is now also spreading southwards, are then continued by the separate pairs. The nest, which is built mainly by the female and is placed on the ground, is made of grass, heather and aquatic plants. The 3 olive-brown to greenish kinds of berries. Some of the western population winter in the North Sea and Mediterranean regions, but the majority on the coasts of western Europe. Only about 2% migrate across inland

so that its breeding range stretches deep into Poland, Germany and France and even into Switzerland, Austria and former Czechoslovakia. It thus does not nest only on the coast, but also on inland lakes in mountains and valleys, beside large rivers, in swamps and on moors. It usually forms colonies, but sometimes nests singly. The birds return to their nesting sites in March or April, already paired. At first they assemble on elevated ground for joint courtship ceremonies, which eggs, marked with dark olive-coloured spots (2), which are laid in May or June, are incubated for 22–25 days by both the parent birds. The parents also both look after the young for about five weeks. The Common Gull lives on various marine invertebrates, dead fish, refuse and various Europe; some of these remain there during the winter. Autumn migration takes place from July to November. In the spring the Common Gull (1) has a grey mantle and has a white patch on the otherwise black wingtips; its beak and legs are greenish-yellow; in the winter there are greyish-brown streaks on the top and back of its head. It is somewhat larger than the Black-headed Gull. Its call is a penetrating 'keeow' and 'gek-gek-gek'.

2

231

Lesser Black-backed Gull
Larus fuscus

The Lesser Black-backed Gull is distributed over a much smaller area than many other gulls, which stretches from Iceland, the British Isles and the French and Spanish shores of the Atlantic to

2

a few days, are tended for four to five weeks by both parents; they are not sexually mature until their third or fourth year. Autumn migration takes place from August to October. The Lesser

the Baltic republics of the former USSR. A few British birds remain in their nesting area during the winter; the rest migrate along the coast of western Europe or across continental Europe to the Mediterranean region or to Africa and return to their nesting sites in April. They nest in colonies on the coast, on islands, in river deltas, and inland beside fresh water not too far from the sea. The nest, which is made of grass, moss, lichen, seaweed and other plant material, is on the ground, generally on a grassy island,

bank or dune and far less often on a rocky cliff. There are usually 3 eggs, which are laid in May or June and are very variably coloured – yellowish, brownish, greenish or greyish, with dark brown spots (2). They are incubated for 26–28 days, both parents taking turns to sit. The young, which leave the nest after

Black-backed Gull is about the size of a Mallard. It lives mainly on various marine animals and their remains, steals eggs and kills small mammals and the young of other birds. In the spring it has a grey to black mantle and wings and a yellow beak and legs, the beak with a red spot near the tip (1); the only difference in the winter is the dark grey-brown streaks on its head and neck (in western populations). Its call is a mewing 'kyow' and a deeper 'gek-gek-gek'.

Herring Gull
Larus argentatus

The Herring Gull is the commonest gull. It inhabits practically the whole of the northern hemisphere and lives on coasts and beside inland seas and lakes. Some populations are resident (e.g. in western Europe), others are nomadic (south European birds), while those from northern Europe migrate far to the south. They all usually nest in colonies, some of which are composed of thousands of pairs. The Herring Gull is not fussy in its choice of a nesting site and the nest may be, in sea-grass on the shore, on a sand dune, on cliffs and rocky

islands or among reeds; it also nests on buildings, even those inland, on such places as the roofs of houses, churches, factories and bridges. The sites are occupied in March or April and nesting is preceded by a very lively courtship ceremony. The nest is a pile of plant material put together by both the partners. The 3 brownish, greenish or greyish eggs, marked with dark brown spots (3), are generally laid from the end of April and are incubated for 26—28 days by both the parent birds in turn. The young are able to fly at six weeks.

They take a long time to reach maturity and do not themselves nest until they are three to five or more years old. From July onwards the birds roam about. They feed on marine animals and various kinds of refuse, and rob other gulls, terns and ducks of their eggs and young; some are

3

so voracious that they even devour their neighbours' young. The Herring Gull is about the size of a Mallard; it has a silvery-grey to dark grey mantle and wings, the latter with black tips and with white spots in the black (1); its legs are flesh-pink or — in the Mediterranean and southeast Europe — yellow, and it has a yellow beak with a red spot near the tip. In its winter plumage, greyish-brown streaks appear on its head and neck. Its call is the same as that of the preceding species, but is much louder. The juveniles (2) are mottled brown.

Great Black-backed Gull
Larus marinus

The Great Black-backed Gull nests on Atlantic coasts and islands, from Iceland, the British Isles and France, via Scandinavia to the Kola Peninsula, and on the east coast of North America. Some birds are resident and remain on the shores of the Atlantic, the North Sea and the Baltic during the winter, but the majority are nomads, whose wanderings take them to the west Mediterranean. In the breeding season they nest chiefly on rocky coasts and islands, less often on flat beaches and sometimes beside large inland lakes. They generally nest in colonies, sometimes together with other gulls, but sometimes singly. Both the sexes build the nest, which is made of seaweed, twigs, grass and heather; it is placed on a rock ledge, in a recess or — though less often — on flat ground, in grass. The 3 eggs are laid between the middle of April and the middle of June; they are brownish, with dark brown spots (2), and the sexes relieve each other during their 26–28 days' incubation. From July to April the birds roam the seashore and open sea. The Great Black-backed Gull has a very wide diet, including fish, crustaceans and other invertebrates, carrion and various kinds of refuse; it also steals eggs and young from seabird colonies. Sometimes it specialises in catching adult birds nesting in holes, such as Storm Petrels and Puffins. The Great Black-backed Gull is the same size as a Greylag Goose and measures 64–79 cm. It looks like a larger edition of the Lesser Black-backed Gull; it has a conspicuous black mantle and wings (1), but its legs are flesh pink. In its winter plumage it has fine brown streaks on its head and the back of its neck. Its call is a deep, gruff 'owk'.

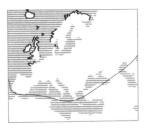

Kittiwake,
Black-legged Kittiwake
Rissa tridactyla

The Kittiwake inhabits mainly Arctic and sub-Arctic parts of Europe, Asia and North America. In Europe it nests in the British Isles, on the coasts of France, Iberia, Denmark and Scandinavia and in Iceland and other large islands of northern seas. Its association with the sea is decidedly closer than that of other gulls. It breeds on rocky islands and shores and otherwise mainly frequents the open sea; it is rare for it to stray inland. In May and June it nests as one of the main species in mixed colonies thousands of birds strong. The nest is built by both the partners on a rocky ledge, in a recess in a sheer cliff and even on the cornices of buildings, in lieu of cliffs. It is a compact structure made of various aquatic plants, moss, seaweed and grasses, reinforced with mud. The

2 greyish-yellow, brown-spotted eggs (2) are incubated for 25—29 days by both the adult birds in turn; the parents also both care painstakingly for the young. Because of where the nest is situated, the young are not nidifugous, but remain in the

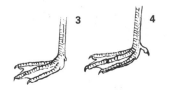

nest until they are fully fledged, i.e. for 38—47 days. When the nesting season is over, the adult birds and the juveniles disperse in all directions, particularly in the northern part of the Atlantic Ocean; those which fly south may stray as far as the Mediterranean. Their diet consists of various marine crustaceans, worms, molluscs and fish. The Kittiwake is a little larger than a Black-headed Gull. In its breeding plumage (1) it has a grey mantle and black-tipped wings; its beak is yellow and its legs are blackish. The hind toe, which in other gulls is normally developed (4), is vestigial in the Kittiwake and usually has no claw (3). In its winter plumage, the Kittiwake has grey smudges on its nape and behind its eyes. Its vernacular name comes from its distinctive 'kitti-wāk' call.

235

Ivory Gull
Pagophila eburnea

The Ivory Gull is a denizen of the high north, living far beyond the Arctic Circle, mostly north of the 75th latitude. In the breeding season it chiefly frequents the rocky shores of Arctic islands and at other times it roams the icy expanses of the Arctic Ocean, near to or far from its breeding area, but mainly at the edge of the drift ice. It arrives at its nesting site between March and May and nests in colonies on cliffs or rocks, usually in places frequented by seals, and sometimes on flat beaches. The nest is similar to the Kittiwake's. Because of the inclement climatic conditions, nesting does not start until mid June or the beginning of July. There are generally 2 olive-brown or greyish, brown-spotted eggs, whose incubation is shared by both the parent birds for just under 30 days. The first young appear at the beginning of August and they are first seen flying at the beginning of September. In September and October the birds start to leave the colony. The Ivory Gull has a rather curious diet; it lives largely on the droppings of seals, walruses and polar bears, which is why it keeps watch at the edge of drift or pack ice, eked out with small fish and marine invertebrates. It has also been observed to catch lemmings, and to practise food parasitism by attacking auks. The Ivory Gull is noticeably larger than the Black-headed Gull, but when on the ground it has the shape of a pigeon. The adult birds (1) are completely white, with black legs; the juveniles have a few black spots on their back, black-tipped wings and a black band on their tail. The call is a sharp, tern-like 'kee-err'.

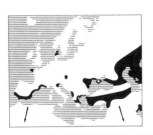

Gull-billed Tern
Gelochelidon nilotica

The Gull-billed Tern lives in the temperate and tropical zone of Europe, Asia, North and South America and Australia. In Europe it nests in scattered localities on the shores of the Mediterranean, from the south of Spain to Turkey, and here and there on the east coast of the North Sea. It also inhabits shallow lakes in steppes, sandy and gravelly islands and the margins of ponds and rivers. It is a gregarious bird and generally nests in colonies, often in the company of other terns or of Black-headed Gulls. Nesting begins in May or June. The nest is a depression in the ground or in short grass, lined with a little grass, small twigs or seaweed.

There are usually 3 light brown eggs with blackish-brown spots, which both the sexes take turns to incubate. The young are hatched in 22—23 days and both the parents care for them until they are fledged, which takes 28—35 days. The Gull-billed Tern lives mainly on insects and small vertebrates, which it gathers on the surface of the water or catches in the grass; it rarely dives head first for food. It is

2

mainly a migrant and winters in the regions south of the Mediterranean — chiefly on the west coast of Africa. It migrates in August or September and returns to its nesting areas in May. The Gull-billed Tern is somewhat smaller than the Black-headed Gull; it has a relatively short and thick, black beak, black legs and an only slightly forked tail: In its spring plumage (1) it has a black cap, a grey mantle and wings and a light grey tail; the rest of the plumage is white. In its winter plumage (2) it has a white head with a lightly black-streaked rear crown and an almost black stripe behind its eyes. Its call is a laughing 'ka-huk, ka-huk'.

1

Caspian Tern
Sterna caspia

2

The Caspian Tern occurs locally on all the continents except South America. In Europe it breeds on the shores of the Baltic, mainly in the Gulf of Bothnia and the Gulf of Finland, on the northern shores of the Black Sea and around the Caspian Sea; it are very close to one another. The nest is a depression in the sand or in low vegetation, lined only with a few remains of plants from the vicinity. In May or June the female usually lays 2 yellowish-grey eggs marked with olive or blackish-brown spots (3), on sea fish, which they catch by diving headlong to the surface, but they also occasionally devour the eggs and young of other birds. The Caspian Tern is the largest member of the tern family and grows to almost the size of a Herring Gull. Its long, angular wings have a light grey upper surface and its white tail is slightly forked. The black feathers in its cap (1) form a distinct crest on the perched bird. In its winter plumage (2) the Caspian Tern has a blackish patch behind the eye and a mottled black and white crown. It has a strikingly large, bright red beak, a large head and

has also nested in other European coastal regions. Although it is mainly a seabird, in Kazakhstan and further east it inhabits inland lakes. Its southern populations are resident and nomadic; northern birds are migrants. In April and May they settle on islets and sandy coastal areas and form large colonies in which the nests which it incubates almost entirely by itself. The young are hatched in 20—25 days and are fledged at four to five weeks. In August the terns leave their nests and by October they have moved to their winter quarters, which lie mainly beside lakes and lagoons in the northern parts of tropical Africa. Caspian Terns live chiefly stumpy black legs. Its call is a raucous 'krray-ee'.

3

Sandwich Tern
Sterna sandvicensis

3

The Sandwich Tern nests on European coasts from the south of Sweden to the Mediterranean, Black and Caspian Seas; it also breeds on the east coast of North and Central America. It is a migrant; some birds winter in the Mediterranean region, but in the autumn birds from northern and western Europe undertake exceptionally long journeys down the coast of western Europe and western Africa to South Africa, where they sometimes round the tip of the continent and continue up the east coast to Mozambique. They return to their nesting areas in April or May, already paired.

Here they frequent sandy or stony beaches, sand dunes and islands. They always nest in colonies, which are sometimes composed of several thousand pairs. The nest is a shallow depression in sand or between stones, thinly lined with straw.

find their own offspring in the throng. At 30–35 days the young birds learn to fly, begin to wander about on their own and between July and September migrate southwards. The Sandwich Tern lives mainly on sea fish, but also eats marine worms and mol-

1

2

The 2 sandy-yellow eggs, marked with brownish-black spots (2), are laid at the end of April or the beginning of May and are incubated for 22–26 days by both the adult birds. At the age of 15–20 days, the young terns collect in a large group under the care of the older birds. It is amazing how the parents always manage to

luscs. Its black cap tapers off in a short crest (3); it has black legs and a black, yellow-tipped beak. In its winter plumage (1) the crest is missing, its forehead is white and the top of its head is spotted (black and white). The adult birds are a little smaller than the Black-headed Gull. Their call is a loud 'kirrrrik'.

Common Tern
Sterna hirundo

The Common Tern inhabits almost the whole of Europe except the most northerly parts, the whole temperate zone of Asia, the northeast east-central parts of America and several places in northern Africa. It is strictly a migrant and the European population winters over a vast area stretching southwards from the Mediterranean. The majority

ance, the partners present each other with fish. The Common Tern nests in colonies, some of which are quite large; sometimes it nests together with other terns

spots (2), which are laid in May or June. Both sexes build the nest, but the female is mostly responsible for incubating the eggs for 20—23 days; the male helps with the feeding and care of the young. The terns leave the colony at the end of July or in August. The Common Tern lives on small fish, insects, crustaceans, molluscs, worms and

of the birds undertake very long journeys down the west coast of Africa to the Cape, often covering distances of over 10,000 km. This species prefers to nest on sandy and gravelly islands, on alluvial deposits beside rivers and lakes, on the coast and by the shallows of large ponds and marshes. It returns to its nesting sites at the end of April or the beginning of May. Courting takes place in the air and on the ground; for inst-

or with gulls, but sometimes singly. The nest is a small depression in the ground or the vegetation and is often lined with dry parts of plants. There are usually 3 brownish-yellow eggs, marked with blackish-brown

echinoderms. In its summer plumage (1) it has a grey mantle and wings, a black cap and a red, black-tipped beak. In the winter plumage (3) it has a white forehead, a white-mottled black crown and a black beak. When perched, its tail does not project beyond the tips of its wings. The Common Tern is the size of a slender Turtle Dove. Its call is a penetrating 'krri-ärr' or 'kirr, kirr-kirri'.

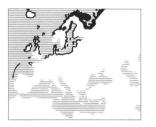

Arctic Tern
Sterna paradisaea

The Arctic Tern is a phenomenal traveller and makes abnormally long journeys southwards, during which it may cover over 20,000 km. It nests chiefly in the most northerly parts of Europe, Asia and North America; in Europe it also nests on more southerly coasts, from Holland to Poland and the Baltic republics of the former USSR. Birds from and islands and occasionally settle beside inland lakes. The nest is a shallow depression lined with a little straw or fragments of shells. The 2 greyish or brownish eggs, with dark brown and black spots (2), are laid in May and are incubated for 20−24 days, generally by both parents. Soon after they hatch, the young terns mingle with the other young in the colony, but their parents always find them with unerring accuracy. The young are fed mainly on fish, together with worms, molluscs, crustaceans and insects. The terns leave the colony at the end of July and

northern Europe migrate southwards along the coast of western Europe, where they are joined by terns from northeastern America; they then all fly together down the coast of western Africa to South Africa and from there to the Antarctic. During these journeys, some birds fly around the whole of the Antarctic in one to two years. They return to their northern breeding areas in April or May. They nest in large colonies on sandy or rocky beaches

3

2

during August. In their breeding plumage (1) they have white cheeks and a grey-tinged underside; the whole of their beak is red. Their legs are strikingly short, but they have a long tail which projects beyond the tips of their folded wings when they are perched. Their winter plumage (3) is similar to that of the Common Tern and the same applies to their size. Their call is rather more monosyllabic and sounds like 'kriä' or 'krirr'.

Little Tern, Least Tern
Sterna albifrons

The Little Tern is distributed very widely, but very irregularly, over a vast area and it nests in Europe, Asia, northern and western Africa, North America and Australia. In Europe it inhabits all the coasts of the southern and western parts, in the north it occurs no further than the south of Scandinavia and the Gulf of Finland, and in some places it also occurs inland. Its winter quarters are on the coasts of western and southern Africa. It nests in medium-sized colonies on sandy and gravelly beaches and islands and on alluvial deposits beside large rivers and lakes, generally apart from other terns and gulls. The Little Tern arrives at its nesting sites in April or May. After mating, the female scoops out a hollow for the nest with its own body and lines it with tiny stones or shells. The 2–3 ochre eggs, with dark brown spots (2), which are laid in May or June, are at first incubated only by the female, but later the male also lends a hand; the young are hatched in 20–22 days. At 20 days they are already able to fly and in July and August they migrate, together with the older birds. The Little Tern lives mainly on crustaceans, small fish and insects. It catches its food in a typical manner (3); when it sights prey, it remains suspended in the air for a short time, flapping its wings, and then drops like a stone, disappearing for a few seconds under the water. Other *Sterna* species have a similar technique. In its breeding plumage (1) the Little Tern has a distinctive white forehead, a yellow, black-tipped beak and yellow legs. In its winter plumage it has a lightly speckled crown and a blackish band from the eyes across the nape. The Little Tern is the smallest tern and is about the size of a Starling. Its call is a high-pitched 'kree-ik' or a grating 'kirri-kirri-kirri'.

Whiskered Tern
Chlidonias hybridus

The Whiskered Tern occurs in Europe, Asia, Africa and Australia. In Europe it nests mainly in the south and the east, but in some years small groups have been found nesting further north and west. It is a migrant and spends the winter in tropical Africa south of the Sahara. It sometimes arrives at its breeding sites at the end of April, but mostly in May; nesting continues into July. Whiskered Terns nest beside muddy rivers and ponds and in swamps. They live in colonies, often together with the Black Tern. The nest, which is built on floating plants in the marginal vegetation at the water's edge, is a fairly large pile of various aquatic plants. The clutch consists of 3 or, less often, 2 greyish or light ochre eggs with dark brown spots; unlike the eggs of other terns, they almost always have a greenish tinge. The parents share in their incubation, which takes about 18 days, and they likewise both rear and feed the young, mostly with insects, insect larvae, worms and other invertebrates and less often with small fish and tadpoles. Migration southwards begins in late July. Adult Whiskered Terns are about one third smaller than the Common Tern. In the spring (1) they have a black cap, white cheeks and sooty-grey underparts. In flight, they show a strikingly large area of white on the underside of their wings and tail. In the winter their underparts are uniformly white and their crown is white with black streaks. Their call is a disyllabic 'ky-ik' and a harsh 'schreea'.

243

Black Tern
Chlidonias niger

The Black Tern inhabits ponds, lakes, swamps and the backwaters and quiet bends of large, slow-flowing rivers. It breeds in the temperate part of Europe (in the north to the south of Scandinavia and the Baltic states of the former USSR, but not in Britain), in western Asia and in North America. It remains in its nesting area only for the time needed to rear the young; it generally does not arrive until May and leaves for tropical Africa as early as July. It nests in colonies, sometimes together with other terns or with gulls. The sexes both build the nest, in thin vegetation, and often among floating, broken or cut plants, at the margin of water.

Nesting losses are consequently high, since a strong wind or a few waves soon destroy the pile of reed, rush and sedge blades of which the nest consists. In May or June the female lays 2—3 yellowish-brown eggs densely marked with brown spots (2) and incubates them for 21—22 days, aided by the male. The parents both look after the young and still continue feeding them after they have learnt to fly. Black Terns live mainly on aquatic insects and their larvae and also on spiders,

leeches, small fish, tadpoles and frogs. When hunting, they usually move over the surface of the water, with their head bent downwards, rising and falling in flight; they do not dive into the water, but only touch the surface. In the spring, the Black Tern is virtually completely dark grey, with head and breast black, except for its white undertail-coverts and the pale grey underside of its wings (1). The most distinctive features of its winter plumage are the dark patch on the sides of its white breast and the black crown and black spot behind the eyes. The bird itself is the same size as a Blackbird. Its call is an unobtrusive 'kirr' or 'kit'.

1

2

White-winged Black Tern

Chlidonias leucopterus

In size and behaviour the White-winged Black Tern closely resembles the Black Tern. In breeding plumage (1) its body is virtually black, but the tail and the upperwing-coverts are pure white. In flight, its underwing-coverts can

marshes with luxuriant vegetation. It nests in colonies, often together with the Black Tern. The nest, which is made of dead aquatic plants, stands in an inaccessible spot in the middle of aquatic vegetation. Nesting be-

They feed them mostly on aquatic insects and insects which they catch on the wing over the water or above clumps of aquatic plants. The White-winged Black Tern lives in eastern Europe and occasionally nests further west;

be seen to be black. In its winter plumage it has a white underside, its head remains black only at the back, and its white rump contrasts with its grey mantle and tail. Its call is a raucous 'kerr' or 'krek'. The White-winged Black Tern inhabits still water and

gins in May or June. The female usually lays 3 yellowish-brown eggs marked with dark brown spots, and while incubating them it receives generous help from the male. The incubation period is 18—22 days. The parents both look after the young.

it also breeds over a wide strip of territory stretching across the whole of Asia as far as Sakhalin. It is strictly a migrant. European birds spend the winter in tropical and southern Africa; they usually set out in August or September and do not return to their breeding areas until May or June.

Lords of Arctic rocks and cliffs and Loud-winged fliers

Auks
Pigeons and
Doves

Auks spend the whole of their life beside the sea, obtain their food (mainly fish) from it and nest on its shores. They are very well adapted for this mode of life. Their torpedo-shaped body is ideal for diving and for swimming under water. Some have a large, deep, flat-sided beak. Their legs are situated at the very end of their body (so that they sit erect on their heels, on the entire area of the tarsus), their front toes are joined together by strong webbing and their first toe is vestigial or absent (Fig. 1). Unlike ducks, grebes and divers, they use their short wings as their means of locomotion when swimming under water; they spread them slightly and 'row' at a rate of 15–20 strokes a minute (Fig. 2). There is only a small amount of air in their bones, so that they are not too buoyant under water. They have a narrow sternum and a long thorax, which stretches far to the back of their body to protect the trunk from the pressure of the water.

Their closely adhering plumage is very thick and its density per area unit is double the value of that for gulls' plumage. Its heat-insulating properties are enhanced by the much greater barb and barbule density of the vanes of the feathers, which are semi-downy at their lower end, by the presence of an aftershaft with a downy vane and by long, thick down. Auks moult twice a year

– partially before nesting and completely afterwards. Their flight feathers are all shed at once, so that for a period they are unable to fly, and until the feathers grow again they remain out at sea. They have a well-developed preen gland for keeping their plumage oiled and, as a result of contact with salt water, they have highly developed nasal glands which secrete salt. There are no differences between the sexes in either coloration or size.

In the nesting season, auks generally form colonies, often numbering thousands of birds, in coastal sites known as 'bird cliffs'. The single large egg is laid on bare rock or in a hole in the ground; its conical shape prevents it from rolling away (Fig. 3). The newly hatched young are clad in a thick coat of down. The offspring of species nesting in the open are nidicolous, but grow quickly and jump down into the sea before they are full-grown, while the young of hole-nesters, which are likewise nidicolous, do not leave the nest until they are full-grown and fully fledged.

Pigeons and doves are a large order of mainly arboreal birds. Their legs, which are adapted for

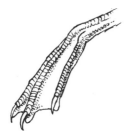

Fig. 1. *Foot of an auk. The three front toes are joined together by webbing; the hind toe is absent.*

Fig. 2. *The Black Guillemot swims under water by means of its wings.*

walking, have a well-developed first toe growing from the same level as the other toes, and a characteristic beak the base of which is covered to beyond the nostrils with a soft, swollen cere and the tip slightly hooked (Fig. 4). Sandgrouse (often treated as a separate order, Ptero-clidiformes) are an exception, since they lack the cere and have only a rudimentary first toe on their short legs. Their dense plumage forms a protection against hot sand.

Pigeons and doves excel as fast and enduring fliers and they have large, highly pneumatic bones. They are densely covered with tough plumage, whose feathers have downy barbs at their lower end, probably because true downy plumage is missing. The flank feathers produce large amounts of powder which replaces the function of the poorly developed preen gland.

There are no differences in plumage between the males and females, though sandgrouse do exhibit sexual plumage dimorphism.

In association with their vegetarian diet, pigeons and doves have a large, bilobate crop for the temporary storage of food, and a large, muscular stomach. The crop has another interesting property; while the young are being fed, the wall of the crop swells and a curd-like substance, which is fed to the young, flakes off from its inner surface. Unlike most other birds, pigeons and doves drink by plunging their beak into the water up to their nostrils and sucking it in. Waxbills, small members of the weaverfinch family (Estrildidae), drink in a similar manner, while sandgrouse suck up water and then tilt their head backwards.

Pigeons and doves nest mainly in trees and usually lay two white eggs; the newly hatched young are naked and blind. Two or three clutches may be laid in a year. Sandgrouse are again an exception; they lay two or three speckled eggs in a depression in the ground and their offspring are soon able to run about, although the parents have to feed them. The young grow very fast and are soon able to fly.

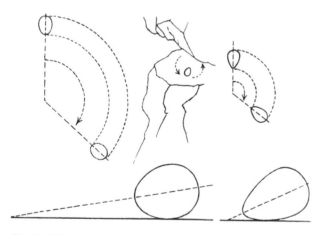

Fig. 3. *The conical eggs of auks rotate over a much smaller area than the eggs of most other birds; this prevents them from rolling off narrow rock ledges.*

Fig. 4. *Pigeon's head; the base of the soft beak is covered with cere.*

The Collared Dove (Streptopelia decaocto) *is a regular inhabitant of town parks.*

Guillemot, Common Murre
Uria aalge

The Guillemot is one of the chief inhabitants of North Atlantic bird islands and cliffs. It frequents mainly the shores of the northern parts of the Atlantic, Pacific and Arctic Oceans, but in Europe it also occurs much further south, to the coasts of France, Portugal and Spain. It is generally resident; only some birds roam the northern Atlantic in various directions and still fewer migrate southwards to the Mediterranean. The Guillemot's typical nesting-sites are precipitous cliffs on seashores or islands, where in some places it nests in colonies a hundred thousand pairs strong. It sometimes returns to the cliffs in December or January, but in the more northerly parts of its range not until March or April. The eggs are generally laid in the middle of May. The birds do not make a nest and the female lays the single egg directly onto a ledge, in a niche or in an empty Kitti-wake nest. The egg (3) is markedly pear-shaped, to prevent it from rolling off the cliff ledge, and is marked with dark green, brown or black speckles on a whitish, greenish or bluish ground. It is incubated for 28—33 days by both the partners in turn; they also both take care of the young bird, which they feed almost entirely on fish caught by skilful diving in the open sea or close to the shore. At 20—25 days, before it is fully fledged, the young bird jumps down into the sea, where it remains a long time in the company of its parents and is fed by them. In its breeding plumage (1), the Guillemot has a chocolate-brown to black back and a white underside; each wing has a narrow white trailing edge. In its winter plumage, its throat, cheeks and the front and sides of its neck are white. It has a tapering, completely black beak. The related Brünnich's Guillemot *U. lomvia* (2) has a shorter, much thicker beak, with a white line along the sides. Both species are about the size of a Tufted Duck.

3

2

Razorbill
Alca torda

The Razorbill is one of the species forming typical colonies on islands and rocky coasts in the north. It lives in the northern part of the Atlantic and in Europe its range extends in the south to Britain, Ireland and France. It is strictly a seabird; it depends on the sea for its food and it nests along the sea coast. It is mainly a resident bird; migrants spend the winter on coasts from western Europe to northwestern Africa and the Mediterranean. They arrive at their nesting sites in February or March and the eggs are laid in May or at the beginning of June. The birds do not build a nest and the single egg lies on bare, hard rock; it is whitish, brownish or reddish and is marked with blurred brown or black spots (2). During the 36 days' incubation, the parents take turns to sit on it, but often leave it unattended for long periods. At the age of about three weeks the young bird leaves its rocky ledge for the sea; it jumps straight down into the water and, since it is not yet able to fly, it often — like young guillemots — receives a severe bruising on the way down. The parents still continue for a time to tend and feed it, mainly on fish. The Razorbill, which measures about 40 cm, looks like a small penguin. In its breeding plumage (1), its head (except for a white line between its eyes and the base of its beak), its neck and the whole of its upperparts are black, while its underside is white. Its flat-sided beak has vertical grooves and white markings across it, and there is also a thin white trailing

2

edge to its wings. In winter plumage, its throat, chin and the front and sides of its neck are white, but the white line in front of its eyes is missing. Young birds have no markings on their beak. When nesting, the Razorbill utters deep growls and grunts.

251

Black Guillemot

Cepphus grylle

The Black Guillemot nests singly and also in loose colonies in northern Europe and Asia and in North America. On European coasts it is to be found from Iceland, Ireland and Britain to Denmark, practically the whole of Scandinavia and the Kola Peninsula and here and there in the Baltic republics of the former USSR. Most of the birds are resident, but some wander to the tends to prefer the lower parts. In May or June the female lays 1—2 greyish or brownish, dark-spotted eggs (2) in a hole or a fissure in a rock, or in a space between boulders, where they lie on the bare stony substrate or at best on a few fragments of shells washed up by the sea. They are incubated for 27—30 days by both the adult birds in turn; both the parents likewise feed the young, mainly on small sea fish, with occasional molluscs and crustaceans. The young remain in the 'nest' for 34—36 days and do not leave it until they are able to provide for themselves. At the end of July the birds vanish from their nesting site. The Black Guillemot is about one fifth smaller than the Guillemot. In the spring it is completely black except for a gleaming white patch on its wings (1);

coasts of Germany and the south of England for the winter. The Black Guillemot nests on rocky coasts and islands, but it also occupies flatter beaches than other auks and on bird cliffs it

in the winter its back is mottled black and white and it has a whitish head and neck and a white underside. When nesting it utters faint whistling sounds and, less often, chirping trills.

Puffin, Common Puffin, Atlantic Puffin
Fratercula arctica

The Puffin is distributed over an area comprising the northeast coast of North America and the coasts of Greenland, Iceland, Spitsbergen, Novaya Zemlya, the Kola Peninsula, Scandinavia, Britain and Ireland, and Brittany in France. When not nesting, it spends virtually all its time on the open sea, when some of its populations reach the Mediterranean. From March onwards, Puffins settle on grassy slopes on islands and sea coasts and either occupy rabbit or shearwater burrows or excavate nesting burrows with plants, in which, in May, the female generally lays a single, large, dingy white egg with yellowish-brown spots (2). Together with its partner, it incubates the egg for a full 40 days. The young bird is also fed in the burrow for about 40 days, and when it is nice and plump the parents abandon it. The young bird starves for about ten days, but then finds its way to the water and begins to fend for itself. Puffins catch their prey, which consists mainly of fish but also includes molluscs, crustaceans and marine worms, mainly under water. The Puffin is about the same size as the preceding species. Its most striking feature is its large, triangular and brightly coloured beak (1), which

their beak and feet. They are very sociable and nest together in colonies numbering tens of thousands of pairs. The burrow is usually 1—2 m long and at its far end there is a roomy chamber lined with dry grass or marine

loses much of its colouring and shrinks a little, however, when the bird assumes its winter plumage (3). The juveniles have a much smaller beak (4). When nesting, the Puffin utters throaty 'arr' or 'ooh' calls.

253

Black-bellied Sandgrouse
Pterocles orientalis

In Europe, the Black-bellied Sandgrouse inhabits Spain and Portugal and the region beyond the Volga, but mainly the area stretching from Asia Minor to Nepal; it also lives in North Africa. Birds living in the northern parts of the range migrate further south in the winter, often as far as India; those which live in the southern parts are resident. In March or April the birds return in small flocks to their nesting sites in semi-desert and grassy, flat or mildly hilly country with clayey or sandy soil and more or less xerophilous plants. They also occur in foothills and in Tien-Shan in mountain steppes. The courting male flies screeching after the female and on the ground paces around it in circles. The breeding season is very long; it lasts from the end of April to the beginning of August and some pairs quite probably rear two broods. The nest is virtually non-existent and the eggs are laid on the ground, sometimes in the shade of a clump of wormwood or some similar plant; it is lined with only a token amount of straw. The brown-spotted eggs are light grey to yellowish-brown; there are usually 3, but occasionally 2. The parents share in their incubation, which starts as soon as the first egg has been laid, doubtless as protection from the burning rays of the sun; the incubation period is 21—22 or more days. The Black-bellied Sandgrouse lives on seeds and shoots. Like other sandgrouse, it needs water in the vicinity; in the morning and evening it flies off and brings back water for the young in its absorbent belly feathers. It is the only sandgrouse with a completely black belly in both sexes (female, 2); in addition, the male (1) has a black throat and an orange-brown chin. In flight, its black belly forms a striking contrast with the black and white underside of its wings. The adult birds are roughly the same size as a pigeon. Their call is a rather deep 'dyürr-rürr-rürr' or 'chow-row'.

2♀

Rock Dove
Columba livia

The Rock Dove inhabits western and southern Europe, northern Africa and most of Asia. Although it also occurs a long way inland, it is found in the largest numbers on the coast, no doubt because there it has the best conditions for nesting. It nests on cliffs and has a special predilection for caves. In many places, the Rock Dove lives in close proximity to man — in old fortifications, in walls and towers and in the upper storeys of inhabited houses. As a rule, it forms large flocks. It is a resident bird and nests during a large part of the year, but mostly from April to July. The nest, which is made of grass and twigs, is built by both the sexes in a niche or hole in rock. They both likewise take turns to sit on the 2 white eggs, which are incubated for 16—18 days, and care for the young for four to five weeks. At first they feed them on a pulpy substance from their crop and later on various kinds of seeds, which form the staple diet of the adult birds. The Rock Dove (1) is mainly grey, with a green and wine-red gloss on its neck, a white rump and two black bars on its wings. It has the same cooing song as domestic pigeons and is in fact their ancestor, however incredible it may seem that all the different races of domestic pigeons, with their variety of colours, outlandish types of plumage, peculiar voices, huge crops and strange facial excrescences are all descended from the modest Rock

Dove. It is nevertheless a fact that even the most exotic domestic pigeon, if allowed to run wild, reverts to a form resembling the grey Rock Dove in a few generations.

255

Stock Dove
Columba oenas

Africa. In western and southern Europe it is a resident bird; over the rest of its range it is a migrant and in September or October it migrates to the European and African part of the Mediterranean region. The pairs, which return to their nesting sites in March, are probably permanent. Courtship takes the form of aerial circling with slow, powerful strokes of the wings, followed by gliding, with the wings held raised above the back. When the partners have found a suitable hole (often an old Black Woodpecker's nest), they line it with dry twigs and straw, often right up to the entrance, but sometimes only sparsely. The nesting season lasts from April to August and in this time the birds manage to rear two to four broods of young. The parents take turns to incubate the 2 white eggs; the male usually broods during the middle of the day. The young are hatched in 16—17 days; for the first eight to ten days they are fed on a curd-like substance secreted by the adult birds' crop, and then on various kinds of seeds which the parents regurgitate from their crop directly into the young bird's beak. Parental care lasts about 25 days. The Stock Dove is more robustly built than the Collared Dove. It is a light bluish-grey colour, with two indistinct black bars on its wings and a black terminal band on its tail; the sides of its neck have a green gloss, its crop a wine-red sheen (1). Its call is a loud hooting or wailing 'hōōh-hōō-hoo-hoo'.

The Stock Dove lives in old woods (mostly deciduous and mixed woods) which provide it with a suitable number of holes to nest in; it seldom nests in conifer forests or in holes in rock or clay faces, but it accepts large nestboxes. It inhabits the whole of Europe (except Iceland and the north of Scandinavia), western Siberia and Asia Minor and a small corner of northwestern

Wood Pigeon
Columba palumbus

2

The distribution of the Wood Pigeon is almost identical to that of the Stock Dove. Its incidence is conditional on the presence of trees, irrespective of whether they stand in a conifer forest or a deciduous wood, in mountains or in lowlands, in a copse, an avenue, a park or a garden. In western Europe and in some parts of central Europe the Wood Pigeon nests in city parks. In western and southern Europe it is a resident or nomadic bird; birds from central and northern Europe migrate to the Mediterranean region between September and November. They arrive at their nesting sites in February or

March, in flocks which soon break up into pairs. These immediately occupy their nesting areas. The courting male often coos at the top of a tree; in its characteristic nuptial flight (3) it soars obliquely into the air, claps its wings together and then sails down again. Very often the male

runs after the female on the ground with expanded crop and spread tail, hopping, bowing and continuously cooing. The nest, a carelessly assembled flat structure made of twigs, is built by both the sexes; it is sometimes

put together so loosely that the 2 white eggs show through the floor. Nesting begins in March and by August the parents are able to rear two to four broods of young. The eggs are incubated for 16—17 days by both the parent birds in turn. For the first five or six days the young are fed on

secretion from the parents'crop and for the next three weeks on softened plant food. At harvest time, cornfields are invaded by flocks of hundreds of Wood Pigeons, but the birds also like conifer seeds, acorns and beech-nuts and gather berries; occasionally they enrich this diet with snails, worms and insects. The Woodpigeon, which measures about 41 cm, is the largest European pigeon (1). It is mainly grey, with white patches (absent in juveniles) on the side of its purple and green neck and a white border on the front edge of its wings, which becomes a wide white band when it flies (2). Its call is a throaty 'roo-cōo-coo-coo-coo'.

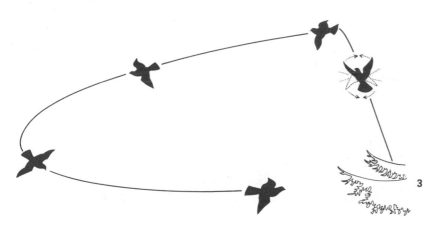

3

257

Collared Dove
Streptopelia decaocto

The Collared Dove originally inhabited southern and eastern Asia and in Europe only the Balkans, but for some reason, during the 1930s, it suddenly began to spread northwards and westwards. In 1932 it appeared in Hungary, in 1936 in former Czechoslovakia, in 1938 in Austria, in 1943 in Germany, in 1947 in Holland, in 1948 in Denmark, in 1949 in Switzerland and Sweden, in 1950 in France, in 1952 in Belgium and Norway, and in 1955 it began to nest in Britain — an advance of over 1,600 km in roughly 20 years. When it colonises a new region, it first of all settles in town parks and gardens and then in their immediate vicinity. It is a resident bird; the pairs are formed during the winter, to the accompaniment of reciprocal pursuit, cooing and bowing. In its nuptial flight, the male rises suddenly into the air, with powerful strokes of its wings, and then glides down again. The pairs are not very demanding in their choice of a site for the nest and they nest in conifers and deciduous trees, on telegraph poles, in drainpipes and on window cornices. Both the sexes build the nest, which is not made only of twigs; in fact, nests made entirely of wire have been found. If conditions are favourable, the birds may nest five times in a year. The 2 white eggs are incubated for 14—16 days by both the parent birds in turn. The young leave the nest at the age of two to three weeks, but are fed for a few days longer by their parents. Collared Doves live mainly on the seeds of field crops; in the winter they often scavenge in towns. The Collared Dove (1) is a little larger than the Turtle Dove. It is greyish-brown and has a black, white-bordered collar on the back and sides of its neck; in flight, it reveals the white underside of the outer half of its tail. Its call is a trisyllabic, throaty 'coo-cōōō, coo' or a kind of mewing or laughing 'hwee'.

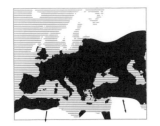

Turtle Dove
Streptopelia turtur

The Turtle Dove is a migrant and does not arrive in its breeding areas until April and May. It frequents parkland, where copses, shrubs and hedgerows alternate with meadows and fields, and nests at the edge of deciduous woods. Its throbbing 'toorrr toorrr toorrr' can be heard as soon as it returns. When the male courts the female, its crop swells and it shuffles its feet and bows repeatedly and mechanically. Occasionally it flies up into the air for a ceremonial flight, loudly clapping its wings, and then glides down again, fanning its tail. It nests in bushes or trees, but usually no higher than 1–5 m. The nest, which is made of dry twigs and straw, is put together so loosely that the 2 white eggs can often be seen from below. The eggs are incubated for 13–14 days by both the parents in turn. The young are fed in the nest for 14–16 or more days. As a rule, the birds manage to rear only one brood, but in Britain they generally nest twice. Turtle Doves feed chiefly on the seeds of cultivated and wild plants. Like other members of the family, their stomach normally contains grit, which helps with mechanical processing of the food. At the end of August or in September they migrate to Africa as far as the Sudan (some winter, rarely, in the Mediterranean region). Otherwise they inhabit the whole of Europe (except the far north and Scandinavia), western Asia and northern Africa. The Turtle Dove (1) is larger and more robust than a Blackbird and measures about 27 cm. It has a rusty-brown, black-spotted back and wings, a wine-red breast and a bluish-grey head; on its neck there is a patch of black and white stripes. In flight it is exceptionally quick and skilful and can be recognised by the narrow white border at the tip of its tail.

Exotic guests and Nest parasites

Parrots
Cuckoos

The most characteristic feature of parrots is their deep, thick beak, whose curved upper mandible overlaps the lower mandible and forms a hook. The upper mandible is not fixed as in other birds, but articulates with the skull by means of a grooved 'joint'. In consequence, the beak is capable of unusual movements and can be used for climbing, as well as for opening and crushing nuts and seeds. At its base, the beak has a wide covering of cere, in which the nostrils are embedded. Parrots are also characterised by feet which are perfectly constructed both for climbing and for grasping food and transferring it to the beak. The toes widen to form pads; the first and fourth toes always point backwards and the second and third toes forwards (Fig. 1).

Parrots generally have brightly coloured plumage and the males and females are generally similar. The feathers are fairly loose and have an aftershaft. The preen gland is poorly developed and in its place the birds produce a quantity of powder, which they sprinkle over their contour feathers. When they shake themselves, some parrots almost disappear in a cloud of powder.

In association with their diet (mainly seeds), parrots have a large crop. They likewise have a remarkable, soft, fleshy tongue (Fig. 2), which is a sensitive tactile organ and is used not only for holding food in place, but also, in some species, for taking nectar from the flowers of tropical plants.

As a rule, parrots keep the same mate for the whole of their life. They nest in holes and the white eggs are laid directly on to the floor of the hole (Fig. 3). The newly hatched young (Fig. 4) are naked and their eyelids are stuck together (Fig. 5), so that they are nest-bound and completely dependent on the parents. They develop slowly and it is a long time before they can leave the nest. Parrots are very gregarious birds and when they have finished nesting they collect together and form large flocks.

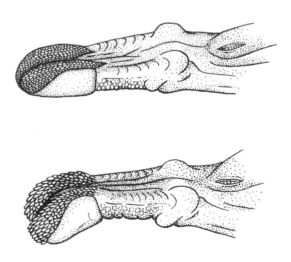

Fig. 1. *Foot of a parrot, showing the padded, widened toes, two of which point forwards and two backwards.*

Fig. 2. *Parrots have a fleshy tongue and in some it is covered with a brush-like layer of tubercles used in the intake of fluid. The tubercles open trumpet-wise only when the bird licks nectar.*

Their gift for imitation and their high intelligence have made parrots very popular as pets.

Parrots form a separate group displaying signs of remote kinship to the order Cuculiformes (cuckoos and touracos).

Cuckoos are mostly medium-sized arboreal birds, with characteristic prehensile feet on which the two middle toes point forwards and the two outer toes backwards; they generally have short tarsi, Their beak is fairly long and wide, with a curving upper mandible, and lacks a cere (Fig. 6).

Cuckoos have extremely thin skin and close-fitting feathers with no aftershaft. They usually have only eight to ten tail feathers, which are generally graduated, so that the longest feathers

Fig. 5. *A one-day-old parrot nestling, still with the egg tooth on its beak.*

Fig. 6. *Head of a Cuckoo.*

are in the middle and the shortest ones on the outside. Cuckoos fly well and swiftly. Those living in the temperate belt are migrants. Their voice is loud and unmistakable. They are predominantly insectivorous.

Most species of the order Cuculiformes are forest-dwellers. The most interesting aspect of their life is undoubtedly their nest parasitism (Fig. 7). Cuckoos do not hatch their eggs themselves, but lay them in the nests of other species and leave the care of their offspring to the foster-parents. This phenomenon is not confined to the order Cuculiformes, but is also to be found among some songbirds (weavers, New World starlings) and woodpeckers (honeyguides, barbets) and even in a South American duck; it is the

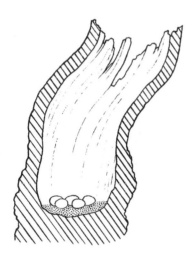

Fig. 3. *Parrots do not line their nest-hole, but lay their eggs directly on the floor.*

Fig. 4. *Parrots have nidicolous young; at hatching the young are naked and blind and are completely dependent on parental care.*

Fig. 7. *Cuckoo laying an egg in a pipit's nest.*

262

most completely developed in cuckoos, however, and it occurs in almost half of all the members of the order. Other cuckoos rear their young normally in nests, like the majority of birds. Our familiar Cuckoo lays its eggs in the nests of small songbirds, but other cuckoo species also leave them to the care of crows or pigeons.

The young cuckoo's body fills the entire nest of its warbler foster-parents.

Ring-necked Parakeet
Psittacula krameri

The Ring-necked Parakeet has a wider distribution than any other species of this genus. It inhabits central and eastern Africa, Egypt, Mauritius, Zanzibar, Aden, Oman, Kuwait, Iraq, Iran, the Indian subcontinent, Indochina and southeastern China. It is likewise the commonest *Psittacula* species kept in captivity. In its natural environment, when not nesting, it usually forms small groups of 10—20 birds; for their midday rest and for excursions in search of food, these groups join forces to form flocks numbering several hundred birds. In the breeding season, the birds nest in solitary pairs or small groups. They nest in tree holes and are not afraid to use trees growing in towns. The 2—6

2♀

eggs are incubated for 22—24 days entirely by the female. The young leave the nest at the age of six weeks, but the parents continue to feed them for two weeks afterwards. Their diet consists of various seeds, cereal grains and fruit, occasionally supplemented by insects and their larvae. The Ring-necked Parakeet measures about 40 cm. Its ground colour is green, but the male (1) has

a black and pink collar and a black chin, which the female lacks (2). Blue and yellow colour mutants of this species have been bred in captivity. In some European countries it also nests in the wild. In England, Ring-necked Parakeets have lived in various London suburbs since 1969—71 and up to 1975 they spread out over the southeastern counties. Today they occur mainly in suburban parks and large gardens with suitable tree holes, but their number in natural surroundings is also increasing. Since 1975, a successful small colony has nested in Trieste, on the border between Italy and former Yugoslavia, and several dozen Ring-necked Parakeets live wild in the Netherlands.

1

Budgerigar
Melopsittacus undulatus

The Budgerigar's true home is the greater part of Australia. In association with its diet, it is explicitly a nomad. The steppe grasses on whose seeds it feeds grow and flower very quickly during the rainy season and that is the time when the Budgerigars appear and occupy every suitable hole, especially in eucalyptus trees. The female incubates the 3−5 white eggs for 18 days; the young leave the nest at the age of 30−35 days. When the supply of grass seeds is exhausted, the huge flocks of Budgerigars move on. In Australia, Budgerigars nest only when sufficient food is available; if there is a shortage, they may go several years without nesting at all. This parakeet was brought to Europe for the first time in 1840. Today it is the commonest bird kept in cages and aviaries, and the number bred in captivity is larger than the number living in the wild. In several European countries, the Budgerigar has been found nesting in the open, but such birds always disappeared again. The most successful attempts to induce the formation of wild colonies were made in England, in particular on Tresco, one of the Scilly Isles. Here the birds lived in aviaries from 1969, were then allowed to fly out, when they occupied nestboxes, and from 1972 onwards they lived completely wild and nested in tree holes. In 1975 there were already over 100 birds living wild and small flocks were also observed on the neighbouring islands of Bryher, St Mary's, St Martin's and St Agnes. Wild Budgerigars are basically light green, with brown vermiculations on their back (1); the front of their head and their throat are yellow, with six black spots on the throat and one blue spot on either cheek. The male (2) has a blue and the female (3) a brownish cere.

2♂   3♀

265

Great Spotted Cuckoo

Clamator glandarius

In shape, the Great Spotted Cuckoo (1) looks rather like a Magpie; it has a long, graduated tail with white-tipped feathers. Its upperparts are brownish-grey, with white spots, and its underside is yellowish-white; on the top of its head it has a clearly discernible light grey crest, which in juveniles is shorter and dark brown. Its call — 'krikrio... karrk, kekeke...' — is very variable. In Europe the Great Spotted Cuckoo inhabits Spain, Portugal, the south of France and western Italy; otherwise it lives in Asia Minor, the Middle East and Africa, where it winters across the centre of the continent. It frequents parkland, the edges of forests, copses and thinly wooded steppes. It lays its eggs in other birds' nests, but in this case the foster-parents are corvids — Magpies, Azure-winged Magpies, Jays, Carrion Crows and Ravens. The 12—15 eggs are similar in colour to those of the host birds, i.e. they are mostly greenish, with brown spots, and the female cuckoo may lay several in one nest. The young cuckoos do not throw the other young out of the nest, but stay in the nest with them until they are fledged, probably because the foster-parents bring so much food that there is sufficient for all. Furthermore, the young cuckoos resemble their foster siblings in form, colour and vocal manifestations, so that there is no danger of their being ejected by the foster-parents. The adult Great Spotted Cuckoo lives on insects and other invertebrate animals.

Cuckoo
Cuculus canorus

The most interesting feature of the Cuckoo's life and habits is its nest parasitism. It does not build a nest of its own, but lays its eggs in the nests of other birds (usually songbirds, in Europe of 25—35 species but over 100 recorded). In about 35—46 days the female lays 15—20 eggs similar in colour and shape to the eggs of the foster-mother, and it always places them (2) in nests of the same species. It always lays the egg directly into the host's nest, usually before the host's clutch is completed, and at the same time eats one of the original eggs. The young Cuckoo is hatched in 12 days, well before the other

2

young, and in about ten hours its inborn instinct to get rid of any obstructions begins to assert itself. It edges its body under an egg or a young bird until it rests on its back, where it is held in place by the Cuckoo's half-raised

featherless wings; the young Cuckoo then retreats to the edge of the nest and, with its head propped on the floor, hurls its load to the ground. It repeats this process until it is the only occupant of the nest. The cuckoo is fledged in 19—21 days, but its foster-parents feed it for a further 14 days or longer. The Cuckoo inhabits the whole of Europe, practically the whole of Asia and the north of Africa. It lives in wooded country, but strays into meadows, fields and riparian woods. After its arrival in April, the male draws attention to itself by its melodious 'cuc-coo' call; when excited it utters a hoarse 'hahahah'. The female's call is a descending bubbling 'quick-quickquickquick'. The adult birds set out on their journey to south-

4♀

ern Africa as early as August, the young birds (1) mostly in September. Cuckoos are about the size of a slim Turtle Dove. The male (3) has slate-grey upperparts, head and breast, and an almost white underside with dark barring across it; the female (4) has a brownish tone to the underside, and a rare variant of the female has rusty-chestnut upperparts.

3♂

267

Silent hunters

Owls

Owls are often thought to be nocturnal birds of prey, but appearances are deceptive and they are actually nothing of the kind. They are not even exclusively nocturnal and many of them hunt by day or in the evening. They are characterised by a large head, a short neck, a hooked beak and short, usually feathered legs with flexible toes, the outermost of which can be turned completely front-to-back (Fig. 1). The toes are armed with sharp claws. The expressive face has large eyes ringed by small, tough feathers forming a mask or facial disc (Fig. 2). As distinct from the eyes of other birds, owls' eyes are not on the sides of the head, but face forwards, so that the angle of vision (about 160 degrees, Fig. 3) is smaller (in other birds 200−300 degrees, Fig. 4). This deficiency is compensated for by the extraordinary flexibility of the head, which can be turned by up to 270 degrees. Owls' eyes can also perceive very faint light, so that they function reliably even in the presence of only a fraction of illumination. The cornea is markedly convex, the iris contracts and expands very quickly, and the receptor cells of the retina consist almost entirely of rods, in the enormous concentration of 56,000 per square millimetre. Naturally, owls can see in daylight just as well as they can at night. They blink with their upper lid, and not with the lower lid as most other birds do. Another interesting feature is that all owls appear to be long-sighted and do not perceive objects that are close at hand. This makes the tactile sense located in the bristly hairs at the base of their beak all the more important, since it is this that enables them to hold and then swallow their prey.

Owls also have remarkably good hearing, which is far more sensitive than that of other birds. It is a tremendous help in the pursuit of prey at night and if it is very dark it is the bird's only guide. The large auditory orifices often occupy the whole lateral part of the edge of the facial disc, which is mounted beside the ears on a fold of skin which sometimes protrudes like a true outer ear. The auditory orifices are positioned asymmetrically and sometimes make the whole skull asymmetrical (Fig. 5). The reason for this asymmetry is that it assures better acoustic location of prey. Auditory sensitivity ranges from 50 to 21,000 Hz, so that owls can hear both deep, hooting voices and the squeaking of mice, voles and shrews.

Fig. 1. *An owl's foot is feathered right down to the claws and the outer toe can be turned backwards as well as forwards.*

Fig. 2. *Large owl's head, showing the facial disc or mask.*

269

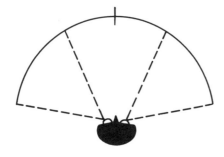

Fig. 3. An owl's eyes face forwards, so that owls have a much smaller range of vision than other birds (about 160 degrees, for three-dimensional vision 60 degrees).

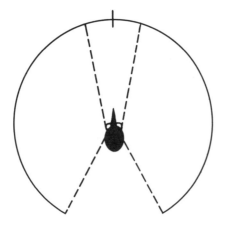

Fig. 4. In most other birds the eyes are on the sides of the head, so that the visual angle is about 300 degrees; the range of three-dimensional vision is only 30 degrees, however.

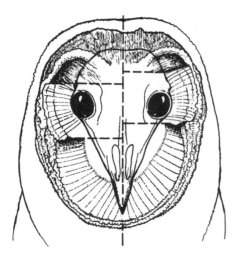

Fig. 5. Asymmetrical structure of an owl's skull. The large auditory orifices are situated asymmetrically; this allows the position of prey to be determined acoustically in the vertical plane.

The flight of owls is proverbial for its silence. On quiet evenings, an owl may fly over us, just above our head, without our hearing a sound. This is due to the soft, thick and fluffy feathers with which most of its usually robust body is covered. Even its flight feathers have soft vanes, and the silence of its flight is probably further enhanced by the pectinate edges of the outer vanes of some of the flight feathers.

Owls are carnivorous and kill their prey by stabbing it with their long, curving claws. They have no crop, their stomach is muscular and thin-walled and their intestine has long, wide diverticula. Owls swallow their prey (except for very large items) whole. The food remains only a short time in the stomach (for instance, a Barn Owl digests a mouse in $2-2\frac{1}{2}$ hours), so that there is no time for the bones to be digested and they are disgorged, together with fur and feathers, in the form of pellets.

Most owls do not build a nest of their own, but lay their eggs in holes, on the ground or in the abandoned nests of other birds. The eggs are noticeably rounded and are always white. A pronounced correlation exists between the rate at which owls reproduce and the available food supply. If there is too little food, owls may not nest at all; if food is abundant, they lay more eggs and may nest twice in the same year. When newly hatched, the nidicolous young are deaf and their eyes are closed; they hatch asynchronously, since incubation starts as soon as the first egg has been laid. There are thus considerable differences between them and, furthermore, they develop very slowly. Most owls are resident birds, but Arctic species and northern populations of several others fly further south for the winter, where there is no snow to prevent them from catching the small rodents on which they mainly live. The only explicit migrant in Europe is the Scops Owl.

Young Tengmalm's owls (Aegolius funereus) *have a characteristic X-shaped mark on their face.*

Barn Owl
Tyto alba

The Barn Owl is found throughout the world, except for the colder parts of North America, northern Europe and a large part of Asia. Originally it inhabited rocks and tree holes, as it still does in Africa, for example. Later, however, it attached itself to human settlements, especially in agricultural regions. It occupies church towers, old barns, lofts and ruined castles. Of late, its numbers in many parts of Europe have diminished, owing largely to the use of chemicals against voles, to the blocking of access to steeples and lofts and to the modernisation of agriculture in general. It likewise does not tolerate winters with severe frosts and heavy snowfalls, since it always uses the same nesting area, does not migrate and often does not survive the cold. Fortunately, there are compensations for such losses. In prolific vole years the Barn Owl nests twice and produces larger clutches. It normally nests in April and May. The 4—6 white eggs are laid in a dark corner on the bare ground or on crumbled pellets and are incubated for 30—34 days by the female owl. In years with successive litters of voles, nesting may continue up to October or November and the clutches may contain as many as 10—13 eggs. The young, which are fed by both the parent birds, are fledged at the age of about two months. Roughly 90% of the prey consists of small mammals, with voles in the majority, and the rest consists of birds, amphibians and insects. The owls catch their prey at night and spend the day in a dark corner in a loft. The Barn Owl (1) has yellow-buff upperparts with white and grey mottling; its underside is very variably coloured, from white to rusty-yellow with dark brown spots. It has a striking, whitish-grey heart-shaped facial disc and long legs covered with short feathers. It is smaller and slimmer than the Tawny Owl. It utters loud shrieks, snores and hissing sounds.

Scops Owl
Otus scops

The Scops Owl is a warm-climate species occurring in southern Europe, southern and western Asia and northwestern Africa. European populations spend the winter in central Africa; they leave at the end of August or in September and return in April. They settle in open country with old trees, in vineyards, in open woods and in orchards close to human settlements. Soon after its arrival, the male occupies a nesting territory, defends it and then attracts a female, which chooses the actual nesting site. This may be a hole in a tree or a wall, a nestbox or even a large old nest; the 3—5 white eggs are laid on the bare floor. It does not build a nest of its own. Nesting takes place only once a year, from May to July. The eggs are incubated for 24—26 days by the female, which the male keeps supplied with food. The female begins to incubate as soon as the first egg has been laid, so that the young are hatched asynchronously and there are marked differences in their sizes. The parents care for them in the nest for about three weeks and for a further two weeks after they have left the nest; they feed them mainly on large insects — beetles, moths, butterflies and caterpillars — and occasionally catch a small mammal or bird for them. They hunt chiefly in the early morning and at night. In the daytime, the Scops Owl, which is about the size of a Song Thrush, sits on a branch of a tree, usually close to the trunk. It has greyish (1) (less often brownish), dark-mottled plumage and a square head with ear tufts. Its eyes have lemon-yellow irises. In the spring, its monotonous 'kyew-kyew' can be heard in the night, at two- to three-second intervals, for hours on end.

Eagle Owl
Bubo bubo

The Eagle Owl is a powerfully built, majestic bird with a wingspan of 170 cm, which flies as silently as a ghost. During the daytime it remains hidden in the shelter of rocks or old trees, but in the evening it goes hunting in open country. It is a resident bird and always nests in the same site. One pair uses the same nest every year, and even if the nest is regularly robbed or is destroyed they move only a little way away. Eagle Owls start to announce their presence in the winter (generally in February). The whole night long the male utters its monotonous 'bōō-hōō', which sometimes changes over to a kind of throaty giggle; the female hoots its reply in a deeper, but quieter voice. The 2—4 white almost spherical eggs are laid between February and April, generally in a shallow hollow on a forest slope, under an uprooted tree or on a sheer rock face and far less often in a hole in a tree or an old nest of a bird of prey or a heron. They are incubated for 35 days by the female, while the male fetches food, which it hands over only at fixed, regularly used sites. The female likewise ejects pellets in special places, which are usually some way away from the nest. The parents care for the young for about nine weeks. Young Eagle Owls are not capable of breeding until they are two or three years old. Eagle Owls live on mammals and birds roughly up to the size of a hare or a pheasant. They inhabit much of Europe (but not Iceland, the Brit-ish Isles and the north of Scandinavia), almost the whole of Asia, and northern Africa, from lowlands up to altitudes of over 4,000 m. The Eagle Owl (1), which is about 70 cm tall, is the largest European owl. It has orange eyes and very pronounced ear tufts. Its plumage is yellowish to rusty-brown and is heavily streaked and spotted with blackish-brown or black.

Snowy Owl
Nyctea scandiaca

in which some birds find their way into central Europe or even to the Black Sea; this happens particularly in severe winters, or when the birds cannot find sufficient food further north. In places where there is an abundance of lemmings, one pair of Snowy Owls may nest within a territory of as little as 1 km². The Snowy Owl is a chiefly diurnal species; in the far north, in places where the sun does not set for a large part of the year, it would anyway be unable to survive as a nocturnal bird. Courting usually starts at the beginning of April, when a loud croaking 'krow-ow' or 'rick rick'can be heard from the owl's nesting area. There are usually 3–8 white eggs, which are laid between April and June in a depression in the ground; the actual number depends on how many rodents are available and may even rise to 14. The female generally begins to brood as soon as the first egg has been laid and from then on the male keeps it supplied with food. The young are hatched asynchronously in 33–37 days, at 18–28 days they spread out over the area around the nest, and at 50–57 days they are able to fly. They are cared for by both the parent birds, which feed them almost entirely on lemmings and voles. Otherwise, when not nesting, Snowy Owls are not afraid to tackle mammals up to the size of a hare and birds as large as a goose, since they are robust owls the same size as the Eagle Owl. The male is almost pure white, with a thin sprinkling of dark brown spots; the much larger female (1) is much more thickly spotted.

The Snowy Owl inhabits lowlands and mountains in treeless Arctic tundra over a narrow strip of northern Europe, Asia and North America and some adjoining islands in the Arctic Ocean. Its distribution is directly correlated to the incidence of lemmings and voles, its main prey. Since the number of lemmings varies from year to year, the Snowy Owl follows them around and nests where the largest numbers are to be found. Approximately every four years, these shifts take on the character of mass invasions,

Pygmy Owl
Glaucidium passerinum

The Pygmy Owl is a typical inhabitant of the Eurasian taiga. The northern limit of its distribution coincides with the edge of the forest belt; in the south, it extends in isolated pockets to the remains of feathers, fur and pellets are carefully removed every day. Only the female incubates, but the male brings it food in the evening and at daybreak. The young are hatched almost a look-out for prey from an elevated perch and hunt mostly in the evening or early morning, but also during the day, especially while rearing the young. The Pygmy Owl (1), as its name im-

parts of central and southern Europe. It inhabits chiefly coniferous and mixed woods in mountains and uplands, but in some places it lives in extensive lowland forests. It is a resident bird and remains in its nesting area the whole year round. The male's voice can be heard from the beginning of March with striking frequency, as it tempts a female to enter its chosen nest hole. In April or May the female lays the 3—6 white eggs in a tree hole (often one made by a woodpecker), always on the bare floor; simultaneously in 28 days. The male hunts for the family; when called up, the female takes over the prey, trims it a little and then, in the nest hole, divides it out among the offspring. The young remain about 30 days in the nest, but the parents continue to tend them for a further three weeks after they have left it. Pygmy Owls live mainly on small mammals and to a lesser extent on birds; they are not afraid to attack birds the same size as, or larger than, themselves. They keep plies, is the smallest owl and is no larger than a Bullfinch. It has dark brown upperparts, spotted and barred with white, and a greyish-white underside marked with dark streaking; it also has a short tail, which it frequently flicks. It has a very trusting nature and allows human beings to come exceptionally close to it (sometimes to within 5 m). In the spring it utters a repeated, melodious whistling 'kew kew' reminiscent of the call of the Bullfinch, and on sunny autumn days it gives forth a series of curious rising notes.

Little Owl
Athene noctua

The Little Owl inhabits open country with rows of trees and copses, old orchards, gardens and parks, open rocky terrain, and does not even shun built-up areas. The pairs remain together the whole of their life. During the courtship period, in March and April, the birds call loudly and frequently. They generally nest in holes in trees, rocks and walls, in steeples and in lofts. The 4–6 round, white eggs are laid in April or May, on the bare substrate; they are incubated for about 28 days, entirely by the female, which the male keeps supplied with food. The young leave the nest hole about four or five weeks after they have hatched, but are still fed outside it for some time afterwards. Little Owls feed mainly on small mammals (particularly voles) and birds (chiefly songbirds), but their diet also includes amphibians, reptiles, earthworms, insects and molluscs. They generally hunt in the evening, but sometimes during the day as well. The Little Owl inhabits the whole of Europe except Ireland and Scandinavia, and also a wide strip of territory across central and southern Asia and the north of Africa; it was introduced into Britain in the late 19th century and has also been introduced into New Zealand.

During the past 30 years or so its numbers in Europe have severely decreased. It is a resident bird, but in the winter some individuals undertake short dispersals.

The Little Owl (1) is roughly the size of a Blackbird; it has a short tail, a wide, flat head, short wings and relatively long legs. It has dark brown, white-spotted upperparts and a whitish underside marked with longitudinal rows of dark brown spots. It flies with undulating movements, usually quite close to the ground (2). When excited it bobs up and down. This owl's spring call is a repetitive 'kee-uw'; if excited it utters a yapping 'keff'.

2

277

Tawny Owl
Strix aluco

The Tawny Owl inhabits the whole of Europe except Ireland and the north, some parts of southeastern Asia and a small portion of northern Africa. It is a resident bird and remains in its nesting area the whole year round. In mild winters it begins courtship as early as December, but mostly not until the middle of February; the resultant union is probably permanent. The pairs nest once a year, as a rule in March and April. They prefer old deciduous woods, but are also to be found in mixed woods and conifer forests and in rows of trees, in parks and in gardens with old trees. They nest in tree holes, large nestboxes and lofts, less often in old nests of birds of prey and sometimes on the ground; they do not build a nest of their own. In March or April the female usually lays 3—4 round, white eggs on the floor of the hole and incubates them itself; while brooding, the only times it leaves the nest are in the evening, to regurgitate pellets, and at night, when it receives food from the male. The young hatch in 28—30 days and for the first ten days or so the female never leaves them; it keeps the nest clean by swallowing their droppings and pellets. The young leave the nest at the age of 28—35 days and undertake short flights at about 50 days. The Tawny Owl has a very varied diet composed mainly of small mammals, together with birds, amphibians and insects. It hunts its prey only after dark. It occurs in a grey (1) and a rust-brown form. In the mating season its call is a melodious tremulous 'hoooo-hoo-hooooo'; its typical normal call is 'ke-wick'.

Ural Owl
Strix uralensis

The Ural Owl inhabits the European and Asian taiga and occurs in isolated pockets in mountain forests of south-central Europe. It is a resident, but individual birds or parts of populations occasionally roam about in the region of their breeding areas. The size of the populations varies with the number of forest rodents; it is largest when this rises, and falls almost to zero when there is a dearth of rodents. The Ural Owl frequents mostly mixed and deciduous woods and has a special predilection for unspoilt beechwoods. Courtship, characterised by deep hooting calls, takes place in February, nesting from March to May. The birds nest in tree holes, often in old nests of birds of prey, in niches in buildings, on rock faces and in nestboxes; they do not build a nest of their own. The number of eggs, which are laid on the bare floor, depends on the amount of food available. In years of plenty there are 4—6 eggs, in lean years only 1—2 or maybe none. The female, which incubates the eggs for 27—29 days, is kept supplied with food by the male. The eggs are laid at three- to five-day intervals. After the young are hatched, the male brings food and the female portions it out. The young remain four to five weeks in the nest and then disperse to neighbouring trees. The whole family wanders about in the vicinity of the nest for about two months; they live on small vertebrates and insects. Ural Owls (1) are essentially nocturnal, but while rearing the young they will also hunt by day, on occasion more so than by night. In appearance they resemble the large, grey-coloured Tawny Owl, but have a distinctly longer tail. In the spring they draw attention to themselves by their hooting 'hoo, wow-wow-wow' call.

279

Great Grey Owl
Strix nebulosa

In Europe the Great Owl lives only in the north of Scandinavia eastwards, and otherwise in the most northerly parts of Asia and North America. In invasion years it spreads to the south of the Scandinavian Peninsula and to Estonia. It nests in dense, tall fir- and pinewoods with an admixture of birches, but hunts in open country, in peat-bogs, on deforested ground and in clearings. Courtship reaches its climax in April or the first half of May; the pairs then begin to inspect old nests of birds of prey and when they have chosen one the female lays the 3—6 white eggs. The actual number of eggs depends on the supply of small rodents, so that in years of abundance there may be more and in deficient years none at all. The eggs are laid at two-day intervals and are incubated for 28—30 days by the female. The young leave the nest at the age of 20—30 days, before they are fledged, and scatter over the nearby branches; at about eight weeks they undertake their first short flights. If the rodent supply is good, the families remain in their nesting area up to the end of October; if it is poor, they soon move on to a more promising place. In the nesting season, 90 % of their diet consists of voles, in particular field voles, but their prey actually ranges from shrews to mountain hares and from small songbirds to Ptarmigans. The Great Grey Owl (1) is almost as large as the Eagle Owl. It is grey to whitish-grey, with rows of pronounced spots down its underside. There are striking whitish and black concentric circles on its face and white semicircular areas between its unusually small yellow eyes; it has a black chin. Its call is a hooting 'hoo-hoo-hoo-hoooh'.

Long-eared Owl
Asio otus

Mice and voles form 90% of the diet of the Long-eared Owl. The best way to confirm this is to watch the birds when they assemble in the winter at the edge of a wood or in a small copse. Very often dozens of these owls roost there during the day for several weeks and hundreds of pellets pile up under the trees. If we were to inspect them, in each

seconds. The pairs nest in old nests made by birds of prey, crows, pigeons and squirrels. The 4–6 round white eggs are laid in March or April and are incubated by the female, which begins to sit after laying the first egg; the incubation period is 27–28 days. The male feeds the female and later brings food for the young, but this is presented

to them by the female. At the age of 21–28 days the young owls (2) crawl out on to the branches around the nest and at night their screeching 'psheea' calls can be heard; at five weeks they are able to fly. In years with a plentiful supply of voles, the adults may nest twice. Long-eared Owls hunt after dusk and during the night. They inhabit practically the

of these pellets we should find several vole or mouse jaws and skulls. In the nesting season, Long-eared Owls frequent woods (often coniferous) alternating with meadows, copses, groups of trees and patches of shrubs. In the spring, the male performs a display flight in which it claps its wings together under its body; its territorial call is a muffled 'hoo-oo', repeated regularly at intervals of about three

2

whole of Europe except the most northerly parts, and also a wide strip of territory across the middle of Asia and North America and a small part of northern Africa; they are partial migrants (mainly migratory in the north of the range). The Long-eared Owl (1) is a roughly half-sized version of the Eagle Owl. It has long ear tufts and yellowish-brown plumage marked with dark brown spots; its eyes are orange.

Short-eared Owl
Asio flammeus

Few owls have such a wide distribution as the Short-eared Owl. It inhabits almost the whole of northern and eastern Europe, the northern half of Asia, North America and part of South America; the southern limits of its range are, however, very variable. Its northern populations are mostly migratory; in more southerly regions its migration, which follows particularly on the heels of rodent population collapses, is sometimes of an invasive character. The Short-eared Owl nests in open country with marshes and wet meadows; in the north it lives in the tundra. The spring display of the male bird is very striking and often takes place during the day. The owl circles higher and higher around the nesting site, gliding from time to time and uttering 'boo-boobooboo…' calls in a hollow voice, and then suddenly swoops, clapping its wings hurriedly several times under its body. This is the only European owl which actually gathers material (dry and green parts of plants) and builds a nest; the nest is always on the ground, in grass, heather, reeds or similar cover. Although the normal nesting season is March to May, in years with a rich supply of small rodents the birds have also been known to nest in the winter. The female lays 4−8 (but sometimes up to 12) white eggs and incubates them for 24−28 days. At the age of 12−17 days the young disperse outside the nest, but are not able to fly for about five weeks. Both the parents look after them. The Short-eared Owl (1) resembles the Long-eared Owl in size and coloration, but it is generally lighter and its yellow eyes are set in a black mask. The ear tufts are short, are usually folded down and are most often invisible. The owl almost invariably perches on the ground; if startled, it flies jerkily away, wavering and rocking as it goes.

Tengmalm's Owl, Boreal Owl
Aegolius funereus

Tengmalm's Owl inhabits mostly extensive conifer forests, but in some place it also nests in completely deciduous woods, beechwoods and oakwoods. In northern Europe and Asia it is distributed over an unbroken area, but in the south it occurs in isolated pockets, which are confined mainly to mountain ranges and their foothills; it also nests in the Caucasus and in Alaska and northern Canada. It is a resident bird, but some individuals living in the north move a few hundred kilometres further south for the winter. The male's display, which usually takes place from March onwards, is accompanied by a tuneful, hooting 'poo-poo-poo-poo-poo' like the call of a Hoopoe or the distant sound of a steam-engine. It nests in tree holes, preferably in old woodpecker holes but frequently in nestboxes. The round white eggs, of which there are usually 4—7, are laid in March, April or May, on the heaped remains of prey and pellets on the floor of the nest hole. They are incubated for 26—27 days by the female, which the male keeps supplied with food. Unlike the Pygmy Owl, the birds do not keep the hole clear of their droppings and pellets, so that by the time they have finished nesting it is in a very sorry state. At the age of 30—35 days the young fly from the nest but are still fed for a long time outside it by the parents. Tengmalm's Owl lives mainly on small mammals and birds, which it catches only at night. It has dark brown upperparts (1) with cream-coloured spots, and a whitish underside with brown mottling, spots and streaks. It is slightly larger than the Little Owl, has a rounder head and a more contrasting facial disc and its legs are feathered right down to the claws. It flies in a straight line, sits upright on a branch, well out of sight, and rarely roosts in a hole, even in the winter.

283

Twilight hunters, Enduring fliers and Birds with rainbow plumage

Nightjars
Swifts
Rollers and Allies

CAPRIMULGIFORMES

APODIFORMES

CORACIIFORMES

Nightjars are active chiefly at night and after dusk. They have a wide, flat-topped head and large eyes (Fig. 1). The corners of their short, wide beak extend back to the eyes or beyond and the beak is made to appear still wider by the projecting bristle-like feathers at its base, an adaptation for catching nocturnal insects on the wing. It has short, slender legs, with three toes pointing forwards and one backwards (Fig. 2). The toes are incapable of grasping a branch properly and perhaps that is why nightjars sit lengthwise on branches, and not across them like other birds. On the ground they are equally awkward.

Like owls, nightjars have soft plumage; it is dark, cryptically marked with spots, streaks and bars in the manner characteristic of nocturnal birds, and it matches the bark of the trees or the colour of the ground. Nightjars have long, narrow wings and usually have a long tail. They fly extremely well, somewhat in the manner of swallows. They have remarkably thin skin.

Nightjars generally nest on the ground, without building a nest. They all lay two eggs and the young are nidicolous. The parents feed the young, beak to beak, on regurgitated food and care for them for a long time.

The order Apodiformes comprises swifts and hummingbirds, although the latter are confined to the American continent. Swifts have long, pointed, curved wings, whose length is determined mainly by the long 'hand', made longer still by the outermost primaries, which are the longest, in relation to body length, of any bird. Swifts are skilful fliers and spend most of their life on the wing. They are wonderfully well adapted to life in the air, where they live on aerial plankton (mainly minute insects and spiders) which they catch in their gaping beak as they fly; they also sleep and mate in the air. Their short, spindly legs are useless for walking and can be employed only for clinging to rocks and walls; when not grasping, all four toes, which have sharp claws, point forwards (Fig. 3).

Swifts generally nest in colonies. At mating time, the remarkably large salivary glands in their beak swell and secrete a substance which hardens on contact with the air and is used for sticking the nest material together; some species make the

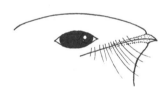

Fig. 1. *The flat head of a Nightjar, showing the short, wide-cleft beak surrounded by tough, bristle-like feathers.*

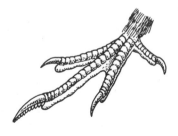

Fig. 2. *The Nightjar has short, puny legs and is therefore very awkward on the ground.*

nest entirely of saliva. As a rule, the clutch consists of only two white eggs; the newly hatched young are naked and blind and are dependent for a long period of time on parental care. In some species, prolonged cold weather, together with a lack of insects, causes the young to fall into a state resembling hypothermia, which enables them to survive until the situation improves.

Rollers and allies are an order of birds showing a great diversity in appearance, but with many features in common as regards their body structure and plumage. Their legs are adapted for an arboreal mode of life and the toes are either free (Hoopoes), or are slightly (rollers, Fig. 4) or markedly (Kingfishers, Fig. 5) fused. Their plumage is usually rather thin, but brightly coloured and often with a metallic sheen; plumage differences between males and females are minimal. Down is usually absent.

Fig. 5. *The foot of a Kingfisher, whose toes are distinctly more fused.*

The members of this order nest in tree holes or in burrows excavated in steep sandy or clayey banks. The eggs are almost always white; both the parents share in their incubation and in the care of the young. The young are nidicolous; when newly hatched, their eyes are closed and they are featherless; Hoopoes, which have downy young, are an exception. The young are nest-bound for a long time. The young of some species are characterised by spiny plumage; this is because the sheaths of the growing feathers rupture relatively late, so that after their long incarceration the feathers are compressed and look like spines.

Fig. 3. *The short, prehensile foot of a Swift. The toes, which all point forwards, including the first, terminate in sharp claws.*

Fig. 4. *The foot of a Roller, showing the partly fused toes.*

The Bee-eater (Merops apiaster) *has a long, awl-like beak, which is very useful both for catching insects and for digging burrows.*

Nightjar, Goatsucker
Caprimulgus europaeus

The Nightjar is a nocturnal bird frequenting the margins of woods, clearings, glades, undergrowth and heaths, which superstition has endowed with many strange properties, the chief one being its supposed habit of visiting farms at night and sucking milk from goats and cows. This is reflected in its vernacular name in many European languages. The Nightjar is strictly a migrant. It does not return from its winter quarters until the end of April or the first half of May, when the male betrays its presence by an alternately rising and falling, churring 'urrrurrrurrr', lasting for minutes on end. During its acrobatic display flight it raises its wings and claps them above its back. In May, June or July the female lays 2 greyish, brown-mottled eggs (2) on the ground, in a depression in conifer needles, moss, heather or sand. It incubates them most of the time itself, briefly relieved in the evening and morning by the male. The young hatch in 18—19 days, remain two or three days in the nest and then run about in the vicinity like chicks. At feeding time they open their beaks very wide, while the parents regurgitate the nocturnal insects they have brought and thrust them deep into their gullet. While the male completes the feeding of the first young, the female begins to sit on the second clutch. The young are able to fly at 16—18 days and are independent at 30—35 days. In August or September the birds depart for tropical and southern Africa. They breed in Europe north to the middle of Scandinavia, in central and southern Asia and in a small area in northern Africa. The Nightjar (1) is a little larger than a Blackbird; it has a large head and large eyes, very short legs, a small, but widely cleft beak, and inconspicuous plumage the colour of bark. It spends the daytime sitting — or rather lying — flat on the ground or on a thick branch.

2

In most of Europe, flocks of Swifts do not appear in towns and villages until the end of April or the beginning of May. They fly in sudden swerves and swoops and draw attention to themselves by their loud cries. Today they are to be found mainly in human settlements, but originally they inhabited cliffs, rocks and hollow trees. They spend the whole of the day in the air, where they not only find food and building material for the nest, but where they also sleep and even mate. The adult birds not only return to the same town and the same building to breed, but they actually use the same nest. The nests are generally built on cornices under eaves, behind rafters, in dark corners and holes and less often in crevices in rocks or in holes in trees. If there are not enough suitable places available, the birds may make do with a Starling's nestbox or a House Sparrow's nest, after first evicting the original occupants, throwing out the eggs or young and rebuilding the nest itself. The Swift's nest is a flat mass of straw, fibres and feathers stuck together with saliva. The 2−3 white eggs, which are laid in May or June, are incubated for 18−20 days by both the parent birds in turn. The young develop very slowly and take 40−50 days to rear, according to the weather and the incidence of tiny insects, which the adult birds present to their offspring in balls of 390−1,500 at a time. As early as the end of July or the beginning of August, Swifts leave for their winter quarters in southern Africa. They nest over almost the whole of Europe, a large part of Asia and the coast of northern Africa. The Swift (1) is somewhat larger than the House Martin, its plumage is almost entirely smoky-black and it has a pale, whitish chin; it has a short, forked tail and narrow, sickle-shaped wings. Its call is a frequent, high-pitched scream 'tsrrreee' or 'sweeree'.

Kingfisher
Alcedo atthis

The Kingfisher frequents clean streams and rivers and less often lakes and ponds. It nests in burrows excavated in the spring in clayey or sandy banks. At the end of February, the birds form pairs the 6—8 round, white, glossy eggs are laid. At first, the eggs lie on the floor of the chamber, but in time a layer of regurgitated fish bones piles up underneath them. The eggs are incubated for Kingfisher inhabits the whole of Europe except the most northerly parts; it also lives in Asia and northern Africa. In the winter it roams about near its nesting area, and only birds from the

after a lively chase alongside the water. The male tries to 'impress' the female with fluttering or gliding flights and then presents her with a fish. When digging the burrow, the birds mostly use their beak; their legs are employed only to throw the loose earth out. The burrow is 5—6 cm across at the entrance, is 30—100 cm long and terminates in a rounded chamber in which 18—21 days by both the parents in turn. They also both feed the young on insects and small fish, which form a substantial part of the diet of the adult birds, too. At the age of 23—27 days the young Kingfishers fly out; the parents look after them for a few days more and then begin to nest a second time. Sometimes they even manage to nest a third time, so that the nesting season is very long — from April to August. The north and east undertake long migrations southwards or westwards. The Kingfisher is brilliantly coloured, with a gleaming bluish-green back and a reddish-orange underside (1). It almost skims the water as it flies, uttering a long, shrill, whistling 'teeeet' or a shorter repetitive 'tittittitt'. The adult birds are a little larger and more robust than a sparrow.

Bee-eater
Merops apiaster

The Bee-eater likes warmth. It inhabits southern Europe, south-west Asia and the north of Africa, but if the spring is exceptionally warm single birds and groups of birds stray north as far as Denmark, the Netherlands and Britain and may even nest there. The Bee-eater is strictly a migrant; it about building the nest burrow (2). They excavate an opening with powerful strokes of their beak and throw out the loose soil with their feet, until they have made a passage 80—200 cm long and 6—7 cm across, terminating in a chamber some 12 cm high and 25—30 cm wide, a feat which takes them eight to 14 days. The 5—6 round white eggs are laid in May, June or July and are incubated for 20—22 days by both the parent birds in turn. The parents likewise both feed the young, 20 days in the burrow and a further 12 days or so outside it. During August or the first half of Sep-

spends the winter in tropical and southern Africa and in recent years has also begun to nest there, as a result of colonisation by previous migrant populations. It nests in sandpits or steep clay banks, generally in large or small colonies and seldom in isolated pairs. The birds usually do not arrive at their breeding sites until May. Their display, which lasts for days, is accompanied by jerking movements of their head and wings; as soon as a pair roosts together, it is a sign that the pair-bond has been firmly established. The partners then set

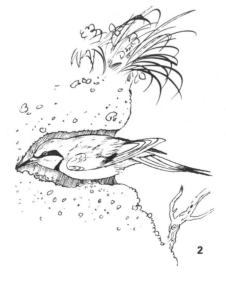

tember, the birds leave the colony. They live entirely on insects, their chief prey being dragonflies, damselflies, wasps, bees, butterflies and moths. The Bee-eater (1) is one of the most gaudily coloured birds. It has a greenish-blue underside, a yellow throat and a reddish and yellowish-brown back. Its two central tail feathers are elongated and taper off to a point. It is about the size of a large thrush, but its flight is more like a Swallow's, interspersed with gliding. Its call is a repetitive 'prruik.

Roller
Coracias garrulus

The Roller inhabits southern and eastern Europe (in the 19th century it nested as far as southeastern Sweden), southwestern Asia and northern Africa. In Europe, its numbers have recently severely decreased. The time spent in its breeding areas is very short; it arrives in April or May and migrates to tropical and southern Africa in August or September. It settles in flat or hilly country with scattered copses and avenues of hollow trees, or at the edge of old deciduous woods bordering on meadows and pastureland. It nests singly, although in suitable places several pairs may nest together. The birds arrive at their breeding sites already in pairs; the male's display consists of aerial acrobatics over the nesting site, with headlong swoops and sudden ascents. The Roller always nests in holes, generally in a tree and less often in a clay-pit or a wall; sometimes it will use a nestbox. The 4—5 eggs are laid in June or July on the floor of the hole; they are incubated for 17—19 days by both the sexes in turn. The adults both feed the young, which leave the nest at the age of 25—30 days, when they are already able to fly.

The parents do not remove the young birds' droppings from the nest, but these dry and harden very quickly, so that the nest is relatively clean. After the young have left the nest, the parents still bring them insects, snails, frogs, lizards and small mammals. In the Roller's plumage we can find every shade of blue and only its back is chestnut-brown (1). It likes to sit on vantage points, such as telegraph posts or wires or the top of a tree, keeping a look-out for prey on the ground. It flies in a similar manner to a Jackdaw. Its call while nesting is a raucous 'rak-rak-rak'. The adult birds are about the same size as a Turtle Dove.

Hoopoe
Upupa epops

The Hoopoe (1) is another handsome member of this order. Its plumage is orange-buff and its wings and tail are conspicuously marked with black and white bars; it also has a long, thin, slightly curving beak and on its head an erectile, fan-like crest of black-tipped feathers (3). It lives in open country with meadows, pastures and fields with scattered copses and groups of trees providing sufficient holes, or at the edge of open deciduous woods. It breeds in Europe, except the north, in the whole southern half of Asia and almost the whole of Africa. In Europe its numbers appear to be steadily declining. It is a migrant; in August or September it leaves for Africa south of the Sahara and for southern Asia, and in April it

1

2

returns to its breeding sites. When courting, the male presents the female with prey. The nest is a hole in a tree, a wall or a pile of stones, and in southern Europe and Africa the Hoopoe also nests around human settlements. There are usually 5–7 greyish, finely dark-speckled eggs (2), which are laid between May and July. They are incubated by the female, which is kept supplied with food the whole time by the male. The young are hatched in about 16 days and remain in the nest for four weeks. At first they are fed only by the female, but after

roughly ten days the male also lends a hand. The nestlings have a curious form of 'chemical defence'; when frightened or in danger, they release an evil-smelling liquid from their cloaca and squirt it over the intruder with unerring accuracy. The parents feed the young on insects and their larvae, spiders, worms

and sometimes small lizards; they collect their food on the ground, often from dung. Their undulating flight is characterised by the peculiar jerking way in which they flap their wings. Their call is a three- or five-syllable 'hoopoopoop'. The adult birds are the size of a Turtle Dove.

3

293

Skilled carpenters

Woodpeckers and Allies

PICIFORMES

The woodpecker order comprises six families of birds differing from one another in appearance. We shall ignore most of them here, chiefly because the majority live in America, although many of them are very interesting, such as toucans (Ramphastidae) with their huge but very light and strikingly coloured beaks, or honeyguides (Indicatoridae), which are characterised by nest parasitism and the ability to live on beeswax by means of symbiotic bacteria in their digestive tract. Here we are concerned with the largest family, the woodpeckers (Picidae), which are specialists in climbing tree trunks and in 'carpentry'. They live mainly on the larvae of wood- and bark-boring insects, but they also eat ants and conifer seeds. Climbing is made possible by their specially adapted feet, on which the first and fourth toes point backwards and the second and third toes forwards (Fig. 1). They move over the trunk in small hops, digging their sharp claws into cracks in the bark. When climbing, they prop themselves on their very strong, flexible, pointed tail feathers (Fig. 2), with their body leaning away from the trunk to allow their head a sufficient range for pecking. Their beak is a perfect woodcutter's tool − axe, chisel and hammer in one. It is thick and wedge-shaped and is covered with a very hard horny sheath. The head is also well adapted for standing the innumerable shocks it must receive as a result of the bird's hacking activities; the bones of the skull are much thicker than in other birds, and the sutures, together with the beak, are fused to form a compact, exceptionally strong capsule protecting the brain from concussion. By tapping the trunk, the woodpecker determines where the tree has been attacked by insects; it can evidently tell, from the different sound made by the wood, those places where a larva is concealed. As soon as the larva

has been located, the bird hacks a hole in the wood and then goes to work with its hard-tipped, barbed, extensible tongue, which is coated with a sticky substance secreted by special salivary glands. Impaled on the tongue, the prey is withdrawn into the bird's oral cavity. The tongue can stretch a long way along the insects' tunnels, since it is connected to the extraordinarily long posterior horns of the hyoid bone, which go right around the skull and back again to the front of the head (Fig. 3).

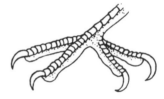

Fig. 1. *A climber's foot, with two toes pointing forwards and two backwards.*

Fig. 2. *Tail of a Great Spotted Woodpecker, with pointed feathers and hard spurs which act as a support when the bird climbs tree trunks.*

From time to time, under a tree in a wood, we may come across a pile of broken cones with their seeds missing. This is probably also the work of a woodpecker. Some species push a cone into a convenient crack in a trunk and when it is wedged in position they pick out the oily seeds, like a blacksmith hammering on an anvil (Fig. 4).

Woodpeckers also use their beak to help them build their nest. They nest in holes which they excavate themselves, mainly in rotting, but sometimes in completely healthy trees. Their eggs are round and, since they do not need to be camouflaged, they are white. The embryos and the young develop very quickly. At first, the young are blind and generally naked and have to be fed by their parents. In most woodpecker species the male and female have differently coloured heads.

Woodpeckers usually have penetrating voices audible over long distances, but their 'instrumental' performances are much more interesting. In the breeding season they drum with their beak on dead branches, tree trunks or stumps at a rate which almost leaves a machine-gun standing. Like their song, the purpose of their drumming is to mark the limits of their nesting area.

Fig. 4. *The way in which an old cone is removed from a woodpecker's 'forge' and a new one is fixed in place.*

The Three-toed Woodpecker (Picoides tridactylus) *usually hacks out its nest holes in dying tree trunks.*

Fig. 3. *The exceptionally long, protrusible tongue of woodpeckers, which has hooks at the tip, is anchored to the forehead by means of the posterior horns of the hyoid bone, which encircle the whole of the skull.*

Wryneck
Jynx torquilla

The Wryneck is the only migratory European woodpecker. It winters in tropical Africa, but it inhabits the whole of Europe except Iceland, the British Isles (where a few nest) and the north of Scandinavia, and also a wide belt of territory across the middle of Asia to Japan and part of northern Africa. Recently, its numbers in Europe have severely decreased. The Wryneck frequents mainly open deciduous and mixed woods, parks, orchards, gardens, and avenues and riverside trees. Immediately after its arrival in April, we can hear its wailing 'quee-quee-quee', repeated 10–20 times; this is part of its advertising display, during which the female may actually call more often than the male. The birds bow to each other, spread their wings and tail and ruffle the feathers on their head and neck. Wrynecks generally nest in tree holes and nest-boxes and less frequently in a hole in a bank or a wall; quite often they take possession of a hollow already occupied by other birds, whose nest material and eggs or young they then throw out. In May or June the female lays 8–11 white eggs on the floor of the hole; the parents conscientiously incubate them for 11–14 days and both care for the young in the nest for 18–21 days. As the young grow, they develop an interesting method of frightening enemies away. If in danger they extend and contract their neck, twist their head, ruffle the feathers on the top of their head and hiss like snakes. While nesting, the adult birds behave similarly and their tactics are in fact often effective. The Wryneck (1) lives mainly on ants and their various stages, caterpillars, spiders and butterflies and moths. It is about the size of a Nightingale or a large sparrow and is an inconspicuous greyish-brown colour, heavily mottled, barred and vermiculated.

Grey-headed Woodpecker
Picus canus

The Grey-headed Woodpecker inhabits eastern and central Europe; it extends westwards only as far as France and northwards to the southwest tip of Scandinavia. Its distribution then continues over a narrow strip across the middle of Asia to the Sea of Japan and it occupies the whole southeastern corner of Asia, including Sumatra. It prefers deciduous and mixed

2♂

woods, but in mountains it inhabits conifer woods almost to the upper tree-limit; it also occurs in old parks and gardens. Its loud voice can be heard from March onwards, and it drums resoundingly on branches, tin roofs and telegraph poles. In the spring it chooses a rotting or dead tree and begins to excavate a nest hole in the damaged softer wood, a labour usually involving more than 14 days of toil. In April or May the female usually lays 5−7 (but sometimes up to 10) gleaming white eggs on the bare floor of the hole. The parents incubate them for 17−18 days, and brood the young birds up to the age of 10−12 days; the young leave the nest at 23−28 days and soon become independent. While feeding the young, the parents bring food and regurgitate it into the gullets of the nestlings in eight to ten successive portions; the Green Woodpecker and Black Woodpecker do the same. The young are fed mainly on ants and their eggs, larvae and pupae and less on beetles and other insects. In the summer the birds eat various fruits and berries; in winter they visit birdtables, particularly in the north. The Grey-headed Woodpecker is about the same size as the Great Spotted Woodpecker; it has greyish-green plumage, with a grey head and neck and a narrow black moustachial stripe. The male (2) can be distinguished from the female (1) by the red patch on its fore crown. It has a soft advertising call, which sounds like 'keekeekeekee', is slower and more melancholic than the call of the Green Woodpecker and generally falls away towards the end.

1

Green Woodpecker
Picus viridis

2♀

The Green Woodpecker resembles the Grey-headed Woodpecker, but is mainly olive-green, with a paler and yellower underside; its rump is yellow. The male (1) and the female (2) both have a completely red crown and a black eye-mask, but the male has a red-centred moustachial stripe whereas the female's is wholly black. The advertising call is a ringing series of laughing 'klee-klee-klee-klee' notes, in which the 'l' is clearly audible. The Green Woodpecker is a predominantly European species and inhabits practically the whole of that continent except Iceland, Ireland and the northern half of Scandinavia; in Asia it occupies only a narrow strip between the Caspian Sea and the Persian Gulf. It lives in open country with copses, avenues, orchards and old gardens and in light, open woods. The nest, which is excavated in a rotting or crumbling trunk by the combined efforts of both the sexes, is often used for several years. In April or May, the female lays 5–7 white eggs with a strikingly glossy shell; they are incubated for 15–17 days by both the parent birds, with the male often brooding at night. At the age of about ten days the young make their way to the opening of the nest and are then fed there by the parents. At about 20 days they climb about outside the hole, but return to the nest for the night, when the male keeps them company. At 27–28 days they are fledged, but the parents still feed them for a further three weeks. Green Woodpeckers live mainly on ants and their developmental stages. They make a hole up to 75 cm deep in an anthill, thrust in their long, sticky tongue among the ants, withdraw it again and swallow their catch. They also eat other insects, but on a smaller scale. They have been reported to peck rings around tree trunks in the spring and to drink the escaping drops of sap. Both male and female are a little larger than the Grey-headed Woodpecker.

Black Woodpecker
Dryocopus martius

The Black Woodpecker inhabits extensive coniferous, mixed and deciduous woods in mountains and lowlands; these must, however, have a sufficient quantity of old, thick trunks in which the birds can excavate their nest holes. Some pairs make a new nest every year, others use the same hole for several years. The birds usually choose an internally damaged tree, but even so it takes them 10–28 days to excavate their hole, which can be up to 60 cm deep and 15–25 cm wide. The 4–5 pure white eggs, which are laid in April or May, lie on a little pile of splinters and rotting wood. Both the parents incubate and they relieve each other every one to three hours. The male has most of the worry, however, since at night it broods alone and later it usually has the task of keeping the nest clear of droppings and of spending the night with the young until they emerge at the age of 24–28 days. The parents continue to care for the young for a further month or more, but then drive them out of their nesting area. The Black Woodpecker hacks its food out of trunks with its powerful beak and hammers rotten stumps to pieces. It lives mainly on wood and bark beetles and their larvae and on *Camponotus* ants. The Black Woodpecker inhabits practically the whole of Europe except Iceland and the British Isles, but in the south and west it occurs only in isolated pockets; it also inhabits a large part of Asia. It is the same size as a crow and is thus the largest woodpecker. Both sexes are black, but, while

2♀

the male (1) has a large red cap, the female (2) has only a small patch of red at the back of its head. Unlike other woodpeckers, this one flies in more of a straight line. Its advertising call, a loud 'kwee-kwee-kwee-kwee', is similar to that of the Green Woodpecker but has a 'wilder' quality; when perched, it also utters a wailing 'klee-eh' reminiscent of the call of a Buzzard.

Great Spotted Woodpecker
Dendrocopos major

While taking a walk in the woods, we may come across a quantity of ragged and seedless cones lying in a pile under a pine tree. Above us, in the tree, we should find a crack in the bark in which a Great Spotted Woodpecker wedges the cones, so that it can pick out the seeds in comfort and then discard the empty cone. In the summer, however, this species lives mainly on insects living in wood and beneath bark, with special emphasis on bark beetles. It also often pecks rings around the trees and drinks the escaping sap. The Great Spotted Woodpecker inhabits every type of wood and forest and also large parks over almost the whole of Europe, a large part of Asia and northwestern Africa. It is a resident and nomadic bird; birds from northern Europe irregularly invade western and central Europe. Both the sexes make the hole for the nest, but the male may do most of the work, which takes two to three weeks. The 5−7 white eggs are laid between April and June and are incubated for 12−13 days by both the parents. The parents feed the young for the first 16 days inside the hole and then at the entrance. Unlike the preceding species, they carry the food visibly in their

4

beak. At the age of three weeks the young fly from the nest, but for a time the parents still bring them food. The Great Spotted Woodpecker is the size of a thrush and measures about 23 cm. It has black and white chequered plumage with a typical pattern and can be recognised by the unbroken black stripe leading from its beak to the back of its head (4), and also by its red vent and undertail-coverts, which stand out sharply against the white of its belly. The male (1) has a red patch on the back of its

head, the female (2) a wholly black crown; the juveniles (3) have a completely red-topped head. The call of the Great Spotted Woodpecker is a short, sharp 'tchick' and occasionally a longer 'kikikiki'. The birds drum in relatively short (less than one second) bursts towards the end of which the drumming grows faster and fainter; they drum particularly actively in the spring and sometimes as early as the end of the winter.

2♀

3

Middle Spotted Woodpecker
Dendrocopos medius

The Middle Spotted Woodpecker inhabits Europe, with the exception of the southern half of Spain, the British Isles and northwards; it also occurs in Asia Minor, Iran and Iraq. It inhabits deciduous or at most mixed woods, in lowlands and uplands, and it has a special predilection for hornbeam and oakwoods. The felling of deciduous woods and their replacement with conifers has led to a marked decrease in its numbers in Europe; in the present century it has disappeared completely from Denmark and recently almost certainly from Sweden. Its nest holes are made chiefly in thoroughly rotten or dry trunks or branches, since its beak is not strong enough to tackle the wood of healthy trees. The work takes up to 20 days. The male starts spending the night in the hole before the first egg is laid. The 5—6 pure white eggs appear in the nest between the end of April and June and are incubated for 11—14 days by both the parent birds in turn. When the young are about 16 days old, the parents begin feeding them in the entrance to the nest and stop removing their droppings. At 20—23 days the young leave the nest and are fed outside it. Middle Spotted Woodpeckers obtain most of their food from the surface of the tree or from cracks in the bark and seldom penetrate the wood. They gather insects at all their developmental stages, and also feed on other invertebrates, berries and fruit and the seeds of trees. In size, appearance and pattern (2), the Middle Spotted Woodpecker closely resembles the Great Spotted Woodpecker, but the male, female and juvenile all have a completely red crown, the pink (not red) colour of the undertail-coverts blends gradually into the white of the belly, and the flanks are lightly streaked (1). This woodpecker's call is a soft 'ptik', joined together in a long series; the courting male utters an unmistakable, nasal, mewing 'wait wait wait' call.

2

303

Lesser Spotted Woodpecker

Dendrocopos minor

and uplands. It is found at the edge of open deciduous woods and in old parks, avenues, gardens, orchards and waterside vegetation, and it shuns woods in which conifers preponderate. It prefers deciduous trees with rotting or damaged trunks and side branches for its nest holes, which are usually excavated by both the sexes but sometimes only by the female; it has also been known to use nestboxes. The 5–6 white eggs are laid in April, May or June and are incubated for about 11 days by both the parents in

The Lesser Spotted Woodpecker, which is the size of a sparrow, is the smallest European woodpecker. It has large numbers of black and white stripes on its wings and back (3), but no red undertail-coverts. The male (1) has a red crown, the female (2) a black and white crown. In the spring the birds utter series of high-pitched, clear 'kee-kee-kee-kee' notes and frequently drum on the trees. Since they choose thin branches, their drumming is fainter and higher than that of related woodpeckers, but the bursts are longer (over

3

one second) and the intervals between the individual bursts are short. Another component of their display is their curious, slow, bat-like flight. The Lesser Spotted Woodpecker lives mostly in open country in lowlands

turn. The parents care for the young for the first 18–21 days in the nest and about 14 days more outside it. The birds live mainly on insects and their various developmental stages, which they generally pick out of cracks in the bark; very often they inspect the ends of the branches in the manner of tits. They dig for prey only if the wood is already crumbling. In the winter their diet also includes seeds. The Lesser Spotted Woodpecker inhabits most of Europe, a large part of Asia and a small area of the northwest coast of Africa.

Three-toed Woodpecker, Northern Three-toed Woodpecker

Picoides tridactylus

The Three-toed Woodpecker is more widely distributed than any other woodpecker. It occupies a continuous belt comprising the whole of northern Europe and a large part of Asia and North America and it also occurs in pockets in central and southern Europe and in some mountain ranges in Asia. It inhabits conifer forests in the taiga and old, unspoilt mountain forests (chiefly coniferous and mixed). The nest hole is most often excavated in a conifer (usually a spruce) which is frequently already dead or dying. Unlike other woodpeckers, this species nests virtually every year in a new hole. The 3—4 white eggs are laid between April and

2♀

June on the floor of the hole, where they are incubated for about 11 days by both the adult birds in turn; the parents both look after the young for 20—24 days in the nest and evidently for some four or more weeks outside it. They gather their food partly from the surface of the tree and from cracks in the bark and partly by digging for it in rotten wood and by peeling away the bark. It is entirely of animal origin and consists mainly of wood-boring beetles and their larvae, but also

3

includes caterpillars and moths. Very often the woodpeckers appear on the scene in large numbers when a bark beetle 'outbreak' is imminent. They also often peck rings around the trees and drink the sap. The Three-toed

Woodpecker is almost the same size as the Great Spotted Woodpecker. It is black and white; it has a white back, broad black cheek stripes (3) and barred flanks; there is no red in its plumage. The male (1) has a bright yellow crown, the female (2) a silvery-grey crown. As its name implies, this woodpecker has only three toes, two directed forwards and one backwards. Its slow, more 'rattling' drumming grows faster towards the end. Its call is a short 'ück'.

305

Birds with gold in their throat

Passerines, Perching birds and Songbirds   PASSERIFORMES

Passerines are by far the largest order of birds and comprise about two thirds of all avian species. They include small to at most moderately large birds; among their European representatives, the smallest, the Goldcrest, weighs about 6 g and the largest, the Raven, about 1,200 g. Most of them have a short to medium-length beak, the shape of which varies with the type of diet. Seed-eaters have a hard, conical beak (Fig. 1), which is sometimes notched (e.g. in buntings, Fig. 2) and is thus well suited for gripping and crushing seeds. Conversely, insectivorous birds mostly have a thin, pointed beak, which is sometimes modified to 'forceps' for extracting insects from cracks in bark (e.g. treecreepers, Fig. 3), and is sometimes flat, with a wide base and with bristles growing from the upper mandible, as an aid to the bird for catching insects on the wing (e.g. flycatchers, Fig. 4). Crossbills have a uniquely formed beak, whose crossed mandibles are used for opening the scales of fir and pine cones to reach the seeds. Passerines have free feet with moderately long toes and sharp claws. Three of the toes are directed forwards and the first toe points backwards (Fig. 5), as adaptation to an arboreal mode of life, since most passerines live in trees. Many inhabit open, unwooded country, however, and live on the ground, in which case the surface of their feet is increased by long, straight claws (e.g. larks, Fig. 6).

Passerines have moderately thick plumage, but poorly developed down. The Dipper is an exception, since it has a thick coat of down, obviously an adaptation to its underwater habits. Most passerines are very good fliers. The length and timing of the moult vary with the species. The length of the complete moult (after nesting, when much of the plumage has been worn away) is very

closely associated with migration. This association is of vital importance, since no bird can undertake the long journey to its winter quarters with tatty wings. The flight feathers may either be changed before the birds leave (e.g. the Pied

Fig. 1. *The conical beak of seed-eaters.*

Fig. 2. *The beak of buntings, with a tooth on the upper mandible.*

Fig. 3. *The forceps-like beak of treecreepers.*

Fig. 4. *The wide, flat beak of flycatchers, with bristles on the upper mandible.*

307

Flycatcher or the Lesser Whitethroat), in which case the moult is very fast and the birds are hardly able to fly at all during it, or they may be shed after the birds have arrived in their winter quarters (e.g. the Spotted Flycatcher and the Garden Warbler). Sexual differences in size and colour are found in a whole range of passerine species.

The vocal manifestations of passerines are exceedingly varied and have a range of seven to eight octaves. Their diversity is associated with a vocal organ (the syrinx) whose structure is very similar in all passerines and is the factor ranking them in one order. The syrinx (Fig. 7) lies at the bifurcation of the trachea (a) into two bronchi (b); it is a small, drum-like structure formed by

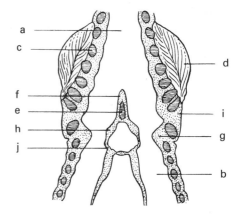

Fig. 7. *Structure of the vocal apparatus (syrinx) of songbirds: a − trachea, b − bronchus, c − cartilage rings, d − song muscles, e − cartilage bar, f − lingula or vocal chord, g − outer glottal labia, h − inner glottal labia, i − external tympanic membrane, j − inner tympanic membrane.*

Fig. 5. *The foot and a cross section of the tarsus of a Starling. The back of the tarsus forms a sharp ridge and is covered with a single layer of horn, without any plates; the claws are curved and sharp.*

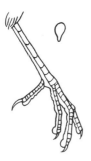

Fig. 6. *The foot and a cross section of the tarsus of a Skylark. The back of the tarsus is rounded and is covered with small plates; the claw on the hind toe is long and straight.*

the fusion of a few tracheal and bronchial cartilages (c) with several pairs of small song muscles (d) inserted on its outer surface. At the spot where the inner walls of the bronchi converge, there is a bar of cartilage (e) which tapers off to form a membranous vocal chord (f). The passage of air through the syrinx is regulated by two glottal spaces, which are controlled by outer (g) and inner (h) glottal labia and are bordered by the tympanic membranes (i,j). The voice is produced by vibration of the membranous vocal chord and stretching of the tympanic membranes by means of the song muscles and is amplified by the surrounding lung sacs, which act as resonators. Passerines include the best songbirds and it may therefore come as a surprise to learn that they also include birds like the Raven, the Carrion Crow and the Jay, whose croaking and screeching can hardly be described as song. Nevertheless, they also are the proud possessors of a syrinx, formed in just the same way as the syrinx of the most celebrated songbirds.

Passerine nests can be found in trees and bushes, in holes and burrows and on the ground. Sometimes they are very simple structures and

sometimes works of art. The size of the clutches is very variable. The young are typically nidicolous; they are dependent on parental care until they are fledged and in some cases for some time afterwards. They beg for food, screaming with their beaks held wide open, and in this respect they differ from the young of most other birds.

Young reared in holes remain there somewhat longer (15−20 days) than those reared in open nests (12−14 days). Premature departure from the nest (in nine days or even sooner) is typical of passerines nesting on or just above the ground. Since enemies have easy access to such nests, dispersal of the young into the surrounding area reduces the danger of the whole family being destroyed; in the worst event only one of the young is captured, and not all of them as would be the case if they remained in the nest. It is thus a kind of defence measure.

The female of the Red-backed Shrike (Lanius collurio) *in its favourite haunt − a thornbush thicket.*

Calandra Lark
Melanocorypha calandra

In Europe, the Calandra Lark inhabits the region around the Mediterranean; it also occurs in the Middle East and northern Africa, but in central and western Europe it is a rare accidental bird. It is a partial migrant and its more northerly populations shift southwards between September and November, sometimes to northern Africa. In February or March they return to their normal environment — dry steppes with thin vegetation, pastureland and fallow fields. The nest, in a hol-

covered with yellowish or greyish-brown spots (2) and are incubated for 16—18 days, chiefly by the female. The young remain only about ten days in the nest and then, with long down still showing above the contour feathers of their head and back, they scatter into the surrounding

vegetation. They are fed mainly on insects, insect larvae and other invertebrates; the adult birds also eat a large amount of plant food (mainly seeds). The Calandra Lark (1) is about the size of a Skylark and it has a similarly coloured back, but its throat and underside are white; it has a large black patch on each side of the neck. In flight, its relatively long, tapering wings can be seen to have a white rear edge. Its contact call is a loud 'chrreet'; its song resembles the Skylark's,

low in the ground or in grass, is made of dry grass and rootlets. In southern Europe the Calandra Lark nests between April and June, often twice. A complete clutch contains 3—5 yellow- or grey-tinted eggs, which are

2

but is louder and contains more trills and more imitations of other birds. It sings in the air and on the ground; in the air, it circles as it sings. At one time the Calandra Lark was quite popular as a cagebird because of its song.

Short-toed Lark
Calandrella brachydactyla

The Short-toed Lark inhabits the southern parts of Europe, particularly the regions bordering the Mediterranean; it also lives in northern Africa and southwestern Asia. It frequents semi-desert regions, sand dunes, steppes and dry and barren fields. It is a migrant and in October or November it flies to northern Africa for the winter, returning again in March or April. The nest is in a depression in the ground and is often hidden under a clump of wormwood or grass;

June or July. They are incubated for about 13 days by the female, aided by the male. The task of feeding and rearing the young is likewise shared. The young usually leave the nest at the age of only 9—12 days and sometimes even sooner, long before they are able to fly. Soon after they have finished nesting, the larks assemble in flocks, roam about the

steppes for a time and then gradually migrate southwards. In the nesting season the Short-toed Lark lives mainly on insects, but later the proportion of seeds in its diet increases. It is interesting to note that this species can go for months without water, but that if it has water nearby it visits it regularly. The Short-toed Lark (1) is much smaller than the Skylark; it has yellowish-brown upperparts streaked with rows of dark brown spots, whitish, unstreaked underparts and small,

it is a carefully built structure made of dry grass blades and leaves and fine rootlets. The complete clutch consists of 3—5 brownish, finely speckled eggs (2); the first batch is laid in April or May and a second clutch in

2

dark brown spots on the sides of its neck. Its call is a sparrow-like 'tchi-tchirrup'; its simple song, of about eight high-pitched whistling notes, is repeated over and over again during its undulating display flight.

311

Crested Lark
Galerida cristata

The Crested Lark is a typical resident bird. It usually spends the winter near human settlements and runs about the streets looking for food. It forms permanent pairs which remain together even during the winter, a rare phenomenon among passerines. In March they vanish from the towns and return to their typical environment — fallow fields and wasteland overgrown with weeds, such as rubbish dumps, building sites and military training fields, etc, where they usually nest twice a year between March and June. The female builds the nest, which is made of grass blades, rootlets and leaves and occasionally of hairs; it is placed in a depression in the ground.

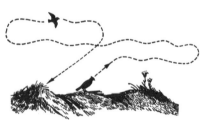

2

The 3—5 yellowish-grey, thickly brown-speckled eggs (3) are incubated for 12—13 days by the female. The young leave the nest after only nine or ten days, long before they are able to fly, and hide in the vicinity. The parents feed them almost entirely on insects and worms, but the predominant components of their own diet are seeds and the green parts of plants. Originally an inhabitant of the steppes of eastern Europe, the Crested Lark

spread over most of the rest of the continent in association with the development of agriculture (in the 14th century it was already a fixture there). Otherwise it inhabits central and southern Asia and northern Africa. In many

3

parts of Europe its numbers have recently severely decreased. The Crested Lark (1) is a typical lark and is the same size as the Skylark, but its head is surmounted by a striking, pointed crest. The male sings from elevations on the ground and often while flying in shallow undulations and wide curves above the nest site (2). The main motif of its song is a repeated 'twee-tee-too', but it also gives excellent imitations of the songs and calls of other birds.

Woodlark
Lullula arborea

The song of the Woodlark is so beautiful and so striking that many people prefer it to the song of the Nightingale. Although this lark also sings during the daytime, its sweet, fluty song, which lasts for at least one minute, can be heard best by moonlight. It sings while on the ground or perched on a tree, but its most characteristic rendition is the one it sings while flying (3); after soaring almost vertically into the air, the male flies around its nesting area and then descends obliquely or vertically to alight on a tree or on the ground. The Woodlark inhabits almost the whole of Europe (except the north), the Middle East and northern Africa. It frequents open areas with scattered trees, such as the edges of conifer forests (especially pinewoods), sunny glades and clearings, heaths and

2

old vineyards, etc. It returns from its winter quarters beside the Mediterranean in February or March and nests twice during the breeding season. The nest, which is on the ground, usually in a place warmed by the sun, is well hidden by loose vegetation; it is made of dry grass and rootlets, and moss, lichen and hairs are sometimes incorporated in it. The 3—5 whitish eggs, marked with brown and grey speckles (2), are incubated for 13—15 days by the female. The parents both care for the young for 10—13 days. At first they live mainly on insects, but later add seeds and the green parts of plants. Migration takes place in September or October. The Woodlark (1) resembles the

3

1

Skylark, but is smaller and has a shorter tail with white-tipped outer feathers; the primaries each have a white-edged black spot at their base, and the whitish superciliary stripe extends to the back of the head. The nestlings can be recognised by the yellow inside of their beak and by their black-tipped tongue, on either side of which there is a large black spot.

313

Skylark
Alauda arvensis

The Skylark originally came from the steppes of eastern Europe and its spread was promoted by the creation of artificial steppes, i.e. fields. Today it is distributed over the whole of Europe, Asia and northern Africa. It typically inhabits unwooded regions from lowlands to mountain meadows. It arrives in its breeding areas as early as the end of February or in March and soon afterwards the males take possession of their nest sites. They are very intolerant of competition and wage numerous battles in defence of their territory. The nest, a loosely woven structure made of blades of grass and rootlets, sometimes together with horsehair and fur, is built by the female in a pre-excavated hollow. The female incubates the 3—5 greyish-yellow eggs marked with grey and brown spots (3) for 12—14 days. The young, which leave the nest at 8—11 days, before they are able to fly, are fed by both the parent birds; their food is at first entirely of animal origin, but later half of plant origin. Almost all the

3

head it has a flat, erectile crest somewhat more noticeable than the crest of the Woodlark. The adult bird measures 18 cm. In the nestlings, the inside of the beak is yellow and there are three black spots on their tongue. Subcon-

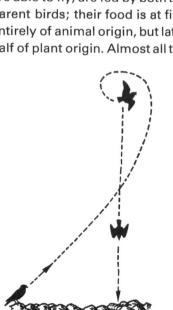

2

pairs nest twice during the season and some of them three times. In September or October the northern and eastern populations migrate to western Europe and the Mediterranean region, but a few remain behind in central Europe. The Skylark (1) has yellow-brown plumage streaked with rows of black spots; its outer tail feathers are white. On its

sciously, people always think of the Skylark in connection with its song, heard practically only while it is flying (2); the male flies almost vertically into the air from the ground, flutters or hovers for a time, gradually drops lower, is suddenly silent and then drops like a stone. In May, the average length of its song is about two minutes.

Sand Martin, Bank Swallow
Riparia riparia

The Sand Martin inhabits a large part of the northern hemisphere, including the whole of Europe, Asia, part of Africa and North America. European birds spend the winter in equatorial and southern Africa and return to

The sexes both work very hard, so that the tunnel is sometimes finished in three or four days. The 4—7 white eggs are laid during May and are incubated for 12—15 days by both the parents in turn. The parents likewise both feed

Erosion and the collapse of riverbanks or the removal of clay or sand in brickworks and sandpits very often leads to the disappearance of a large part or the whole of a colony. During August and September the colonies thin out

their breeding areas in March to May. They frequent perpendicular sandy and clayey riverbanks, the walls of sandpits and brickworks, where they excavate their nest tunnels, first of all with their beak and then with their feet as well. The tunnels are about 1 m long and widen at the far end to form a spherical nest chamber lined with dry grass and feathers.

their offspring, on small insects which they catch on the wing. At the age of 16—23 days the young martins leave the safe shelter of the burrow, but for some time still spend the night in it. Some pairs nest a second time in July. Sand Martins nest in colonies comprising several dozen to several hundred pairs; it is rare for them to nest singly. Tunnels have certain disadvantages, however.

and by the middle of October the place is deserted. Sand Martins (1) are the smallest European members of the swallow family (they are smaller even than House Martins). They have a brown back, a dingy white underside and a brown band below their throat; their tail is only slightly forked. Their call is a dry 'tchrrip' or 'tschrr'.

Swallow, Barn Swallow

Hirundo rustica

The Swallow is one of the most popular birds in Europe, and country folk wait impatiently for its return from tropical and southern Africa at the end of March or in April. It literally seeks out the company of human be-

3

ings. Its nests are generally situated inside buildings – in cowsheds, stables, passages and porchways – and seldom on their outer walls. The basin-shaped nest (2), which is open from above, is made of lumps of mud stuck together with saliva; the gaps are filled with blades of grass or straw. It is usually built

entirely by the female, while the male fetches the material, especially straw. About 750–1,400 lumps of mud are needed for one nest and the rough structure is finished in eight or nine days. The cup is lined with straw, feathers and hair. The 4–6 white eggs with brownish-red spots (3), which are laid in May, June or

July, are incubated for 14–16 days by the female. The parents tend the young for about three weeks in the nest, feed them and teach them how to catch insects for a week or so after they have left it, and then begin a second brood, as a rule in the same nest; some pairs nest a third time. When the breeding season is over, the Swallows gather together in flocks, sometimes numbering tens of thousands of birds, and spend the night in reedbeds around ponds until September or October, when it is time to migrate. The Swallow's enormous range includes Europe, Asia, northern Africa and almost the whole of North America. The Swallow (1) is an elegant metallic

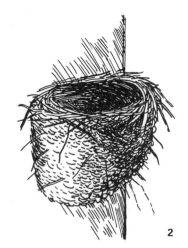
2

dark blue and white bird a little larger than the House Martin, with a deep red throat and forehead. In flight we can recognise it by its deeply forked tail with long streamers. It spends most of its time on the wing and flies tens of kilometres every day. It also catches its food – winged insects – entirely in the air.

Red-rumped Swallow
Hirundo daurica

The Red-rumped Swallow (1) is similar in shape and size to the Swallow. It has blackish-blue plumage, but the nape and the sides of its head, and also its rump, are rusty-yellow to rusty-brown, its underside is creamy-yellow and there are no white spots on its tail feathers; its tail is not quite so deeply forked. In flight, it utters a loud 'queech'

Asia as far as China and Japan. The Red-rumped Swallow has largely retained its habit of nesting on rocks and cliffs, but it often also nests in towns. Its mud nest is stuck beneath a projection on a rock face or below a bridge or a roof. The nest chamber is reached by a long, tubular entrance forming a kind of ante-room (2). The birds nest twice

a year, between April and July. The sexes take turns to sit and the 3—5 white eggs are incubated for about 14 days. The young are fed in the nest for about three weeks. The Red-rumped Swallow lives on winged insects caught in the air. It is a migrant, leaving for its African winter quarters in September or October and returning to its nesting sites in April.

and a warning 'kēērr'. It inhabits parts of the south European peninsulas (Spain and Portugal, Italy and the Balkans), the extreme south of France, some of the Mediterranean islands, northwest Africa and the south of

317

House Martin

Delichon urbica

The House Martin inhabits Europe, Asia and northern Africa. It nests in close proximity to human beings, although, like the Swallow, it originally nested on rock faces (and in some areas still does). As distinct from the Swallow, its nests are built on the outer walls of buildings, under eaves, cornices and balconies or in the shelter of bay windows. The sexes both build the nest, which is made of lumps of mud mixed and stuck together with saliva; 690—1,495 such lumps are needed for one nest, which is

the nest, already able to fly. The pairs usually rear two or more broods of young in one season in the same nest, and if the latter remains in place it is repaired and used for years. House Martins have a greater tendency than

Swallows to nest in colonies and their nests are often crowded together, side by side. Before migrating, the martins collect in flocks, when they can be seen perching on telegraph wires, often together with Swallows, and at the end of September they leave for Africa; they return in April or May. The House Martin (1), whose tail has a shorter fork than the Swallow's, has bluish-black upperparts and a white underside and rump. Its short legs are covered with white feathers right to the claws. The bird itself measures about 13 cm.

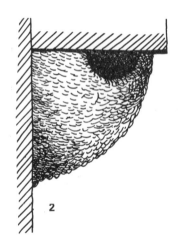

neater than the Swallow's nest and contains no admixture of plant material. It is an almost closed structure and is entered by a small opening at the top (2). It takes 10—12 days to build, and when it is finished the birds add a soft lining of feathers, fur and grass, which never show outside; if they can be seen from outside, it is a sign that the nest is occupied by sparrows. The 4—6 pure white eggs (3) are incubated for 14—16 days by both the parent birds in turn. After three weeks' feeding, the young leave

June and the female incubates them for 13—14 days. After roughly the same length of time the young leave the nest and are fed for a time in its vicinity by the parents; they are evidently fed entirely on small insects and other invertebrates. Some pairs probably nest a second time, so that the nesting period lasts from May to July. At the end of August and during September, the pipits migrate to Africa. The adult Tawny Pipit (1) has light brown, almost unstreaked plumage; a distinct, whitish superciliary stripe

Originally a steppe bird, the Tawny Pipit is also to be found on stony hillsides, on barren ground, on heaths and in large fields. It likes warmth and normally shuns wet areas. It inhabits central and southern Europe, northern Africa and the temperate parts of Asia, to which it returns from its winter quarters in April or May. The nest, built by the female, is made of dry grass and rootlets and has a few hairs in its lining; it is placed in a depression in the ground, in the shelter of a clump of grass or heather or of a bush. Unlike those of other pipits, the 4—5 eggs (3) are only sparsely covered with dark brown spots, so that the greenish, greyish or brownish ground colour is often visible; they are usually laid in May or can be seen on its head. It has a slim body, a fairly long tail and long, pale yellowish-brown legs. Most of the time it struts about on the ground and frequently 'stands to attention'. It has a fairly distinctive voice; its call note is a 'tzeep, tzeep' and its song is a repeated 'chivee, chivee' or 'tsirlooee, tsirlooee', rendered by the male, usually as it flies in undulations from bush to bush, but sometimes from the ground (2). All pipits are a little smaller than the Skylark.

3

Tree Pipit

Anthus trivialis

The Tree Pipit has a predilection for clearings or the edges of deciduous woods and conifer forests in mountains and lowlands, for open woodland and bushy hillsides and meadows. It occurs mainly in Europe, but its range extends to Siberia and central Asia. Tree Pipits return from their winter quarters in the Mediterranean region and the whole of Africa in April or May. The nest is made of grass blades, leaves and moss and stands on the ground, always well hidden by a clump of grass or a clod of earth. The 4—6 eggs are very variably coloured, from whitish to greyish-blue or brownish-pink, and are thickly speckled with greyish-brown spots (4). The female incubates them unaided for 12—13 days. The parents both feed the young for roughly the same length of time, on insects and other small invertebrates. Many pairs rear a second brood in June or July. Tree Pipit families migrate in August or September, when they are to be seen in fields and meadows, searching for seeds. The Tree Pipit (1) has an olive-brown back streaked with dark brown, a yellowish-buff, conspicuously dark-spotted breast and a whitish belly. The claw of the hind toe is about 3 mm shorter than the toe itself and is markedly curved (2).

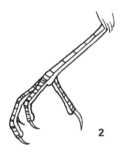

The Tree Pipit is one of the best European songbirds. The male sings mostly while in flight (3). It flies up obliquely from the top of a tree, begins to sing and then comes down again in a curve or a spiral, spreading its wings and tail, to the same or another treetop, where it concludes its song with a loud and characteristic 'seeah-seeah-seeah'; its alarm call is a high-pitched 'seep, seep'.

Meadow Pipit
Anthus pratensis

tween March and May the birds return in small flocks to their nesting sites, and from September to November they migrate to their winter quarters. The nesting period is April to August. The nest, which is always well

brownish eggs with dark grey or dark brown spots (4) are incubated for about 13 days by the female. The young leave the nest at 12–14 days and the male helps the female to rear them. Some pairs nest a second time. Like other pipits, the Meadow Pipit (1) lives chiefly on small beetles, hymenopterous insects and spiders, etc, but occasionally also eats seeds. In colouring it is almost indistinguishable from the Tree Pipit, but it has a darker,

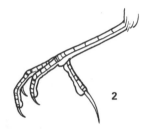

The Meadow Pipit inhabits large stretches of meadowland, bogs and heaths in mountains and wet lowlands. It breeds over almost the whole of the northern half of Europe and in western Siberia; its range in southern Europe is patchy and sporadic. It winters mainly in western Europe and the Mediterranean region, but northern birds sometimes remain in central Europe, primarily near ice-free rivers and streams. Be-

hidden in grass, is made of dry grass and moss and is lined with fine plant fibres and sometimes with hairs. The 4–6 greyish or

more greyish-green back, an only faintly buffish breast with smaller but denser black spots, and light flesh-coloured legs. The claw of the hind toe is only slightly curved and is generally the same length as, or longer than, the toe itself — i.e. usually over 10 mm (2). The Meadow Pipit remains mainly on the ground, but if flushed it utters a piercing 'ist, ist' and flies around in small circles. Its alarm call is a shrill 'tissip'. Its fine, bell-like song, frequently sung in the air (3), is also different; the male flies up, begins to sing and towards the end of its song sinks almost perpendicularly to the ground, or perches on a tall herbaceous plant or a bush.

Water Pipit
Anthus spinoletta

separate species. Members of the form *spinoletta* arrive at their nesting sites in March or April, when the mountain tops are still covered with snow; they usually nest from May to July. The female builds a hollow under overhanging grass, or under a stone or shrub; it is made of grass, moss and lichen and sometimes contains hair. The female incubates the 4—5 eggs, which are thickly marked with fawn or russet speckles on a greyish or greenish ground (2), for 14—16 days. Together with the male, it rears the offspring for about two weeks. In September,

2

the pipits usually descend to lower altitudes, where they sometimes remain during the winter near water; the majority, however, migrate to western Europe or the Mediterranean. In its breeding plumage, the Water Pipit (1) has a grey crown and nape, a white superciliary stripe and an unspotted, pink-tinted breast; its legs are dark brown. Its call note and song are similar to those of the Meadow Pipit; its song, 'tsip-tsip-tsip', grows faster and faster, becoming a trill, and then ends with a long-drawn-out 'titti-dee-eh'. As a rule, the male sings while fluttering or gliding from one boulder to another, but also while perched on a stone, a post or a telegraph wire, etc.

The Water Pipit forms two ecologically and taxonomically differentiated groups of subspecies. Montane forms (*'spinoletta'*) inhabit terrain above the tree-line — boulder fields, mountain meadows, stony loess and precipitous rocks — usually beside fast-flowing streams. They live in the alpine zone of mountain ranges in southern and central Europe, the Balkans, Asia Minor, eastern Asia and a large part of North America. Littoral forms (*'petrosus'*) inhabit rocky coasts in western and northern Europe. The two forms are now considered to be two

Yellow Wagtail, Blue-headed Wagtail
Motacilla flava

The Yellow Wagtail inhabits a vast breeding range covering the whole of Europe and Asia and extending to North America and northern Africa. Over this area it has formed more than 20 subspecies. In the subspecies *M. f. flava*, the male (1) has a bright yellow throat and underside, an olive-green back and a blue-grey head with a white superciliary stripe; the female has a brownish crown and cheeks and a whitish or buff throat. In *M. f. thunbergi*, the male (2) has a dark grey head and blackish ear-coverts; in the British subspecies *M. f. flavissi-*

2♂

3♂

4♂

5♂

ma (3) it has a yellowish-green head with a yellow superciliary stripe; in *M. f. cinereocapilla* (4) a grey head and a white throat; and in *M. f. feldegg* (5) a jet-black head and a yellow throat. The Yellow Wagtail has a shorter tail than other wagtails. It likes to sit on protruding plants and the top of bushes, uttering its call note 'tsoueep' or simply singing 'tseep-tseep-tseep-tsipsi'. It returns from its winter quarters in tropical Africa in April and settles in damp meadows, swamps and marshes, beside ponds and rivers and in fields and other places overgrown with weeds. In May, June or July, the female builds a nest made of grass, rootlets, moss and hairs, placed on the ground surrounded by vegetation, and lays 4−6 whitish, fawn-speckled eggs (6), which it incubates with occasional help from

the male for 13−14 days. Some pairs manage to raise two broods. The Yellow Wagtail lives mainly on insects, together with spiders, worms and small molluscs. When they have finished nesting, the birds collect in flocks and spend the night in reed-beds, together with Pied or White Wagtails; in August or September they set out on their long journey southwards. Although roughly the same length as the Skylark, wagtails are distinctly slimmer.

6

323

Grey Wagtail
Motacilla cinerea

The Grey Wagtail inhabits almost the whole of Europe except the north, and also occurs in Asia and northern Africa. It is always to be found near water, since it lives chiefly on aquatic insects and other small aquatic animals. Although it prefers mountain torrents, it also nests beside rocky submontane streams and in lowlands it is satisfied with a weir or a stony sluice with a stretch of fast water, the outlet of a pond or

2♀

Most pairs have a second brood in June or July. The birds move to lowlands and to southern Europe and northern Africa in September or October, and return to the breeding sites in March or April; many south and west European birds are resident, and Grey Wagtails can also be encountered in the winter in central Europe, usually near ice-free water. The Grey Wagtail is sometimes mistaken for the

a millrace. The nest usually lies in a hollow near a stream — between stones or roots on the bank, in a hole in a small bridge, near a sluice or a culvert — and even in the wall of a house or on rafters, far away from any water. Both the sexes build the nest, which is made of grass blades, leaves, rootlets and moss and is lined with fine plant fibres and, as a rule, with hair. In April or May, the female (2) lays 4—6 yellowish

or greyish, russet-speckled eggs (3), which are incubated for 12—14 days by both the parent birds in turn; they both feed the young in the nest for approximately the same length of time.

3

Yellow Wagtail, but it has an ash-grey back, a much longer tail and light brown legs; in addition, in the spring plumage the male has a black throat (1). Furthermore, the two species live in different environments and a yellow-coloured wagtail beside a fast-flowing stream is almost certainly a Grey Wagtail. The Grey Wagtail's flight is deeply undulating and it usually utters a sharp 'tsit, tsit'.

White Wagtail, Pied Wagtail
Motacilla alba

The White Wagtail is mostly to be seen near water, but it does not always live there; it also nests near isolated cottages in woods and pastureland, in quarries, in farm buildings and in large human settlements, and at high as well as low altitudes. It inhabits the whole of Europe, Asia and part of northern Africa. It occupies a nesting territory and defends it furiously against all comers. It raises two or three

2♂

nice or a ledge. The 4—6 greyish or bluish eggs, which are marked with dark brown speckles (3), are incubated for 12—14 days by the female. The nestlings are fed for

and eastern populations migrate between September and November to winter quarters between the Mediterranean region and equatorial Africa, returning in March, but some birds in central Europe remain there, near ice-free water, during the winter; birds living in western and southern Europe are resident and nomadic. The breeding plumage of the White Wagtail (1) is a vivid mixture of black, grey and white,

broods during the breeding season, which lasts from April to August. The relatively large nest, which is made of straw, rootlets, leaves, twigs and moss and is lined with fur, horsehair and sometimes feathers, is built by both the sexes. It is generally situated in a recess in a building or a rock, in a space in a pile of timber, etc, or on a rafter, a cor-

3

but after their summer moult the birds lose their black chin and throat and only their breast remains black (2). Britain and Ireland and part of western Europe are inhabited by the Pied Wagtail (*M. a. yarrellii*), a subspecies with a black instead of a pale grey back. The White Wagtail flies in long undulations, uttering a disyllabic 'tzi-wirrp, tzi-wirrp'.

325

Waxwing, Bohemian Waxwing

Bombycilla garrulus

The Waxwing inhabits conifer forests and Arctic-type mixed forests, i.e. taiga and wooded tundra, in Europe, Asia and North America, where it nests once a year, at the end of May or in June. The nest, which both the sexes build on a tree, 2—20 m above the ground, is made of

small twigs, grass, moss and lichen and is lined with hair and feathers. The 4—6 bluish eggs, thinly marked with brown and black spots (2), are incubated for 12—15 days by the female. Both the parents care for the nestlings for 14—16 days, feeding them on the same diet as they themselves eat, i.e. mainly mosquitoes, which infest the taiga and tundra in vast numbers. Later they change to a diet of berries. Their berry consumption is enormous, since the food passes very quickly through their stomach and intestine and is excreted only half digested; the birds' droppings contain large quantities of seeds, so that Waxwings are very effective in helping to propagate many ligneous plants. Further south, Waxwings are usually seen only in the winter, roughly between November and March, when they roam about in search of food. In some years their visits are more like invasions (flocks of several hundred can be observed); this is evidently because they have overmultiplied further north, resulting in reduction of their 'Lebensraum' (living space) and consequent undesirable competition. After such invasions, only a proportion of the birds find their way home in March or April; the rest die on the way. The Waxwing (1) has rich, silky plumage, which is mainly buffish-brown with a reddish tinge, is decorated with vivid black, yellow, white and red markings and is completed by a striking crest. It is about the same size as a Starling. The call note, uttered while flying, is a metallic 'zhreee'.

Dipper, Water Ouzel

Cinclus cinclus

The Dipper occupies a special position among passerines in that it is completely at home in water, where it catches most of its food — mainly the larvae of aquatic insects, crustaceans and small molluscs. In shallow water it wades and only its head is submerged, but in deep water the whole bird is submerged. Holding on to stones with its sharp claws or 'rowing' under water with its wings, it scours the bed for prey, turning over small stones and throwing them aside as it goes. When it surfaces, it is absolutely dry, since the water slides off its plumage, which is thoroughly waterproofed with oil from its preen gland. Nest material is usually collected under water and if any is gathered on the bank the bird usually immediately wets it. The nest is almost always above water level; it is often situated under a small bridge, in a hole in the ground, among roots under the bank or under a weir, where it can often be reached only through water. It is large and spherical and is entered by a side opening; its outer wall is made mainly of moss and its inner wall of stems, leaves and rootlets; it is lined with dry leaves. The 4—6 white eggs are incubated for 15—17 days by the female. The young, which are fed by both parents, leave the nest at the age of about three weeks. Most pairs nest twice a year, between March and June. The Dipper inhabits much of Europe, Asia and northwest Africa. It is a resident bird and during the winter generally remains in the region of the 0.5—1 km of stream or river which forms its nesting territory. It is the same size as the Blackbird, but has a conspicuously short tail (1), which it holds erect and jerks from time to time; it frequently bobs up and down. It has blackish-brown plumage with a vivid white 'bib'. Its call is a sharp 'zit, zit' and its loud song can also be heard in the winter.

Wren, Winter Wren
Troglodytes troglodytes

2

The Wren inhabits Europe, Asia and the north of Africa. It occurs anywhere where it can find dense thickets. It is a solitary nester, finds its way about nimbly in the tangled vegetation and seldom flies out. The nest, which is disproportionately large in relation to the size of the bird, is built in the thickest tangle of roots or branches, in various open cavities, in an uprooted tree or under an overhanging bank. It is a spherical structure made of moss, grass, twigs and leaves and is entered from the side. It is built by the male, which starts to build several such nests (during the year, up to 12) in its territory. The female, attracted by its song, inspects them all, chooses one and lines it with hair and feathers.

In April or May it lays 5—7 white, finely red-speckled eggs (2) and incubates them unaided for 14—16 days. The young are fed first of all by the female and later also by the male; in 15—17 days they leave the nest. In June or July the pairs nest again and then we can witness one of the most remarkable phenomena in the life of passerines, when the older siblings begin to look after the second brood of young and, together with the parents, bring them insects, spiders, centipedes

and small snails. The Wren is a resident bird and lives a mainly sedentary life. Some pairs remain together the whole of the year, but polygamy is not uncommon and one male may live with up to three females. The Wren (1) is one of the smallest birds and weighs only 9 g. It has rust-brown plumage with dark brown barring. It holds its short tail noticeably cocked and often bobs up and down. In relation to its size it has an abnormally loud voice. Its song begins with fluty whistles and ends with a loud chirping trill; its contact and alarm calls, 'tserr, tserr' and 'zek, zek', are likewise very penetrating. The Wren is one of the few passerine birds that also sing in the winter.

328

Dunnock, Hedge Sparrow, Hedge Accentor
Prunella modularis

1

2

The Dunnock inhabits most of Europe except the most northerly and most southerly parts and its range also extends to Asia Minor. It leads a secretive life in dense conifer woods, and easily escapes notice, but it is also found commonly in other types of woods and in neglected gardens, parks, cemeteries and scrub; it is likewise a typical bird of the sub-alpine birch zone in mountains. The presence of thickets is always the decisive factor, however. The Dunnock returns to its nesting sites in March or April. The female makes the nest almost entirely of moss and lines it with fine grass and hair (often from roe deer), frequently adding the russet-red stems and spore cases of moses. The nest is carefully hidden away in the densest vegetation, usually up to 1.5 m above the ground, and is often situated in bushes or in a young spruce. The 4−6 bluish-green eggs (2) are incubated mainly by the female, relieved only occasionally by the male. The young are hatched in 12−14 days and after 12−13 days' parental care they leave the nest. The pairs regularly nest twice a year, between April and July. Dunnocks are partial migrants, and only birds from the north are wholly migratory; in September or October they fly to southern and western Europe (and sometimes to northern Africa), but some birds spend the winter in low-lying country in central Europe. In the summer, Dunnocks live mainly on spiders and small snails, in the winter on small seeds and berries. Both the male and the female are about the same size as a sparrow; they have a bluish-grey head and breast, and a dark brown back and wings streaked with black-ish-brown (1). The tail feathers are plainly coloured, whereas in the Alpine Accentor the tips have large white or buff spots.

Siberian Accentor,
Mountain Accentor
Prunella montanella

The Siberian Accentor inhabits only one strip of territory in northern Siberia, leading from the Urals (the only place where it touches Europe) to the Chukotsk Peninsula, and another one in central Asia, stretching from the Altai Mountains to Lake Baikal. It is a migratory species and in September or October it migrates to southeastern Asia, roughly to the region embracing northern China and Korea. In March or April it returns to its nesting sites in open conifer woods in the taiga with plenty of dense undergrowth, in birchwoods at the edge of the tundra and in thickets alongside mountain streams. The pairs nest solitarily; the males mark out their nesting territory by singing energetically from the top of bushes and trees. The nest is usually situated low down, in dense shrubs, and is made of small twigs, rootlets, straw and (chiefly) moss; it is lined with the finer parts of mosses and their stems, usually together with hairs. The clutch consists of 4–6 plain bluish-green eggs and the nesting period lasts from May to July. The young are probably hatched in 11–12 days, but no further details of their development are known. The Siberian Accentor lives partly on invertebrate animals and partly on small seeds and berries. It has black ear-coverts, a prominent light ochre superciliary stripe and throat and a russet back only faintly marked with black streaks (1). Its voice, size and habits are similar to those of the Dunnock.

Alpine Accentor
Prunella collaris

The Alpine Accentor is a typical montane passerine bird inhabiting the mountain ranges of central and southern Europe, northwest Africa and Asia from Iran to Japan. It nests above the tree-line on stony slopes and rocky mountain tops. The nest is always carefully hidden in a crack in a rock or in stony rubble and less often under a boulder or a bush in a mountain meadow. Isolated nests have been found in the retaining walls of mountain chalets. The nest is put together rather loosely, and if one tries to remove it from its hole it often falls to pieces. It is made of straw, moss, rootlets and hair and is built by both the sexes. The 3—5 bright bluish-green eggs (2) are incubated for 13—15 days by both the parent birds in turn. The young leave the nest at the age of 13—15 days. It has regularly been observed that the number of young that leave the nest (usually one to three) is fewer than the number of eggs laid. The nesting period lasts from May to July and some pairs are therefore able to nest twice. In the summer the Alpine Accentor lives on insects and other invertebrates; later there is an increase in the amount of grass and other seeds in its diet. With the advent of colder weather, the birds collect near mountain chalets and hunt for food on scrap heaps and rubbish dumps, where they sometimes remain the whole of the winter. Sometimes, however, in October or November, they descend to lower altitudes, often far away from their nesting sites, returning again in April. The fore part of the Alpine Accentor's body is grey; it has a white, black-speckled throat and its flanks are heavily streaked with rusty-brown (1). Its song is reminiscent of the Skylark's and the male usually sings it from the ground. The bird is also much the same size as the Skylark.

2

Rufous Bush Robin, Rufous Warbler, Rufous Bush Chat

Cercotrichas galactotes

The Rufous Bush Robin inhabits the southern part of the Iberian and Balkan Peninsulas, but its range stretches across Asia as far as India and it also occurs in Africa. It is a migratory bird, wintering in tropical Africa and southwest Asia, and its rare appearances in central and western Europe are accidental. It nests in bushes, preferably on sunny slopes, in vineyards, gardens and palm and olive groves, on the edge of deserts and in steppes with scattered shrubs. The nest is situated in a bush or in a cactus or palm thicket, usually close to the ground. It is built by both the sexes, is made of small twigs and grasses and is lined with fluff and feathers. The 3—5 greyish or yellowish, brown- and grey-speckled eggs (2) are incubated entirely by the female, which at first broods only at night, but after the clutch is complete she sits all around the clock and is fed by the male. Incubation lasts for 13—14 days and the chicks are fed for a similar period in the nest. This is a slender, long-legged bird similar in shape to a Nightingale. Its most distinctive feature is its long, fan-like chestnut-brown tail with a black and white tip; it has

a rust-brown or grey-brown back and a pale sandy underside. The Rufous Bush Robin (1) sits ostentatiously on the top of a bush or on the ground with drooping wings and with its tail cocked and spread (3). Its pleasing song, with short motifs reminiscent of the Skylark, is sung from a perch or as the bird slowly descends in flight.

Robin
Erithacus rubecula

The Robin is a typical bird of deciduous and coniferous woods with dense undergrowth, but it also lives in gardens, parks and cemeteries. The males are very quarrelsome, especially when defending their nesting territory in the spring, when they are particularly 'sensitive' to any red-breasted birds and will even attack a dummy with a red spot painted on it. The nest, which is built by the female, is made of dry leaves, plant fibres and green moss (visible around the outside) and is rather scantily lined with very fine rootlets and hair. It is situated close to the ground, in a bank, a dense spruce, a heap of brushwood or a hollow stump, or even in a depression in the ground itself. Twice a year, between April and July, the female lays 4—6 yellowish, brown-spotted eggs (2) and incubates them for 13—14 days. After two weeks of parental care the young leave the nest before they are able properly to fly. The birds live on various invertebrate animals — mainly insects — and in the autumn they eat berries. The Robin inhabits the whole of Europe (except the most northerly parts of Scandinavia), and also western Siberia, Asia Minor and northwestern Africa. It is a partial migrant, but west and south European birds are mostly resident and occasional individuals even remain in central Europe throughout the winter; the rest migrate in September or October to western and southern Europe or to northern Africa and return to their breeding areas in March. The Robin (1) is a little smaller than a sparrow. With its orange-red face and breast, it is unmistakable. It has strikingly large, round eyes, enabling it to look for food in the half light of dense thickets. The male sings from various perches, often until dusk and later. Its sweet song consists of fluty passages alternating with soft, almost inaudible notes.

2

333

Thrush Nightingale, Sprosser

Luscinia luscinia

The Thrush Nightingale is the east European counterpart of the Nightingale. In central and south-east Europe, the ranges of the two species partly overlap; in such places mixed pairs are sometimes formed and the song of the hybrid offspring contains elements of both repertoires. The breeding range of the Thrush Nightingale stretches to the extreme south of Scandinavia in the north and across Asia to the River

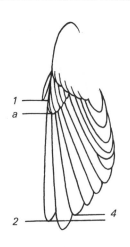

remain only 11—12 days in the nest and scatter into the surrounding vegetation before they are able to fly; the male then also takes a hand in tending and teaching them. The birds live mainly on small invertebrate animals, but in the late summer they add various kinds of fruit to their diet. The Thrush Nightingale (1) has brown plumage, a rusty-brown tail and faint grey spotting across its throat and breast. Its

Ob in the east. The Thrush Nightingale is a typical migrant; in August or September it flies to eastern Africa, returning in April or May. It inhabits dank woods with luxuriant undergrowth, river valleys and swampy lowlands with dense thickets. It tends to frequent damper places than the Nightingale. The nest is built by the female in the shade of dense shrubs, usually on or close to the ground. Dry leaves from the pre-

vious year form the foundations and the deep cup is made of straw, rootlets and moss, sometimes together with fluff and hair. The 4—5 brown eggs (2), laid in May, are incubated for 13—14 days by the female. The young

1st primary is discernibly shorter than the primary coverts (a) and is very narrow and sharp-tipped; its 2nd primary is the same length as the 4th, or a little longer (3). Its song lacks the initial slurred whistle of the Nightingale's song and the typical crescendo, but it is characterised by a terminal 'srrrrr', which is to be heard in the song of practically all the males. Both nightingales are the same size as a sparrow.

2

Nightingale

Luscinia megarhynchos

For most people the Nightingale (1) is the epitome of the songbird; many people are familiar with its song, but have no idea of what the bird itself looks like and are surprised when they see how plain its plumage is. It is completely light brown, except for its rusty tail and rump. The relative lengths of its primaries (3) differ from those of the Thrush Nightingale. Although the Nightingale also sings during the daytime, it

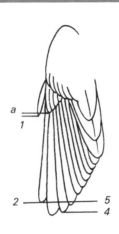

3

and southern Europe, northern Africa, the Middle East and central Asia; it returns from its winter quarters in tropical Africa in April or May. The birds arrive during the night: first of all the males, which immediately begin their nightly concerts, to attract the females when they arrive several days later. The 4–5 olive-brown to coffee-coloured eggs (2), which are laid in April, May or June, are incubated entirely by

is its nocturnal concerts that make the greatest impression. The males do not all sing the same song, however. Some are really masterly singers, others are less gifted. The Nightingale's song is not inborn; it has to be learnt by ear and its quality therefore depends on how good the young bird's teachers are. The

Nightingale is to be encountered mostly in deciduous and mixed woods, beside rivers and ponds and in overgrown parks and gardens. It inhabits western, central

2

the female. The young are hatched in 12–14 days and 11 days later they disperse into the surrounding vegetation, where both the parents take care of them. The Nightingale lives on the same kinds of food as the Thrush Nightingale. In August or September it migrates, silently and inconspicuously.

Bluethroat
Luscinia svecica

In shape and behaviour the Blue-throat resembles the Robin. It is just as active and agile, likes to run about on the ground, and flicks its tail and bobs in the same manner. The adult male is a very attractive bird. Its back and wings are dark brown, but it has a strik-ing, bright blue 'bib', which is separated from the white of its underside by a black and chest-nut breast band. In the middle of the blue 'bib' there is a patch, which in the Scandinavian Red-spotted Bluethroat (*L. s. svecica,* 2) is chestnut and in the central European White-spotted Blue-throat (*L. s. cyanecula,* 1) is white. The russet colouring of the base

3

of the tail feathers is another characteristic feature. After moulting and donning their win-ter plumage, the males lose their bright colours, and the blue 'bib', with its black and chestnut stripes, fades; young males in their spring plumage sometimes have the same, duller, appear-

ance. The female (4) has a white throat, bounded laterally and ventrally by a band of blackish-brown spots. The juveniles are brown and speckled, but already show signs of the reddish bases to the outer tail feathers. The Bluethroat is a talented singer. Its song begins with 'deep-deep-deep-deep' notes and con-tinues with a medley of warbling, squeaking and other varied sounds mixed with imitations of other bird calls. The male can also mimic animals such as frogs. Its call note is a sharp 'tac-tac' or a soft 'hweet'.

The Bluethroat inhabits Europe and Asia and has infiltrated into

Bluethroat
Luscinia svecica

western Alaska in North America. It nests only patchily in central, southern and western Europe, where its occurrence is more of a relict character, representing residues of what were once continuous populations which were broken up by lowland drainage and loss of suitable environments.

The Scandinavian subspecies lives chiefly in the tundra or in mountainous regions in the south of its range. Further south it is mostly seen only during its spring (March and April) or autumn (August and September) migration, during which the birds generally follow the banks of rivers, the sides of ponds and even the courses of small streams and drainage channels. The central European subspecies usually occurs in swampy regions overgrown with reeds, sedge and shrubs.

The nest is usually very carefully

4♀

hidden away in a depression in the ground among dense vegetation. It is made of the leaves of trees, grass blades, moss and rootlets and is lined with fine grass and occasionally with fur or a few feathers. It is built by the female, sometimes assisted by the male. The 5–6 brown or olive-green eggs, which are marked with blackish-brown speckles and blurred spots (3), are incubated for 13–14 days, entirely by the female. The young leave the nest at the age of 13–14 days, although they are still unable to fly. The parents feed them on insects, worms, spiders and other invertebrates, which also constitute their own diet. In the autumn, when Bluethroats migrate to northern Africa, they not infrequently eat the berries of various trees and shrubs.

2

337

White-throated Robin

Irania gutturalis

The White-throated Robin inhabits Transcaucasia, Asia Minor and a narrow but long strip of territory reaching into central Asia. It is a migrant, spending the winter in the southern part of Arabia and in eastern Africa and returning to its nesting sites in April. As a rule it frequents bushy mountainsides, ravines, mountain river valleys and stony or grassy inclines in fields; in mountains it occurs at altitudes of up to 2,300 m. The nest, which is built in a bush quite close to the ground, is made of twigs, dry straw, pieces of bark and grass and is lined with plant fluff and animal hair and fine grass. The 4—5 greenish-blue eggs are covered with rusty-buff speckles and are laid in April or May. The female incubates alone for about 14 days and both parents care for the young in the nest for a further two weeks. The birds' diet has not been studied very thoroughly, but it evidently consists of various invertebrates and also, in the autumn, of berries and other fruit. The male White-throated Robin (1) has black lores and cheeks, a white throat and superciliary stripe, a slate-grey crown and back and a rust-brown underside. The female lacks the black colouring on the head and the white superciliary stripe and its back is grey-brown rather than grey, but it has a whitish throat. These birds, which are about the size of redstarts, frequent bushes, but also like to perch on boulders in the open. They are very wary; if disturbed, they raise themselves erect, let the ends of their wings droop, and slowly raise and lower their tail in a regular rhythm. Their song, often given in flight (when the russet underside of their wings can be seen), is composed of loud, tinkling notes reminiscent of the sound of sleigh-bells.

Black Redstart
Phoenicurus ochruros

The Black Redstart originally inhabited rock faces and rocky slopes and boulder fields in mountains. It seems to have acquired a liking for the company of human beings, however, since today there are more Black Redstarts in human settlements than there are in their original environment. Even those which still live in mountainous regions show a tendency to keep close to man. Montane birds nest in rock crevices, in holes under stones or in small caves. Urban birds nest under the eaves of houses, barns and sheds, in recesses and holes in walls and in half-open nestboxes. The nest is built by the female and is made of dry grass, leaves, rootlets, moss and a quantity of feathers and hair. The female incubates the 4–6 white eggs unaided for 13–14 days; the male helps with the care of the young. The young leave the nest at the age of 12–16 days, but remain some time in its vicinity. The adult birds nest twice during the summer. The Black Redstart inhabits central and southern Europe, a strip of territory leading from Asia Minor to China and a small part of northwest Africa. In September and October the birds migrate to western and southern Europe and northern Africa, and return in March; south and west European populations are resident. This and the following redstart both measure about 14 cm. The male (1) is almost completely greyish-black; it has a white patch on its wings and a rufous rump and tail. The female is dark grey-brown and has no white

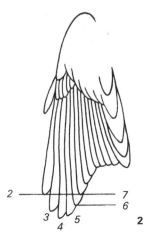

patch on its wings. The second primary is shorter than the 6th, the 4th and 5th are roughly the same length (2) and the 3rd to the 6th primaries have a narrow outer vane. The male draws attention to itself by continuously 'quivering' its tail, by frequently bobbing up and down and by its unmusical, grating song which it usually sings from a rooftop. Its contact call is a sharp 'fitt' or 'fitt-teck-teck'.

339

Redstart
Phoenicurus phoenicurus

The Redstart inhabits deciduous and mixed woods, well-lit pinewoods, copses and avenues; it also nests in parks, orchards and gardens, i.e. in proximity to man, although it never occurs in human settlements in the same numbers as the Black Redstart. The nest is usually built in a tree hole, but may be situated in a hole in a building or in a nest-box; sometimes it is found in the open, in a niche, on a beam or on green moss incorporated into its upper edge. As a rule the birds nest twice, between April and June, and the 5—7 bright bluish-green eggs (3) in each clutch are incubated for 12—14 days by the female; the male helps to look after the young. The Redstart is distributed over the whole of Europe and a large part of Asia and also occurs in northern Africa. Its winter quarters lie between northern and equatorial Africa; live on a diet of insects, spiders, worms and small molluscs, enriched in the summer and autumn by berries and other soft fruit. In its breeding plumage, the male (1) has a white forehead, a black throat and cheeks, an orange breast, a rufous rump and tail, a white belly and a greyish-blue crown and back. The female is plain grey-brown, but is always paler than the female Black Redstart. The Redstart also bobs its

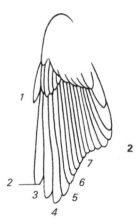

body and 'quivers' its tail. The 2nd primary is the same length as or longer than the 6th, the 3rd and 4th are the longest (2) and the 3rd to the 5th primaries have a narrow outer vane. The Redstart's alarm call is 'phwheet-teck-teck'; its song begins with a single high note and two deep notes, 'hee, tra-tra'.

a cornice, etc. It is built largely by the female and is made of straw, leaves, rootlets, hair and feathers; it can be recognised from the its autumn migration takes place in September and October, its spring migration in April. Both this and the preceding species

Güldenstädt's Redstart
Phoenicurus erythrogaster

The distribution of this species is divided into two parts. One subspecies inhabits the mountains of the Caucasus and northern Iran, while the other lives in the mountains of central Asia. The birds nest very high up, in the alpine zone and in stony mountain steppes. They normally nest at altitudes of up to 3,000 m and even as high as 5,000 m. They are resident, but at the beginning of October, and sometimes sooner, they descend to valleys further down the mountainside; they return to their domain above the clouds in February or March. The nest is built in a fissure in a rock, in a space between large stones or in the midst of rubble; it is made of dry parts of plants and is lined with wool, hair and single feathers. The nesting season lasts from May to July and the female alone evidently incubates the 4–5 creamy-white, finely russet-speckled eggs. Otherwise little is known about the nesting biology of this species. During the breeding season the birds live on small invertebrates, which they frequently catch in alpine meadows and to which, in the autumn, they add berries and fruit. Güldenstädt's Redstart is the largest member of the genus. It is very active and, like other redstarts, it continuously 'quivers' its tail. The vividly coloured male (1), with its black face, throat and back, almost white crown, large white wing patch and rufous underside, tail and rump, is well visible from a distance. The mod-

estly garbed female, on the other hand, can hardly be detected among the stones; it is mainly grey-brown, has a light-coloured throat and its tail and rump are much less vivid. Juvenile males already have a white wing patch.

Whinchat
Saxicola rubetra

The Whinchat inhabits the greater part of Europe, from the Arctic Circle to the north of the Iberian Peninsula, Italy and the Balkans; it also lives in a large part of Asia. It is a typical migrant, spending the winter in equatorial Africa. It returns in April or May to settle along ditches and beside

3

1

vegetation. It is made chiefly of straw and grass, sometimes together with a little moss; as distinct from the Stonechat's nest, there are few hairs in its lining. The clutch usually consists of 5—6 bluish-green eggs (2), sometimes marked with minute blackish-brown speckles, which are laid between May and July and are incubated for 12—14 days by the female. The young are fed by both the parents and leave the nest at the age of only 11—14 days. At the end of August or in September, the birds migrate southwards. The typical features of the male Whinchat (1) are a brown-streaked head and back, a light rusty-brown underside and broad, white superciliary stripes; the base of its outer tail feathers is also white (3). The female's colouring is somewhat duller. Both are the same size as the Redstart. In their nesting territory, the adult birds can mostly be seen perched on the top of a bush, a tall herbaceous plant or a telegraph pole or wire, or flying from one to the other in short undulating movements; when they settle, they flick their wings and half spread their tail. Their song is a mixture of scraping and whistling notes and sometimes contains imitations of the songs of other birds. Their contact call is an explosive 'tic-tic'.

footpaths in fields, in meadows and pastureland with scattered bushes and in bogs and mountain meadows. The nest, which is built entirely by the female, is always on the ground in dense

2

Stonechat
Saxicola torquata

The Stonechat likes sunny slopes, stony hillsides, embankments, ditches, wasteland, heaths, dry meadows and pastures overgrown with scattered bushes. The pairs nest twice a year, first in April and again in June or July. The nest, which is built mostly by the female and is

rest migrate in October and return in February or March. Their winter quarters stretch from the British Isles to the Mediterranean region and from there to equatorial Africa. The male (1) has a black head and blackish-brown back, sharply contrasting white patches on its neck and wings,

made of dry grass, moss and rootlets lined with fine grass and hair, sometimes together with feathers, is placed on the ground, usually on or at the foot of a slope, well hidden in a hollow under overhanging grass or other herbaceous plants. The 5—6 bluish-green eggs with small russet spots (3) are incubated for 13—14 days by the female; after the young are hatched, the male also lends a hand. The young receive the same food as the parents: insects, spiders, small worms and molluscs. The Stonechat inhabits a large part of Europe and Asia and northwestern and southern Africa. South European and African populations are resident; the

a whitish rump (4) and a rust-brown breast. In the female (2), the black colouring is replaced by brown. Both birds are the same size as Redstarts. The male sits strikingly upright on an elevation to sing its rather grating song, which is reminiscent of the song of the Redstart; its call note is a hard 'fitt-tack-tack'.

343

Wheatear
Oenanthe oenanthe

Although the Wheatear is a typical bird of stony mountainsides and rocks, it is also to be encountered at lower altitudes, in quarries, in stony and sandy fields and on wasteland covered with thin vegetation. It is a thorough cosmopolitan, whose distribution forms a belt of varying

the male (1) has a grey crown and back, a striking black eye-mask and a yellow-buff underside; the black markings in the male are replaced by brown or grey in the female. In all their plumages the birds have a white rump; their tail is also white at the base and has a black inverted T-shaped mark at

breadth across Europe, Asia, northern Africa and North America. European Wheatears migrate in September or October to equatorial Africa and return at the end of March or in April. The nests are to be found in piles of stones, in holes or cracks in walls or rocks, in holes in the ground and even in such unexpected

places as bird and mammal burrows or derelict machinery. The two sexes collect a mass of grass blades, rootlets, twigs and moss and carefully line the nest with fine plant fibres, hair and feathers. The 5—6 unspotted greenish-blue eggs (2), which are laid in April, May or June, are incubated for 13—14 days by the female. The young leave the nest at only 10—15 days. They are fed by the parents on insects, spiders, centipedes, worms and small molluscs; in the summer and autumn more berries and other kinds of fruit are added to the diet. In its breeding plumage,

the end (3). The Wheatear's short song is composed of fluty notes mixed with twittering tones; its alarm call is a sharp 'yiff-yiff' or 'yiff-tack'. The nestlings have a yellow-lined beak and a black band across their tongue (4).

2

4

Pied Wheatear
Oenanthe pleschanka

In its breeding plumage, the male Pied Wheatear (1) is distinguished from other European wheatears chiefly by its black back; its chin and throat, the upper breast and the end of its tail are also black. Its crown, nape and upper back, its rump and its belly are white. After its autumn moult (2), the top of its head becomes brownish and the black feathers on its wings and back acquire cream-coloured edges. The female is browner and more uniformly marked, and the whole of its underside is whitish; it closely resembles the female Wheatear. The alarm call of this species is a harsh 'seck'; its song is fast and high-pitched. The Pied Wheatear occurs in the south of eastern Europe, but the greater part of its range lies in Asia; it seldom strays into central and

to its nesting sites in March or April. The males are the first to arrive, followed about one week later by the females. The nest is built on the ground among stones, in a crack in a rock or under the eaves of buildings; it is made of coarse grass blades and

spots, are laid in May or June. The young are hatched in 12—14 days and spend approximately the same length of time in the nest. In August the birds begin to leave their territories, but do not actually migrate to their winter quarters in the Arabian Peninsula

western Europe. It inhabits rocky coasts, stony hillsides with scattered shrubs and dry steppes; in Asia it ascends mountains to altitudes of up to 3,000 m. It returns

leaves and is lined with finer material, usually including fur and horsehair. The 4—6 bluish eggs, which are thinly marked with brownish-red and grey

and central and eastern Africa until October. The Pied Wheatear lives chiefly on small invertebrates, but also eats fruit and berries (e.g. mulberries).

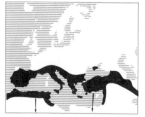

Rock Thrush
Monticola saxatilis

The Rock Thrush inhabits central and southern Europe, northern Africa and a strip of territory stretching from Asia Minor to Lake Baikal. It is not a strictly montane bird and is satisfied with dry rocky hillsides, quarries and even ruined castles at low altitudes. It is very timid, wary and secretive, so that it often escapes notice even when it nests in a constantly busy quarry. The nest, which is built by the female in a crevice or recess in a rock or rock face, between boulders or in a hole in a wall, usually where it is almost inaccessible, is made of stems, rootlets, leaves, moss and grass and has no hair or feathers in its lining. The 4—5 bluish-green eggs (2) are laid between April and June and are incubated for 14—15 days by the female. Both parents care for the young in the nest for 12—15 days. Rock Thrushes return to their breeding areas in April, but in August or September they leave again for the warmth of equatorial Africa and Arabia. Their diet consists of various invertebrate animals, which they gather on the ground or catch in the air; in the summer and autumn they enrich it with fruit and berries. The Rock Thrush is the size of a Blackbird, but has a very short tail. In its breeding plumage, the male (1) has a slate-blue head and shoulders and a rufous-chestnut underside; its rusty-brown tail and white rump also help in its iden-

tification. The brown-speckled female likewise has a rusty-

brown tail. The Rock Thrush is an excellent vocalist; its song is composed of fluty notes mixed with the tunes of other birds. The male often sings while 'dancing' on a rock face, with its wings and tail fully spread.

sures in rocks, among stones and in holes in walls. It is not a good builder and the nest is an untidy heap of grass blades, rootlets, moss and lichen. The nesting season lasts from April to June and some pairs appear to nest twice during that time. The 4—5 light blue eggs (2) are incubated for about 15 days by the female. The parents both care for the nestlings for 14—18 days, bringing them insects, spiders, worms and berries. With its slate to cobalt-blue coloration, the male Blue Rock Thrush (1) is easily recognisable; in the winter it becomes blacker. The female (3) has a bluish-brown back and

3♀

The Blue Rock Thrush is a typical south European species inhabiting all the countries bordering the Mediterranean and the southern part of Asia. It frequents dry, rocky regions with sparse vegetation and nests on mountainsides and coasts, in quarries and on the outskirts of human habitations; it does not usually ascend to such altitudes as the Rock Thrush, however. It is a partial migrant; populations from the northern part of its range migrate

2

in September to the southern part or still further south, to northern Africa and southern Asia, and return to their nesting sites in April. The Blue Rock Thrush nests in holes and fis-

a lighter underside barred with fine grey scale marks. Both sexes are very slightly larger than the Rock Thrush. The Blue Rock Thrush likes to sit on rocks with its wings half drooping, but it is very timid and vanishes if a human being approaches. Its alarm call is a sharp 'tchack' or a protracted 'tseeh'. Its loud, fluty song sometimes resembles the Blackbird's, but is simpler. The male sings while perched on a rock or, rarely, in flight.

Ring Ouzel

Turdus torquatus

by the female and is carefully concealed, preferably among the dense branches of a young spruce, but often in a taller tree. In form and structure it is similar to the Blackbird's nest, but has more thin twigs in its foundations. The 4—5 bluish or greenish eggs, which are thickly marked with rust-brown spots (2) and closely resemble Blackbird eggs, are laid in May or June. They are incubated for 14 days, mostly by the female; both the parents care for the young in the nest for approximately the same length of time. The birds occasionally rear two broods. This thrush is a migrant, arriving at its nesting sites in March or April and migrating to southern Europe or northern Africa in September or October. The male Ring Ouzel (1) is the size of a Blackbird, but is more brownish-black and has white-edged feathers, especially

The Ring Ouzel breeds mainly in the mountains of central and southern Europe, but also nests in large parts of Scandinavia, Britain and Ireland and in Asia Minor. It is not a purely montane bird and quite often it occurs on hills and moors at altitudes of less than 400 m and sometimes even lower, e.g. on cliffs on the coast. It has a preference for submontane and montane conifer forests, where it ascends high up into the alpine spruce zone; it does not nest so often in areas of deciduous and mixed woods at lower altitudes. It hunts for food on the ground, in open spaces — in meadows, pastureland and clearings. The nest is built chiefly on its wings and on the underside of its body. Its most distinctive feature is the wide white crescent-shaped area on its breast. The female has browner plumage and the 'half-moon' patch is also tinged with brown. The Ring Ouzel's song is less tuneful than the Blackbird's and contains jarring tones.

Blackbird

Turdus merula

Everybody is acquainted with the Blackbird, whose personality and song enliven even the biggest cities. Despite this, it is by rights a forest bird and some Blackbirds still live in their original environment. Forest-dwelling and Scandinavian Blackbirds are migrants and leave for west Europe and the Mediterranean region in the autumn; urban populations and west and south European Blackbirds are mostly resident. In addition, the Blackbird inhabits northwestern Africa and an area leading eastwards from Asia Minor to China. Unlike urban birds, forest Blackbirds are very timid and easily frightened, so that they are often heard rather than seen. The nest is usually built in a bush or a tree, up to a height of 2 m, but

urban birds will nest anywhere – in guttering, on a cornice, on a gravestone, or simply on a pile of logs. The outer wall of the nest is made of grass, leaves, moss, rootlets and twigs, the inner lining of fine grass and rootlets; the two are sandwiched together with mud (3). It takes the female 4–6 days to build the nest. The eggs are bluish-green and the whole of their surface is evenly speckled with small rust-brown spots (2). There are usually 4–5, the female incubates them for

13–14 days and, together with the male, feeds the young birds in the nest for roughly the same length of time. The pairs nest twice or three times during the season, which lasts from the end

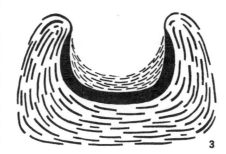

of March to the end of June. The male (1) is completely black, with a yellow to orange beak and yellow-ringed eyes. The female has a brownish-black back and lighter underparts with a spotted throat. The adult birds measure about 25 cm. The Blackbird is one of the first heralds of spring and often sings its mellow, fluty song, mixed with dissonant sounds, from an elevated perch while there is still snow lying on the ground. Its alarm call is a noisy 'chick-chick-chick'.

Fieldfare
Turdus pilaris

Unlike other thrushes, the Field-fare is a sociable bird. Although some pairs occasionally nest singly, the majority nest in colonies of about 30 pairs. The Field-fare likes parkland; it frequents old trees beside rivers, streams and ponds, old parks, copses and the outskirts of woods adjoining damp meadows and pastures. It inhabits mainly northern and central Europe and Asia, but lately it has shown a distinct tendency to spread westwards and southwards. It is largely a mi-grant. Scandinavian and some central European birds migrate to western and southern Europe in September and October and return to their nesting areas in March or April. The Fieldfare's nest closely resembles the Black-bird's. Its outer layer consists of grass, moss and twigs; inside this there is a layer of mud, which does not reach quite to the upper edge of the nest, quickly dries and hardens and is lined with a layer of fine grass (3). It is built entirely by the female; the female likewise receives no help with the incubation of the 4—6 eggs (2), which are almost indistinguish-able from the Blackbird's and from which the young hatch in 13—14 days. The parents feed the young for 13—15 days in the nest and continue their duties a fur-ther two weeks after the offspring have left it. Some pairs nest once during the season, others twice. Fieldfares live on both animal and plant food; in the winter their flocks descend on rowan berries and on other berry-bearing

trees and shrubs. The Field-fare (1) is the most brightly col-oured thrush. It is the same size as the Blackbird and its most distinctive features are its slate-grey head and rump, its brown back and black tail and the white under surface of its wings. Another good identification mark is its loud contact call, 'tchak-tchak-tchak', which can of-ten be heard as it flies. The male sometimes also sings in flight; its song is a mixture of twittering and whistling notes.

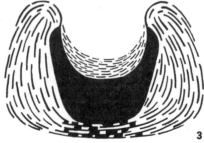

Song Thrush
Turdus philomelos

The Song Thrush inhabits most of Europe and a large part of Asia. It lives in various types of woods (more on their outskirts than inside them), in copses and in groups of trees beside rivers and streams. During the past few dec-

a surprise. Song Thrushes nest from the end of April to the beginning of July. The female builds the nest unaided, generally in a tree or a bush, less often in a recess in a wall, on a cornice or

on a beam, etc. It is easily recognisable, since the cup is faced with woody pulp mixed with saliva (2); it is hard and unlined. The 4—5 blue to bluish-green eggs are marked with a few scattered black speckles (3); they are incubated for 12—13 days by the female. The young are tended for about 14 days in the nest, this time with participation by the male. When the first young are independent, the adult birds begin to nest a second time. The Song Thrush (1), which measures about 23 cm, is somewhat smaller than the Blackbird; its back is olive-brown, its creamy-yellow breast is thickly marked with brown spots and the under surface of its wings is yellow (4). Its song is characterised by several repetitions of each of the various motifs, which are uttered explosively, with a kind of barking effect. Its call note is a piercing 'tsik, tsik'. Song Thrushes (and sometimes Blackbirds) betray their presence by the stones, tree stumps or branches on which they smash snail shells to extract their contents.

ades it has begun to infiltrate into human communities, but its urbanisation has not progressed anywhere near so far as in the case of the Blackbird. The vast majority of Song Thrushes are still migrants; they leave for southern and western Europe or northern Africa in September or October and usually return in March. Since they arrive during the night, their sudden loud song on a cold morning comes as

351

Redwing
Turdus iliacus

The Redwing normally breeds in Scandinavia, Iceland, Scotland, the north of the European part of the former USSR and Siberia, but it occasionally nests in central Europe and the limit of its distribution seems to be steadily

shifting further south. In the north, it is a typical taiga bird; in the south it likes wet ground, the banks of rivers and streams and the outskirts of woods with damp meadows in the vicinity. In the autumn, usually in October or November, large flocks of Redwings migrate to southern and western Europe or to northern

Africa; many of them stay in central Europe, however, often in the company of Fieldfares. They return in March or April and nest in May or June. The nest (2) is generally in a tree or a bush, but in the far north it is often on the ground; it is made of grass, leaves and rootlets and is reinforced with a layer of mud, which, as in the Fieldfare's nest, reaches to the bottom and attaches the nest to the branches on which it is built. The interior is lined with fine grass and rootlets. It is built by the female, but the male evidently helps to brood the 4—6 Blackbird-like eggs (3),

whose incubation takes 12—14 days. The young leave the nest prematurely, at only 10—12 days; the adult birds still look after them for a time and then nest again. The Redwing (1) is a little smaller than the Song Thrush, from which it differs by its striking whitish superciliary stripes and the reddish colouring of its sides and the under surface of its wings, which is particularly noticeable when it flies (4). The migration of Scandinavian Redwings can be followed quite well at night; their whistling contact call, 'see-ip', can be heard frequently, especially during the first half of the night.

Mistle Thrush
Turdus viscivorus

The Mistle Thrush inhabits practically the whole of Europe, the western part of Asia and the region of the Atlas Mountains in Africa. It is mainly a forest-dweller, with a special predilection for tall conifer woods, but is also occasionally found in deciduous woods and in old large parks; in western Europe it even infiltrates into human settlements. Southern birds are resident; northern populations migrate to southern and southwestern Europe in the autumn, but at the end of February or in March, before the snow has melted, they return and start singing from their favourite

perch at the top of a tree. The nest, which is built by the female, generally quite high up in a tree, has three layers in its structure: an outer layer made of dry grass, leaves, moss and lichen, a middle layer of mud (which can often be seen around the rim of the nest) and an inner layer of fine grass and rootlets (2). The female incubates the 4–5 greenish or bluish eggs marked with violet-grey and reddish spots (3) for 13–15 days. At the age of 12–16 days the young hop out of the nest and are then fed in its vicinity by the parents. Finally, they are left in the care of the male, while the female builds a new nest for the

next brood. This thrush lives on roughly the same diet as other thrushes: insects, spiders, worms and molluscs, etc in the spring and summer, and mainly berries and other fruit in the autumn and winter. The Mistle

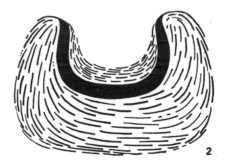

Thrush (1), which is a little larger than the Blackbird, is the largest thrush. Compared with the Song Thrush, it has a greyer back and a whiter underside with bolder spots; the under surface of its wings is white (4). Its song is similar to the Blackbird's, but is divided into short, simple phrases. Its alarm call is a rattling 'tsrrr' or 'shnurrr'.

353

Cetti's Warbler
Cettia cetti

Cetti's Warbler (1) looks rather like an unstreaked *Acrocephalus* warbler, but its back is a darker brown and it has a narrow, light superciliary stripe; its underside is greyish-white and the end of its tail is widely rounded. It is smaller than a sparrow. It lives secretively in dense vegetation and is

Cetti's Warbler is a resident, or at most a nomadic, bird inhabiting southern and western Europe as far as the south of Britain, Holland and Switzerland, southern Asia and the north of Africa. It lives and nests in reeds and in dense low vegetation, mostly beside water. It usually nests twice

during the breeding season, which lasts from April to June. The cup-shaped nest is made of straw, grass and moss and is carefully concealed in the thickest tangle of plants, close to the ground. There are usually 3–5 brick red, unspotted eggs (2), which are incubated for 13–14

seldom seen. It is given away mostly by its voice, with short 'chi-wik' and 'chik' calls, or by its short and very loud song — tchi-tchi-tchuitt! tchuitti-tchuitti-tchuitti' — which begins unexpectedly and ends very suddenly.

days by the female. The young leave the nest at the age of 12–14 days, but the parents feed and look after them for a further 14 days. Cetti's Warbler lives chiefly on insects and other small invertebrates.

2

Fan-tailed Warbler

Cisticola juncidis

The Fan-tailed Warbler (1) is only slightly larger than the Goldcrest. It has a very short, round-ended tail. Its crown and its back are brown to rust-coloured, streaked with rows of dark spots; its rust-brown rump is unspotted. It lacks a pale supercilium and its outer tail feathers have black and white tips. Its underside is white and its breast and flanks have a rusty-yellow tinge. The Fan-tailed Warbler is extremely retiring, but is usually betrayed by its song, 'dzeep dzeep dzeep', sung as it flies in undulating curves over its nesting area; the song is synchronised with the movements of its wings, each note coinciding with an upstroke. The Fan-tailed Warbler inhabits southern Europe, northern Africa and part of Asia Minor. It is a resident bird and nests in damp meadows, swamps and ricefields, but also in dry steppes and in cornfields. The pear-shaped nest is a beautifully woven structure made of straw, grass, leaves and fluff and is carefully hidden in dense vegetation close to the ground. The breeding season is from April to July and the pairs usually nest twice. The 4—6 white, russet-spotted eggs (2) are incubated for 10—11 days by both the sexes. The young leave the nest after roughly the same length of time and are fed by the parents in the surrounding vegetation for about two weeks longer. This species lives on insects and other invertebrates.

Grasshopper Warbler
Locustella naevia

The Grasshopper Warbler breeds mainly in damp meadows with tall herbaceous plants and scattered shrubs, or ponds and the flood areas of large rivers with similar vegetation; it occurs less often in overgrown clearings and rape or clover fields. It arrives at its nesting sites in April or May. The relatively deep nest, which is evidently built by both sexes, is made chiefly of grass and is placed on or just above the ground in a dense tangle of plants; gossamer is often woven into the walls and the lining consists of fine dry grass and a small quantity of hair. The 5−6 eggs (2) are marked with small rusty-red speckles on a reddish ground. The sexes take turns to sit and the incubation time is 12−14 days.

The parents likewise both feed the nestlings for 10−12 days, mainly on insects and less often on other small invertebrates. Between May and July the pairs usually manage to nest twice. In August or September the birds migrate to Africa. They breed over a wide range stretching from northern Spain, across the whole of Europe, to southwestern Siberia and inner Asia. The adult birds both have a greenish-brown back streaked with rows of blackish spots and a yellowish-white underside. The Grasshopper Warbler (1) is very secretive; if alarmed, it darts into the thickest vegetation like a mouse rather than a bird. As it sings, the male sidles its way up to the top of a reed or a bush, and if we catch sight of it we at once notice its wide-open beak, from which an unbroken, chirping 'seeerrrr' issues forth, often for as long as one to three minutes. It is a metallic sound, all in one key, and continues without discernible interruption. The members of this genus are all somewhat smaller than a sparrow.

River Warbler

Locustella fluviatilis

The River Warbler nests in thickets beside streams, rivers and ponds, in the dense undergrowth of riparian woods, in marshy meadows with luxuriant vegetation and occasionally in fairly dry overgrown clearings. The nest is always skilfully concealed in dense vegetation close to the ground; its outer layer is formed of leaves, dry grass and thick stems of various herbaceous plants and its inner layer is made of fine grass, occasionally together with hair. The nest is sometimes provided with a small ramp. The 4—5 whitish, russet-speckled eggs (2) are laid in May or June; they are incubated for about 13 days by the female, occasionally relieved by the male. The young, which are fed by both the parent birds, leave the nest in about 11—15 days and two weeks later they are independent. Some pairs nest twice during the breeding season. River Warblers migrate to their winter quarters on the east coast of Africa at the end of August or in September. They return in April or May. The River Warbler inhabits a rather small area stretching from Germany in the west to the Urals in the east and from the south of Sweden in the north to the Black Sea in the south. The male and the female both have an olive-brown back and a whitish underside with sparse streaking on their throat and breast. The River Warbler is secretive and nimble, and flits unobserved through the dense undergrowth in a characteristic attitude, with its body and head held level (1). When it sings, however, the male climbs up the highest branches of bushes or the tallest herbaceous plants. Its song, a persistently repeated 'dzedzedzedze' divided into verses of varying lengths, has a fast rhythm similar to a sewing-machine; it is never so long or so fast as the song of the Grasshoppers Warbler.

2

Savi's Warbler
Locustella luscinioides

In Europe, the breeding range of Savi's Warbler extends north to southernmost Britain and the Scandinavian countries; it also comprises a small part of Asia and northern Africa. Recently, this species has spread north and northwestwards and there has been a distinct increase in its numbers in central Europe. It nests only in swampy regions, mostly with beds of reed, rush and sedge. It is strictly a migrant, appearing in its typical nesting sites at the end of April and migrating to its winter quarters in tropical Africa in August or at the beginning of September. In the meantime, some pairs manage to nest twice. The nest is carefully hidden in dense swamp vegetation, usually just above water; it

is not anchored to the surrounding plants, however, but is rather pressed into them. It is built by both the sexes, is made virtually entirely of strips of reed, rush or sedge leaves 0.5—2.5 cm wide and is characterised by a paucity of fine material in its lining. The 3—4 eggs (2) resemble those of the River Warbler; they are incu-

bated by the female, helped by the male. The young hatch in 12—13 days and after approximately the same length of time they leave the nest. Savi's Warbler (1) has a brownish-russet back and a rusty-white underside with a lighter throat. A typical feature of this and other *Locustella* species is the tail, which is graduated, producing a very rounded tip, and has long under-tail-coverts. The long, monotonous song is a frequently interrupted 'urrrr-urrrr', deeper than the song of the Grasshopper Warbler. As a rule, the male sings while climbing to the top of a reed blade; like other members of the genus, it also sings unremittingly in the evening and at night.

Moustached Warbler

Acrocephalus melanopogon

2

In Europe, the Moustached Warbler inhabits the regions around the Mediterranean and the Black Sea; it also occurs in southwestern Asia. Its eastern populations migrate; other populations are evidently resident. Many birds spend the winter in the southern part of the range; others fly on to northern Africa, the Middle East or India. Autumn migration takes place in September and October, spring migration in March and April. When they return, the birds settle in the vegetation beside ponds and lakes or in large marshes with a permanently high water level, sedge or grass undergrowth and the flattened remains of the previous year's vegetation. The nest is evidently built by the female, which sus-

pends it between thick reed blades close to the surface of the water, but supported by broken blades from below and covered with vegetation from above. The adults nest twice a year between April and June. The 3–5 greyish or yellowish eggs, which are thickly covered with brown spots

(2), are incubated for 14 days by both the parent birds in turn; the nestlings are tended for about 12 days, again by both the adult birds, which feed them mainly on insects and other small invertebrates. The Moustached Warbler (1) is similar in coloration to the Sedge Warbler, but its darker crown is marked with rich brown and black stripes and it has a more pronounced, whitish superciliary stripe; if alarmed it holds its tail erect like the Wren. Its song resembles the song of the Reed Warbler, but contains 'dee-dee-dee' notes reminiscent of the crescendo tones of a Nightingale. This, and all other *Acrocephalus* species except the Great Reed Warbler, are the size of a sparrow.

Sedge Warbler
Acrocephalus schoenobaenus

1

The male Sedge Warbler often rounds off its song with a display flight, during which it flies high up into the air and then, with open wings and spread tail, glides obliquely down again (2); the only other reed warbler that does this is the rare Aquatic Warbler *Acrocephalus paludicola*. The Sedge Warbler nests at the edge of ponds overgrown with reeds, sedge, tall grass and shrubs; it also occurs in marshy meadows with isolated bushes, overgrown depressions and drainage channels and sometimes far away from any water, in cornfields and rape fields. Its range includes virtually the whole of Europe (except the Iberian Peninsula) and Siberia as far as the Yenisei. The nest is not suspended from the stems of plants, as it is in most other species, but is simply pressed into a thick layer of old grass, sedge or reeds. The sexes both build it together; they construct an outer layer of dry grass and reed blades and leaves and an inner layer formed mainly of reed down, plant fluff and hair. The

2

4—6 greyish-yellow eggs, which are marked with fine black streaks at their blunt end (3), are incubated for 12—13 days; the young leave the nest after 10—15 days' parental care. The adult birds often nest twice in the same season. In September or October, Sedge Warblers migrate to tropical Africa, returning again in April or May. Both sexes have dark brown streaking on their back and a rusty-brown, unstreaked rump. The top of their head is dark brown and finely striped and they have striking creamy-buff superciliary stripes (1). The male's song is rendered hurriedly and always contains a typical fluty 'wheet-wheet' phrase; the male also sings at night and sometimes incorporates mimicry of other birds into its song.

3

Marsh Warbler
Acrocephalus palustris

birds live mainly on insects and their larvae and spiders, supplemented in the autumn by small berries. During August, they vanish, one by one, from their nesting areas. The Marsh Warbler is a European bird whose range stretches from England and France to the Urals; it is absent from Portugal, Spain, Italy and most of Scandinavia. The male and the female (1) both have an olive-brown back and a creamy-yellow underside; their rump never has a rusty tinge. The tip of their 8th primary does not reach to the level where the inner vane of their 2nd primary narrows (2). The interior of their beak is orange-yellow; their legs are a reddish-flesh colour. The Marsh Warbler's sweet, tuneful song is reminiscent of the song of the Icterine Warbler, but usually contains a typical 'witt-witt-witt' and mimetic motifs; it can also frequently be heard at night.

The Marsh Warbler is not associated with damp environments so strictly as other members of the genus and it is to be found in rape fields, cornfields, clover fields, dry thickets in fields and dense growths of weeds (often stinging-nettles), as well as beside ponds, rivers and streams. By occupying rubbly wasteland, it often breeds near towns. Marsh Warblers return from their African winter quarters in May and soon begin building their nests, which they anchor in the typical reed warbler manner to stems or twigs not too far above dry ground. The nest is made of dry grass blades and leaves, plant fibres and fluff and sometimes hair. The 4−5 bluish or greenish eggs are marked with a few brown spots; they are incubated for 12−13 days by both the parent birds in turn and the nestlings are fed for approximately the same length of time. Like most reed warblers, the

Reed Warbler
Acrocephalus scirpaceus

The Reed Warbler inhabits the whole of Europe except Ireland, the north of Britain and the north in April or May. It is a typical inhabitant of reedbeds, but sometimes appears among bulrushes.

around supporting reed stems; the latter are sometimes new and green and sometimes old and dry. The nest is usually 25—100 cm above the water or the ground; it is made of strips of reed leaves and plant fibres and is lined with parts of reed tops. As a rule, the female lays 4 greenish or bluish, brown- or grey-spotted eggs (2), which both the parents incubate for 12—13 days. The adult birds likewise both care for the young, which remain 9—13 days in the nest. Some pairs nest twice during the season. The Reed Warbler (1) looks so much like the Marsh Warbler that they can normally be differentiated only by their voices and by their appearance in their respective different environments during the nesting season. The Reed Warbler has a more rusty-brown rump and darker, grey legs. As in other members of this genus, the young have two elongate black spots on their tongue. In this species, the tip of the 8th primary reaches to the level of the narrow part of the inner vane of the 2nd primary. The Reed Warbler keeps strict time while singing and its song always contains the triple repeated motif 'tirri, tirri, tirri — churr, churr, churr — chirruc, chirruc, chirruc'. The bird climbs up a reed blade as it sings.

of Scandinavia; its range also extends to southwestern Asia and northern Africa. In September or October it migrates to tropical Africa, and returns again rushes. It also nests in small patches of reeds far away from water. The sexes both participate in the building of the nest, which is a deep basket skilfully woven

2

Great Reed Warbler
Acrocephalus arundinaceus

The Great Reed Warbler inhabits the whole of Europe except Scandinavia and the British Isles; it also occurs in northern Africa and Asia Minor. Further subspecies (according to some authors further species) are found in Asia as far as the Philippines and over the whole of Australia. The Great Reed Warbler lives in reed (less often bulrush) thickets with permanent water in the vicinity. European birds are typical migrants and do not arrive at their nesting sites until May. The nest (2) is made by the female, which successively weaves strips of reed leaves around several reed or rush stems, binding them so firmly that they appear to be growing through the walls of the nest. The nest itself is up to 20 cm

they are not yet able to fly, but they climb about nimbly among the tangled reeds, where they are

fed for two more weeks by their parents. Cases of polygyny, in which one male nested with up to

deep and its upper edge, like that of the Reed Warbler's nest, is folded inwards, so that the eggs cannot fall out even in a strong wind. The nest is always suspended 25—75 cm above the water and usually takes five days to build. The 4—5 eggs (3) are larger replicas of the Reed Warbler's eggs. They are incubated for 12—15 days by the female, which the male keeps supplied with food. At the age of 10—12 days the young hop out of the nest;

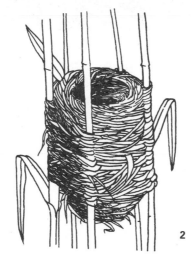

three females, are known. The birds set out on their long journey to equatorial and southern Africa in August or September. The Great Reed Warbler (1) is the largest member of the genus; it is the size of a slim thrush. It has a plain brown back and a whitish, ochre-tinged underside. In reed-beds it gives itself away by its harsh, 'squawking' song, characterised by constant repetition of a clearly distinct 'karra, karra — keek, keek' motif.

363

Olivaceous Warbler
Hippolais pallida

The Olivaceous Warbler (1) has brownish-grey upperparts, a whitish underside and a white superciliary stripe. It also has fairly short wings (62—72 mm),

water. It is a migrant and winters in the African savanna belt north of the equator. It returns in April or May and mating and nest--building begin soon afterwards. The nest is built mainly by the female, sometimes helped by the

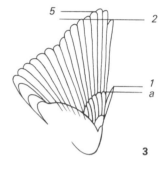

male; it is placed low down in a bush, is made of rootlets, grass, leaves, plant fibres, moss and lichen and the lining contains fluff and horsehair. The 4—5 light grey, pink-tinted eggs, marked with fine black streaks and spots (2), are incubated for 14—15 days. The nestlings are fed for about 15 days, mainly on insects. The adult birds do not nest a second time and in August they leave their nesting areas. All *Hippolais* species grow to sparrow size; the only exception is the Olive-tree Warbler, which is slightly larger.

on which the 1st primary is longer than the primary coverts (a) and the 2nd primary is shorter than the 5th (3) (in the Olive-tree Warbler the wings measure 79—93 mm, the 1st primary is shorter than the primary coverts (a) and the 2nd primary is longer than the 5th: (4). In Europe, the Olivaceous Warbler lives only in the Balkans and the south of Spain; otherwise it occurs in northern Africa and the south-western part of Asia. During the past few decades it has also spread from the Balkans into Hungary. The Olivaceous Warbler likes an uneven terrain, with bushes, trees, parks and gardens; it is often to be found near

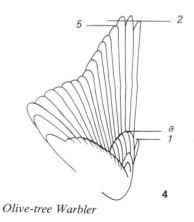

Olive-tree Warbler

Olive-tree Warbler
Hippolais olivetorum

The Olive-tree Warbler (1) has generally grey plumage. It is the largest member of this genus; it also has a much thicker and longer beak, which is yellow at its base, and bluish-grey legs. Its back is grey, its tail and wings are greyish-brown (the secondaries have clearly discernible white edges) and its underside is whit-

2

in orchards. The nest, which is built on a forked branch, is a neat, strongly woven structure made of straw, rootlets, strips of bark,

larger than the eggs of the Icterine Warbler; they are reddish-violet and are marked with blackish brown spots (2). The young hatch in 13—14 days. No details of their further development are known, but it is probably similar to that of the Icterine Warbler. The birds live mainly on insects and insect larvae gathered from

ish. Its distinctive song is louder, slower and deeper than the song of other *Hippolais* species. The Olive-tree Warbler occurs only in the southern part of the Balkans and in Asia Minor, where large numbers of these birds live in olive groves and oakwoods and

thistle down and cobwebs and softly lined with fine grass, root fibres and plant wool (but no feathers). The adults nest only once a year, between May and July, and the female has never been known to lay more than 4 eggs. These are somewhat

the branches and leaves of trees and bushes. At the end of August, Olive-tree Warblers leave for their winter quarters in northern and northeastern Africa (as far as Ethiopia); they return to their breeding areas at the end of April.

Icterine Warbler

Hippolais icterina

The nest of the lcterine Warbler is one of the most attractive of all birds' nests. The sexes build it together, always in a deciduous bush or tree. The twigs to which it is attached are firmly incorporated in the walls of the nest, which is a skilfully woven structure made of dry grass, rootlets, fragments of moss, plant fluff and cobwebs; it is faced with white strips of silver birch bark and is softly lined with hair and feathers. The 4—5 eggs, which are

same length of time. The adults are unable to nest more than once, because at the end of August they leave again for central and southern Africa. In May, when they return, they settle in open deciduous woods with un-

2

Siberia. It lives mainly on small insects, to which a fair amount of berries and other fruit is added in the autumn. The adult birds (1) have a brownish-green or greenish-grey back, a yellow underside and bluish-grey legs. They have the profile characteristic of all *Hippolais* species, i. e. with a long, broad-based beak, a sloping forehead and a high crown. The lcterine Warbler is an outstanding singer. Its resounding song consists of fluty and

laid at the end of May or in June, are rose-pink and are marked with thinly scattered blackish-brown and black spots (2), so that they are easily identified. They are incubated for 13—14 days by both the sexes in turn and the young are fed in the nest for the

dergrowth, on densely overgrown banks beside water and in parks and gardens. The lcterine Warbler is a primarily European bird whose range stretches eastwards from northern and eastern France and Scandinavia and sends out spurs to the River Ob in

churring tones with triple motifs, including its call note, 'deederoid, deederoid, deederoid', which is so typical that the bird can always be identified from it. The lcterine Warbler is also a master in the art of imitating the voices of other birds.

366

Melodious Warbler
Hippolais polyglotta

The Melodious Warbler (1) closely resembles the Icterine Warbler and when seen in natural surroundings is almost indistinguishable from it. It has browner legs, however, and shorter, rounded wings measuring only 59—70 mm, in which the 1st primary is over 3 mm longer than the primary coverts (a) and the 2nd primary is shorter than the 6th primary (2); in the Icterine Warbler the wings measure 69—85 mm, the 1st primary is the same length as, or only slightly longer than, the coverts (a) and the 2nd primary is shorter than only the 3rd to 5th (3). The song of the Melodious Warbler is somewhat softer and more tuneful than that of the Icterine Warbler; it has no harsh tones, but

spends the winter in the savannas of western Africa and returns in April or May. The nest, which is smaller than that of the Icterine Warbler, is built in a copse, a thicket, an orchard or a garden. The 4—5 rosy, black-speckled eggs are incubated for about 13 days, entirely by the female. The parents both feed the nestlings for a further 12—13 days, mainly on insects. The birds leave for their winter quarters in August or September.

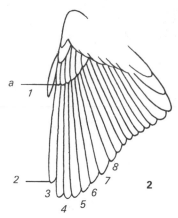

mimics other birds' motifs equally well. This species inhabits western Europe, roughly westwards from Italy, and also lives in northern Africa. In places where its range overlaps that of the Icterine Warbler, the males fight battles for nesting territories and in such places mixed pairs can evidently be formed. The Melodious Warbler is a migrant; it

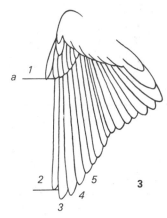

Icterine Warbler

Dartford Warbler
Sylvia undata

The Dartford Warbler is distributed over a relatively small area. It inhabits the warm southern and western parts of Europe, i. e. the Iberian Peninsula, France, Italy, Sardinia and Corsica and the southernmost parts of Britain, together with the north coast of Africa. It nests in dry localities with dense scrub. The nest, which is usually built low down in a thornbush, is generally made of grass blades and leaves. The 3—4 whitish, finely brown-speckled eggs (2) are incubated for 12—13 days, mostly by the female; the nestlings are fed for 11—13 days by both parents. The young birds then leave the nest and learn to be independent, aided by the adult birds. They live almost entirely on insect imagos, larvae and pupae and sometimes on small spiders. The adult birds then nest again and rear a second brood, despite the shortness of the nesting period (April to June).

The Dartford Warbler (1) is a resident bird and even after nesting it does not usually roam very far afield. It is a small sylviid and is about the size of the Lesser Whitethroat; it has a much longer, round-ended tail, however, and darker plumage. Its back is dark grey-brown, and its underside reddish-brown with a white belly; the female's underside is lighter. It has small white spots on its throat. Its song is rather like the song of the Whitethroat and the male likewise sings it from a perch or in flight. All sylviids are small birds measuring 13—15 cm.

2

Spectacled Warbler
Sylvia conspicillata

The Spectacled Warbler (1) closely resembles the Whitethroat. Its plumage is largely brownish-grey, but it has a darker head, a striking white throat, a redder breast and reddish-brown wings; the narrow white ring around its eyes can be seen only at close quarters. Its song is relatively quiet, again like the Whitethroat's, and the male sings it from a perch or during its display flight. Its dry, rattling alarm call is characteristic. The Spectacled Warbler is confined to southern Europe (Portugal, Spain, the south of France and Italy) and the northern part of Africa. European birds are migrants and cross to Africa for the winter. In the spring they return to their nesting areas, for which they prefer flat ground beside water, densely overgrown with low shrubs. The nesting season usually lasts from April to June and the nest, which is made of straw, rootlets, thin twigs and grass, is carefully concealed in thick vegetation, close to the ground. The 4—6 eggs are incubated by both the parent birds, which afterwards both care for the young for about two weeks in the nest and some time after they have left it. Their initial diet (mainly insects and other small invertebrates) is later supplemented with berries and fruit.

Sardinian Warbler
Sylvia melanocephala

The Sardinian Warbler occurs mainly in the Mediterranean region, i. e. on the coast of southern Europe and in a small part of Asia and northern Africa. It is a resident, or at most a nomadic, bird nesting in dry, scrubby country, in pinewoods and holm-oak copses with plenty of undergrowth and in vineyards and gardens. From April to June it nests in low shrubs, and the nest, which is made of dry stalks and grass, is hidden away in the thickest tangle of branches only a little way above the ground. The 3—5 yellowish-white eggs, which are thickly speckled with russet spots (2), are incubated for 13—14 days by both the parent birds in turn. The parents likewise both feed the nestlings for 11—12 days and continue to feed the young in the surrounding bushes for some time after they have left the nest. When the young are independent, the adult birds nest again. During the nesting season, Sardinian Warblers live mainly on insects and spiders; later, they eat more berries and fruit. The male (1) has a grey back, a whitish underside and grey-tinged flanks; the outer feathers of its rounded tail are white. Its most distinctive feature is its glossy black hood, which extends down over its crimson-ringed eyes; the female is browner and has a grey-brown cap. Its song is rather like the Whitethroat's, but is longer and more resonant and is occasionally interrupted by

a staccato, warning 'cha-cha-cha-cha'. The male sings while perched, or during its brief display flight.

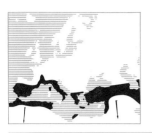

Orphean Warbler
Sylvia hortensis

The Orphean Warbler is one of the larger sylviids and is the same size as the Barred Warbler. Its back is dark grey-brown, its throat, the middle of its belly and its outer tail feathers are white and its flanks are buff to pink. Its

most striking features are its white eyes and (in the spring) the male's dull black hood (1), which reaches down over its eyes. Its call note is a sharp 'tac tac' or 'terrr'; its song is loud and tuneful, with four to five repetitions of 'chiwirroo' and 'tittiwoo' motifs somewhat reminiscent of the Song Thrush. The Orphean Warbler inhabits the countries of southern Europe around the Mediterranean (its most northerly limit is the southwest of Switzerland), southwestern Asia and northern Africa. It frequents dry and mostly hilly country with copses, thickets, olive and lemon groves, parks and gardens. On its arrival, in April or May, it immediately takes possession of a nesting territory and starts building. The nest, which is generally built on a branch of a tree and less often in a bush, is a firmly woven structure made of blades and rootlets. The 4−5 white or pale green eggs thinly marked with black spots (2) appear in the nest in May or June; they are incubated for about 12 days by the female, with occasional help from the male. The young, which are fed by both parents, also leave the nest at about 12 days. Orphean Warblers live chiefly on insects and other small invertebrates found on the branches of trees and bushes, together with berries and fruit. During August they leave their territories and in October they migrate to their winter quarters in Africa, in the savanna belt south of the Sahara.

2

Barred Warbler

Sylvia nisoria

The Barred Warbler inhabits central and eastern Europe and Asia as far as Mongolia. It frequents open country with dense thickets (particularly thorn-bushes), copses, hedges and the vegetation on the outskirts of woods and beside water. As distinct from many other sylviids, it shuns human settlements. Its nest is often to be found quite close to the nest of the Red-backed Shrike, which other passerines usually avoid. It is situated on a branch of a dense shrub, usually not more than 1 m above the ground; it is built mainly by the female, is made of dry stems and rootlets and is lined with fine grass and animal hairs. The parents take turns to brood the 4—5 yellowish or greenish, grey-spotted eggs (2), which are incubated for 12—15 days. In the initial phase of nesting, the Barred Warbler is very timid and often abandons the nest and eggs at the slightest disturbance. The parents care for the young for 11—16 days in the nest and then roam the neighbourhood with them. They do not nest a second time and in August they migrate to eastern Africa, returning again at the beginning of May. The Barred Warbler's coloration is reminiscent of that of the Cuckoo or the Sparrowhawk and, like the latter, it has unusual, bright yellow eyes, which give it a predatory appearance. The male (1, behind) has a slate-grey back; its flanks and the whole of its underside are light grey and have grey vermiculations across them. The female (1, in front) is browner and the markings are less distinct. The Barred Warbler's song resembles the song of the Garden Warbler, but is shorter and sharper and contains an occasionally interspersed, characteristic hard 'tcharrr' call note. The male sings from the top of a bush or the shelter of branches, but occasionally it marks out its domain by a dancing song flight over the bushes.

2

Lesser Whitethroat
Sylvia curruca

The Lesser Whitethroat is more of an open country bird and avoids large forest areas. It can be encountered in copses, on bushy hillsides, on the outskirts of woods and in clearings, parks, gardens and cemeteries, but for nesting it will also make do with a group of bushes beside a footpath in a field. It nests over most of Europe and Asia, usually returns to its nesting sites in the middle of April and is among the first sylviid birds to be heard in the spring. Its nesting season lasts from the end of April to the beginning of July. The nest, which is built in a bush, usually at a height of about 1 m, is a rather rickety structure made of loosely interwoven dry stalks, grass blades and leaves and rootlets, with cobwebs in the outer layer. The parents take turns to brood the 4–5 yellowish or greenish-white, brown- and grey-spotted eggs (2), which are incubated for 10–13 days; nest care lasts the same length of time. Many pairs rear a further brood during the season. In September or October, they all migrate to north-eastern Africa. The Lesser Whitethroat (1) has a brownish-grey back, dark brown wings, distinctive dark grey ear-coverts, a white throat and white outer tail feathers. The male sings while exploring the tops of trees and bushes. Its song is in two parts – a fine, twittering prelude, which is so soft that it can be heard only at close quarters, and a fast, rattling main song, 'chikka-chikka-chikka-chik', which some birds sing in sparkling tones and others like the clattering of a sewing-machine.

2

Whitethroat
Sylvia communis

The Whitethroat nests in shrubs at the edge of woods or clearings, in copses, parks and gardens, in groups of bushes in meadows and fields and even among dense tall herbaceous plants (e. g. nettles) growing in ditches. The birds return to their nesting areas in April or May. The first to arrive are the males; as soon as they have taken possession of a nesting territory, like other sylviids they immediately begin to build a nest (or several nests), to which they try to attract a female. The female either uses this nest, or builds a new one, aided by the male. The nest is built in a dense tangle of branches or a clump of herbaceous plants, usually not more than 1 m above the ground; it is made of dry stalks, grass blades and rootlets and is often faced with insect cocoons and cobwebs. The parents take turns to brood the 4—5 greenish, brown- or grey-speckled eggs (2), which are incubated for 11—13 days; they likewise both care for the nestlings for 10—13 days. They manage to rear two broods in one season. Whitethroats migrate in September to the savannas of tropical Africa. They inhabit virtually the whole of Europe, a large part of Asia and the north coast of Africa. In recent years there has been a sharp decrease in their numbers in practically the whole of western and central Europe. The male (1) has an ash-grey head, a grey-brown back and a whitish, pink-tinged underside; its wings are bright russet. The female has a brownish head and lacks the pink-tinted breast. The Whitethroat's song has short verses, is rendered hurriedly and ends on a loud interrogative note. While singing, the male often flies up and then sails down into the bushes again, spreading its wings and holding its tail erect.

2

Garden Warbler
Sylvia borin

The Garden Warbler (1) inhabits Europe except the most northerly and most southerly parts and its range extends eastwards to western Siberia. It lives on the thicketed edges of damp woods (mainly deciduous and mixed woods) and in clearings, in thickets beside rivers, streams and ponds and less often in parks, cemeteries and gardens. It returns from its winter quarters in tropical and southern Africa in May. Soon afterwards, the sexes build a thin-walled, cup-shaped nest low down in dense bushes. It is made practically entirely of dry round grass stalks and is lined with dry finer grass. The 4—5 very variably coloured, grey- or brown-spotted eggs (2) are incubated for 11—14 days by both the parent birds. When only 9—12 days old, the young leave the nest, although they are not yet fully able to fly. The Garden Warbler lives mainly on insects, but in the summer and autumn, like other *Sylvia* species, it also eats soft berries and fruit. At the end of August or the beginning of September, the birds migrate to warmer regions. The Garden Warbler is a plain brownish-grey colour, with a dark back and a light underside; its legs are grey. As distinct from young Blackcaps, the nestlings have a black spot between their beak and their eyes; the lining of their beak is dingy red, the edges are yellowish-white and on the tongue there are two indistinct elongate grey spots. The male usually sings from the cover of

a tree or bush. Its pleasing, tuneful song is composed of fairly long verses and is rendered the whole time at almost the same pitch; it thus lacks the arresting pure fluty tones of the Blackcap.

Blackcap
Sylvia atricapilla

The Blackcap is the most typical forest-dweller of the entire genus. It inhabits both deciduous woods and conifer forests, but is also to be found in copses, waterside vegetation, overgrown parks, cemeteries and gardens. Its nest is almost always built in the most shady spot, usually close to the ground; it is a loosely woven structure made of small twigs and grass blades and leaves and is lined with fine grass, rootlets and fur. The female does most of the building itself. The 4—5 almost uni-

spend the winter in western Europe and the cold climate of central Europe (this is possible because the Blackcap's diet contains a larger proportion of plant material, such as common and scarlet-berried elder, privet and bird cherry, than the food of other sylviids). Its small cap makes identification of the Blackcap easy. In the adult male the cap is black and glossy (1), in the female (2) and juveniles it is rusty-brown. The Blackcap is one of the best songbirds. Its song consists of a muted twittering prelude,

followed by a rich-toned, fluty warble (counterpoint) with an ascending finish. The whole song gives the impression of being slower than the song of the Garden Warbler.

3

coloured brownish, or lightly brown-speckled eggs (3) are incubated for 11—15 days by both the parent birds in turn; the young are tended for 11—14 days in the nest. The adults usually rear two broods during the summer. The Blackcap inhabits the whole of Europe, Asia as far as western Siberia and the coast of northern Africa. It is a migrant, arriving in April and leaving for the Mediterranean region or the northern part of Africa in September or October. Occasional birds, in particular males, also

Bonelli's Warbler
Phylloscopus bonelli

Bonelli's Warbler inhabits chiefly western and southern Europe, but also some of central Europe. Since 1940 it has spread northwards and today it inhabits the Iberian Peninsula, France, Switzerland, the southern part of Germany, the south of Belgium, part of Holland, Austria and Italy; it also lives in a narrow strip of the Mediterranean coast of northern Africa. A somewhat different race inhabits the whole of the Balkans and part of Asia Minor. Bonelli's Warbler is a migrant. In April or May, the male announces its arrival by a simple short trilling song which can be heard from the tree canopy. It is similar to the Wood Warbler's song, but is rendered more slowly and consists of clearly separate single notes. When the female arrives, it soon begins to build the nest, which is always on the ground and has a side entrance like a little door. It is made of leaves, moss and grass and is very carefully concealed somewhere in a wood on a dry slope. The 5—6 white eggs, which are thickly covered with russet spots (2), are incubated for about 13 days, entirely by the female. The male lends a hand with the young, however, and both parents look after them in the nest for roughly the same length of time. The young are given the same food as other young of the genus, i. e. mainly insects and small spiders. The adults nest only once a year and in August or September they migrate to their winter quarters in the acacia steppes of western Africa. Bonelli's Warbler (1) has a greyish-brown back and a white throat, breast and belly; its yellowish rump is clearly distinguishable from the colour of its back and its tail feathers are also a yellowish shade. Its pale ear-coverts are fairly conspicuous.

2

Wood Warbler
Phylloscopus sibilatrix

The Wood Warbler inhabits practically the whole of Europe except the Iberian Peninsula and the northern part of Scandinavia. It lives in tall deciduous and

mixed woods and seldom occurs in conifer forests. The nest (3), which is built by the female, usually in two to four days, has a side entrance and almost always lies on the ground in the shelter of grass or fallen leaves. Unlike the nest of the Chiffchaff and the Willow Warbler, it is never lined with feathers. The 5—7 white eggs are marked with fairly large dark brown or grey spots (4), denser and more distinct than the markings on the eggs of other *Phylloscopus* species; they are laid in May or June and are incubated for 12—14 days by the female. The young are fed by both parents and remain 12—13 days in the nest. About four weeks after the young have left the nest, the families break up; the adult birds do not usually nest a second time. In August or September they all migrate to equatorial Africa, returning to their nesting areas in April or at the beginning of May. The Wood Warbler (1) is the largest and most colourful *Phylloscopus* species. It has a yellow throat and breast and a fairly wide, sulphur-yellow superciliary stripe. Its belly is white, its back is yellowish-green and its legs are a light yellowish-brown. The length of its primaries (2) is an important distinguishing character. The 2nd primary is longer than the 5th and the 1st is distinctly shorter than the primary coverts (a). The Wood Warbler's song is composed of a series of 'stip-stip-stip' notes, sung at the same pitch, which grow faster and faster and end with a trilling 'shreeeee'. It is sung by the male while perched, or as it flies from one branch to another, usually quite low in the tree canopy. The song is also accompanied by fluty 'piu-piu-piu' notes.

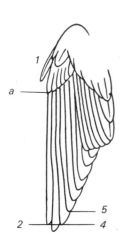

Chiffchaff
Phylloscopus collybita

Early in the spring, usually in March, we can hear from the crowns of the trees a simple, persistently repeated and easily remembered bird's song sounding like 'chiff-chaff, chiff-chaff'. It is the song of the Chiffchaff, which has just returned from southern Europe or northern Africa and announces its presence in copses, large parks, cemeteries and old gardens. The female builds the nest on or just above the ground, in bilberry plants, in new undergrowth, in a thicket or on a young fir; it is a spherical structure with a side entrance (3); like other *Phylloscopus* nests, it is made of dry grass, twigs, leaves, moss and strips of bark and is lined with feathers. The nesting period lasts from May into July. The 5—7 white eggs, which are covered with small red-brown speckles (4), are incubated for 13—14 days by the female. The female also rears the young unaided, while the male busily sings in the vicinity. The young are fed for 13—16 days in the nest and the female

still cares for them for several days after they have left it. When the young are independent, the adults generally nest again. In September or October they all fly southwards or westwards. The Chiffchaff is a European species, but it extends a long way into Asia and also occurs in part of northwestern Africa. The male and the female (1) both have a greyish-green back and a dingy white to yellowish underside; their legs (and the juveniles') are blackish-brown. The 6th primary appears at the tip of the wing, the second is shorter than, or the

same length as, the 7th and the 1st is distinctly longer than the primary coverts (2-a). The male sings as it explores the tops of trees and bushes and its song can be heard at the end of the summer and in the autumn, as well as during the nesting period.

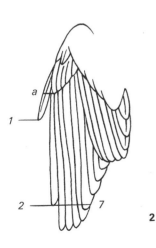

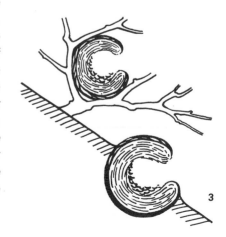

Willow Warbler
Phylloscopus trochilus

The breeding range of the Willow Warbler lies somewhat further north than that of the preceding species; in Asia it stretches a long way into Siberia. This bird lives in deciduous woods and conifer forests, particularly with small trees and undergrowth. The spherical nest (3), which is almost always on the ground, is made of the same material as the Chiffchaff's nest, but is usually better concealed in the new shoots of various trees and bushes, in brambles or in clumps of grass. It is built entirely by the female, which also incubates the 5—7 whitish eggs, which are marked with tiny russet or brown spots (4). The male, however,

helps to rear the young for 12—15 days in the nest and about one week more after they have left it. The adults do not usually nest a second time. If we come across a nest with young and have

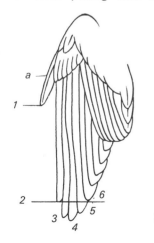

doubts as to whether it is the nest of a Willow Warbler or a Chiffchaff, it is a help to remember that Willow Warbler parents both feed their young, so that during this time the male's song is seldom heard, and that the juveniles — like the adult

birds — have light-coloured legs. In September or October, Willow Warblers migrate to central and southern Africa; they return in April. Compared with the very similar Chiffchaff, the Willow Warbler (1) has yellow-tinted plumage, a more pronounced superciliary stripe and lighter-coloured legs (flesh-pink or light brown). In identification in the hand, the 3rd to the 5th primaries form the tip of the Willow Warbler's wing, the 2nd is approximately the same length as the 6th and the 1st is much longer than the primary coverts (2-a). The Willow Warbler's song is rather like the song of the Chaffinch, but it is flutier, softer, slower and sadder, with steadily descending tones ending in a flourish.

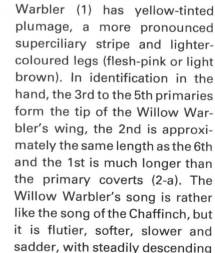

Goldcrest
Regulus regulus

laid in June, usually contains only 5—8 eggs. The female incubates them unaided for 14—16 days; both the parent birds care for the nestlings, which are fed for 14—18 days on small insects, plant lice and spiders. The Goldcrest inhabits practically the whole of Europe, northern and central Asia and North America. It is a partial migrant; in the autumn and winter, Scandinavian birds roam southwards for varying distances, starting roughly in October; they return to their nesting areas in March or April. The male has an orange-coloured crown bordered with black stripes which do not converge on its forehead (3) (in the Firecrest, which also has a black

With a body weight of only 5—6 g, the Goldcrest and the Firecrest are the smallest passerine birds (hummingbirds are smaller, but are not passerines). The Goldcrest lives in conifer forests (mainly firwoods) from lowlands to the upper tree-limit and builds its nest almost entirely on fir trees. The nest is a thick-walled, spherical structure supported from below by long horizontal fir branches, whose perpendicular twigs and needles are cleverly woven into its walls. It is situated 4—12 m above the ground and is concealed so well that it cannot be seen at all from

below. It is built by both the sexes, usually in about 20 days; it is made mainly of moss and lichen, small twigs, grass and cocoon silk and is lined with fur and feathers. In April or May the female lays 8—11 yellowish eggs marked with small light brown speckles (2); the second clutch,

stripe through the eye, they do: (4). The female has a yellow crown (1). The Goldcrest's song is a rising and falling series of fine tones sounding like 'tseetseedui-tseetseedui-tseetseedui'. Its thin call note, 'sitt-sitt', is often the only bird's voice to be heard in conifer forests in the winter.

3

4

Firecrest
Regulus ignicapillus

The Firecrest inhabits conifer forests, but also — though less often — lives in mixed or even deciduous woods. It is distributed over a much smaller area than the

the bottom of the side branches of fir trees (2). The nest is made chiefly of moss and its upper edge turns sharply inwards, giving the nest the shape of a sphere

birds; their average weight is 0.72 g and they measure 13.5 × 10.5 mm. The whole clutch thus weighs about 7.2 g, i. e. 140% of the female's body

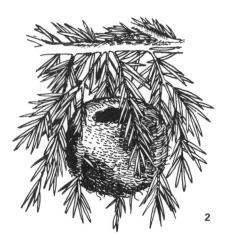
3

weight. It is puzzling, to say the least, how the female, in only 10—11 days, manages to produce more matter than it possesses itself, twice a year. The female incubates the eggs for 14—16 days; the male only helps to rear the young. The male (1) has an orange-red crown bordered by black and white stripes which meet on its forehead; the female has a yellow crown. Through each eye there is also a black stripe forming a vivid contrast to the white superciliary stripe; the shoulders are golden-yellow. The Firecrest's song is a series of 'zeezeezeezeee' notes, all in the same key.

preceding species. Central European populations migrate to the Mediterranean region for the winter; they leave in October and return in March or April. Soon after arriving, the male takes possession of a nesting territory; it is joined later by the female, which then begins to weave a nest into

with an opening on top. The purpose of this arrangement is to prevent the eggs or nestlings from falling out if the branch is caught by a strong wind. The 7—11 eggs (3) are redder than those of the Goldcrest. *Regulus* eggs are smaller than those of any other European passerine

2

Spotted Flycatcher
Muscicapa striata

The Spotted Flycatcher inhabits the whole of Europe, northwest Africa and southwestern Asia. It is strictly a migrant, spending the winter in tropical and southern Africa and returning to its nesting areas at the end of April or in May. It lives mostly at the edge of deciduous woods, in old avenues and in orchards, parks and gardens. The nest is usually built only by the female, in various kinds of niches, in a crack in a tree, on a forked or broken branch and (in towns and villages) in spaces and recesses in walls, or quite openly on rafters. It is a dish-like structure made of rootlets, straw and moss and is softly lined with feathers or fur. The 4—5 bluish or greenish, grey- or red-spotted eggs (2) are incubated for 13—14 days by the female, with only occasional help from the male. The young birds, which leave the nest at the age of 12—14 days, are fed by both the adult birds. Two broods in one year are relatively rare. The family remains in the region of the nest almost until it is time to migrate (in August or September). The Spotted Flycatcher (1) has a dark greyish-brown back and a lighter, greyish-white underside; brown streaks are present on its forehead, crown, throat and breast. Its short, thin legs are not of much use except for perching and, indeed, we most often see the Spotted Flycatcher sitting insect, returning immediately to the same or a similar perch. It flies very skilfully and catches its prey in the air. Its call note, a sharp 'tzee', is uttered to the

stiffly erect on dry branches, fences and telegraph poles and wires, from which it suddenly shoots upwards to catch some accompaniment of flicks of its wings and tail. Its song is short and inconspicuous and easily goes unnoticed.

Red-breasted Flycatcher
Ficedula parva

The Red-breasted Flycatcher is a typical inhabitant of submontane and montane beechwoods, but it is also to be found in old beech- and oakwoods at low altitudes. Its breeding range stretches from central Europe, across the Urals and Asia, to Kamchatka and Sakhalin in the east; isolated populations live in the Caucasus and the Himalayas. It arrives at its nesting sites in May, the males a few days before the females. The nest, which is made of dry leaves and grass, fine rootlets, moss, cobwebs and hair, is generally built by both the sexes in a recess (often only a crack) or hole in a tree, or even on a thick forked branch. The 5–7 whitish eggs are marked fairly densely with rusty-brown spots; they are incubated for 13–15 days by the female. The parents both feed the nestlings for 13–14 days and then accompany them outside the nest until they are fully able to fly. The Red-breasted Flycatcher nests only once a year, sometimes in May, but more often in June. In August or September the birds migrate to their winter quarters in distant India. At first glance, the male Red-breasted Flycatcher looks rather like a Robin, but is much (about one fifth) smaller. It is olive-brown, with a whitish underside and an orange-red throat and breast. This applies only to older males (1), however; juvenile males (up to the age of about two years) lack the red and resemble the females (2), which have only a yellow-tinged breast. The outer tail feathers are white at their base; this is most clearly visible when the birds are excited, fan their tail and fold it over their back, uttering a typical disyllabic 'teedle, teedle'. Their rather loud song is composed of a descending series of notes reminiscent of the song of the Willow Warbler.

Collared Flycatcher
Ficedula albicollis

The range of this species is confined to central and southeastern Europe and the western part of Asia Minor. The Collared Flycatcher inhabits open deciduous woods, parks, orchards and gardens. It nests in tree holes, but readily accepts nestboxes, which are one way of attracting both it and the Pied Flycatcher into towns. If provided with nestboxes it will even settle in pinewoods. Soon after its arrival in April or May, the male tempts a female to enter the chosen nest hole, partly by singing and partly by means of visual signals, e. g. by repeatedly flying into the hole itself and spreading its wings and tail in the entrance. The female incubates the 5—8 bluish-green eggs (3) for 13—15 days unaided; the nestlings are fed for 14—16 days on insects by both parents. Superfluous singing unpaired males are sometimes to be found near the holes, where they actually help to feed the young of other adults. Polygamy is also a fairly frequent phenomenon. The birds leave for their winter quarters in distant tropical Africa at the end of August or in September. The male Collared Flycatcher (1, in front) has a white collar, white patches on its wings, a white spot above its beak and a white underside. In the winter it loses its black colour and resembles the grey-brown female (1, behind). In its wings, the 2nd primary is longer than the 5th and there is white on the outer vane of the 3rd to the 5th primaries (2). In the field, it is often difficult to distinguish between female Collared and Pied Flycatchers (and grey male Pied Flycatchers). If in doubt, the alarm call of the Collared Flycatcher — a protracted 'seep, seep' — is a decisive character; its song is a series of high-pitched whistling notes.

Pied Flycatcher
Ficedula hypoleuca

The Pied Flycatcher inhabits an extensive breeding range stretching from the coast of northern Africa across the whole of Europe and western Asia to the Altai Mountains. Its spring migra-

3

Pied Flycatcher is an exhibition of black and white contrast (1); the bird's underside, the patch on its wings, the spot above its beak and, as a rule, the outer vanes of its outer tail feathers are white and the rest is black. This does not apply in central Europe (Germany, former Czechoslovakia and Poland), however, where the males have a more or less grey-brown back like the females. In the wings, the 5th primary is longer than the 2nd and the white colouring starts on the 6th primary (2). The alarm call of the Pied Flycatcher is a short, rapidly repeated 'whit, whit'. Its song resembles the song of the Redstart and contains repeated sounds like 'whootee-whootee-whootee'. The behaviour of the two black and white flycatcher species is also very similar. They both like sitting on dry branches and when excited they flick their tail and their wings – and not only both wings at once, but often just one wing, which they raise above their body. Lastly, they are both the same size (roughly the size of the Spotted Flycatcher).

tion, in April and May, is often very noticeable, since Pied Flycatchers appear all over the place, stay a few days and then disappear again. Their autumn migration in August and September, when they fly to northern and central Africa, passes virtually unnoticed except on the coasts. The Pied Flycatcher nests only once a year, preferably in old deciduous and mixed woods, but also in parks and gardens.

The nest is made almost entirely of dry grass and strips of bark, like the Collared Flycatcher's nest. The eggs (3) are also similar in appearance and the course of nesting in the two species is practically the same. The Pied and Collared Flycatchers sometimes interbreed, usually where birds of the one species appear in an area containing many individuals of the other species. The breeding plumage of the male

Bearded Tit,
Bearded Reedling
Panurus biarmicus

The Bearded Tit lives in Europe, where in some places its distribution is very patchy. Its whole life is spent in extensive reedbeds. It prefers reeds with a constant water level and with an underlying layer of sedge or an adequately deep layer of old, flattened reeds; it also nests in reedmace beds, though not to the same extent. In April, in a sedge bed or a clump of reeds or bulrushes, the birds build a nest made of the wider leaves of these plants and line it with the remains of reed tops and often with feathers. The nest is merely pressed down into a dense layer of old plants in such a manner that it is always covered over. The sexes take turns to brood the 5—7 eggs, which are marked with dark or reddish-brown speckles on a white ground (2). The young hatch in 12—13 days and the parents care for them for 10—13 days in the nest and then for about two weeks outside it. At the end of May or the beginning of June they nest again. Other pairs, and evidently the first young, sometimes help to rear the second brood. When the nesting season is over, the birds collect together in small flocks in which new pairs are formed; as distinct from most passerines, Bearded Tit pair-bonds are of long duration. Bearded Tits are mostly resident birds, but some undertake short journeys southwards for the winter. At this time of year they live mainly on the seeds of reeds and other aquatic plants; otherwise their diet consists chiefly of insects, spiders and small snails. The adult birds are the size of sparrows, but have a strikingly long tail. The male (1) has a bluish-grey head with a conspicuous black moustachial stripe; its back is rusty-brown and there are two longitudinal white patches on its wings. The female has a brown head and no moustachial stripe. Because of its retiring habits, practically the only thing that may betray the presence of the Bearded Tit in its reed jungle is its clear and fairly loud call note, 'tching-tching'; its song is a soft chirping.

Long-tailed Tit
Aegithalos caudatus

3

4

graduated tail. Its head is white (north European subspecies: 1, 4) or white with a curved black superciliary stripe (west European subspecies: 3); in central Europe we find mixed populations, the result of subspecies

The Long-tailed Tit lives primarily in open deciduous and mixed woods, on trees growing beside water and in large parks and old gardens. It is one of the best builders among the birds, and although it is one of the smallest (it weighs only 7–10 g) its nest measures 23 × 12 cm. The nest is a solid, bag-shaped structure with a narrow side entrance at the top and it takes the sexes about 9–13 days to build it. Its walls, which are 1.5–2.5 cm thick, are made almost entirely of moss, lichen and bark fibre and the surface is perfectly masked by pieces of bark, cobwebs and cocoon silk, so that it is indistinguishable from the trunk or branch to which it is attached. Another remarkable thing is where the birds find the enormous number of tiny feathers (up to 2,000) with which the inside of the nest is upholstered. The male helps to brood the 6–12 white, red-speckled eggs (2), which are incubated for 12–13 days. The young remain 15–18 days in the nest and then fly out. They stay with the parents, however, and help them to rear the second brood of young. Pairs with no young of their own do the same, so that it is not uncommon to find young being fed by three, four and even six adult birds. The Long-tailed Tit inhabits the whole

of Europe except the most northerly parts; in Asia it occurs over a wide belt extending to Japan and Kamchatka. It is a resident bird, but Scandinavian populations shift slightly southwards in the winter, when their movements are of an invasive character. The Long-tailed Tit's most distinctive features are its white, black and deep pink colouring and, of course, its long,

interbreeding. The most familiar vocal manifestation of the Long-tailed Tit is its rolling call note, which sounds like 'tsirrr' or 'chrrr'.

2

One of the most interesting characteristics of the Marsh Tit is that the pairs are very closely knit and remain together during the autumn and winter, when they may form flocks together with nest holes in the trunks of trees or in thick branches, usually near the foot of the tree. Nestboxes are not used so often; rarely, the females excavate their own nest holes. The nest is made mainly of sects, including a large proportion of beetles. They inhabit deciduous and mixed woods, groups of trees beside ponds and rivers and sometimes parks and gardens on the outskirts of towns. The distribution of the Marsh Tit is very interesting; it occurs in Europe and Asia Minor and then thousands of kilometres away in the most easterly parts of Asia. The male and female both measure about 11—12 cm. They are greyish-brown, but have a glossy black crown, white cheeks and a small black spot below their chin (1). The underside of their tail is only slightly graduated and the outer tail feathers are at most 4 mm shorter than the longest feathers (3), whereas in the Willow Tit they are over 5 mm shorter (4). The Marsh Tit's contact call is a sharp 'pitchew-chew' or 'psi-ddedde'; its song is a monotonous, repeated 'schip-schip-schip'.

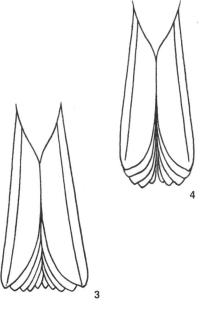

other tits. As a resident bird, the Marsh Tit spends the winter near its nesting site. In the spring, as a rule in April, the females begin an intensive search for suitable moss, together with lichen, grass, animal hairs and feathers, and is built by the female. The 7—10 eggs with a sprinkling of red spots (2) are incubated for 12—15 days, also by the female; the male sometimes feeds the brooding female and helps with the feeding of the young, which leave the hole at the age of 17—20 days. Unlike other tits, Marsh Tits usually nest only once during the season. They live on various in-

Willow Tit
Parus montanus

carpenters as woodpeckers, however, and their beaks are not really fitted for such work, and so it takes them, on an average, about 13 days. Despite this, about 90% of the occupied nest holes are new ones (in the case of the Marsh Tit only a little over 10%); some pairs use nestboxes. The nest is made of the same materials as the Marsh Tit's; the appearance and number of eggs (2) and other aspects of nesting are also the same. When they have finished nesting, the birds roam about, but only for short distances; Scandinavian populations are partly migratory, however. Like the Marsh Tit, the Willow Tit lives chiefly on insects and other small invertebrates, but the plant component of its diet — the seeds of forest trees, bushes and other plants, such as thistles, timothy and dock — is also important. The Willow Tit (1) closely resembles the Marsh Tit,

The Willow Tit is probably the most widely distributed tit, since it inhabits the whole of Europe and Asia, except the most southerly parts. It is a more frequent nester in conifer forests than the Marsh Tit and in mountains it is often to be found up to the upper tree-limit; in addition, it inhabits damp deciduous and mixed woods and trees growing beside water, particularly groups of alders, willows and birches. The pairs remain together during the winter and the following spring they excavate a hole for their nest in a suitable rotting tree or stump. They are not such good but it has a dull black crown, a larger chin spot and pale-edged secondaries forming a clearly discernible light panel. Its contact call is a protracted 'chay-chay-chay'; its song is a high 'tsee-ay, tsee-ay, tsee-ay, tsee-ay, tsee-ay' of five or six double notes.

Siberian Tit
Parus cinctus

The Siberian Tit (1) looks rather like a large, 'untidy' Marsh Tit. It has a brown back, a dingy white underside and rusty flanks. Its most striking features are its brownish-grey cap and its large greyish-black chin spot. It seems less lively than other tits. Its song consists of long 'deeh' notes repeated four or five times. The Siberian Tit inhabits the far north of Europe and Asia, in Europe only the northern half of Scandinavia and the most northerly European part of the former USSR. It is a resident bird; in the winter it occasionally strays to St Petersburg or even to Moscow, but is very rarely seen in central Europe. It inhabits dark taiga forests with firs, larches and cembra pines, but also occurs in riverside deciduous and mixed woods and Scandinavian birchwoods. The birds nest only once during the breeding season, which lasts from May to July. The Siberian

Tit nests in abandoned woodpecker holes, but is capable of making its own improvements to a hole in the soft wood of a dead trunk. The 6–10 glossy white eggs are marked with fairly large, scattered brownish-red spots (2); the female begins sitting when they have all been laid. The male brings food during the incubation period (13–15 days) and after the young have been hatched; later, both the parents care for the young. In September, the families collect together in small flocks and lead a nomadic existence. Siberian Tits live on insects and seeds.

391

Crested Tit

Parus cristatus

The Crested Tit inhabits almost the whole of Europe, except the north of Scandinavia, the greater part of the British Isles and Italy. It prefers various types of conifer forests, but in southern and western Europe it also lives in deciduous woods. The female usually builds the nest in an existing hole, but sometimes makes one

tively small and usually consists of only 5–7 white, red-spotted eggs (2); they are incubated for 14–17 days by the female, while the male fetches food. The

fer seeds in its diet increases. It takes its name from the characteristic black and white crest on its head. Its back is brown, its underside is whitish-grey, its head is white, with a black horseshoe mark behind the eyes, and its chin and throat are black; the female's crest is greyer and shorter than the male's. The

itself near the foot of a rotting trunk or stump; it is comparatively rare for it to use a nestbox. The hole is lined mainly with moss, but contains more grass than the nests of other tits; the cup of the nest is lined with animal hairs. The nesting period lasts from April to June. The clutch is rela-

young, which remain 17–21 days in the safety of the nest, are fed mainly on insects, in particular bark beetles, weevils and other pests. Only a few pairs nest a second time. The Crested Tit is a resident bird, but displays nomadic tendencies in the autumn and winter, when the amount of coni-

Crested Tit is the same size as the Marsh Tit. The male's (1) song is muted and inconspicuous; while courting the female, it continually opens, fans and folds its crest. Its most striking vocal manifestation is its loud, purring call note, which sounds like 'tzee-tzee-choor-r-r'.

Coal Tit
Parus ater

The Coal Tit typically inhabits conifer forests, and in mixed woods it prefers places with a preponderance of conifers; in mountains it occurs right up to the upper tree-limit. It also occurs in gardens. It is found over virtually the whole of Europe and a large part of Asia and in mountain forests in the Atlas Moun-

natural tree holes in conifer woods as in deciduous woods, it often makes do — far more than other tits — with holes in the ground, mouse holes, hollows in

2

those of other tits; like other tits, when it leaves the nest it covers them with nest material. The young are hatched in 14—16 days, remain 16—19 days in the nest and are then fed for a time in its vicinity by the parents. The adults usually nest twice during the season, which lasts from April to June. The Coal Tit also lives

tains in northern Africa. In the southern part of its range it is a resident bird; further north it has a strong tendency to migrate southwards, leaving in September or October and returning in March or April. Coal Tits are also hole-nesters, but, since there are not nearly so many

tree stumps and cracks in walls and rocks. It is also grateful for nestboxes, but relatively few of these are erected in conifer woods. The nest, which is made chiefly of moss and animal hair, is built by the female. The female also incubates unaided the 6—10 eggs (2), which are similar to

on insects; in the winter, conifer (mainly spruce and silver fir) seeds form a large part of its diet. It has a black head, white cheeks and a large white nuchal patch (1) and is the same size as the Marsh Tit. The male attracts attention by its simple, but frequent song: 'tsitsi, tsitsi, tsitsi'.

Blue Tit
Parus caeruleus

The Blue Tit inhabits the whole of Europe except the north of Scandinavia and the most northerly parts of the former USSR, and also the region of the Atlas Mountains in northern Africa. It lives in deciduous and mixed woods, in avenues, in groups of trees beside ponds and rivers, in copses and in parks, wherever it can find a suitable tree, i. e. sufficiently old and with holes in it. It is often attracted to nestboxes in gardens and orchards. The female carries moss — and sometimes a little dry grass — into the hole and hollows out a nest which it lines with hair and small feathers. In April, May or June, it lays a single white, red-spotted egg (2) every day until there are 7—13 and sometimes as many as 18; it then incubates them for 13—15 days. With such a large brood, the parents are kept busy fetching food; at the age of 15—20 days the young leave the nest within the space of only three days, since they are all at the same stage of development. The female may then lay a second clutch of eggs, but this time not so many. Most Blue Tits remain in the same general area and do not migrate for the winter, but in some winters those living in the north make long excursions southwards. The most distinctive feature of the Blue Tit (1) is its bright blue cap; its wings and tail are also blue. The blue contrasts vividly with its yellow throat, white cheeks and olive-green back. Its call note is a clear 'tsee, tsit', its alarm call a vibrating

'tserrrrettettett'. In the autumn it forms roving flocks with other tits, and in the winter the Blue Tit, together with the Great Tit, is one of the most frequent visitors to birdtables. Although it appears smaller, it is the same size as the Marsh Tit.

2

Great Tit
Parus major

The Great Tit (1) lives in virtually the same places as the Blue Tit, but in many town parks and gardens it is definitely commoner. In mountains, its distribution extends to the upper tree-limit. The whole of its range is considerably larger than that of the Blue Tit, since it inhabits practically the whole of Europe, Asia and northern Africa. It is a resident species, but Great Tits living in the north sometimes undertake journeys so long that they can be described as migration, e. g. when birds from the Moscow region appear in central Europe. Spring migrations (or wanderings) take place in March or April and autumn migrations approximately in October. Early in the spring, the females choose a hollow or a hole and pad it with a thick layer of moss in which they make a deep hair-lined cup. They also accept nestboxes and even (like Blue Tits) nest in the most outlandish places, such an unused pump, metal tubing, a letterbox, a watering-can, an empty tin or an old boot. The female first of all lays 7–12 (and sometimes more) white, red-speckled eggs (2) and then begins incubating. It sits on the eggs very determinedly for the whole 13–15 days and is kept supplied with food by the male. At the age of about 14–20 days the young leave the hole; the parents continue to feed them for two more weeks and may then produce a second, smaller, clutch of eggs. With the first hint of spring, town-dwellers, as well as countryfolk, will recognise a rhythmical metallic 'teecha-teecha' or 'teechūwee, teech-ūwee', the song of the male Great Tit as it begins courtship. The male has a glossy black head and white cheeks; its yellow underside is divided in half by a broad black stripe running from its throat to its tail; in the female the stripe is narrower and ends on the belly. Both birds are the size of a slim sparrow.

2

Nuthatch
Sitta europaea

The Nuthatch has many remarkable habits and characteristics. It is at home on tree trunks and thick branches, which it climbs with great dexterity, but which it can also descend head first — a feat of which not even woodpeckers or treecreepers are capable. Its building instincts are also admirable. It nests in tree holes and the female always adapts the entrance to fit the size of its own body, walling it up with a mixture of mud and saliva until only the bird itself can wriggle through (2). If, as is often the case, it uses a nestbox, it blocks up any spaces in the walls and under the roof; minor adjustments while the female is brooding are made by the male. The nest is made almost entirely of fine flakes of pine bark (up to 2,500); in deciduous woods, other kinds of bark and dry leaves

are occasionally used, but if the Nuthatch can find at least one pine tree in the neighbourhood it will fly there for its nest material. The 6—8 white, russet-spotted eggs (3) lie in a shallow depression in a bed of bark fragments, where they are incubated for 15—18 days. The male helps the female to rear the young, which do not leave the nest hole until they are 23—24 days old. The Nuthatch is a strictly resident bird and usually remains in its nesting area all through the winter. It has a very varied diet, which is mainly of animal origin in the summer, but in which seeds begin to preponderate in the autumn. Its distribution covers most of Europe (except the most northerly regions) and a large part of Asia; it also occurs in northwest Africa. The Nuthatch (1), which is about the size of a sparrow, has a bluish-grey back, a brownish-yellow underside and a black eye-stripe. In the spring it draws attention to itself by its whistling.

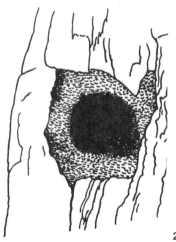

Wallcreeper
Tichodroma muraria

The Wallcreeper is a typical bird of high mountain peaks and sheer rock faces. The male chooses a suitable crack or hollow in a rock and then draws the female's attention to it by acrobatic performances in the entrance. The actual nest is built by the female; it is made mainly of dry grass, lichen and moss and is lined with hair or wool (often from chamois and sheep) and sometimes with small feathers, and is finished in about five days. The 3—5 russet-speckled eggs (2) are laid in May or June; they are incubated for 18—20 days by the female, which is kept regularly fed by the male. Both the parents feed the young, which remain 21—29 days in the nest hole and when they leave it are already able to fly and climb. The Wallcreeper is a largely resident bird, but from July onwards the young birds start to roam about and in September they begin to descend to lower altitudes. In the winter the Wallcreeper can also be seen, mostly singly, but occasionally in pairs, on lonely rocks and in quarries and ruins in low-lying country. It does not shun the company of human beings, however, and explores the walls of castles, mansions and other tall buildings in towns. It lives on insects, spiders and other invertebrate animals, which it catches in crevices in rocks and walls. The Wallcreeper (1) is larger than a Treecreeper; it has mainly grey plumage, but its throat and breast, the tips of its wings and its tail feathers are black and it has large patches of crimson on its wings. When it flies it has a fluttering action, and this makes its crimson wing-coverts and the white spots on its primaries (3) — invisible on the sitting bird — all the more conspicuous. Its song is composed of rising, whistling 'zizizizui' notes.

Treecreeper, Brown Creeper

Certhia familiaris

The Treecreeper is perfectly adapted for climbing trees. It does not come down them head first like the Nuthatch, but its long, sharp claws give it a firm hold on the bark and its thick, tough tail feathers are a reliable support, like a woodpecker's tail. When examining bark, it starts at the foot of the tree and climbs up it in jerking hops, in an irregular spiral, until it reaches the top; it then flies down to the foot of another tree and starts all over again (2). In addition to Europe and Asia, the Treecreeper inhabits North America from Canada to Mexico. It prefers conifer forests and mixed woods, but in Britain also occurs in deciduous woods and parks and gardens. The nest is usually situated in a hollow, cracked or broken trunk, behind peeling bark or in a woodpile. It is almost the same as the nest of the Short-toed Treecreeper and is built by the female, which is only sometimes helped by the male. The female also incubates the 5—7 white eggs, which are

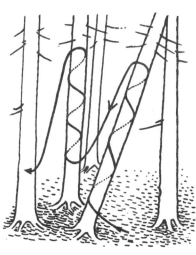

2

join flocks of tits. The Tree-creeper (1) has a tobacco-brown back and a completely white underside. The claw of its hind toe is

marked with red spots of various sizes (3), for 13—15 days. The young are fed for 14—16 days in the nest by both the parent birds. The adults nest first in April and often again in June or July. Both treecreepers are resident birds; in the autumn and winter they

over 8 mm long; it is usually longer than the toe itself and is only slightly curved. Its call note is a soft 'tsee, tsee'; its song is higher-pitched and longer than the song of the Short-toed Tree-creeper and ends with a rolling trill like the Blue Tit's song.

Short-toed Treecreeper
Certhia brachydactyla

The Short-toed Treecreeper frequents the margins of old deciduous and mixed woods; it is most typically to be found in riparian

4

lichen, hair and feathers. The eggs (4) are similar in shape and colouring to the Treecreeper's eggs and the incubation period and parental care are likewise the same. Almost all pairs nest twice during the season. The two treecreeper species live on the same type of diet. With their long, thin beak they probe cracks in the bark for insects and other invertebrates (chiefly spiders); in the winter they also eat a small quantity of seeds. Both species are smaller than sparrows. The Short-toed Treecreeper (1) has a greyish-brown back, a greyish belly and brownish flanks. Its beak is longer than the Treecreeper's and is noticeably curved, while the claw of its hind toe is shorter (it measures at most 7.5 mm) and more curved. Another important feature, visible only if the birds are handled, is the dark spot on the inner wing, at the base of the 1st primary (2), which is absent in the Treecreper (3). Its song is shorter, has no trill and sounds like 'teet, teet, teer-rooititt'.

woods and does not as a rule penetrate deep into large forests. On the other hand, it likes copses, parks, gardens and avenues with old trees. It is confined to central, southern and western Europe, northern Africa and Asia Minor. The nest is situated in the same places as that of the preceding species. Considering how small the bird is, it is a large structure made of a quantity of dry twigs put together in a hole or behind peeling bark in such a haphazard manner that it is easily damaged. The foundations of the nest are sometimes up to 40 cm high; at the top there is a neat little 'well' — the actual nest — made of grass, strips of bark fibre, moss,

2

3

399

Penduline Tit
Remiz pendulinus

1

The suspended, pouch-like nest of the Penduline Tit is unique among the nests of European birds and is a real architectural work of art. To human beings it is known better than the bird that builds it. It looks like a 'mitten glove' hanging from a thin vertical twig, with the entrance leading through the thumb. It takes 12—20 days to build. The work is started by the male, sometimes at the end of April, but usually in May; it makes the pear-shaped skeleton of the nest out of long fibres, often from wild hops or stinging-nettles, and the female fills in the gaps with plant fluff mixed with saliva. Before the nest is finished, the female lays 5—8 pure white, noticeably elongate eggs and adds a tubular entrance, the main sign that the nest is at last complete. The male then departs and begins to build another nest for another female. The male's nest-building instinct is so strong that it builds up to five further 'play' nests. The eggs are incubated for 14—15 days, entirely by the female, which likewise cares unaided for the young for 17—20 days. The Penduline Tit lives mainly in the lowlands of eastern and southern Europe and also inhabits a strip of territory leading from Asia Minor to Japan. Since it requires water, it occurs mainly in regions with fishponds or beside rivers bordered by trees and thickets. In the south it is a resident bird; northern populations sometimes migrate southwards for the winter. It lives chiefly on insects, supplemented in the autumn and winter by seeds. The Penduline Tit (1) has a greyish-white head with a black mask and a russet back. It usually draws attention to itself by its call note, a very thin, protracted 'seeee-seeee'.

Golden Oriole
Oriolus oriolus

2

The Golden Oriole is the only member of the tropical Oriolidae family to have settled in the north. Today it inhabits Europe as far as the southern part of Britain and Sweden and its range stretches to southwestern Siberia; it also lives in part of northwestern Africa and in Asia Minor. Evidence of its tropical origin is provided by its glowing colours and by the fact that it is strictly a migrant, whose sojourn in Europe is of very brief duration. It is one of the last birds to arrive, usually at the beginning of May, when it settles in deciduous woods, old parks, gardens, avenues and tall trees beside rivers and ponds. Its nest is a strongly woven basket made of grass stems and leaves, plant fibres and strips of bark and lined with fine grass, wool and feathers; it hangs from a fork near the tip of a branch, usually at the top of a tree. The 3—5 white or faintly pink-tinged eggs, thinly marked with blackish-brown or black spots (2), are laid in May or June; they are incubated for 14—15 days, as a rule entirely by the female. The young leave the nest after the same length of time, but remain with their parents until August, when they all leave for tropical Africa. Golden Orioles live mainly on insects, together with spiders and small snails; towards the end of the summer they also peck the soft fruit of

various woody plants. The male oriole (1) has vivid black and yellow plumage and red eyes;

3♀

the female (3) has a yellowish-green back and a whitish-grey, streaked underside. Both are about the same size as the Blackbird. When the male arrives in the spring, it immediately announces its presence by a loud fluty whistle, 'weela-weeō', which it repeats over and over again. Sometimes, from a tree, it utters a sharp, raucous 'krāāk', which seems to come from an altogether different bird.

Red-backed Shrike

Lanius collurio

The Red-backed Shrike, which is a typical migrant, spends only four or five months in its breeding areas. It arrives in May and leaves for its winter quarters in eastern and southern Africa at the end of August or in September. It inhabits a large part of Europe, from the north of the Iberian Peninsula to the middle of Scandinavia, and a considerable part of Asia. It likes open country, with thickets, hedges and bushy hillsides, the margins of woods and copses, etc, and is less fond of orchards and gardens. The nest is usually built in a thicket, often in a thornbush. It is a massive, thick-walled structure made of rootlets, blades and stalks, often with moss in the middle, and is lined with fine grass and rootlets, hairs and sometimes feathers. It is built by both the sexes, but only the female broods the 4—6 eggs, which are incubated for 14—16 days. The eggs are very variably coloured and the brown spots with which they are marked are denser at the blunt end, or form a ring around it (2); they are laid in May or June. The young are fed and tended for 12—15 days in the nest, but parental care continues for three or four weeks afterwards, when the young are already able to fly. The Red-backed Shrike lives primarily on insects and less on small vertebrates; in the summer it varies its diet with fruit and berries. It has the characteristic habits — common to all shrikes — of laying up a stock of food by impaling its prey on thorns and of regurgitating indigestible food particles in pellet form. Red-backed Shrikes are about one fifth larger than a sparrow. The male (1, in front) has a light grey head with a black mask, a chest-nut back and a grey rump; the female (1, behind) is mainly rust-brown and has vermiculations on its flanks and breast. The male sings rather rarely, softly and scrapingly, but its vocal range is large and it is an excellent imitator of other birds' voices. Its alarm call is a harsh, barking 'chack, chack'.

2

Lesser Grey Shrike
Lanius minor

The Lesser Grey Shrike inhabits open country with scattered trees or groups of trees, copses, avenues and sometimes orchards and the edges of woods. It has a clear preference for deciduous trees, although now and again it nests in coniferous trees; in the following species the reverse is rather the case. The nest is quite large and is built by both the sexes; it is made mainly of coarse grass and stalks, rootlets and twigs and is lined with hair, feathers and fluff. The nest of the Lesser Grey Shrike can sometimes be recognised from the presence of a large quantity of green plants in the middle layer, which may show through. The 5—7 greenish, brown-spotted

eggs (3) are incubated for 15—16 days, chiefly by the female, which is relieved by the male only when it goes in search of food. The young are fed by both the parents, for 14—19 days in the nest and for some time in its vicinity after they have left it. The Lesser Grey Shrike lives practically entirely on flesh, but does not impale its prey on thorns so often as other shrikes. Its breeding distribution begins in France and stretches across southern and central Europe to Asia, to the banks of the Yenisei. In its nesting areas, it spends approximately only the four months needed to nest and rear the young. It arrives at the beginning of May and leaves for its winter quarters in Africa, south of the equator, at the end of August. This shrike is somewhat smaller than a Blackbird. It has a pink-tinted breast and its black mask also covers its forehead (1). Its primaries are an important distinguishing character. The 1st is roughly the same length as the primary coverts (a), the 3rd and 4th are the longest, and the 2nd is thus longer than the 5th (2). As distinct from other shrikes, the Lesser Grey Shrike flies in a straight line and not in undulations. Its alarm call is 'tseck tseck' or a shrill 'kveell'; its song is like that of the Woodchat Shrike.

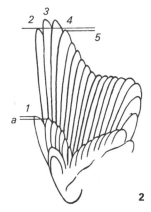

Great Grey Shrike, Northern Shrike
Lanius excubitor

The Great Grey Shrike breeds on every continent but Australia: in Europe except the British Isles, Italy and the Balkans, in Asia, in northern Africa and in the northern part of North America. Unlike other shrikes, it is only a partial migrant, since only birds from the north fly south for the winter. We may then come across them in fields and meadows, sitting on bushes or treetops and keeping a look-out for small rodents, their

titudes. The large nest is a solid structure made of dry twigs, stalks, rootlets and moss; both sexes build it, in a tree, and line it with plant fluff, feathers and hair.

3

The 5–7 greyish-green eggs, evenly covered with brown spots (3), are incubated for 15–16 days by the female. The parents both feed the young for 19–20 days in the nest, chiefly on insects. The Great Grey Shrike (1), which is the largest member of the genus, is about the size of a Blackbird. Both the sexes have a grey back, a white belly and across their eyes a black band which ends at their beak and does not extend to

1

main prey. In years when food is plentiful, their stocks of food – voles impaled on thorns and here and there a small bird – may be found. Sometimes the prey is simply hung up in forked branches. The Great Grey Shrike inhabits open country with groups of trees and copses and less frequently on the outskirts of woods, particularly in damp regions and places at higher al-

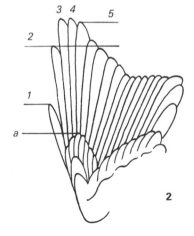

2

their forehead. The 1st primary is roughly half the length of the 2nd, but is substantially longer than the primary coverts (a), the 3rd and 4th are the longest and the 2nd is distinctly shorter than the 5th (2). When hunting, the birds often hover, fluttering their wings and spreading their tail like a Kestrel. Their song is a mixture of churrs and whistles; their alarm call is a harsh 'wick-wick'.

Woodchat Shrike
Lanius senator

The Woodchat Shrike lives in western, southern and central Europe, northern Africa and the Middle East. In Europe its numbers have severely decreased since the last century. It is a strictly migratory bird and winters in the tree savannas of tropical Africa, returning again in April or May. It frequents the edges of deciduous woods, copses, avenues of old trees, orchards and gardens, even on the outskirts of

a side branch. It is made of straw and rootlets and the edge is decorated with green plants. The lining contains a layer of feathers, fur and plant fluff. The 4—6

2

wards both parents feed the young, almost solely on insects. The young leave the nest in 16—18 days, but the parents keep an eye on them and teach them to hunt for a further three or four weeks. The families remain together until the end of August or the beginning of September and then migrate. The Woodchat Shrike (1) is the same size as the Red-backed Shrike. With its russet crown and nape, its black

1

villages. It is an explicitly warmth-loving bird, preferring places exposed as long as possible to the sun, and avoids damp and shady spots. Soon after arriving in the spring, the adults begin to build a nest, almost always on a tree and often on

greyish, brown-spotted eggs (2) are laid between May and July and are incubated for 14—16 days by the female, which the male keeps supplied with food. For the first week after the young are hatched, the male fetches food for the whole family, but after-

mask, its black wings with a large and a small white patch in them, its white underside and rump and its white-bordered tail, it is the most brightly coloured member of the genus. Its grating song contains whistling notes and mimetic motifs.

405

Jay
Garrulus glandarius

The Jay is a very cautious bird and its sharp, screeching 'retch, retch' call often warns the other inhabitants of the forest of the approach of a human being before we can catch sight of it. It also often utters a mewing 'pee-oo, pee-oo', like a Buzzard. It is a master in the art of imitating other birds' voices and even the most unexpected sounds, such as the bleating of a goat, the barking of a dog or a squeaking door. The Jay lives in every type of wood, including large copses and old large parks. The nest, which is built by both the sexes, is relatively small and flat; it is made of twigs and stalks and is lined with dry grass and rootlets. The 5—7 greyish-green, brown-spotted eggs (3) are usually laid in April or May and are incubated for 16—19 days, evidently only by the female. At the age of three weeks, the young are sufficiently independent to be able to leave the nest. The parents bring them various invertebrate animals, small forest rodents and birds' young and eggs. From the summer to the winter, the birds live predominantly on berries, beech-nuts, hazelnuts and acorns. The Jay inhabits the whole of Europe, northern Africa and Asia (except the south). It is mostly a resident bird, but Jays living in the north and northeast sometimes form large flocks and migrate southwards and southwestwards, occasionally in immense numbers. The male and the female both measure about 34 cm; their plumage is reddish-brown (1) with a white rump, but their most typical feature is their shimmering blue, black-striped wing-coverts, which are also often marked with intermediate white stripes (2). Adult birds have 10—12 such stripes (not counting the last one); birds aged under one year have only six to eight.

Siberian Jay
Perisoreus infaustus

In Europe, the Siberian Jay occurs in Scandinavia and the north of the former USSR; otherwise it lives in the northern part of Asia. During the past few decades it has noticeably retreated northwards and has disappeared from the south of Finland and the Baltic republics of the former USSR. It inhabits the conifer forests and birchwoods of the taiga, is a resident bird, but often comes close to villages in the winter. Some birds wander southwards in the autumn and a few sometimes stray far into the heart of Europe. The nesting season begins early in the spring, before the snow has melted. The nest is built on a tree,

often a pine, beside the trunk; it is made chiefly of twigs and is lined with lichen and hair for warmth. The 3−4 greenish or greyish eggs, irregularly speckled with brown or russet spots (2), are laid in April or May. The young hatch in 16−17 days and remain three to four weeks in the nest. The families generally stay together until the following spring. They

live partly on insects, small rodents and the eggs and young of forest birds and partly on conifer (especially pine) seeds and berries. The Siberian Jay (1) is larger than a Blackbird. It has a short, conical beak with white bristle-like feathers around it. Its plumage is mainly greyish-brown, with a darker, smoky-brown cap; its rump and the sides of its tail are rusty and on its wings there are rusty-red areas, which are particularly noticeable in flight. The Siberian Jay is a generally silent bird, but sometimes it utters a mewing 'gee-ah', a harsh 'chair' or a disyllabic 'kook, kook'.

407

Magpie, Black-billed Magpie
Pica pica

The Magpie inhabits the whole of Europe, a large part of Asia and northwestern Africa. Its favourite environment is parkland, where fields and meadows alternate with copses, avenues, groups of trees and bushes and waterside build several nests and then choose the best one; they nest from the end of March until May. The 5—8 brownish or greenish, brown-spotted eggs (2) are incubated for 17—18 days by the female; it is rare for the male to young remain 22—27 days in the nest; after leaving it, they mostly stay with their parents until the following spring. The Magpie is a resident bird, so the young often build their own nests quite close to the parental nest. With its

vegetation; it even infiltrates into human communities. The nest is usually built high up in a tree; if other trees are scarce, it may be built in a fruit tree or in a thicket. The foundations are made of brushwood; the nest itself is a 5-cm layer of mud and turf with a cup lined with rootlets, grass blades, leaves and hair. It is covered with a characteristic canopy of dry twigs. Magpies generally brood, but it always helps to feed the ever-hungry young. While rearing their family, Magpies raid other birds' nests and devour small rodents, molluscs and insects, to which they later add fruit, grain and berries. The striking appearance, black and white plumage and long tail, the Magpie (1) could hardly be mistaken for any other bird. It draws attention to itself by its loud, cackling 'chack, chack, chack' calls; in the spring it also chatters in a muted voice. The Magpie has earned itself a certain notoriety because of its inquisitiveness and its propensity for appropriating and hiding glittering objects.

2

Nutcracker
Nucifraga caryocatactes

The Nutcracker is a taiga bird by origin and it inhabits a wide strip of territory stretching from Scandinavia, across Siberia, to Japan. In addition, small populations live in conifer forests in European mountains and recently they

out to form the foundations and then add a characteristic layer of rotting wood, sometimes together with lichen; the nest itself is lined with dry grass, moss and occasionally a few feathers. The 3—5 greenish, brown-speckled

lared Dove. Its plumage is dark brown, with white drop-shaped spots; there is a large white patch on the underside of its tail, and at the tip of its tail it has a white band which is 15—25 mm wide at its outer edge. This distinguishes

have shown a distinct tendency to spread to unbroken conifer woods at lower altitudes. The nest is built in March, when the forest floor is still covered with snow. It is made by both the sexes and is almost always built in dense branches, beside the trunk. The birds break off twigs — often fresh ones — directly from the trees, straighten them

eggs (2) are incubated for 16—18 days by the female; both the parents look after the young in the nest for a total of 22—25 days. Nutcrackers live chiefly on conifer seeds, beechnuts and acorns and in the autumn mainly on hazelnuts, which they hold in their feet and crack open with their beak. Like most corvid birds, Nutcrackers have the habit of laying up a stock of seeds. Their memory is remarkable and they usually manage to find most of their stores. In addition, they eat insects, worms, molluscs and occasionally small mammals and young nestlings. The Nutcracker (1) is the same size as the Col-

European birds (*N. c. caryocatactes* — 4) from Siberian Nutcrackers (*N. c. macrorhynchos*). which come to Europe for the winter and whose white tail band is 25—33 mm wide (3). The call of the Nutcracker is a moderately loud, hoarse 'krair, krair'.

Alpine Chough
Pyrrhocorax graculus

The Alpine Chough is an exclusively montane species inhabiting the mountains of southern Europe, northwestern Africa, Asia Minor and the Caucasus; it also lives in the mountains of inner Asia. It is a resident bird, but in the winter it descends to lower altitudes and is to be seen near human dwellings; it returns to its nesting areas on bare rocks above the tree-line, as far the snow-limit, in March or April. The birds usually nest gregariously, as a rule in small colonies of up to 20 pairs, but quite often the pairs nest singly. The nest is in a hole or a crevice in a rock face. The brushwood foundations are surmounted by a layer of straw and rootlets and the nest itself is softly lined with hair and sometimes with feathers. Once a year, generally between April and June, the female lays 4–5 yellowish-grey to greenish-grey eggs thickly marked with dark brown spots (2), which it incubates unaided for 18–21 days; the male helps to feed and rear the young, which leave the nest at the age of 31–38 days, but stay with the parents long afterwards. Later on, the families unite to form flocks, which remain together until the end of the winter. In the spring and summer, Alpine Choughs live on insects, worms, spiders, molluscs and small rodents and occasionally they steal the eggs and young of other birds. In the autumn and winter they also eat berries, fruit and seeds and feed on refuse and carrion. The male and the female both have glossy black plumage, a yellow beak and red legs (1); they are somewhat larger than a Jackdaw; the juveniles have dull black plumage; their legs and beak are brownish. The call note of the Alpine Chough is a clear 'skree' or 'tchiup', it also utters a thin, high-pitched whistle.

Jackdaw
Corvus monedula

The Jackdaw inhabits the whole of Europe except the most northerly parts, extends deep into central Asia and occurs in one or two places in northwestern Africa. It is a mainly resident bird, but northern populations usually migrate. The birds converge on their nesting sites in February or March; they frequent localities with an adequate number of old trees, but also live on cliffs, in ruins, towers and steeples and in lofts and chimneys in towns. The nest is built by both the sexes in a hole in a tree, rock or building, but sometimes quite openly in a loft. With long use and frequent additions, it can grow to a huge structure 0.5 m high and 1 m across. The foundations are a pile

of twigs broken off directly from a tree, mixed with the blades of various plants and with mud; inside it is lined mainly with dry grass, hair and feathers, and in towns with rags and paper. The 4—6 greenish or bluish eggs (2), whose brown or blackish-brown spots are more pronounced than those on the eggs of other corvid birds, are incubated for 15—20 days, mostly by the female. The young, which are fed by both the parent birds, are fledged in

32—36 days. The colonies are usually vacated after the middle of June and the young birds, together with the adults, roam the neighbouring countryside. In the autumn, they join flocks of Rooks and spend the night with them. The whole year round the adult birds live largely on cereals, fruit and berries, while the young birds eat mainly insects, molluscs, worms and other invertebrates and occasionally small vertebrates. The Jackdaw (1) is black, with a slate-grey nape and neck and white irises; it is the same size as the Collared Dove. Both when perched and in flight, it utters a clear 'kyaa-kyaa'; it can also learn to imitate various sounds and even words.

411

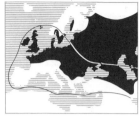

Rook
Corvus frugilegus

The Rook inhabits the greater part of western and central Europe and a large part of Asia. It prefers open country with scattered copses and groups of old trees beside water, but it also nests on the outskirts of woods and even in parks in the centre of towns. It almost always nests in colonies. Rooks repair their old nests in March, or build new ones from broken twigs, mud, moss, leaves and dry grass. The nest is built by both the sexes, but later on one of them must always stay on the spot to make sure that the building material is not stolen by neighbours. The 3—5 greenish, brown-spotted eggs (3), which are laid in March or April, are incubated for 17—19 days by the female, which the male keeps regularly supplied with food. The parents feed the young for four to five weeks in the nest. In June the birds begin to leave the colony and to roam the countryside. West European Rooks are mostly resident or nomadic, but those from the north and the northeast spend the winter in central and southern Europe, in flocks numbering thousands of birds. During the daytime they scour fields, meadows and even towns for food and in the evening they all return to their common roosting site, at the same time and by the same routes. These large flocks remain together from about October to March, when they return to their individual nesting colonies. Rooks live on a very varied diet, including insects, worms, snails, small mammals and cereals, fruit, berries and the remains of potatoes, etc. The Rook has completely black plumage with a violet-blue gloss and from its second year it has a patch of bare skin at the base of its beak (1). The feathers on the top of its head are wide and have rounded ends (2). Rooks have a higher-pitched 'caw' than Carrion Crows, and often add a short, deep 'gack-gack'. They are also the same length as crows, but are slimmer.

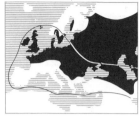

PASSERIFORMES
CORVIDAE

Carrion Crow, Hooded Crow

Corvus corone

In Europe there are two sub-species of this crow. The Carrion Crow (*C. c. corone*) inhabits the western part, roughly as far as the Elbe and the Vltava and from there via Vienna and the Alps to the north of Italy (the black area). Further east, as far as eastern Siberia, it is succeeded by the Hooded Crow (*C. c. cornix*, shaded area). In the wide contact zone where the two species meet, mixed pairs are formed. Crows frequent the margins of forests and small copses in the middle of fields and meadows, but they also nest in the centre of large towns (especially in the case of the Hooded Crow). They never form colonies like Rooks. The pairs are permanent and are parted only by the death of one of the birds. Both the sexes build the nest, which is situated high up in a tree; it is made of broken dry twigs filled in with mud and moss, and sometimes with string and paper, and is lined with dry grass and fur. The 4—6 eggs (3) resemble Rook's eggs and are incubated for 17—20 days by the female. The young crows are at first fed only by the male, while the female keeps them warm, but after about a week the female also begins feeding them. In four to five weeks the young leave the nest and roam the neighbourhood with their parents until the winter comes. The Carrion Crow is a resident bird; the Hooded Crow makes longer and more frequent excursions during the winter. Both are omnivorous, but prefer a flesh diet. They measure about 47 cm. The Carrion Crow has completely black plumage with a green and purple gloss; the Hooded Crow (1) has a black head, wings, tail and tibiae, but the rest of its body is grey. Crows have a deeper and more massive beak than Rooks and they lack the long thigh feathers. The feathers on their crown are narrow and pointed (2).

3

2

Raven,
Common Raven
Corvus corax

The Raven is distributed over the whole of Europe and Asia, North America and the northern part of Africa, but in Europe its range is discontinuous owing to its extinction in many places in previous centuries. It is resident or at most a nomadic bird. It nests mostly in mountains, but also in

2

food which they carry in a pouch in their throat. Ravens live mainly on carrion and will fly 10 km and more in search of it, but they also eat live prey, from insects to animals the size of a hare; they are likewise not above scavenging near mountain chalets and villages. The Raven (1) is the

wooded regions at lower altitudes. The pairs remain together the whole of their lives. In February or March, on a tall tree or a steep cliff, they build a nest made of thick twigs, with a middle layer of thin twigs, rootlets and dry grass; the inside is smeared with mud and is lined with grass, moss, wool and hair. The actual building is done by the female, while the male fetches

the material. Continuous additions to the nest can give rise to a structure up to 1 m high and over 1 m across. The 4—6 bluish-green eggs, marked with blackish-brown spots (2), are incubated for 20—23 days by the female, while the whole time the male keeps watch and brings food. The young birds grow slowly and the parents feed them for a full six to seven weeks on

largest European passerine bird; it weighs 1—1.5 kg and has a wingspan of up to 1 m. It has a strikingly deep, thick beak, and on its throat long, pointed feathers which it often ruffles. Both sexes are jet-black. When they fly, their silhouette is characterised by the wedge shape of their tail. Their contact call is a deep 'korrk-korrk', their display call a throaty 'klong-klong'.

The Starling returns to its nesting areas in February and March. At first the birds remain together in small flocks, but as soon as the weather improves a little the males appear at their chosen holes, where they break into joyful song, with half-spread wings and open beak. They have a dis-

to time, symbolically brings building material, i. e. twigs, straw, rootlets, grass blades and

a fair quantity of feathers. The female always broods the 4–6 greenish-blue eggs (3) at night; during the daytime it is relieved by the male. The young hatch in 12–14 days and are fed for 18–22 days in the nest. In August or September, Starlings form flocks numbering several thousand birds, which roost in reedbeds beside ponds, or at the top of trees, until October, when northern and eastern populations migrate to western Europe and to the Mediterranean region. In the nesting season Starlings live mainly on insects, from the late summer onwards predominantly on fruit. The Starling is a largely European species, whose breeding range stretches from Iceland to the Urals. Emigrants, however, took it with them to South Africa, Australia, New Zealand and North America, which it colonised completely (2) in only 70 years (from 1890). At the beginning of the spring the Starling has black plumage with a metallic lustre, and white speckles (1) formed by the white tips of the individual feathers. During the spring the white tips are worn away, however, so that by June the Starlings are completely black.

tinct preference for nestboxes, which have undoubtedly contributed to the marked increase in the Starling population. Originally, Starlings inhabited deciduous woods; today they also nest in holes in rocks and – in increasing measure – in the walls and roofs of buildings. The nest is built by the female; the male, from time

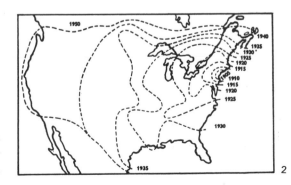

Rose-coloured Starling
Sturnus roseus

The Rose-coloured Starling (1) is the same size as the Starling, but has a pink body, a black head with a flat crest, black wings and a black, very slightly forked tail. The juveniles are yellowish-brown, with a spotted breast and yellow beak (young Starlings are grey-brown and have a brown beak). The vocal manifestations and behaviour of the two species are very similar. The Rose-coloured Starling inhabits the southeastern corner of Europe (Hungary and Italy form its western limit) and southwestern Asia. It nests chiefly in places where its staple food, locusts, is most abundant in that particular year. It is a migrant and often joins flocks of Starlings. It inhabits

mainly steppes, extensive pastures, lowlands in Europe and mountains in central Asia. It is a very sociable bird and lives in flocks the whole year round; its nesting colonies sometimes consist of several thousand pairs. It arrives in its nesting areas rather late, in May or June. The nest is an untidy structure made of twigs, grass blades, rootlets and feathers and is built in a pile of stones, sticks or brushwood, or in a hole in a wall, a quarry or the ground. The 5—6 bluish eggs (2), which are noticeably lighter and glossier than those of the Starling, are laid at the end of May or in June. They are incubated for 11—14 days by the female, but both the parents care for the

young in the nest for 14—19 days. Rose-coloured Starlings eat other insects as well as locusts; they attach themselves to herds of cattle, whose hides they keep clear of parasites. They also like fruit and berries. They leave their breeding areas in August, as soon as they have finished nesting, and spend the winter in Pakistan and India.

House Sparrow
Passer domesticus

2

The House Sparrow, whose natural range is the Palaearctic region, has been spread by man over practically the whole of the globe. It is a markedly synanthropic species and even lives in cities, surrounded by nothing but concrete and stone, where other birds would be unable to subsist. Its courting rituals, in which, as a rule, several ruffled, excitedly twittering males hop around a female in a joint display, can be observed from February onwards. The adults nest three, sometimes four and very occasionally five times in the course of the year. The nest is generally built in a hole or a recess in some kind of building, either outside or inside; sparrows also often settle in House Martins' and Swallows' nests, in the walls of White Storks' nests, in nestboxes and in holes in trees and rocks, but seldom nest openly in the crown of a tree. The nest is a large, untidy spherical structure with a side entrance; it is built by both the sexes, is made of dry grass, straw, string, paper and rags and is lined with a large quantity of feathers. It is always built from the inside outwards and its outer wall is never tidied up. The 4–6 variably coloured, greyish, brownish or greenish eggs, densely brown-spotted (2), are incubated for 12–13 days by both the parents in turn; they likewise feed the nestlings in turn, for 14–17 days. The young are fed primarily on insects. The adult birds have a mainly vegetarian diet, in particular seeds; they also nip off leaves and buds and consume refuse. House Sparrows are resident birds and are strictly loyal to their birthplace. The male (1) has a grey-topped head, white cheeks and a black throat; the female is light brown and buff, with dark brown spots. Both birds measure about 15 cm.

417

Spanish Sparrow

Passer hispaniolensis

The male Spanish Sparrow can be distinguished from the very similar House Sparrow by its chestnut crown, the much larger black patch on its throat and breast and its black-spotted flanks (1). The female and juvenile are almost indistinguishable from female House Sparrows, but some may have a streaked breast and flanks. The two species have similar voices. The Spanish Sparrow inhabits northern Africa, Asia Minor and central Asia. In Europe it lives in Spain, Italy and the Balkans, where it has spread in recent years to the south of Romania. It is not so closely associated with human communities as the House Sparrow. The birds nest gregariously, often in very large colonies, on bushes and trees in avenues lining country roads, in river valleys and open woods and on trees in towns and villages. Occasional pairs nest singly in the lower part of a stork's nest, an eagle's eyrie or the nest of some other large bird, or in a Swallow's nest. Sometimes the colonies are unmixed, sometimes they also contain House Sparrows. The nest resembles that of the House Sparrow, but is softly lined with feathers, horsehair and fluff. The adults evidently nest twice a year, between May and July. The clutches consist of 4—8 whitish, fawn-spotted eggs (2). After leaving the nest, the young remain for a time with the parents, but then form flocks which roam the countryside in search of food (largely the seeds of crops and weeds). When feeding their young, Spanish Sparrows also catch insects. The Spanish Sparrow is a mainly resident bird, but its most northerly populations wander southwards for the winter.

2

1

Tree Sparrow
Passer montanus

Many people are only vaguely aware that there are other sparrows besides the familiar urban House Sparrow. Tree Sparrows (1) of both sexes have a completely chestnut-brown crown and a black crescent-shaped spot on either cheek. They are only very slightly smaller than the House Sparrow. Their call note is a 'chee-ip, chee-ip' or 'chick, chick' and their song is a medley of similar sounds. The Tree Sparrow is hardly ever seen in built-up areas; at best we may find it in parks and gardens with old trees. It likes country where open spaces alternate with groups of old, hollow trees, such as the edges of deciduous woods, old orchards, avenues and riverside copses; it is thus bound much more closely to a green and natural environment than the House Sparrow. Its nests are mostly to be found in tree holes and nestboxes. The adults fill the hole with straw, hay, rootlets, moss and fragments of leaves, giving rise to a shaggy spherical structure softly lined with feathers. About three times a year, the female lays 4–6 eggs (2), variably coloured like those of the preceding species, which are incubated for 12–13 days by both the parent birds in turn. The young leave the nest at the age of 14–16 days; ten days later they are able to fend for themselves and form joint flocks together with the adult birds. The flocks roam the countryside and sleep in dense thickets, in the crowns of trees and in reedbeds, but the pairs remain together the whole time. The Tree Sparrow inhabits almost the whole of Europe, Asia and northern Africa. Its diet contains more insect than plant food. The Tree Sparrow and the House Sparrow occasionally interbreed.

2

Rock Sparrow
Petronia petronia

The male and female Rock Sparrow (1) resemble the female House Sparrow. They have dark brown stripes on the crown of their head and a yellow spot on their throat, but the latter can be seen only at close quarters, when the bird raises its head. At the tip tains of the central and eastern parts; it ascends mountains to altitudes of 3,000—4,000 m. It nests on sunlit rock faces and stony mountain slopes, in ruins and in human settlements. The nest is built in a rock crevice, under a boulder, in a hole onies, sometimes of 100 pairs. They usually nest twice a year, between April und June. The nest is made of stalks, grass blades and rootlets and is lined with feathers and hair. The 4—7 whitish eggs, which are marked with greyish-brown spots (2), are in-

of their tail feathers they have round white spots which are particularly visible in flight. Juveniles lack the yellow spot on the throat. The Rock Sparrow's call is a somewhat croaking disyllabic 'pey-i'; sparrow-like sounds can also be heard in its song. On the ground, the Rock Sparrow walks, i.e. it does not hop like other sparrows. It inhabits southern Europe, northern Africa and Asia as far as the steppes and moun- or crack in a wall or under eaves. The birds preferably nest in col- cubated for 12—14 days by both the parent birds in turn; the parents likewise both feed the young for about 20 days in the nest. When they leave the nest, the young at first remain with their families, but in the autumn they form separate flocks which live nomadically when searching for food. Otherwise the Rock Sparrow is a resident bird whose diet consists of seeds, berries and various insects.

2

Snow Finch
Montifringilla nivalis

The distribution of the Snow Finch is very interesting. It lives only in the alpine zone of the mountains of southern Europe and central Asia. In Europe it inhabits the Pyrenees, the Apennines, the Alps and the mountains of the western Balkans, tween May and July, generally in a rock crevice or a hole in a wall, or under the eaves of a mountain hut. It is built by both the sexes, is made of dry grass, rootlets and moss and is lined with fine grass, feathers or fur. In some places the adults nest twice a year; they roads. The Snow Finch (1), which is larger than the House Sparrow, has a grey head, a brown back, a black throat patch and a whitish moustachial stripe; there is a broad white patch on its wings, and its tail is white with blackish-brown feathers in the centre and

from former Yugoslavia to the north of Greece. It is a resident bird. When the nesting season is over the families form small flocks and usually ascend to still higher altitudes; they do not return to their nesting areas until snow has fallen and they only exceptionally stray to the foothills. The birds nest on stony or grassy ground on ridges and peaks above the tree-limit. The nest is built be- both incubate the 4—5 pure white eggs for a period of 13—14 days. The young, which are likewise fed and reared by both parents, leave the nest at the age of 18—21 days. The adult birds feed them on small insects; otherwise the Snow Finch is largely a vegetarian, although it also forages in various kinds of waste in the vicinity of chalets and beside a black border at the tip. In the adult bird's winter plumage and the juvenile's, the black throat patch is missing and the beak is yellow instead of black. The Snow Finch flies fast, with undulating movements, and never perches on trees. Its contact call is 'tsweek' or 'keek', its alarm call is 'shray' and its song, rendered while perched or in flight, sounds like 'sittitshay-si-tittshay'.

Chaffinch
Fringilla coelebs

and cocoon silk, it blends perfectly with its surroundings. It is softly lined with hair, horsehair and small feathers. The 4—6 reddish or bluish-green eggs, which are marked with spots of different sizes (3), are incubated entirely by the female. The young are hatched in 12—14 days and leave the nest after about two weeks' parental care. The adults then nest again, sometimes in the same nest. The Chaffinch's breeding range stretches from Europe to western Siberia, central Asia and northern Africa. It lives wherever it can find trees and bushes and is even to be

2♂

Most Chaffinches are migrants, but many stay in their nesting areas during the winter. Such birds are mainly males, and when the famous naturalist Linnaeus noticed this he gave the Chaffinch the specific name *'coelebs'* (= widower). Most Chaffinches spend the winter in southern and western Europe; they migrate in September or October and return in March or April. The Chaffinch builds one of the prettiest nests; it is a strong, densely woven structure made of moss, fine grass blades and rootlets, and, since it is masked by a layer of lichen collected by the female from branches in the immediate vicinity and by cobwebs

3

found in villages and towns. Three quarters of its diet consists of seeds and the rest is made up of insects, most of which it catches while rearing the young. In its breeding plumage, the male (1, behind) has a bluish-grey head (in the autumn, after moulting, a brown head: 2), a claret-coloured underside and a green rump; the female (1, in front) is greenish-grey. Both sexes have two white bands across their wings. They are the same size as a sparrow.

Brambling
Fringilla montifringilla

The Brambling inhabits forests in northern Europe and Asia. In the taiga it replaces the Chaffinch and where their ranges overlap the two species occasionally interbreed. Every year, starting roughly in October, flocks of Bramblings migrate southwards, sometimes to southern Europe. They are then to be seen, at times together with other finches, in stubble-fields, meadows and fallow and stony fields and around food provided for Pheasants, where they gather weed seeds and grain; in addition, they eat birch, alder and conifer seeds. They also frequent beechwoods,

3♂

1

2

since they are very fond of beech-nuts, but they usually retire to coniferous trees to roost. The nest resembles that of the Chaffinch; it is built entirely by the female, which also incubates the 5–7 eggs (2), similar to the Chaffinch's, unaided. The young are hatched in about 14 days and both the parents feed them for about 11 days in the nest; they are fed mainly on insects, which at this time form a substantial part of the adult birds' diet. Because of the shortness of the

summer in the far north, Bramblings are able to rear only one brood of young. When the nesting season is over, the families join forces and begin to live together in flocks again. In its

breeding plumage, the male (1) has a jet-black head and back, an orange breast and shoulders and a white belly and rump (3). In the winter, the black colouring is broken by the grey and brown fringes of the individual feathers. The female has a browner and more spotted crown and back; the sides of its head and neck are grey. Both sexes are the same size as the Chaffinch. The contact call of the Brambling when flying is a broad 'que-e-eck' or a softer 'yick'.

423

Red-fronted Serin
Serinus pusillus

The Red-fronted Serin inhabits the Caucasus and Asia from Asia Minor to the Tien-Shan Mountains. It lives at moderate to high montane altitudes (in the Caucasus up to 3,000 m). It settles on rocks, on moraine, in mountain valleys with rocky outcrops, on stony mountain steppes with barberry, wild roses and rhododendrons growing on them and in open birchwoods and pinewoods. It is a resident bird, but in the winter small flocks

2

of Red-fronted Serins descend to wide river valleys at lower altitudes and to the foothills of the mountains. At the beginning of May the flocks break up into pairs, which nest in close proximity to one another. Egg-laying starts at the end of May and a second family is reared in July. The nest is a strongly built structure made of grass, moss and rootlets and lined with feathers and hair; it is situated in a rock fissure, on a ledge of rock, or in a low, dense bush. The 3—5 bluish eggs, marked with brownish-black spots and streaks, are incubated for about 14 days by the female. The young remain 15—17 days in the nest and after they have left it they are fed for a further five to seven days in its vicinity, mostly by the male. The Red-fronted Serin lives mainly on the small seeds of mountain plants, alders and birches. It is one of the smallest, but one of the prettiest, finches (it is smaller than the Serin). Its head, throat and breast and the back of its neck are black, its back is cinnamon-brown, with black streaks, its belly and flanks are yellowish- grey, with black spots, and its rump is orange. Adult birds (1) have orange-red caps, juveniles (2) have a dark brown head. Old females are sometimes more brightly coloured than young males, but the red area is usually smaller and there is less black on the breast.

1

Serin
Serinus serinus

Originally a Mediterranean bird, in the last century the Serin suddenly began to spread northwards and has now reached Scandinavia. Its eastward advance is slower, so that it has reached only the marginal parts of the former USSR. It is a migrant and in October it leaves for the countries bordering the Mediterranean. Individual birds overwinter with increasing frequency in central Europe, however. In April, Serins begin to take possession of their nesting sites in open country, in avenues, beside water and on the outskirts of forests; they also nest in gardens, orchards, parks and cemeteries. Soon after the courtship ceremony, the female begins to weave the neat little nest, which is made of fine rootlets, grass blades, bark fibres and lichen, is lined with fluff, fur and feathers and is situated on a forked or dense branch of a bush or tree. The 3—5 bluish eggs, which are marked with rusty and dark brown spots (2), are incubated for 12—14 days, mainly by the female, with occasional help from the male. Both the parents feed the young, but, unlike other passerines, they do not swallow or remove their droppings, which accumulate at the edge of the nest and are thus a good criterion for its identification. In 14—16 days the young leave the nest and the adult birds nest again. The nesting season as a whole lasts from the end of April to the beginning of July. When Serins have finished nesting, together with other granivorous birds they form flocks which live mainly on the seeds of weeds and crops.

2

The male (1, standing) has a bright yellow forehead, breast and rump; otherwise it is greyish-yellow and streaked. Its long, rather jingling song, in which its disyllabic call note, 'tir-rititt', can frequently be heard, is sung from an elevation or during the bird's elaborate display flight. The female, (1, sitting) is browner and more striped. Serins are noticeably smaller than House Sparrows; they measure about 11.5 cm.

Greenfinch
Carduelis chloris

Outside Europe, the Greenfinch occurs only in northern Africa, Asia Minor and the Middle East. Birds from the northern and northeastern part of its range migrate in the autumn to central and southern Europe; birds living further south are nomadic. Migrants return to their nesting areas in March and April. They have a preference for country of a parkland type, with thickets and groups of trees, for the edges of woods and for parks, gardens and cemeteries; they also penetrate into the centre of large towns. Like other finches, they must have open spaces close at hand, where they can find food. Their relatively large nest is made of twigs, rootlets, grass blades and moss (which usually shows through the walls) and is lined with very fine rootlets, hair and feathers. In the spring it is built by the female in a conifer before the deciduous trees burst into leaf; if the birds nest a second or third time it is often built in a deciduous tree. The 4–6 bluish eggs, which are sparsely marked with large greyish-violet spots and small russet spots (2), are incubated for 12–14 days, entirely by the female. The male fetches food for the brooding female and helps to rear the young, which leave the nest at the age of 14–16 days. The adult birds feed them mostly on plant food pre-softened in their own crop, with only an occasional caterpillar or beetle. The male (1) is olive-green, but the edges of its wings and tail are bright yellow. The female is more greyish-green and the yellow is less distinct. Both sexes are the size of a sparrow. The male's twittering and wheezing song is rendered from elevations and during flight. Its call note is a tinkling 'giggiggi' or a rough, drawling 'itsch'.

Goldfinch, European Goldfinch
Carduelis carduelis

2

The Goldfinch likes open parkland with an adequate number of trees. It inhabits orchards, gardens, parks, avenues and open deciduous woods over a large part of Europe and Asia. The nest is built by the female, almost always on a deciduous tree (very often a fruit tree), and usually at the end of a terminal branch at the periphery of the crown. The thick-walled nest, whose upper edge turns slightly inwards, is a carefully woven structure made of fine grass blades, rootlets and moss, intermingled with cocoon silk and lichen from nearby trees, so that it blends perfectly with its surroundings; it is lined with thistledown and fur. The 4—5 whitish eggs, which are marked with reddish underlying spots and russet surface spots and streaks (2), are incubated for 12—14 days by the female, which is fed the whole time by the male. At first, the parents feed their offspring on insects; later, they give them seeds pre-softened in their own crop. At the age of 12—14 days the young leave the nest; when the young have become independent, the adult birds nest again and finally, in the late summer, the whole family joins other families to form a flock. The flocks visit waste ground, meadows and fields overgrown with weeds, such as thistles and dock, where the birds find their favourite food. Nimbly negotiating thin twigs, they also gather seeds from birch nuts and alder cones. Some Goldfinches remain near their nesting areas throughout the winter, but in October or November some of them undertake long journeys to southern Europe, returning again in March or April. The striking white, red, black and yellow colouring of the Goldfinch (1) makes it easy to identify. Very often, especially while flying, it utters its clear call note, 'tswitt-witt', which can also be heard in its twittering, tinkling song. The Goldfinch is smaller than the House Sparrow.

Siskin
Carduelis spinus

The Siskin inhabits central, eastern and southern Europe, Asia Minor and eastern Siberia. It prefers conifer forests, but occasionally nests in mixed woods and, in exceptional cases, in deciduous woods. The nest is built by the female, usually high up in the densest part of a conifer, at the end of a side branch. It is made of thin twigs, rootlets, dry grass, moss and lichen, cleverly interwoven with cocoon silk, and is softly lined with fluff, hair and feathers. Twice a year, between April and July, the female lays 4−5 bluish eggs marked with blurred russet spots and a few blackish spots and streaks, which it incubates for 12−14 days,

while the male fetches food. Both parents feed the young for 13−15 days in the nest, at first almost solely on insects. After rearing a second brood, the adult birds, together with the young, form flocks and from August onwards begin to roam about. Siskins from the north always migrate further south for the winter; they either remain in west or central Europe or proceed to the Mediterranean region. Mountain Siskins descend to the lowlands, where they mainly frequent groups of birches and alders, whose seeds are their chief winter food. Migrants always return to their nesting areas in March. Siskins are about the same size

as the Serin. The male (1, on right) has a generally yellowish-green appearance; it has a black cap (some males also have a black chin spot) and two yellow bands on its wings. The female (1, on left) has no black markings on its head, is rather a greyish-green shade and is more noticeably streaked. The Siskin's song is a mixture of wheezing and twittering interspersed with short whistling tones; the male often sings while flying in a bat-like manner above the trees. Its contact call, uttered in flight, is a thin, characteristic 'tsi-ee'.

Linnet
Carduelis cannabina

The Linnet inhabits practically the whole of Europe, a small part of western Siberia, northern Africa, Asia Minor and central Asia. It has a preference for parkland, where bushy slopes, hedges and copses alternate with spaces overgrown with herbaceous vegetation, where the birds find their food. It also lives at the edges of woods and in cemeteries, parks and gardens; several pairs often nest close together. Linnet pairbonds are stronger than those of other finches. Wherever the one partner goes the other follows after, and the pairs do not separate even in the winter flocks. The nest is built by the female, usually low down in a dense thicket; it is made of grass blades, stems and rootlets, various plant fibres, wool and animal hair. The 4—6 bluish, brown-speckled eggs are incubated for 12—14 days, largely by the female, which now and again is relieved for a short time by the male. The young remain 10—12 days in the nest; when they leave it, they are cared for mainly by the male, since the female is busy building a new nest for the next clutch of eggs. Linnets live on herbaceous plant seeds much more so than other finches. When the nesting season is over, the birds assemble in flocks, which sometimes remain near their nesting areas for the whole of the winter, but sometimes migrate to west Europe or the Mediterranean region and return in March or April. The male (1) has a crimson breast and forehead, grey cheeks, a grey neck and a chestnut back; in the autumn, when it moults, the red colouring disappears. The female is brown, heavily streaked with dark brown. Both are the same size as the Goldfinch. With its rich and varied song, the Linnet is undoubtedly the best vocalist among the finches.

Twite
Carduelis flavirostris

The distribution of this species is of great interest. In Europe, the Twite breeds in Britain and Ireland and in Norway, Sweden and Finland; otherwise it lives in the mountains of Asia Minor and central Asia. According to some theories, it found its way into Europe from central Asia after the last post-glacial period, along the head of the retreating ice sheet, which thawed and thus divided its area in two. It is a resident, nomadic and migratory bird, which spends the winter in northwest Europe and sometimes as far as the Mediterranean region. In the north it inhabits unforested places at high altitudes, with low herbaceous vegetation and shrubs, and coastal regions and islands. When migrating, it frequents stubble-fields, moors, fallow fields and wasteland. It nests in small, loose colonies. The nest is built on the ground, in a recess in a rock or under a boulder, or a little way above the ground. It is fairly large, is made of dry grass and moss and is lined with hair and feathers. The 4–6 bluish, russet-speckled eggs (2) are laid between May and July and are incubated by the female. The parents both feed the young for about 15 days in the nest, and when they are independent the adult birds sometimes nest again. When the nesting season is over, the birds group together in flocks and from October onwards migrant populations set out on their journey southwards; they return in February or March. The Twite (1), which is smaller than the House Sparrow, is streaked with black and brown.

2

Its throat is buff or cinnamon-brown and the male has a reddish rump; its beak is yellowish-grey in the summer and yellow in the winter. Its contact calls while flying are a soft 'dja-dja-dja' and a loud 'chweek'; its song resembles the Linnet's.

1

Redpoll, Common Redpoll
Carduelis flammea

The Redpoll lives primarily in the tundras of Europe, Asia and North America; it also occurs in the British Isles and the mountains of central Europe, where it nests mainly in the subalpine birch zone. Recently, however, it has spread to lower altitudes and has settled in birch and pine

2

May and July. The Redpoll's diet is very similar to the Siskin's and the two species often form mixed flocks. Every year, roughly from October onwards, northern Redpolls migrate to central and southern Europe, where their appearance is sometimes of an irruptive character. The Redpoll

1

growths on peat-moors, in willows and alders growing near water and even in town and village parks and gardens. Several pairs usually nest together. The nest is built by the female, accompanied and sometimes supplied with material by the male. It is generally placed low down on a conifer or a deciduous tree; it is made of thin twigs, dry grass, rootlets and moss and is lined with horsehair, hair and feathers. The 4—5 bluish eggs, marked with light brown spots and russet speckles (2), are incubated for 12—14 days by the female. The male feeds the brooding female and helps to rear the young, which leave the nest in 11—14 days. Central European Redpolls generally nest twice between (1) has greyish-brown plumage streaked with blackish-brown; it has a red forehead, a black chin spot and two light bars on its wings. The male has a reddish breast. Its typical contact call is 'chuch-uch-uch', sometimes interspersed with a chirruping 'irrre' Redpolls, Linnets and Twites are small birds and are all approximately the same size.

431

Arctic Redpoll
Carduelis hornemanni

is made of thin twigs, rootlets and grass and is lined with hair, feathers and fluff. Because of the severity of the Arctic climate, the adults are able to nest only once. The 4–6 eggs (2) resemble those of the Redpoll. The incubation period and the care of the young in the nest are each presumably for 12–14 days. Arctic Redpolls live on the seeds of various plants, on alder and birch seeds and on small insects. They are irregular migrants; in some winters they migrate in varying numbers southwards, particularly to the Baltic region and the middle of Russia, but sometimes to Britain and central Europe, where they are most likely to be found from November to February. The Arctic Redpoll (1) resembles the Redpoll, but is distinctly paler. The adult male has a white, unspotted rump, a whitish under-

The Arctic Redpoll inhabits the most northerly parts of the tundra of Europe, Asia and North America. In Europe it occurs only in the north of Scandinavia and the European part of the former USSR. It nests in thickets, both at quite high altitudes and in river valleys and coastal regions. The nest is usually built in a stunted birch or willow thicket; several pairs usually nest together. It side and a light grey, dark-streaked back. Both sexes have a crimson forehead and the male has a pink breast. The voice and habits of the Arctic Redpoll are the same as those of the Redpoll.

Crossbill, Red Crossbill

Loxia curvirostra

The Crossbill inhabits spruce and silver fir forests in Europe, Asia and North America and also lives in northern Africa. Its whole life is dependent on spruce cones (less on silver fir and larch cones), or, to be precise, on the seed yield from the cones. In association with this peculiarity, the Crossbill is the only bird which always nests in the winter, when the cones ripen. Its main nesting season is from January to April, although Crossbills can actually breed at any time of year. Since they nest in the winter, the Crossbill's nest is a very substantial structure with walls over 4 cm thick. It is built by the female, high up in a conifer, is made of twigs, grass blades, moss and lichen and is thickly upholstered with dry grass, hair and feathers. The 3—4 whitish, russet-spotted eggs (3) are incubated by the female, which, because of the inclement weather, begins brooding as soon as it has laid the first one, hardly leaves the

nest for the whole 14—16 days and is kept supplied with food by the male. At first, the young are fed only by the female, but after a time the male also lends a hand. In 14—20 days the young leave the nest, but stay with their parents. The Crossbill is a resident and nomadic bird; its movements literally follow the cone supply and are sometimes of an irruptive character, so that in places swarming with Crossbills in one year we may look for them in vain the next. The adult male Crossbill (1) usually has brick-red plumage, but younger males are yellowish-green like the females (2). The young are brownish-grey and do not acquire the crossed mandibles until they are about three weeks old. The adult birds are somewhat larger than a sparrow. The best known sound made by the Crossbill is its loud 'chip-chip' contact call.

2♀

3

433

Crimson-winged Finch

Rhodopechys sanguinea

The Crimson-winged Finch has an interesting distribution. It lives in southwestern Asia (it comes closest to Europe in Turkey and Transcaucasia) and otherwise occurs only in the Atlas Mountains in northwestern Africa. It is a resident bird, but changes altitude with the season. In the spring it ascends high up into the mountains and in the winter it seeks the shelter of the valleys. It inhabits rocky places at alpine altitudes, where the surface of the mountain is broken up; in some places it nests at somewhat lower altitudes. As a rule it does not descend below 1,200 m, but it nests at altitudes of up to 3,200 m. At present, we know very little about its family life. It evidently nests between May and July and its 4—5 eggs are white, with greenish-grey and grey spots concentrated more near the blunt end; the lengths of the incubation and fledging periods are not known for certain. The Crimson-winged Finch lives on a largely vegetarian diet, primarily on the seeds of various kinds of plants. In size and shape the male bird (1) resembles the male Hawfinch and it likewise has a short, thick beak, but the beak is yellow. It has a brownish-grey, dark-spotted back, a black crown, a rusty-grey underside and large, deep pink areas on its wings. The female closely resembles the male, but it has a browner crown and the pink areas on its wings are lighter. The Crimson-winged Finch has a similar voice to the Linnet.

Desert Finch
Rhodospiza obsoleta

In Asia, the Desert Finch has a distribution similar to that of the Crimson-winged Finch, but it does not nest in Africa. Northern populations migrate to the shores of the eastern Mediterranean for the winter; the rest are resident. Desert Finches inhabit orchards and gardens, oases, the vegetation beside natural water and irrigation canals, dry steppe and wooded steppe formations and desert outskirts with an incidence of woody plants; they must always have water within flying distance, however. The pairs nest in close proximity and fly together in search of food and water. The nest is built in a tree or a bush, usually not more than 2 m above the ground, and is neither hidden nor disguised. It is easy to identify. The outer wall is made of quickly assembled and interwoven sticks and twigs, which are surprisingly thick considering the size of the bird (it is only slightly larger than a sparrow). The lining, however, is made of the finest material possible, including plant fluff and animal hairs (usually from camels or sheep). The first 5—7 bluish, dark-spotted eggs are laid in April and the parent birds take turns to incubate them; the first clutch is usually followed by a second. When the young have left their nests, all the birds collect together in a flock and roam about in the vicinity; they live on various kinds of seeds, but are particularly fond of the seeds of thistles. The Desert Finch is about the size of a Greenfinch; it is mainly greyish-brown, has black, white-bordered wing and tail feathers and pink-coloured patches on its wings. The male (1, in front) has black feathers at the base of its beak and black lores; in the female (1, behind), these markings are brown. The call note of the Desert Finch is a soft 'fink-fink'; its song resembles the Greenfinch's.

435

Scarlet Rosefinch, Scarlet Grosbeak

Carpodacus erythrinus

The Scarlet Rosefinch inhabits a broad range extending from eastern Europe to western Siberia; it also lives in the mountains of Asia Minor and recently it has begun to spread to southern and western Europe. It is a migrant and spends the winter in the region between Asia Minor and India. It leaves at the end of August or during September and does not return to its nesting areas until May or even June. It usually nests near water − in overgrown stream and river valleys, in damp meadows with a scattering of bushes and in mountains. In some places it even inhabits tangled gardens and parks in villages and towns. The somewhat carelessly constructed nest is built by the female low down in a thicket or in herbaceous vegetation; it is made of thick grass blades and thin twigs and is lined with fine grass, rootlets and fur. The 4−6 bright blue eggs, which are marked with a few blackish-brown spots (3), are laid in June. The young hatch in 12−14 days and leave the nest at 11−13 days, before they are fully able to fly. The eggs are incubated only by

the female, but both the parents feed the young, chiefly on small seeds, which they pre-soften in their own crop, and partly on insects. The adult birds have a mainly vegetarian diet and live on the seeds, buds and leaves of

various herbaceous plants and trees. They grow to the size of a sparrow. In its full breeding plumage, the male (1) has a crimson head, breast and rump and a pink-tinted belly. During its autumn moult it loses its red plumage and afterwards resembles the olive-brown, dark-spotted female (2). Up to their second year, young males likewise lack the red colouring. The song of the Scarlet Rosefinch is a tuneful, whistling 'tiu-tiu-fi-tiu'.

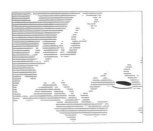

Great Rosefinch
Carpodacus rubicilla

The only place where the Great Rosefinch touches Europe is in the mountains of the Caucasus; otherwise it inhabits the mountain massifs of central Asia at altitudes of roughly 2,500 m and

specific movements and by hopping on a ledge of rock or a stone; it droops its wings, spreads its tail and sings loudly the whole time. The pairs nest singly or in small colonies. The nests are

branches of squat bushes; they are made of plant material. The 4—5 bluish-green eggs, which are marked with a few brown speckles, are laid at the end of May or the beginning of June and are incubated for about 13—14 days; little is known of the bird's family life, however. It lives on the seeds and berries of various mountain herbaceous plants and bushes. The Great Rosefinch (1) is the largest member of the genus *Carpodacus*. The adult male in full breeding plumage (2) (at least two years old) is dark crimson, with white spots on its head and underside. Young males are brownish-grey and do not turn red until their second year. The females are also largely brownish-grey and their underside is thickly marked with dark spots. The song of the Great Rosefinch is very loud and can be heard over a distance of up to 1 km. It is composed of seven to nine whistles, the first two or three of which are particularly loud and high, while the rest descend, decrescendo and diminuendo, until they fade away.

over. It frequents alpine meadows, sunny rocky slopes carpeted with mountain plants and conifer woods and deciduous woods at high altitudes. It is a resident bird; in the autumn it descends to mountain valleys, though seldom below 1,000—1,500 m, and spends the winter there in small flocks. At the beginning of April the flocks begin to break up, as the birds return to higher altitudes. The courting male draws attention to itself by

usually hidden in fissures in the rocks or low down in the

2♂

Bullfinch
Pyrrhula pyrrhula

The Bullfinch inhabits almost the whole of Europe and a broad belt stretching across Asia north of the Himalayas as far as Japan. It has a predilection for montane conifer forests, but also nests in off itself) and is lined with fine rootlets, dry grass, lichen and hair. The 4—5 pale blue eggs are marked with grey spots and blackish-brown surface spots and streaks (3); they are incubated by

birds migrate quite a long way southwards for the winter, when they live entirely on the seeds of herbaceous plants, trees and bushes and peck the buds of woody plants. Bullfinches are the same size as a sparrow. They have a black head, a grey back, a white rump and a white band on their wings. The male's underside is red (1), the female's is greyish-brown (2). The most familiar vocal manifestation of the Bullfinch is its soft call note, 'deu-deu', which is easily imitated and can be used to decoy the bird itself. Its song is an inconspicuous twitter; the female also sings, but its song is even softer than the male's. The pairs often remain together throughout the winter.

conifer and mixed woods at lower altitudes and sometimes in old large parks, cemeteries and gardens. In March the pairs take possession of their nesting territory and in April the female, accompanied by the male, begins to build the nest, which is situated at a moderate height, usually beside the trunk of a dense spruce. It is a shallow structure made of loosely assembled twigs (which the bird breaks the female, which, while sitting, is fed by the male. The young, which hatch in 13—15 days, leave the nest at the age of 14—17 days. The parents both feed them on a pulp of small seeds and fruit regurgitated from their own crop, together with a small quantity of insects and spiders. About half the birds nest again in June or July. In regions with a temperate climate, Bullfinches are resident or nomadic, but Scandinavian

Hawfinch
Coccothraustes coccothraustes

The most distinctive feature of the Hawfinch is its large nutcracker beak, which is a match for even the hardest plum and damson stones — not to mention our fingers, if we are rash enough to

finch (1) inhabits most of Europe, north to the southern part of Scandinavia; it also lives in northern Africa and in Asia, in a strip of territory south of the conifer taiga as far as Japan.

Most central European Hawfinches fly further south for the winter and their place is taken by birds from the north; southern Hawfinches are resident. The Hawfinch's beak is bluish-grey in

handle one of these birds. Hawfinches also eat hard-coated seeds, and if it comes to the worst they will make do with weed and hip seeds and the pips of apples and pears. They preferably inhabit light deciduous and mixed woods, copses, old gardens and orchards. The female begins to build the nest in April, usually on a deciduous tree. It is a fairly large structure made basically of long, thick twigs, which often protrude from the sides; next comes a layer of rootlets and grass blades and lastly the lining, which is made of fine rootlets and sometimes of hair. The 4—6 bluish eggs, which are marked with grey spots and greyish-brown speckles and streaks (3), are incubated for 12—14 days, mainly by the female, which is meanwhile fed by the male. The parents both feed the young for 10—14 days in the nest and accompany them for a long time after they have left it. The Haw-

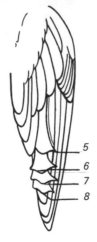

the summer and yellowish-brown in the winter. It has a yellowish-brown head with a black chin patch, a grey nape, a dark brown back and a large white area on each wing. The outer vane of the 5th to the 8th violet-glossed primaries terminates with an obtuse angle, the inner vane is rounded inwards (2). The Hawfinch is the same size as the Starling. Its call note is a sharp 'tzik-tzik'.

439

Pine Grosbeak
Pinicola enucleator

The Pine Grosbeak inhabits the north of Europe, Asia and North America. It nests in conifer forests with an admixture of birches and alders, and in mountainous country also in birchwoods. The female builds the nest at a moderate height on a tree or bush; it is made of twigs, rootlets and grass and is lined with moss, lichen and horsehair. The nest usually contains 4 bluish-green eggs, marked with brownish-black spots (2), which are laid between the end of May and July. They are incubated for 13—14 days by the female, which the male keeps supplied with food.

2

The young remain about 14 days in the nest and are cared for by both parents. When the birds have finished nesting, they form small flocks comprising several families. They live mainly on conifer seeds and buds, crawling to the end of twigs with the dexterity of parrots to nip them off; they enrich this diet with berries and invertebrate animals (mainly plant lice). The Pine Grosbeak is a migrant and a nomad. Its northern populations fly southwards for the winter, usually to the southern part of Scandinavia and the Baltic, but in years of mass invasions some flocks, or individual birds, also find their way to central Europe. The Pine Grosbeak is one of the largest finches (it is the size of a Starling). It has a strikingly thick beak, whose upper mandible has a hooked tip overhanging the lower mandible.

Old males have a crimson head, neck, breast and rump; the females and juveniles are olive-green to yellowish-green (1). The song of the Pine Grosbeak is composed of soft, fluty tones and nasal sounds.

440

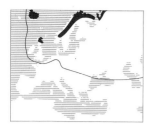

Snow Bunting
Plectrophenax nivalis

The Snow Bunting nests further north than any other passerine bird. It inhabits stony tundra and rocky riverbanks and coasts in the north of Europe, Asia and North America. In the most southerly parts of its range in Europe – e. g. in Scandinavia and Scotland – it occurs only at high altitudes, above the tree-line. It is a migrant and in September and October it flies southwards. In the winter, its flocks can be found

nest until June or July (in Scotland in May). The nest, which is built by the female, is made of grass, moss and lichen and is lined with hair and feathers. It is

reddish ground (2). They are incubated for 12–14 days by the female, which is sometimes fed by the male. In the summer the Snow Bunting lives mainly on insects and in the autumn on seeds. The male's breeding plumage is vividly black and white; its winter plumage (1) is white and light brown. The female's plumage is similar to the male's winter plumage. At all times of the year the birds have

chiefly on the North Sea coast, but it also strays inland into the heart of Europe, where it frequents fields and, quite regularly, mountain meadows above the forest-limit. It returns northwards in March or April, but does not

carefully concealed in a rock crevice, under a boulder, in a pile of wood or even in a derelict building. The 4–6 eggs are very variably coloured, with rust-red to purplish-brown spots on a greenish, bluish, yellowish or

striking white areas on their wings and black flight feathers. This bunting's call note is a rippling 'brrree'; its melodious song, 'teuri-teuri-teuri-teurivee', can be heard frequently during its display flight.

441

Pine Bunting
Emberiza leucocephalos

Despite the differences in their coloration, the Pine Bunting is very closely related to the Yellowhammer and over the wide zone where their ranges overlap, the two species interbreed. The Pine Bunting's range stretches from the Ural Mountains to China; in Europe it nests only in the region of the River Pechora. Southern populations are resident; northern birds fly, mainly in Sep-

2♂

tember and October, to central Asia and from there to Iraq and Nepal. Only stray birds appear in central and western Europe. The Pine Bunting nests in light conifer woods but frequently settles in deciduous woods and in parkland with copses and thickets. The males immediately occupy a nesting territory, sing their hardest and wage numerous battles. The nesting season lasts from May to July and during it the adults usually nest twice. The nest, which is built on the ground, in grass or under a bush, is made of grass blades and rootlets and often has horsehair in its lining. The 3—6 pink- or green-tinted eggs are thickly marked with brown streaks and spots; they are incubated for about 13 days by the female. Both parents look after the young, which leave the nest in 9—13 days, before they are able to fly. The adult birds feed them mainly on insects; later, the plant component of their diet (in particular seeds) preponderates. In its breeding plumage, the male (2) has a white crown and cheeks, a white band across its breast and a white belly; its wide superciliary stripe and its throat and rump are chestnut; in its winter plumage (1), the amount of white is much smaller. The female resembles the female Yellowhammer, except that the Yellowhammer's yellow areas of plumage are white in the Pine Bunting. The voice, size and behaviour of the two species are likewise similar.

442

Yellowhammer
Emberiza citrinella

The Yellowhammer nests over virtually the whole of Europe and in western Siberia; an isolated population also occurs in the Caucasus. This bunting likes open country with fields and meadows, groups of bushes and trees, copses, trees growing beside rivers and streams, the edges of forests and forest clearings; it also frequents the outskirts of human communities. From April to August it can be seen singing on elevated perches such as trees and bushes, telegraph wires, or even on nothing more than a stone or a clod of earth. The male defends its chosen territory extremely energetically and few birds can equal it for belligerence. The female builds the nest, which is made of grass blades and leaves, thin twigs, rootlets and moss and is

lined with fine grass, horsehair or hair. It is generally on the ground, in grass, under a piece of turf or a bush, in a hedge or in a ditch. The 4—5 eggs are dingy white or reddish and are covered with brown or black streaks and scribbles (2). They are incubated for 12—14 days, mainly by the female. Both the parents feed the young in the nest for the same length of time. When the first young are independent, the adults nest a second — and sometimes a third — time. Three quar-

ters of the Yellowhammer's diet consists of weed, grass and cereal seeds and the green parts of plants, but the young are fed chiefly on insects and other invertebrates. The Yellowhammer is a partial migrant; birds from the north and northeast spend the winter in central and southern Europe. Spring migration takes place in March or April, autumn migration in October or November. The male (1, on right) has a golden-yellow head and underside and a chestnut rump; the female (1, on left) is browner and more noticeably streaked. The Yellowhammer's song is a series of notes of the same pitch with a somewhat higher, protracted finish note, 'tiutiutiutiutswee'. All buntings are more or less the same size as the House Sparrow.

Cirl Bunting

Emberiza cirlus

The Cirl Bunting lives in southern and western Europe, where its northernmost point is the south of England; in addition, it inhabits northern Africa and Asia Minor. It frequents hilly, sunny country and is found on thinly overgrown slopes and in copses, vineyards and gardens. Its habits are similar to those of the Yellowhammer. The nest, which is made of grass blades and dry twigs, sometimes together with a little moss and fragments of leaves, is lined with hair and is built by the female; it is generally hidden in a thicket and is only rarely to be found on the ground or just above it. The egg-laying period lasts from April to the end of July or the beginning of August, so that there are least two clutches, each composed of 3—5 eggs. The eggs themselves are greyish-white or greenish and are covered with black and brown spots and lines (2); they are incubated for 11—13 days by the female. The female is also largely responsible for the care of the young, although the male helps; the young birds fledge in 11—14 days. The parents feed them chiefly on insects, but in the autumn the birds eat more grass and weed seeds and various kinds of berries. The Cirl Bunting is a resident bird. From the end of the summer the families group together and form small flocks which roam hillsides and fields until the end of the winter. The adult male (1, on left) has a black chin and throat and its yellow face is divided in two by a black eye-stripe. Its yellow breast is crossed by a band of grey which stretches to its neck and its dark-streaked crown; its rump is olive-grey. Its song is a monotonous rattle. The female is marked with streaky brown spots (1, on right).

2

1

Rock Bunting
Emberiza cia

The Rock Bunting inhabits southern Europe and a few parts of central Europe, Asia Minor, a strip of territory leading across Asia as far as China and the extreme north of Africa. It likes sunny, rocky slopes with a scattering of trees and bushes, warm hillsides and vineyards and it even ascends high up into the mountains. It is a mostly resident bird, but some populations are nomadic. Mountain-dwellers descend to lower altitudes for the winter and northern birds migrate southwards as far as northern Africa. The birds evidently appear in their nesting areas in April and disappear in September. The nest is made of dry grass and small twigs and is lined with fine rootlets and hair. It is usually built on the ground, in a space between stones, under an overhanging clump of grass or in a hole in a stone terrace of a vineyard. It appears to be built entirely by the female, which is sometimes accompanied by the male. The eggs are laid mostly between May and July; some pairs rear two broods of young. The 4—6 greyish or bluish eggs, which are marked with dark brown or black spots and lines (2), are incubated for 12—14 days,

2

apparently entirely by the female. Both parents care for the young, however. They feed them for 10—13 days in the nest, at first mainly on insects; the vegetable component of their diet consists largely of grass and other seeds. The male (1) has a bluish-grey, black-striped head (the stripes meet at the rear of the ear-coverts), a pale throat and a grey breast; its rump and underside are rust-brown, and the rest of its plumage is brown streaked with blackish-brown. The female is similar but much duller, lacks the sharpness of the head pattern and has faint brown spots on its breast and flanks. The Rock Bunting's call note is a sharp 'tzit' or 'tseee'; its song sounds like 'tzi-tzi-tzi-tzirrr'.

1

445

Ortolan Bunting
Emberiza hortulana

The Ortolan Bunting did not settle in Europe until the 17th century. Today it inhabits virtually the whole of that continent, but in many places its occurrence is very patchy, or is beginning to decline again. It also occurs in the Middle East and central Asia. Although in some languages its vernacular name has been taken from the Latin *'hortulana',* meaning 'pertaining to gardens', the closest it comes to nesting in a garden is an orchard or a vineyard. It likes agricultural country with large fields and scattered trees or shrubs, roadside avenues, copses, the edges of open woods adjoining fields, and warm, dry hillsides with thickets. The nest, which is built by the female, is made largely of dry grass blades and leaves, rootlets,

horsehair and hair. The 4—5 whitish or pinkish eggs are marked with grey spots and occasional dark dots and lines (3); they are incubated for 12—14 days by the female. Both parents care for the young, which leave the nest in about 12 (but sometimes only 9—10) days. When the young are independent, the adult birds evi-

dently nest again. The diet of the young and of the adult birds is similar to that of the Yellow-

hammer. The Ortolan Bunting, which is a migrant, spends the winter mainly in eastern Africa; it

leaves at the end of August and returns at the end of April or in May. The male (1) has a greenish-grey head, a yellow throat and moustachial stripe and a cinnamon-brown underside. The female (2) is distinctly browner and lighter. At all times of year, the yellow ring around the eyes and the reddish beak are important identification marks. The song is reminiscent of the Yellowhammer's song, but has a slower rhythm and dies away with a melancholy 'teu-teu-teu-tyeh'. When singing the male flies in a characteristic way (4).

Grey-necked Bunting

Emberiza buchanani

The range of the Grey-necked Bunting is confined to the Middle East and Central Asia and it does not appear any further west than Transcaucasia (Armenia). It frequents dry, stony country at the foot of mountains and also lives at moderate montane altitudes. It usually settles on rocky slopes covered with xerophilous which they defend by singing from the tops of bushes. The nest, which is built on the ground, is generally well hidden by the vegetation. It is made – not very skilfully – of grass blades and leaves and is lined with hair. The nesting season lasts from May to July and during it some pairs manage to rear two ciently reliably. Soon after the nesting period is over, the families join forces and form flocks; at the end of August or in September, these set out for their winter quarters in India. Their diet consists mainly of seeds. The Grey-necked Bunting (1) resembles the Ortolan Bunting. The top and back of its head are

grasses and thinly scattered shrubs. It ascends to altitudes of up to 2,500 m. It does not appear in its nesting areas until April and often not until May. The pairs usually nest singly. As soon as they arrive, the males take possession of a nesting territory, broods of young. One clutch usually contains 5 light bluish-green eggs, which are marked with dark grey to black spots and scribbles. The incubation and fledging periods and the role of the male in the rearing of the young have not yet been determined sufficiently bluish-grey; its throat and the whole of its underside are russet. It has a yellow ring around its eyes. Its melancholy song, which is rather like the Ortolan Bunting's song but is longer, first of all rises and then descends, ending 'tsi-tsi-tsi-tsi-tsi-oo'.

Rustic Bunting
Emberiza rustica

As distinct from other buntings, the Rustic Bunting has a pure white throat, which is separated from its similarly coloured underside by the cinnamon-brown band on its breast; its chestnut-brown back is marked with black streaks. In its breeding plumage, the male (1) has a black head with a wide white superciliary stripe; in the winter it has a brown head (2) and only a trace of the breast band. On the female's head, the black is replaced by brown. The head feathers are occasionally erected to form a kind of crest. The song is more like a warbler's song than a bunting's. The Rustic Bunting inhabits the taiga belt of Europe and Asia. In Europe it lives only in the north of the Scandinavian Peninsula and of

3

the former USSR; in the east its range stretches to Sakhalin. It is a forest-dweller, nesting in the thinner and marginal – and often boggy – parts of the taiga, in

peat-bogs and on riverbanks with adequate vegetation. The nest, which is built on the ground and is well hidden in dry grass from the previous year, is made of dry blades and rootlets. Once a year, in May or June, the female lays 4–5 greenish eggs, which lack the typical bunting lines and scribbles and are covered with round grey spots (3); they are incubated for 12–13 days, mainly by the female. The young remain 14 days in the nest. Rustic Buntings live on grass, sedge and other seeds and in the breeding season on insects as well. In September they form flocks and in October they migrate to southeastern Asia; they usually return to their north European breeding areas in May.

2♂

448

Little Bunting
Emberiza pusilla

In Europe, the Little Bunting occurs in the north of Scandinavia and the most northerly part of the former USSR. It inhabits shrubby tundra with willow and birch growths, riverbanks with alders and willows and marshy forests rich in undergrowth. The birds generally arrive at their nesting sites in May. The nest is built on the ground in grass, often under a bush or a grassy overhang; it is made of dry grass blades, moss and lichen and is lined with soft grass and hair (mainly from reindeer). The eggs are usually laid in the middle of June, and since nestlings have been found as late

as August it would appear that many pairs nest twice during the season. There are usually 4–6 eggs and they are so small that they cannot possibly be mistaken for other buntings' eggs. They are very variably coloured, from reddish-grey to greyish-green, and have characteristic bunting markings consisting of black to russet spots, lines and squiggles; they are incubated for 11–12 days by both the parent birds. The young leave the nest at the age of only six to eight days, long before they are able to fly; the parents both look after them and by the time they are about 12

days old they have learnt to fly. The Little Bunting lives chiefly on small seeds, but when feeding the young it also eats insects. In September or October the birds migrate to southern and eastern Asia. The Little Bunting is about the size of a Linnet. The male (1) is mainly brown, with black spots, but the crown of its head and its cheeks are reddish-brown with black markings; the female's colours are duller. The Little Bunting's call note is a short 'phuick' or 'chick'; its song is soft and of a typical bunting character.

449

Yellow-breasted Bunting
Emberiza aureola

Originally a Siberian species, the Yellow-breasted Bunting spread to northern Europe in the last century. It is a migrant and spends the winter in southeastern Asia; it leaves its nesting areas in August and does not return until May or June. Individual stray birds are regularly found in other parts of Europe, as far as Britain and France. The Yellow-breasted Bunting inhabits waterside thickets and herbaceous vegetation, damp meadows and the edges of swamps; it also lives in steppes and near human settlements. The nest is usually on the ground or in a low bush. It is built by the female, is made of dry grass blades and rootlets and is lined in most cases with horsehair. The 3–5 eggs are generally not laid until June; they are greyish-green to olive-brown, are marked with brown spots, speckles and squiggles (2) and are incubated for about 13 days, chiefly by the female, but with help from the male. The adults nest only once a year. The young leave the nest at the age of 9–13 days, before they are fully fledged. The parents feed them mainly on insects, but themselves live largely on seeds. The Yellow-breasted Bunting always has a yellow underside, whatever the time of year. The adult male (1) has a black face and forehead; its crown, back and the band across its breast are dark chestnut and there is one wide and one narrow white bar on its wings. The female lacks the dark mask and

2

the breast band and the middle of its crown is ochre; there is only one narrow white bar on its wings. The call note of this species is a sharp 'tsipp' or a softer 'trssit'; its song resembles the song of the Ortolan Bunting, but is faster and more fluid.

450

Reed Bunting
Emberiza schoeniclus

The Reed Bunting likes wet ground with a few willows beside ponds and rivers, swamps and marshes overgrown with reeds, sedge and other swamp plants and wet meadows with osier thickets. The nest is situated on dry ground or just above it, where it is always well concealed by flattened reeds, under a dry

grass overhang, in a sedge bed or in a willow bush. It is built by the

female, sometimes with help from the male; it is made of dry grass blades and leaves, moss and the leaves of aquatic plants and is lined with fine grass and animal hair. The pairs nest twice (some of them perhaps three times) a year, between April and July. The 4—5 eggs are marked with dark spots and the lines and scribbles characteristic of all bunting eggs, on a very variably coloured yellowish, greenish or reddish ground (2). They are incubated for 12—14 days, chiefly by the female. Both the parents feed the young, which leave the nest at the age of 10—13 days; they feed them on insects and small molluscs and crustaceans gathered on the ground, from plants and from the surface of the water; their own diet consists mainly of various kinds of seeds. The Reed Bunting inhabits the whole of Europe and the greater part of Asia. Southern populations are resident; birds from the north and northeast, and particularly from central Europe, migrate in October to west Europe and the Mediterranean region; they return to their nesting areas in March. In its breeding plumage, the male (1) has a sharply defined black head and throat, a white collar and moustachial stripe and a white underside. In its winter plumage it resembles the female, which is brownish, with brownish-black streaks and spots, and has a greyish-white throat and black and white moustachial stripes. The Reed Bunting's song is short, slow and faltering, and sounds like 'tseek-teet-tai-tississisk'.

Red-headed Bunting

Emberiza bruniceps

The Red-headed Bunting inhabits a small area east of the Caspian Sea; during the past 100 years it has spread westwards, in Europe roughly from the lower a bush, or at least on thick, dry grass or reeds from the previous year, and never directly on the ground like most buntings' nests. It is built by the female, is an but exact details of the incubation and nest-care periods are not available. Their food consists of seeds and various insects; the latter are fed mainly to the young.

Volga to the southern spurs of the Ural Mountains. In central and western Europe it is a rare accidental bird and there are speculations as to whether such specimens are escapes, since there is quite a brisk trade in Red-headed Buntings. The Red-headed Bunting prefers steppes and semi-desert regions overgrown with shrubs, but also lives in riparian thickets and in reed-beds. The nest is always built on untidy structure made of plant material (often green) and the outer walls are frequently adorned with wilted flowers; it is lined with fine grass, rootlets and hair. The 4—5 whitish eggs, irregularly marked with brown and grey spots, are laid between April and July. They are evidently incubated entirely by the female, although the male is never very far away. The adults usually rear two broods of young in one season, The male (1) has a striking chestnut face, throat and breast; its back is olive-green with blackish-brown stripes, and its underside is yellow. The female is olive-brown above with blackish streaks, and has a dull whitish underside. The Red-headed Bunting's call note is a pleasant 'tweet'; its song, which resembles the song of the Corn Bunting, is a tuneful, repeated 'tschek-tschek-dree-drah-dree'.

Corn Bunting
Miliaria calandra

The Corn Bunting frequents the margins of fields and damp meadows with scattered trees and bushes and often lives beside streams and rivers. The field or a cornfield, at the edge of a ditch or a hedge, and there builds a nest made of the stems of various herbaceous plants, grass blades and leaves, rootlets and a small amount of hair. The 4—5 eggs, which have typical bunting markings on a reddish ground (2), are laid in May or June and are incubated for

12—14 days by the female. At first, the female also has the whole work of looking after the offspring, but this is later shared by the male. The young buntings hop out of the nest at the age of only 9—12 days, before they are able to fly, so that the parents continue to feed them for some time afterwards. Some pairs nest a second time. The Corn Bunting lives on the same type of diet as the Yellowhammer. It inhabits the whole of Europe south of southern Scandinavia, and also northern Africa, Asia Minor and the Middle East. Lately, however, its numbers in many places have severely decreased. It is mainly a resident species, but northern birds form flocks and migrate to central and southern Europe. The Corn Bunting (1), which is distinctly bigger than the House Sparrow, is the largest of the buntings; in appearance it is rather similar to a lark. Exceptionally for this family, the female has the same coloration as the male. Unlike other small birds, the Corn Bunting, during short flights or when alighting, lets its legs dangle (3). The male sings its simple, rattling song, 'tseek-tseek-tseek-shnirlrlrl', from a perch, either elevated or low down.

males begin singing at their nesting sites in March or April, while awaiting the arrival of the females. As a rule, they are polygamous. The female looks for a suitable depression in the ground, in a meadow, a clover

453

Nests and eggs

In order to demonstrate the nidification of a given species of bird, we sometimes need to look for the actual nest. In no case, however, should this involve disturbing the bird to such an extent as to cause it to abandon the nest. Nevertheless, a knowledge of nests and eggs can help the ornithologist to identify the species and for this reason we have illustrated various nests, together with the eggs, representing the largest number of families possible.

Where and how the nest is built is a matter of heredity and we should hardly expect a swallow, for instance, to build its clay nest in a tree, or a woodpecker to lay its eggs in grass. Occasionally we may come across nests in unusual places — a Tawny Owl nesting on the ground, a Mallard in the deserted nest of a bird of prey, or a kestrel on a building — but they are only the exceptions that confirm the rule.

There are only a few birds which do not build a nest at all and lay their eggs either directly on the ground (auks, the Nightjar), or at the bottom of a hole (most owls and woodpeckers). Some waders and gulls make a simple hollow in the ground and line it with just a few blades of grass, or with stones or broken shells. Conversely, ducks, geese, game birds, rails and some songbirds (e.g. larks and pipits) build elaborate, neatly finished and properly lined ground nests. The commonest type of nest is shaped like a cup or a basket and is held in place — sometimes firmly, sometimes loosely — in the branches of a tree or a bush. The most skilled builders are warblers (whose nests are closed structures with a side entrance) and Long-tailed and Penduline Tits (which build artistic nests in the shape of a sphere or a mitten). Swallows and House Martins build characteristic clay nests and nuthatches wall up the entrance to their nest-hole with clay. Woodpeckers hack out holes in tree trunks; when the woodpeckers have finished with them, they furnish accommodation for many other species of hole-nesters (owls, Stock Doves and Starlings).

Birds' eggs differ as regards their size, shape, colouring, gloss and the structure of the shell. White eggs are usually laid by birds which nest in holes (all woodpeckers, owls and the Swift), in burrows (the Kingfisher, the Sand Martin, the Bee-eater) or in closed nests (the Penduline Tit, the Dipper). Again there are exceptions, however, and some hole-nesters, such as the Starling, Pied Flycatcher and Redstart, lay brightly coloured eggs, but they are all species which once built open nests. The eggs are most frequently spotted, sometimes very variably; for instance, we should be hard put to find two Meadow Pipit, Tree Pipit or Black-headed Gull eggs which are exactly alike.

The size of the clutch is species specific and is sometimes absolutely constant. With auks, shearwaters, flamingos and vultures, one egg is the rule. Divers, eagles, cranes, bustards and nightjars lay two eggs, gulls three and waders four; in other species the number of eggs is variable.

Nests and eggs

Great Crested Grebe – *Podiceps cristatus*
Cormorant, Great Cormorant – *Phalacrocorax carbo*

Bittern – *Botaurus stellaris*
Grey Heron – *Ardea cinerea*

Mute Swan – *Cygnus olor*
Gadwall and Tufted Duck
– *Anas strepera* and *Aythya fuligula*

Greylag Goose – *Anser anser*
Pochard – *Aythya ferina*

Nests and eggs

Black Kite − *Milvus migrans*
White-tailed Eagle − *Haliaeetus albicilla*

Marsh Harrier − *Circus cyaneus*
Goshawk − *Accipiter gentilis*

Peregrine Falcon – *Falco peregrinus*
Kestrel – *Falco tinnunculus*

Hazel Hen – *Bonasa bonasia*
Partridge, Grey Partridge – *Perdix perdix*

Nests and eggs

Water Rail − *Rallus aquaticus*
Coot − *Fulica atra*

Black-winged Stilt − *Himantopus himantopus*
Pratincole − *Glareola pratincola*

Little Ringed Plover – *Charadrius dubius*
Kentish Plover – *Charadrius alexandrinus*

Lapwing – *Vanellus vanellus*
Woodcock – *Scolopax rusticola*

Nests and eggs

Black-tailed Godwit – *Limosa limosa*
Black Tern – *Chlidonias niger*

Whiskered Tern – *Chlidonias hybridus*
Turtle Dove – *Streptopelia turtur*

Eagle Owl – *Bubo bubo*
Pygmy Owl – *Glaucidium passerinum*

Nightjar – *Caprimulgus europaeus*
Swift – *Apus apus*

Nests and eggs

Wryneck – *Jynx torquilla*

Wood Lark and Cuckoo – *Lullula arborea* and *Cuculus canorus*

Swallow, Barn Swallow – *Hirundo rustica*
Water Pipit – *Anthus spinoletta*

Alpine Accentor − *Prunella collaris*
Nightingale − *Luscinia megarhynchos*

Redstart − *Phoenicurus phoenicurus*
Whinchat − *Saxicola rubetra*

Nests and eggs

Rock Thrush – *Monticola saxatilis*
Ring Ouzel – *Turdus torquatus*

Song Thrush – *Turdus philomelos*
Thrush Nightingale – *Luscinia luscinioides*

Great Reed Warbler – *Acrocephalus arundinaceus*
Icterine Warbler – *Hippolais icterina*

Barred Warbler – *Sylvia nisoria*
Wood Warbler – *Phylloscopus sibilatrix*

Nests and eggs

Goldcrest – *Regulus regulus*
Red-breasted Flycatcher – *Ficedula parva*

Bearded Titmouse – *Panurus biarmicus*
Great Tit – *Parus major*

Nuthatch – *Sitta europaea*
Short-toed Treecreeper – *Certhia brachydactyla*

Golden Oriole – *Oriolus oriolus*
Woodchat Shrike – *Lanius senator*

Nests and eggs

Jay − *Garrulus glandarius*
Chaffinch − *Fringilla coelebs*

Serin − *Serinus serinus*
Crossbill, Red Crossbill − *Loxia curvirostra*

Scarlet Rosefinch – *Carpodacus erythrinus*
Hawfinch – *Coccothraustes coccothraustes*

Rock Bunting – *Emberiza cia*
Reed Bunting – *Emberiza schoeniclus*

Systematic classification

With a very few modifications, every bird described in this book belongs to the relevant order and family to which it is ascribed in the internationally known nomenclatural review 'List of Recent Holarctic Bird Species' by Professor K. H. Voous (1977).

Gaviiformes (Divers)

Gaviidae – Divers   p. 30

Large diving birds whose long, cylindrical body is submerged to a considerable depth when they swim. They dive frequently and for long periods. They have webbed feet, a sharp, dagger-like beak and a very short tail. Their wings are rather narrow and pointed and when they fly their feet extend beyond the end of their tail. The sexes are identically coloured. Four species live in Europe.

Podicipediformes (Grebes)

Podicipedidae – Grebes   p. 31

Diving birds the largest of which is the size of a duck, with a long neck and a more robust body than divers. The beak is pointed. The toes are not joined together by webbing, but are bordered by tough skin. Grebes have short, narrow wings; they seldom fly, but when they do, their feet show beyond the tip of their short tail. The sexes are similarly coloured. Five species nest in Europe.

Procellariiformes (Tubenoses)

Procellariidae – Shearwaters   p. 40

Birds the size of a gull, with long, narrow wings, a beak composed of horny platelets and external nostrils produced to tubular structures. They fly and glide with outstanding skill over the open sea. The sexes are identically coloured. The three species which nest in Europe live gregariously in colonies. They brood the single egg and care for the young bird for a very long time.

Hydrobatidae – Storm Petrels   p. 42

The smallest birds frequenting the open sea and outstanding fliers which literally dance over the waves. The males and females are both predominantly greyish black, with a whitish rump; their slender beak has tubular nostrils. They likewise live in colonies and lay only one egg. Only two species nest in Europe.

Pelecaniformes (Pelicans and Allies)

Sulidae — Gannets   p. 44

Large, slim-bodied sea birds with a large, pointed beak, long, narrow wings and a pointed tail. All the toes, including the first toe, which points forwards, are joined together by webbing. Gannets catch their prey by a headlong dive into the water. The sexes are identical in appearance. The only species inhabiting Europe nests in large colonies on rocky shores or islands.

Phalacrocoracidae — Cormorants   p. 45

Large, dark-coloured sea birds with a long neck and a hook-tipped beak. They are excellent divers. Their feet are constructed in the same way as those of Gannets. They live on inland waters and on the sea. Very often they sit with their wings half-spread to let their feathers dry. They nest together in colonies. The male and female are the same colour. Three species nest in Europe.

Pelecanidae — Pelicans   p. 48

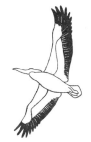

Large water birds the size of a swan, with broad wings and a talent for gliding. They fly with their head retracted on to their back. Their lower mandible is equipped with a pouch and their toes are all joined together by webbing. The colouring of the male and female is the same. Only two species live in Europe.

Ciconiiformes (Herons and Allies)

Ardeidae — Herons   p. 54

Long-legged birds with a long neck and a long, pointed beak, living mainly in shallow fresh water. When flying, they hold their head withdrawn between their shoulders, their neck curved like a letter S and their legs stretched out behind them. In their display plumage, their head, neck and shoulders are generally decorated with ornamental feathers. In appearance the sexes are the same (except in the case of the Little Bittern). They mostly nest in colonies. Nine species live in Europe.

Ciconiidae — Storks   p. 62

Large birds with long legs, a long neck and a long, straight beak. Unlike herons, they hold their neck stretched forwards while flying. The sexes are similarly coloured. Only two species nest in Europe.

Threskiornithidae — Ibises   p. 64

Medium-sized birds resembling herons or storks in form and likewise with a long, but differently shaped, beak. Two dissimilar species live in Europe — the white Spoonbill, which has a long, spatulate beak, and the brown Glossy Ibis, whose beak is long and thin and curves downwards. In both species the sexes are the same colour and both nest in colonies.

Phoenicopteriformes (Flamingos)

Phoenicopteridae — Flamingos   p. 67

Large, slim-bodied birds with white and pink plumage, abnormally long legs, a long neck and a short, striking-looking hooked beak curving downwards at an obtuse angle. They fly with their neck and legs extended. Their wings are marked with scarlet and black. In appearance the sexes are the same. They are represented in Europe by a single species.

Anseriformes (Swans, Geese and Ducks)

Anatidae — Swans, Geese and Ducks   p. 72

A large family with very different types of birds whose feet are adapted for swimming and have webbing between the three fore toes.

Swans: Very large birds which can swim, but not dive. In Europe, the adult males and females are always white. Three species nest in Europe (one black species has been introduced).

Geese: Large aquatic birds which often fly over the countryside in search of food. They have a long neck and are generally larger than ducks. The colouring of the male and female is the same. Seven species nest in Europe and one (the Canada Goose) has been imported from North America.

Shelducks: Goose-like ducks with features of both geese and ducks. The colouring of the male and female is not the same in every species. Two species nest in Europe and a third (the Egyptian Goose) has been introduced there.

Dabbling ducks: Dabbling ducks have only a small 'draught' and hold their tail out of the water; they do not dive for food and at most just dip their head under water. To fly, they take off from the water directly. As a rule, they have a brightly coloured speculum on each wing and in the nesting season the male usually wears colourful plumage. Eight species nest in Europe and others (the Wood Duck and the Mandarin Duck) have been introduced there.

Diving ducks: Diving ducks swim deeper in the water and their tail is almost level with the surface. They dive in search of food and run over the water before taking off; they have no specula on their wings. The male and the female are usually differently coloured. Twelve species nest in Europe.

Stifftails: Small 'ducks' of the genus *Oxyura* which often swim with their tail held vertically erect. The sexes are differently coloured. One species nests in Europe; *Oxyura jamaicensis* has been imported from North America.

Mergansers: In form, these birds look more like swimming cormorants and they likewise have a slender, hook-tipped beak; they catch their food by diving. The male and female are differently coloured. Three species nest in Europe.

Falconiformes (Birds of Prey)

Accipitridae – Vultures, Eagles, Buzzards, etc p. 116

A heterogeneous family comprising large to medium-sized (but occasionally small) birds of prey, most of which catch vertebrates, although some eat carrion. In keeping with this diet they have a curved, hooked beak.

Vultures: Large birds with a scantily feathered or featherless small head and neck. Their very long, broad wings show that they are outstanding gliders and, indeed, they can circle at high altitudes for hours without any movement of their wings. They live on carrion. The colouring of the sexes is the same. Four species nest in Europe, on rocks and on trees.

Kites: Slim-bodied, moderately large predators with relatively long wings and a more or less forked tail; they are good gliders. They have short legs, the tarsus being roughly the same length as the middle toe. The male and female are similar in appearance. Their diet consists largely of carrion. The two European species nest on trees. This group also includes the genus *Elanus*.

Eagles: Big birds of prey with long, broad wings, eagles are excellent gliders. They have a powerful, curved beak and short, thick legs with large talons. They nest on trees and rocks and they catch their prey alive or content themselves with carrion. Five true eagles (genus *Aquila*) nest in Europe, but because of their similarity we have extended this group to include the genera *Haliaeetus, Circaetus* and *Hieraaetus* (i.e. it is not a genuine systematic group).

Hawks: Medium-sized and small birds of prey with rounded wings and a long tail. They fly fast, generally close to the ground, zigzag skilfully between trees and pounce on their prey. Their relatively long legs terminate in sharp talons. The female is larger than the male. All hawks, including the three European species, nest on trees.

Buzzards: Moderately large birds of prey with broad wings and a wide, rounded tail. Since they spend a great deal of time in the air, they can mostly be observed as they glide and circle. They nest on trees and rocks, but occasionally on the ground. The male is smaller than the female but their plumage are similar. Three species live in Europe (and because of its marked similarity, we add the genus *Pernis* to them).

Harriers: Medium-sized predators with a slender body, long, narrow wings, a relatively long tail and long legs with sharp talons. They fly low over the ground, holding their wings above their body in a shallow V position. The males and females are quite differently coloured. Harriers nest on the ground or in reed-beds. Four species live in Europe.

Pandionidae – Ospreys   p. 138
This family comprises only a single species which is distributed all over the globe. The Osprey is a large predator with long, narrow, strikingly angular wings. It usually flies along the course of rivers or circles over lakes and ponds and catches fish by diving headlong with its talons outstretched. Its long, sharp claws, the rough skin on the underside of its toes and the fact that its fourth toe can be turned backwards or forwards help it to grip slippery prey. It nests on trees and steep rocks. The male and female are identical.

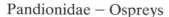

Falconidae – Falcons   p. 139
Exceptionally fast fliers, moderately large and small birds with long, narrow, pointed wings, falcons hunt vertebrates or catch insects. At the tip of their upper mandible they have a typical 'tooth'. The male often differs from the female in colouring and sometimes in size. Falcons nest on trees or rocks and sometimes on the ground, but never build a nest of their own. Ten species live in Europe.

Galliformes (Game Birds)

Tetraonidae – Grouse   p. 150
Robust ground-dwelling birds with rounded wings, feathered legs and toes and a thick beak with a curved tip. They fly reluctantly and generally only for short distances. The male differs distinctly from the female. They nest on the ground. Five species live in Europe.

Phasianidae — Pheasants, Partridges and Quails p. 155

Medium-sized to small ground-dwelling game birds with a thickset body and unfeathered legs adapted for scratching. The tail is either long and wedge-shaped (pheasants) or short. The sexes are very similar or the same in appearance, except for male pheasants, which are very brightly coloured. These birds are ground-nesters. Seven original species live in Europe, another (the Ring-necked Pheasant) is now fully established there and several more have been introduced, with varying success.

Gruiformes (Rails and Allies)

Rallidae — Rails, Crakes and Coots p. 168

A family with two different types of birds. Rails are small and live secretively in reeds and similar dense growths; they have a somewhat flat-sided body, short, rounded wings and a short tail which they frequently jerk erect. Five species live in Europe. Moorhens and Coots are mostly sturdily built swimming birds with short, rounded wings. Like rails they are not very keen fliers and when they do fly, they also let their long-toed legs dangle behind them. Coots have a patch of a different colour on their forehead. These birds nest in reed-beds or on the ground. Four species live in Europe.

Gruidae — Cranes p. 174

Large ground-dwelling birds with a stork-like body, but a shorter beak. They fly in echelon formation or in single file, with their long neck and legs extended. They nest on the ground. Two species live in Europe.

Otididae — Bustards p. 176

Moderately large to large birds like long-legged fowls in appearance, living in steppes and extensive fields. They fly with their neck stretched out, showing the black and white underside of their wide wings. Both European species nest on the ground; the males are markedly different from the females.

Charadriiformes
(Waders, Gulls, Terns and Allies)

Haematopodidae — Oystercatchers p. 182

Medium-sized, strikingly black and white waders whose red, flat-sided beak is longer than their head; their short legs are minus the hind toe. Only one species nests in Europe.

Systematic classification

Recurvirostridae — Avocets and Stilts
p. 183

Large black and white waders whose legs and beak are long to very long. They live beside shallow water, mainly in places with a warm climate, and only two species occur in Europe. The male is somewhat different from the female in appearance.

Burhinidae — Stone Curlews
p. 185

Moderately large waders with long, thick legs, three short, thick toes and long, sharp wings. Their large eyes indicate that they are active after dusk and partly at night. The only European species inhabits warm localities. The male and female resemble one another.

Glareolidae — Pratincoles
p. 186

Smallish birds with very long, sharp-pointed wings and a deeply forked tail reminiscent of a swallow's (like swallows, pratincoles also catch insects on the wing). The top of their head is noticeably rounded, their beak is short and wide and their legs, which are also short, have a well developed hind toe. Two species nest in southern Europe.

Charadriidae — Plovers and Lapwings
p. 187

Relatively small waders with a short neck, a large head, a short beak and large eyes. Differences between the appearance of the male and female are usually small. Nine species live in Europe.

Scolopacidae — Snipes, Sandpipers, Godwits, etc
p. 195

The members of this large and multiform family generally have a long beak and long legs; their wings are mostly pointed and angular. As a rule, there are no distinctive characters in their plumage, but their nesting (nuptial) and resting plumage differ. The males and females are usually alike; phalaropes, Ruffs and Turnstones are exceptions. Twenty-seven species live in Europe (11 nest regularly in central Europe).

Stercorariidae — Skuas
p. 222

Large sea birds like gulls in appearance and mostly with a dark back (although dark and light forms both occur). Their beak has a hook-like tip; the horny portion of the upper mandible is composed of three parts. Their wings are long and narrow and in the adult birds the middle tail feathers project beyond the rest, giving the tail a characteristic shape. Skuas often snatch food away from other birds. The sexes are the same in appearance. The four species inhabiting the northern part of the Atlantic are seldom to be seen on the mainland.

Laridae — Gulls p. 225

Long-winged birds with mainly white plumage, or with a grey back. Their upper mandible overlaps the lower mandible and is often hooked. Gulls live mostly along the coast, but sometimes occur on inland waters; they live in colonies. The male and female look alike. Fifteen species live in Europe (11 of them nest in central Europe).

Sternidae — Terns p. 237

Slender birds resembling gulls, with long, narrow wings and generally with a forked tail, with short legs and a straight, sharp-pointed beak. Terns are mainly white and seldom predominantly dark. Most of them swoop on their prey from a height. The male and female are the same in appearance. Ten species form colonies in Europe.

Alciformes (Auks)

Alcidae — Auks p. 250

Small to medium-sized black and white sea birds with short, narrow wings and with their legs so far back on their body that they sit erect. They dive in search of food, 'rowing' under water with their wings. Their beak is narrow and usually has flattened sides. There are no differences in the appearance of the sexes. Auks nest in colonies on rocky coasts; six species nest in Europe.

Columbiformes (Pigeons and Doves)

Pteroclididae — Sandgrouse p. 254

Birds resembling pigeons in appearance, but with a short, hard beak more like the beak of a gamebird. Their very short legs are feathered right down to the toes; the hind toe is vestigial or absent. The wings and the long tail are pointed. The males and females are differently coloured. Sandgrouse nest on the ground in steppes and deserts; two species live in Europe.

Columbidae — Pigeons and Doves p. 255

Moderately large birds with a small head and a soft beak which is horny only towards the tip; the hind part is covered with skin, which also overlaps the nostrils from above. The characteristic voice is a deep-throated cooing. The male and female are similar. The five European species are mainly tree- or hole-nesters.

Psittaciformes (Parrots)

Psittacidae – Parrots   p. 264

Mostly tropical and subtropical birds with a high, thick, strikingly hooked upper mandible and with two toes pointing forwards and two backwards. As a rule, the male and female are different. Parrots are generally hole-nesters. Two species have been induced to nest in Europe.

Cuculiformes (Cuckoos)

Cuculidae – Cuckoos   p. 266

Slender birds with a long tail and narrow wings; on their feet, two of the toes point forwards and two backwards. The sexes are generally the same in appearance. The two species nesting in Europe are noted for nest parasitism.

Strigiformes (Owls)

Tytonidae – Barn Owls   p. 272

Owls with a heart-shaped facial disc terminating below their beak, small eyes facing forwards and slim legs. Their long wings stretch beyond the tip of their tail. They are nocturnal hunters. The sexes are the same colour. Only one species occurs in Europe.

Strigidae – Owls   p. 273

Owls with a circular facial mask, a large head and large eyes facing forwards. Their short, thick legs terminate in strong claws and are thickly feathered. They hunt their prey (mammals, birds and insects) mainly after dusk or at night. The female is usually larger than the male. Twelve species nest in Europe.

Caprimulgiformes (Nightjars or Goatsuckers)

Caprimulgidae – Nightjars   p. 288

Slim-bodied birds with long, narrow wings, which hunt insects by night and catch them on the wing. They have a large head, large eyes and a short, widely gaping beak. They usually spend the day crouching motionless on the ground or along a branch (their legs and toes are too short for them to sit across it). The sexes are the same in appearance. Only two species nest in Europe.

Apodiformes (Swifts)

Apodidae — Swifts   p. 289
Small, slender birds with a similar form to a swallow's. The long
wings are curved and sickle-shaped; the tail is short and forked.
Swifts spend the greater part of their life in the air; their short legs are
adapted for clinging and they are unable to alight on the ground. The
male and female are alike. Three species nest in Europe.

Coraciiformes (Rollers and Allies)

Alcedinidae — Kingfishers   p. 290
Brightly coloured, small to medium-sized birds with a relatively
large head, a longish, thick, straight beak, a short tail and short legs.
The sexes resemble each other. The birds nest in burrows dug by
themselves in the ground. Only one species nests in Europe.

Meropidae — Bee-eaters   p. 291
Gaily coloured, small, slim birds with a long, thin, slightly curved
beak, long, pointed wings and — in some species — long middle tail
feathers; the male and female are alike. They catch insects in the air,
usually live in colonies and nest in burrows. Only one species occurs
in Europe.

Coraciidae — Rollers   p. 292
Brightly coloured, small to moderately large tree-dwellers resembling corvid birds in form. They have a thick, slightly curved beak
and short, thick legs and in flight their wings are rounded. The sexes
are similarly coloured. The single European species nests in
tree-holes.

Upupidae — Hoopoes   p. 293
Medium-sized birds with chequered plumage and an unmistakable
erectile crest, a long, thin, slightly curved beak, a very short tongue
and short, thick legs. In flight their wings are broad and have
rounded ends. The male and female are the same in appearance. The
only species living in Europe is a hole-nester.

Piciformes (Woodpeckers)

Picidae — Woodpeckers   p. 298
Small to moderately large birds with feet adapted for climbing (two
toes point forwards and two backwards) and with hard tail feathers.
They have a strong, straight beak like a chisel and a long, sharp,

protrusible tongue. They nest in tree-holes which they excavate themselves and winkle insects out from under the bark. Most species drum on the trees. Except for the Wryneck, which is brown, they are vividly coloured and the males generally have some red on their head. Ten species nest in Europe.

Passeriformes (Passerines)

Alaudidae – Larks   p. 310

Small birds inhabiting open country. They are generally brown and spotted and spend most of their time on the ground; the males usually sing while flying. The horny skin on their legs is divided by a row of small plates into a front and a hind part; the claw on their hind toe is usually longer than the others. When not nesting, they often form flocks. The male and female look the same. Nine species live in Europe.

Hirundinidae – Swallows   p. 315

Small, slender passerines with long, pointed wings and generally with a forked tail. Elegant fliers which catch insects on the wing with their short, wide beak. Their legs are short and thin. They like to nest together and often form large colonies on buildings, rock faces and the walls of sand-pits. The male is coloured similarly to the female. Five species nest in Europe.

Motacillidae – Pipits and Wagtails   p. 319

Small, slim and usually long-tailed birds with a thin, awl-like beak, thin legs and long toes armed, as a rule, with claws (especially the hind toe). They are mostly to be found in open country or beside water and live mainly on insects. Pipits are generally brown and the male and female look alike; wagtails are vividly marked and the male often differs form the female. Five pipit species and three wagtail species live in Europe.

Bombycillidae – Waxwings   p. 326

Passerine birds the size of a Starling, with a robust form and dense plumage. With their reddish-brown colouring, the coloured markings on their wings and their conspicuous crest they are unmistakable. The male and female look alike. The single species inhabiting northern Europe occasionally invades central Europe.

Cinclidae – Dippers   p. 327

Small passerines with a thickset body and a short tail. Among all the members of the order they are the best adapted to a life near running water, since they can dive and then run along the bed of the stream, catching small aquatic animals. They fly dartingly, generally just above the surface. The male and female of the single European species are both dark brown, with a large white 'bib'.

Troglodytidae – Wrens p. 328

Small, brown-spotted birds with an awl-like beak, short, rounded wings and a very short tail which is often held erect. The male and female are the same in appearance. Only one species lives in Europe.

Prunellidae – Accentors p. 329

Small and mainly greyish-brown passerines, with somewhat brighter shades of colour on the underside of their body. They are the same size as sparrows, but have a thin, sharp-pointed beak. They live inconspicuously in dense thickets or high up in the mountains. The males and females are very much alike. Two species nest regularly in Europe; one of them is only found in mountainous regions.

Turdidae – Thrushes p. 332

A large family comprising small to medium-sized songbirds with a relatively thick, slightly curved beak, strong legs and a fairly long tail. Although they are very variably coloured, the colouring of the sexes is the same, or almost the same. Thrushes are tree-dwellers, but often come down to the ground to catch invertebrate animals or (in the autumn) to gather berries; 23 species live in Europe.

Sylviidae – Warblers p. 354

Small, slim and generally inconspicuously coloured songbirds with a thin, sharp-pointed beak. The male and female are the same or only slightly different from each other. Many species are visually hard to tell apart and their song is therefore an important determinant character. All sylviids frequent trees and bushes and live mainly on insects, supplemented outside the nesting season by berries; 37 species live in Europe.

Muscicapidae – Flycatchers p. 383

Small passerines with a relatively large head and a flat beak whose widened base is further emphasised by the large bristle-like feathers in the corners; their legs are short and thin. Flycatchers frequent trees, where they keep a look-out for passing insects, which they catch on the wing. The male and female are usually differently coloured. Four species nest in Europe.

Systematic classification

Timaliidae – Babblers p. 387

A very heterogeneous group of small to medium-sized passerines living chiefly in central and eastern Asia. They are thinly feathered, their thickish beak curves slightly downwards and they have sturdy legs. The behaviour and movements of the only species living in Europe, which is specialised for life in extensive reed-beds, are reminiscent of those of titmice. The male is coloured differently from the female.

Aegithalidae – Long-tailed Tits p. 388

Small passerines with a strikingly long tail, a distinctly round head with a short beak, short, rounded wings and thin legs. The vivid markings are the same in both sexes. These birds, which are tree-dwellers, live very sociably in families. Only one species occurs in Europe.

Paridae – Titmice p. 389

Small passerines with a relatively short, thick, sharp-pointed beak and sturdy legs. They are tree birds and climb nimbly about among the branches, chiefly in search of animal food. They are hole-nesters. The vivid colours and markings of the males and females are practically the same. Nine species live in Europe.

Sittidae – Nuthatches p. 396

Small, thick-bodied passerines with a short tail, a large head, a rather long, strong and straight beak and short, thick legs with strong, sharp claws. They climb skilfully up trunks and branches (and even rocks), generally descending head first. They are hole-nesters and partly wall up the entrance to the nest to make it narrower. The fairly bright colouring of the sexes is almost identical. Three species live in Europe.

Tichodromadidae – Wallcreepers p. 397

The only member of this family which nests in Europe has a long, slim body and a thin, downcurving beak. In flight, its wide, rounded wings are very conspicuous. Wallcreepers resemble treecreepers and these characters are adaptation for climbing rock faces in the mountains. The male is more brightly coloured than the female.

Certhiidae – Treecreepers p. 398

Small passerines with a slim body, a long, thin, downcurving beak and short, sturdy legs with long, sharp claws. Treecreepers climb up trees looking for small invertebrates in cracks in the bark. Both European species have brown mottled markings, which are the same in both sexes.

Remizidae – Penduline Tits   p. 400

Small passerine birds resembling tits in appearance and habits. They have a round head and a small, straight beak produced to a very fine point. They live in the vegetation around water and reed-beds and build very distinctive pouch-like nests with a tubular entrance. The male and female are almost identical in appearance. Only one species lives in Europe.

Oriolidae – Orioles   p. 401

Songbirds the size of a thrush, with a large head and a fairly long, strong and slightly curved beak, which live in the crowns of trees and hang their nests below forks in the branches. They are very vividly marked and coloured, but the females are plainer, as a rule, than the males. The centre of the incidence of this family is the tropics of the Old World and only one species lives in Europe.

Laniidae – Shrikes   p. 402

Because of their appearance and behaviour, shrikes are 'predators', as it were, among the passerines. They have a strong beak with a hooked tip and a notched upper mandible. Their moderately long legs have strong toes with sharp claws. They inhabit open country, where they sit erect on a high perch, waiting for prey, which they often impale on thorns. They are vividly marked, but the female is usually more plainly coloured. Five species nest in Europe.

Corvidae – Crows   p. 406

This family comprises the biggest passerines with glossy black plumage or contrasting colours, which are the same in both sexes. They have a large head, a strong, slightly rounded or straight beak and thick legs with large claws. Their voice is harsh and raucous. Eleven species nest in Europe.

Sturnidae – Starlings   p. 415

Robust songbirds with a short tail and noticeably pointed wings. Their beak is strong and is usually straight and sharp-pointed and they likewise have strong legs and toes. Their plumage is often glossy and is sometimes brightly coloured; the male and female are either the same in appearance or are only slightly different. These markedly gregarious birds frequently form large flocks. They look for their food mainly on the ground. Three species nest in Europe.

Passeridae – Sparrows   p. 417

Small, thickset songbirds with somewhat plainly coloured plumage, which in the male is somewhat brighter in appearance. They have

a strong, short, conical beak, strong legs and, in flight, pointed wings. As a rule they are very sociable and like to nest in colonies. Five species nest in Europe.

Fringillidae – Finches p. 422

Small songbirds with a short, conical beak, living mainly on grain. They are very brightly coloured and there are often marked differences between the sexes. They build cup-like nests which stand unattached on trees and bushes. They mostly live solitarily, but after they have finished nesting they collect together in flocks; 22 species live in Europe.

Emberizidae – Buntings p. 441

Small, stout passerines resembling finches. They have a short, straight beak with a thick base; the edges of their jaws curve inwards and are notched. The majority are seed-eaters and generally live solitarily. When they have finished nesting they form flocks. The males are generally more brightly coloured than the females. Thirteen species occur in Europe.

Key to the determination of orders

1 (18) The toes are joined together by webbing, which in the case of the second and fourth toe reaches at least half-way along them.

2 (3) Webbing not only joins the front toes, but also stretches from the second to the inturned first digit . . . . Pelicans and Allies (Pelecaniformes)

3 (2) Only the front toes are joined by webbing; the first toe is free.

4 (7) The beak has serrated edges; the teeth are usually wide and lamelliform.

5 (6) The tarsus is roughly the same length as the middle toe. The beak is straight or slightly curved and has a wide or narrow sharp nail at the tip of the upper mandible . . . . Ducks, Geese and Swans (Anseriformes).

6 (5) The tarsus is several times longer than the middle toe. The beak, which has no nail, is bent at an angle in the middle. Large birds with white and pink or whitish-grey plumage and with black flight feathers . . . . Flamingos (Phoenicopteriformes).

7 (4) The edges of the beak are smooth.

8 (9) The nostrils lie at the end of one or two tubes leading along the beak from its base . . . . Tubenoses (Procellariiformes).

9 (8) The nostrils open directly on the beak and not at the end of tubes.

10 (13) The first toe is absent.

11 (12) The legs are situated near the rear end of the body. When folded, the relatively short, narrow wings slightly overlap the base of the short tail . . . . Auks (Alciformes).

12 (11) The legs are situated almost in the middle of the body and are also bare above the tarsus. The folded wings stretch beyond the tip of the tail . . . . Kittiwake Rissa tridactyla, order Skuas, Gulls and Terns (Charadriiformes: Lari).

13 (10) A first toe is present.

14 (15) The outermost toe is the longest. The flat-sided tarsi have a sharp ridge down the front. The legs are situated almost at the rear end of the body. The short wings do not extend to the end of the short tail . . . . Divers (Gaviiformes).

15 (14) The middle toe is the longest. The tarsi are only slightly flat-sided. The legs are situated roughly in the middle of the body. There are no feathers on the lower parts of the tibiae. The long wings generally extend to or beyond the end of the tail.

16 (17) The beak is straight or slightly curved; it is roughly the same length as, or shorter than, the head . . . . Skuas, Gulls and Terns (Charadriiformes: Lari).

17 (16) The beak curves very noticeably upwards and is roughly double the length of the head . . . . Avocet Recurvirostra avosetta, order Waders (Charadriiformes: Charadrii).

Key to the determination of orders

18 (1) *The toes are not joined together by webbing, but a rudimentary membrane may be present at the base of the front toes (usually between the third and the fourth).*

19 (24) *The front toes are edged with strong skin.*

20 (21) *The skin fringing both sides of the front toes forms a border of equal width* . . . . *Grebes (Podicipediformes).*

21 (20) *The skin bordering both sides of the front toes forms lobes.*

22 (23) *On the forehead, the beak merges into a white or yellowish-grey horny shield. Large unicoloured (dark grey) birds with a thickset body* . . . . *Coot* Fulica atra, *order Rails and Allies (Gruiformes).*

23 (22) *The slender beak springs from a normally-feathered forehead. Small, delicate birds with a long body* . . . . *Phalaropes* Phalaropus, *order Waders (Charadriiformes: Charadrii).*

24 (19) *The front toes are not edged with skin.*

25 (52) *The feet are feathered down to the tarsus and sometimes as far as, or including, the toes.*

26 (27) *Only three toes are present* . . . . *Three-toed Woodpecker* Picoides tridactylus, *order Woodpeckers (Piciformes).*

27 (26) *The feet have four toes.*

28 (29) *All four toes on the short feet when at rest point forwards* . . . . *Swifts* Apus, *order Swifts (Apodiformes).*

29 (28) *The toes are differently positioned.*

30 (49) *Three toes (2—4) point forwards, the first toe backwards. (This also includes species which are able to direct the outermost toe forwards, sideways or backwards.)*

31 (32) *The straight beak is about $1\frac{1}{2}$ times to double the length of the head; the eyes appear to be set a long way back* . . . . *Woodcock* Scolopax rusticola, *order Waders (Charadriiformes: Charadrii).*

32 (31) *A beak and eyes with different characteristics.*

33 (36) *A hooked beak covered at the base of the upper mandible with a strikingly coloured cere. Curved claws, which are usually long and very sharp.*

34 (35) *A very wide head, approximately the same width as the body. The eyes face forwards. The nostrils are surrounded by bunches of tough, flexible feathers. The tarsus and generally the toes as well are thickly feathered; the outermost toe is double-jointed.* . . . . *Owls (Strigiformes).*

35 (34) *The head is distinctly narrower than the body, the eyes face sideways and the area around the nostrils is bare. The toes are unfeathered.* . . . . *Birds of Prey (Falconiformes).*

36 (33) *A beak and claws with other characteristics.*

37 (38) *The beak is short and thick; the upper mandible curves slightly downwards, is very occasionally hooked and is always without a cere. The claws are thick, gently curved and blunt* . . . . *Game Birds (Galliformes).*

38 (37) *A different beak and claws, generally flatter and thinner in relation to length.*

39 (40) *The beak is straight and relatively short; a white or greyish bulging cere is present at the base of the upper mandible* . . . . *Pigeons and Doves (Columbiformes).*

40 (39) *There is no bulging cere at the base of the beak.*

41 (44) *The toes are more or less fused together.*

42 (43) *The toes are fused as far as the claws and are thickly feathered; the underside of the foot is covered with thick, warty skin* . . . . *Pallas's Sandgrouse* Syrrhaptes paradoxus, *family Sandgrouse (Pteroclididae)*

43 (42) *The toes are fused together only at their base* . . . . *Rollers and Allies (Coraciiformes).*

44 (41) *The toes show no discernible signs of fusion.*

45 (46) *The outer toes (2 and 4) are relatively short compared with the third. The claw on the third toe has a pectinate inner surface. The beak is wide and gaping and at the base it is surrounded by a ring of bristly hairs* . . . . *Nightjars or Goatsuckers (Caprimulgiformes).*

46 (45) *The outer toes (2 and 4) are the same length as the third, or only slightly shorter; the third toe has a smooth claw.*

47 (48) *The head is crowned with a long, erectile comb of feathers* . . . . *Hoopoes (Upupidae), order Rollers and Allies (Coraciiformes).*

48 (47) *There is no comb on the head (but there may be a differently shaped, usually pointed, crest)* . . . . *Passerines (Passeriformes).*

49 (30) *Two of the toes (2 and 3) point forwards and the other two (1 and 4) backwards.*

50 (51) *The beak is wedge-shaped and pointed. The 12 tail feathers (the outer ones of which are short) are almost always tough and pointed* . . . . *Woodpeckers (Piciformes).*

51 (52) *The beak is slightly curved. The ten tail feathers are graduated in length* . . . . *Cuckoos (Cuculiformes).*

52 (50) *The beak is deep and thick; the tip of the hooked upper mandible overlaps the lower mandible and both articulate with the powerful skull. The nostrils are surrounded by a wide cere. The short, thick tarsi and prehensile toes are covered with small horny plates* . . . . *Parrots (Psittaciformes).*

53 (25) *The tarsi and the lower part of the tibiae are unfeathered.*

54 (55) *The lores, and often the skin around the eyes, are bare of feathers* . . . . *Herons and Allies (Ciconiiformes).*

55 (54) *A lore with feathers.*

Key to the determination of orders

56 (57) *The first primary to develop is the longest, or is the same length as the second; the wing is pointed . . . . Waders (Charadriiformes: Charadrii).*

57 (56) *The first primary to develop is shorter than the second.*

58 (59) *The outer end of the wing is wide and rounded; on the head there is a pointed crest formed of a few tapering feathers . . . . Lapwing* Vanellus vanellus, *order Waders (Charadriiformes: Charadrii).*

59 (58) *There is no long crest on the head.*

60 (61) *The legs are long and the tarsus is several times longer than the middle (third) toe. Big birds . . . . Cranes (Gruidae), order Rails and Allies (Gruiformes).*

61 (60) *Short legs; the tarsus is shorter than, or roughly the same length as, the middle toe. Small to medium-sized birds . . . . Rails and Allies (Gruiformes).*

Bibliography

Austin, O. L. 1963. *Birds of the World*. London.

Bruun, B., Delin, H. and Svensson, L. 1986. *The Hamlyn Guide to Birds of Britain and Europe*. London.

Campbell, B., and Lack, E. 1985. *A Dictionary of Birds*. Calton.

Cramp, S., *et al*. 1977 − . *The Birds of the Western Palearctic*. Oxford. Vols. 1−5, further vols. in prep.

Ferguson-Lees, J., Willis, I., and Sharrock, J.T.R. 1983. *The Shell Guide to the Birds of Britain and Ireland*. London.

Flegg, J. 1986. *Birdlife: insights into the daily lives of birds*. London.

Grant, P. J. 1986. *Gulls: a guide to identification*. Calton.

Hammond, N., and Everett, M. J. 1980. *Birds of Britain and Europe*. London.

Harrison, C. 1982. *An Atlas of the Birds of the Western Palaearctic*. London.

Harrison, P. 1986. *Seabirds: an identification guide*. London.
− − − 1987. *Seabirds of the World: a photographic guide*. London.

Hayman, P., Marchant, J., and Prater, T. 1986. *Shorebirds: an identification guide to the waders of the world*. London.

Heinzel, H., Fitter, R., and Parslow, J. 1979. *The Birds of Britain and Europe with North Africa and the Middle East*. London.

Hollom, P.A. D. 1962. *The Popular Handbook of British Birds*. London.

Perrins, C. 1987. *Collins New Generation Guide to the Birds of Britain and Europe*. London.

Peterson, R. T., Mountfort, G., and Hollom, P. 1983. *A Field Guide to the Birds of Britain and Europe*. London.

Porter, R. F., *et al*. 1981. *Flight Identification of European Raptors*. Berkhamsted.

Redman, N., and Harrap, S. 1987. *Birdwatching in Britain: a site by site guide*. London.

Witherby, H. F., *et al*. 1938−41. *The Handbook of British Birds*. London. 5 vols.

Index of Common Names

Numbers in bold refer to main entries

Index of Scientific Names

Numbers in bold refer to main entries